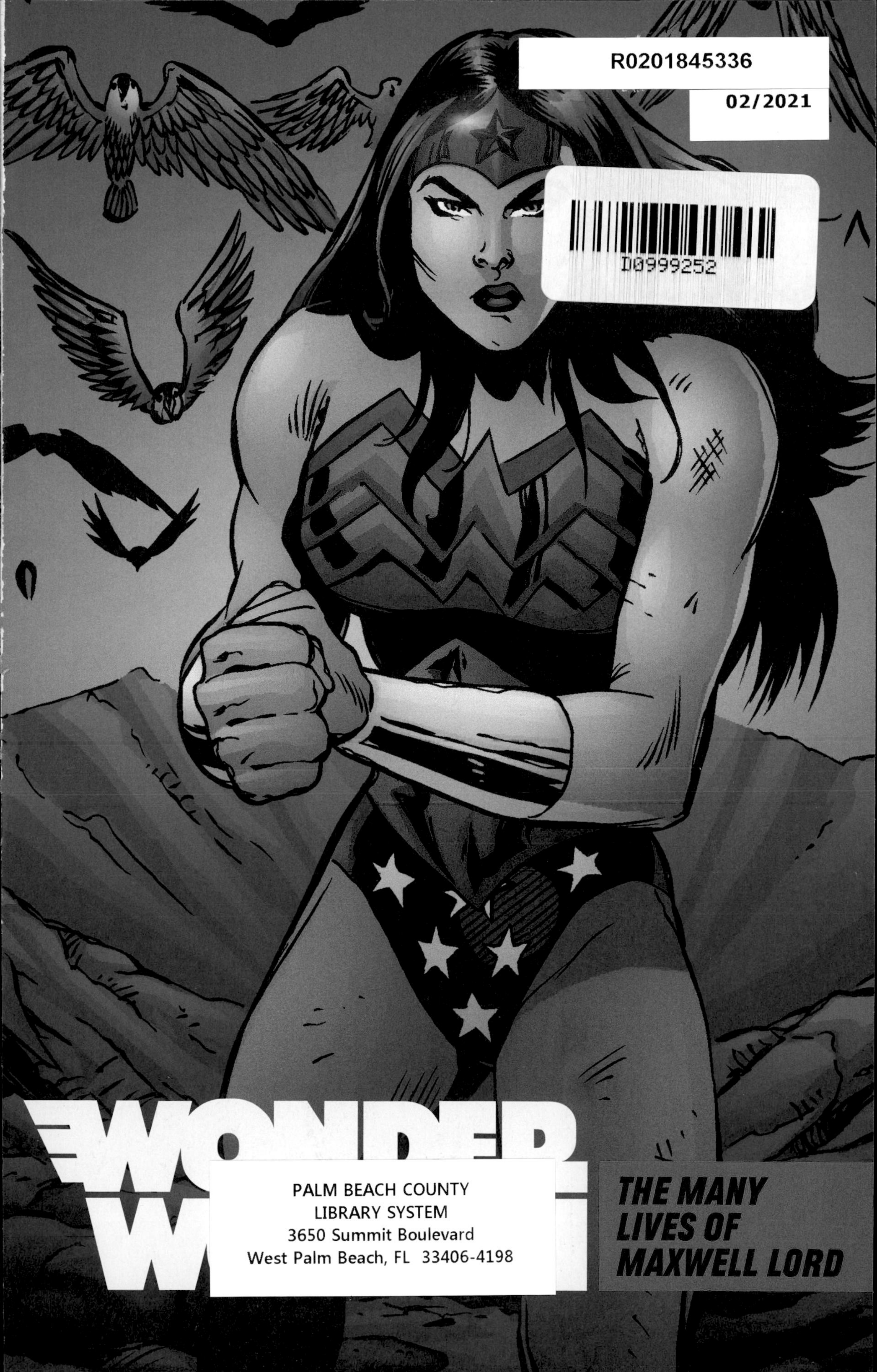
WONDER W
THE MANY LIVES OF MAXWELL LORD

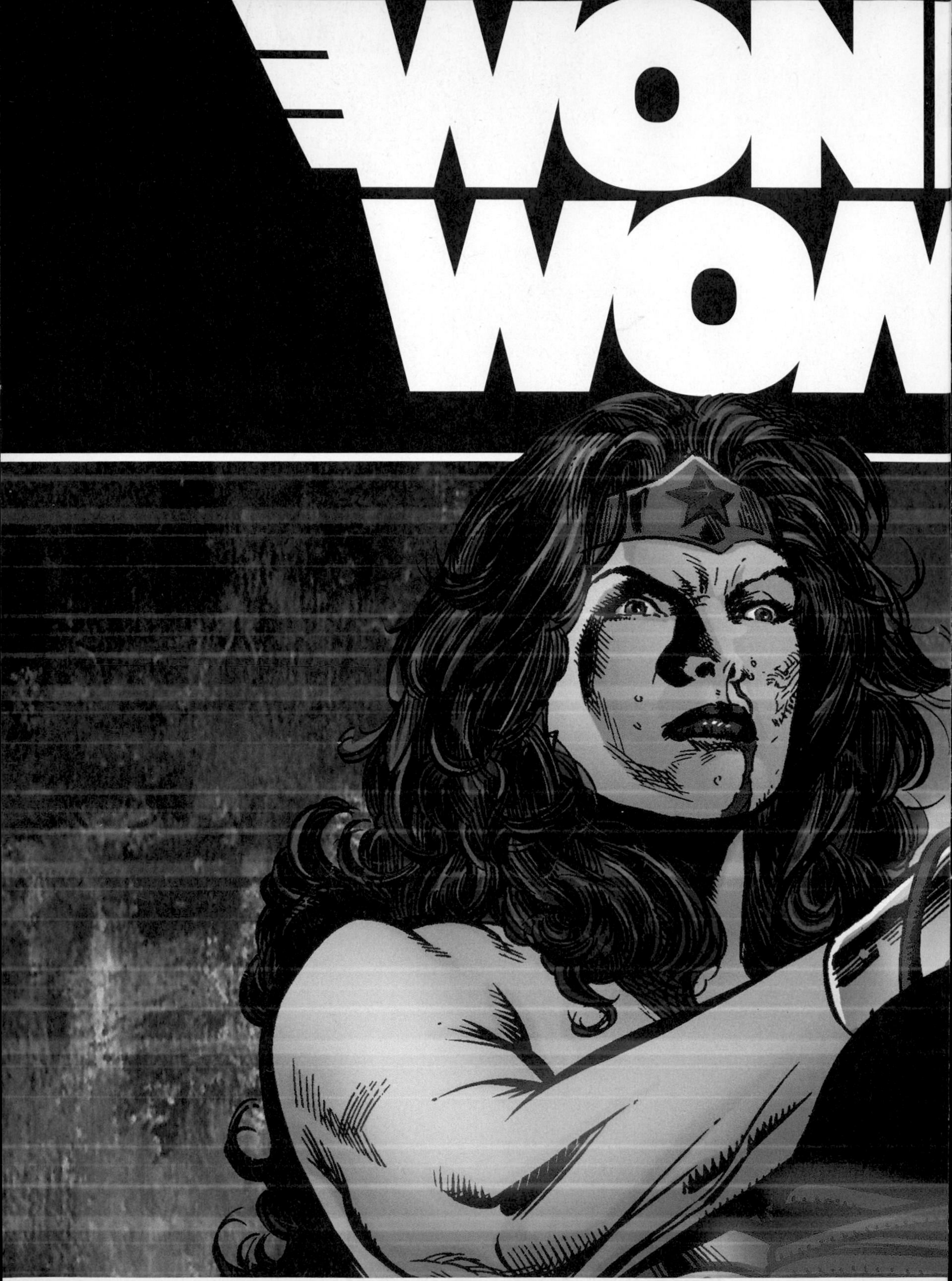

JASON FABOK

collection cover artist

THE MANY LIVES OF MAXWELL LORD

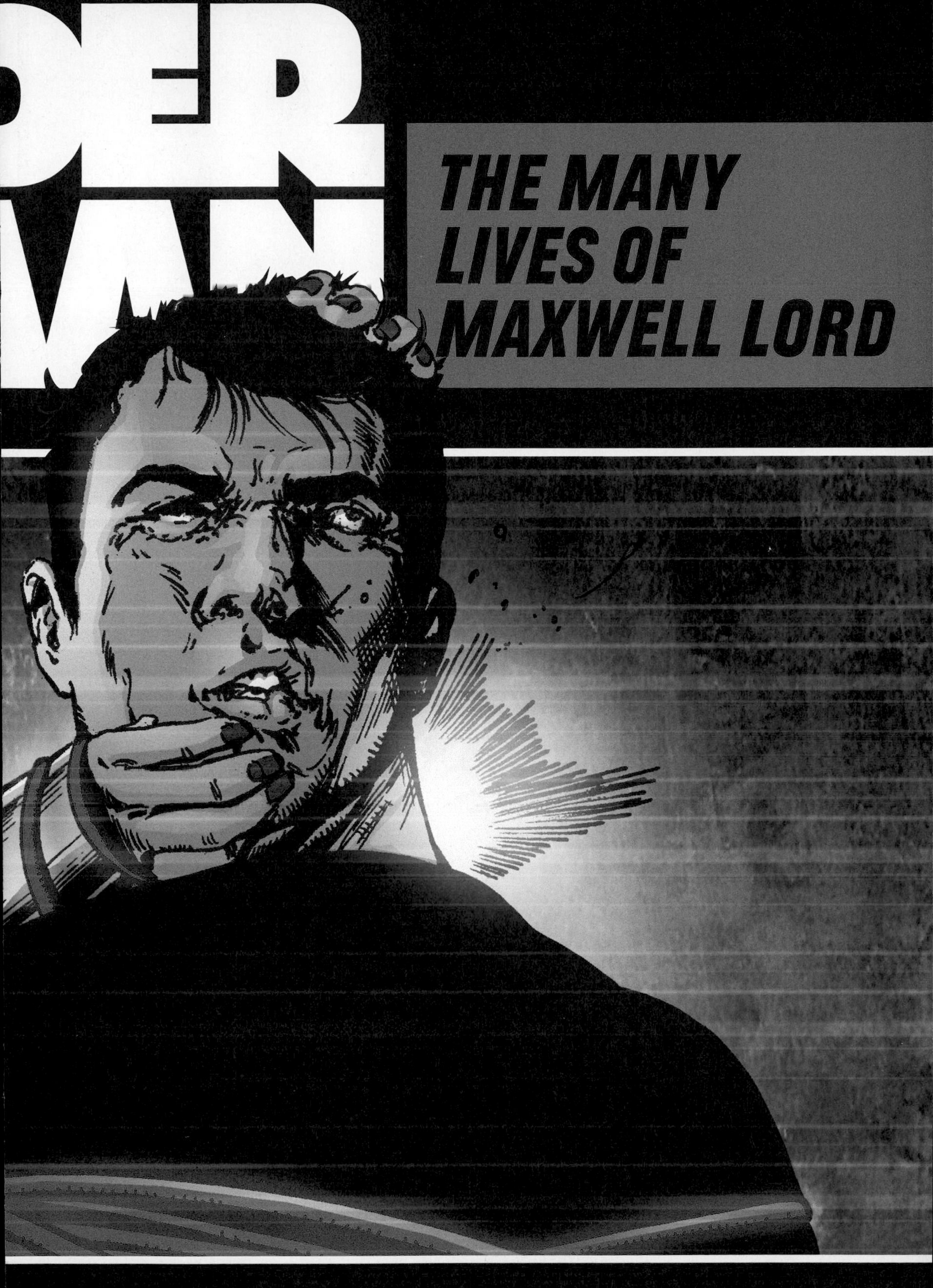

SUPERMAN created by **JERRY SIEGEL** and **JOE SHUSTER**
By special arrangement with the Jerry Siegel family

IVAN COHEN, BRIAN CUNNINGHAM, ANDREW HELFER, JUAN HILTY Editors – Original Series
RACHEL GLUCKSTERN, JANN JONES, DIEGO LOPEZ, REX OGLE, AMEDEO TURTURRO Assistant Editors – Original Series
JEB WOODARD Group Editor – Collected Editions
STEVE COOK Design Director – Books
MEGEN BELLERSEN Publication Design
SUZANNAH ROWNTREE Publication Production

BOB HARRAS Senior VP – Editor-in-Chief, DC Comics

DAN DiDIO Publisher
JIM LEE Publisher & Chief Creative Officer
BOBBIE CHASE VP – New Publishing Initiatives
DON FALLETTI VP – Manufacturing Operations & Workflow Management
LAWRENCE GANEM VP – Talent Services
ALISON GILL Senior VP – Manufacturing & Operations
HANK KANALZ Senior VP – Publishing Strategy & Support Services
DAN MIRON VP – Publishing Operations
NICK J. NAPOLITANO VP – Manufacturing Administration & Design
NANCY SPEARS VP – Sales
JONAH WEILAND VP – Marketing & Creative Services
MICHELE R. WELLS VP & Executive Editor, Young Reader

WONDER WOMAN: THE MANY LIVES OF MAXWELL LORD

DC Comics, 2900 West Alameda Ave., Burbank, CA 91505
Printed by LSC Communications, Kendallville, IN, USA. 7/3/20. First Printing.
ISBN: 978-1-77950-609-2

Library of Congress Cataloging-in-Publication Data is available.

PEFC
PEFC/29-31-337
PEFC Certified
This product is from sustainably managed forests and controlled sources
www.pefc.org

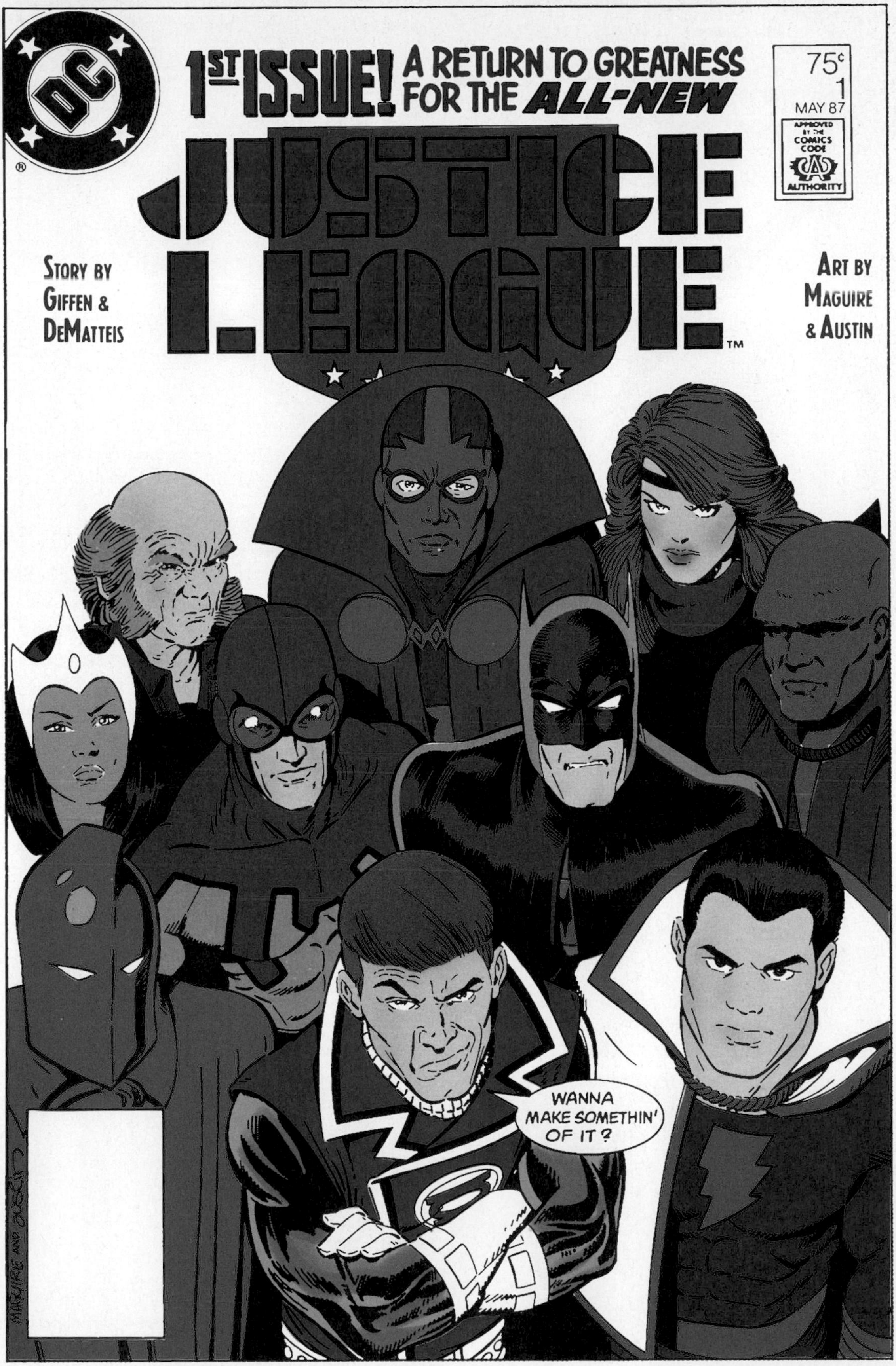

1ST ISSUE! A RETURN TO GREATNESS FOR THE ALL-NEW
JUSTICE LEAGUE
75¢
1
MAY 87
APPROVED BY THE COMICS CODE AUTHORITY
STORY BY GIFFEN & DeMATTEIS
ART BY MAGUIRE & AUSTIN
WANNA MAKE SOMETHIN' OF IT?

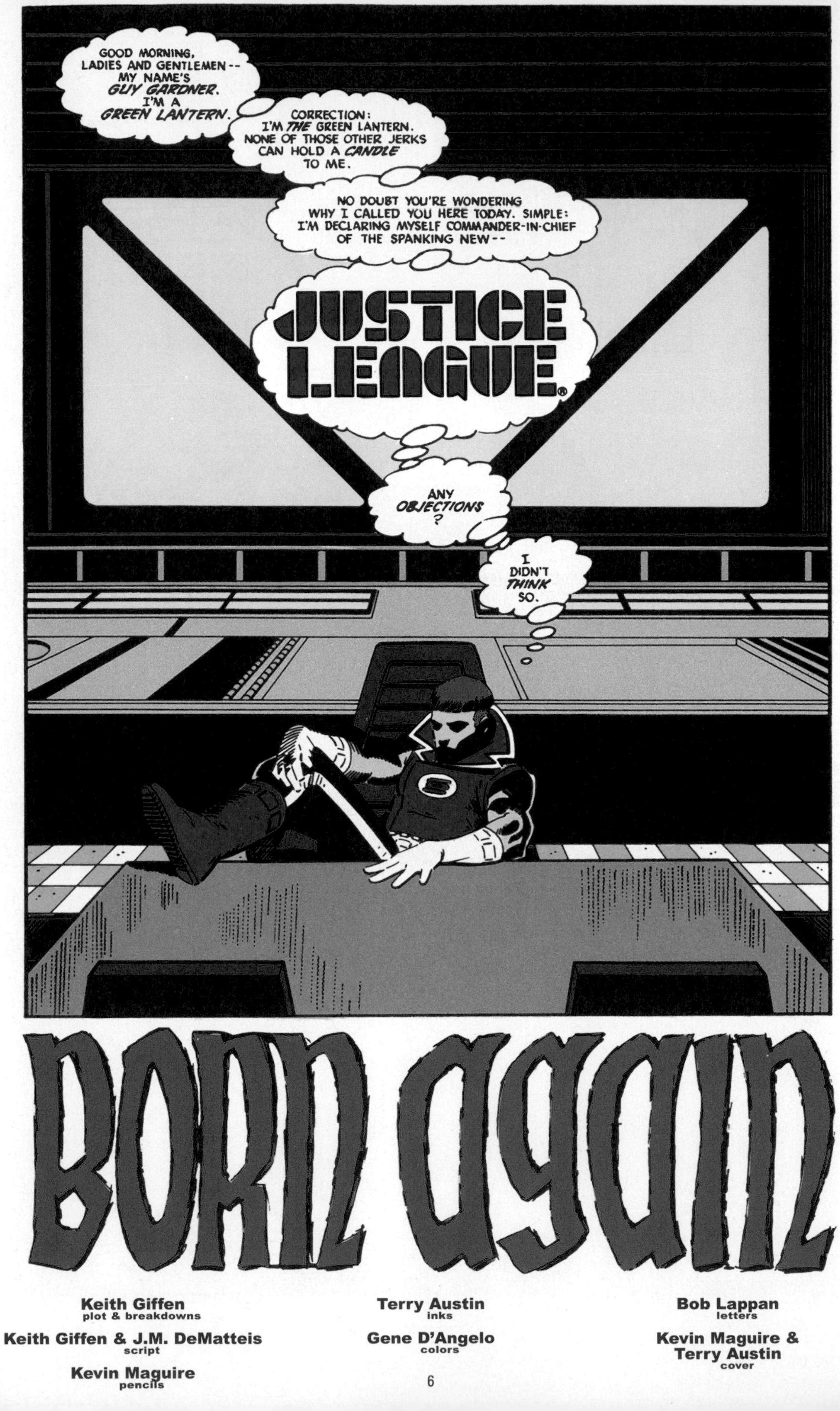
GOOD MORNING, LADIES AND GENTLEMEN-- MY NAME'S GUY GARDNER. I'M A GREEN LANTERN.
CORRECTION: I'M THE GREEN LANTERN. NONE OF THOSE OTHER JERKS CAN HOLD A CANDLE TO ME.
NO DOUBT YOU'RE WONDERING WHY I CALLED YOU HERE TODAY. SIMPLE: I'M DECLARING MYSELF COMMANDER-IN-CHIEF OF THE SPANKING NEW--
JUSTICE LEAGUE®
ANY OBJECTIONS?
I DIDN'T THINK SO.

BORN AGAIN

Keith Giffen plot & breakdowns
Keith Giffen & J.M. DeMatteis script
Kevin Maguire pencils
Terry Austin inks
Gene D'Angelo colors
Bob Lappan letters
Kevin Maguire & Terry Austin cover

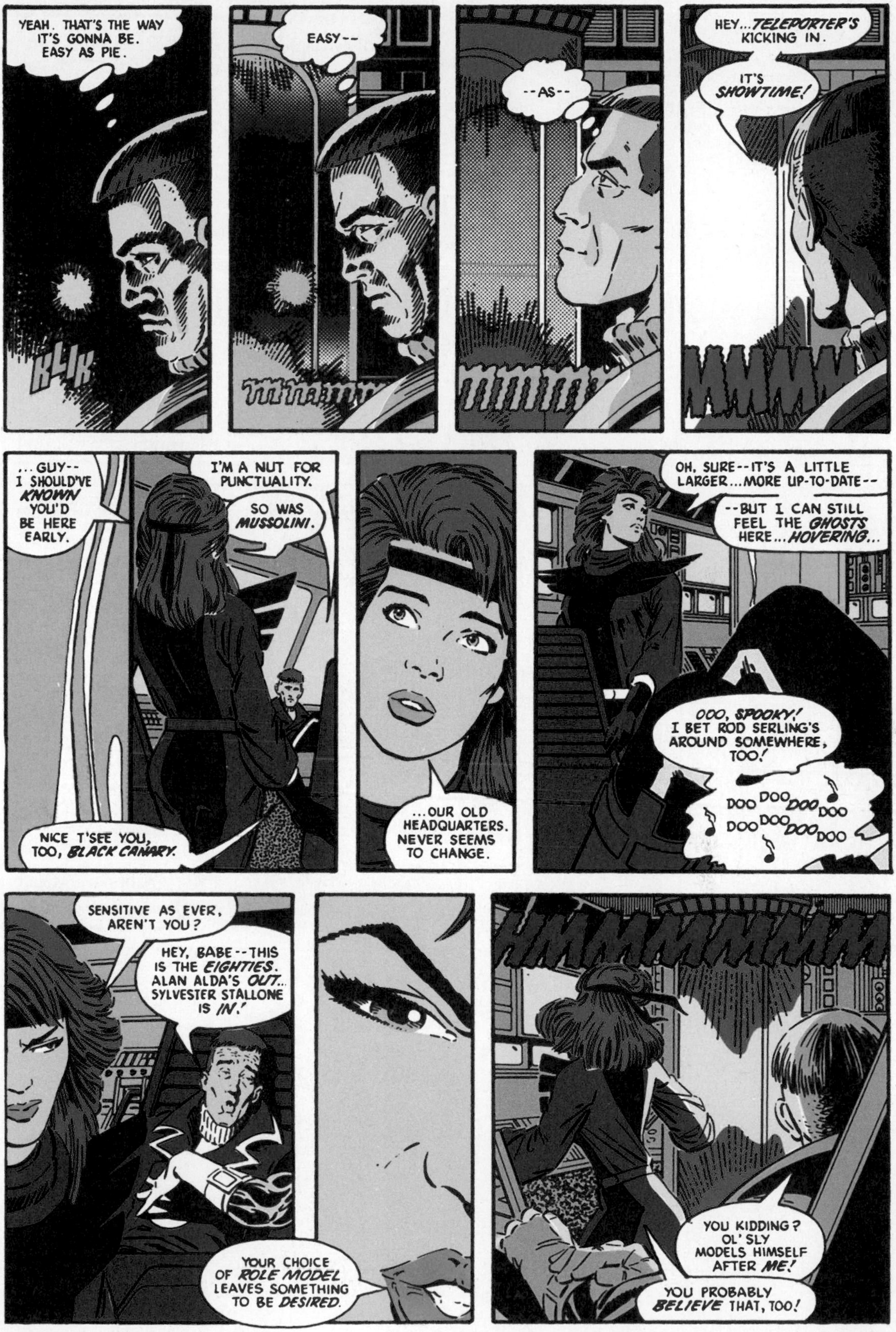
YEAH. THAT'S THE WAY IT'S GONNA BE. EASY AS PIE.
KLIK
EASY--
MMMMMM
--AS--
MMMMMM
HEY...TELEPORTER'S KICKING IN.
IT'S SHOWTIME!
MMMM
...GUY--I SHOULD'VE KNOWN YOU'D BE HERE EARLY.
I'M A NUT FOR PUNCTUALITY.
SO WAS MUSSOLINI.
NICE T'SEE YOU, TOO, BLACK CANARY.
...OUR OLD HEADQUARTERS. NEVER SEEMS TO CHANGE.
OH, SURE--IT'S A LITTLE LARGER...MORE UP-TO-DATE--
--BUT I CAN STILL FEEL THE GHOSTS HERE...HOVERING...
OOO, SPOOKY! I BET ROD SERLING'S AROUND SOMEWHERE, TOO!
DOO DOO DOO DOO
DOO DOO DOO DOO
SENSITIVE AS EVER, AREN'T YOU?
HEY, BABE--THIS IS THE EIGHTIES. ALAN ALDA'S OUT... SYLVESTER STALLONE IS IN!
YOUR CHOICE OF ROLE MODEL LEAVES SOMETHING TO BE DESIRED.
HMMMMMMMMM
YOU KIDDING? OL' SLY MODELS HIMSELF AFTER ME!
YOU PROBABLY BELIEVE THAT, TOO!

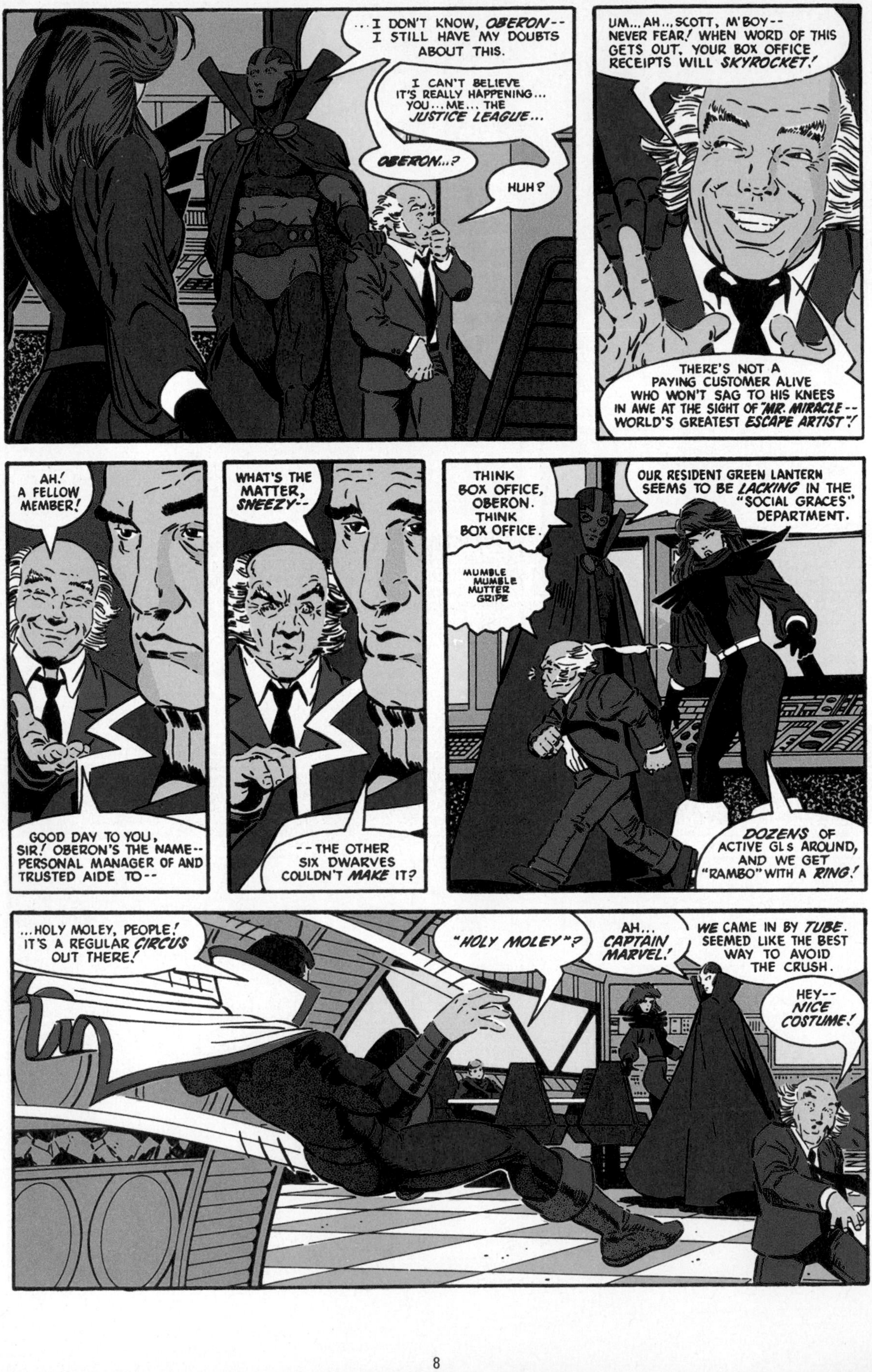

...I DON'T KNOW, OBERON--
I STILL HAVE MY DOUBTS ABOUT THIS.
I CAN'T BELIEVE IT'S REALLY HAPPENING... YOU...ME... THE JUSTICE LEAGUE...
OBERON...?
HUH?
UM...AH...SCOTT, M'BOY--NEVER FEAR! WHEN WORD OF THIS GETS OUT, YOUR BOX OFFICE RECEIPTS WILL SKYROCKET!
THERE'S NOT A PAYING CUSTOMER ALIVE WHO WON'T SAG TO HIS KNEES IN AWE AT THE SIGHT OF "MR. MIRACLE--WORLD'S GREATEST ESCAPE ARTIST"!
AH! A FELLOW MEMBER!
GOOD DAY TO YOU, SIR! OBERON'S THE NAME--PERSONAL MANAGER OF AND TRUSTED AIDE TO--
WHAT'S THE MATTER, SNEEZY--
--THE OTHER SIX DWARVES COULDN'T MAKE IT?
THINK BOX OFFICE, OBERON. THINK BOX OFFICE.
MUMBLE MUMBLE MUTTER GRIPE
OUR RESIDENT GREEN LANTERN SEEMS TO BE LACKING IN THE "SOCIAL GRACES" DEPARTMENT.
DOZENS OF ACTIVE GLs AROUND, AND WE GET "RAMBO" WITH A RING!
...HOLY MOLEY, PEOPLE! IT'S A REGULAR CIRCUS OUT THERE!
"HOLY MOLEY"?
AH... CAPTAIN MARVEL!
WE CAME IN BY TUBE. SEEMED LIKE THE BEST WAY TO AVOID THE CRUSH.
HEY--NICE COSTUME!

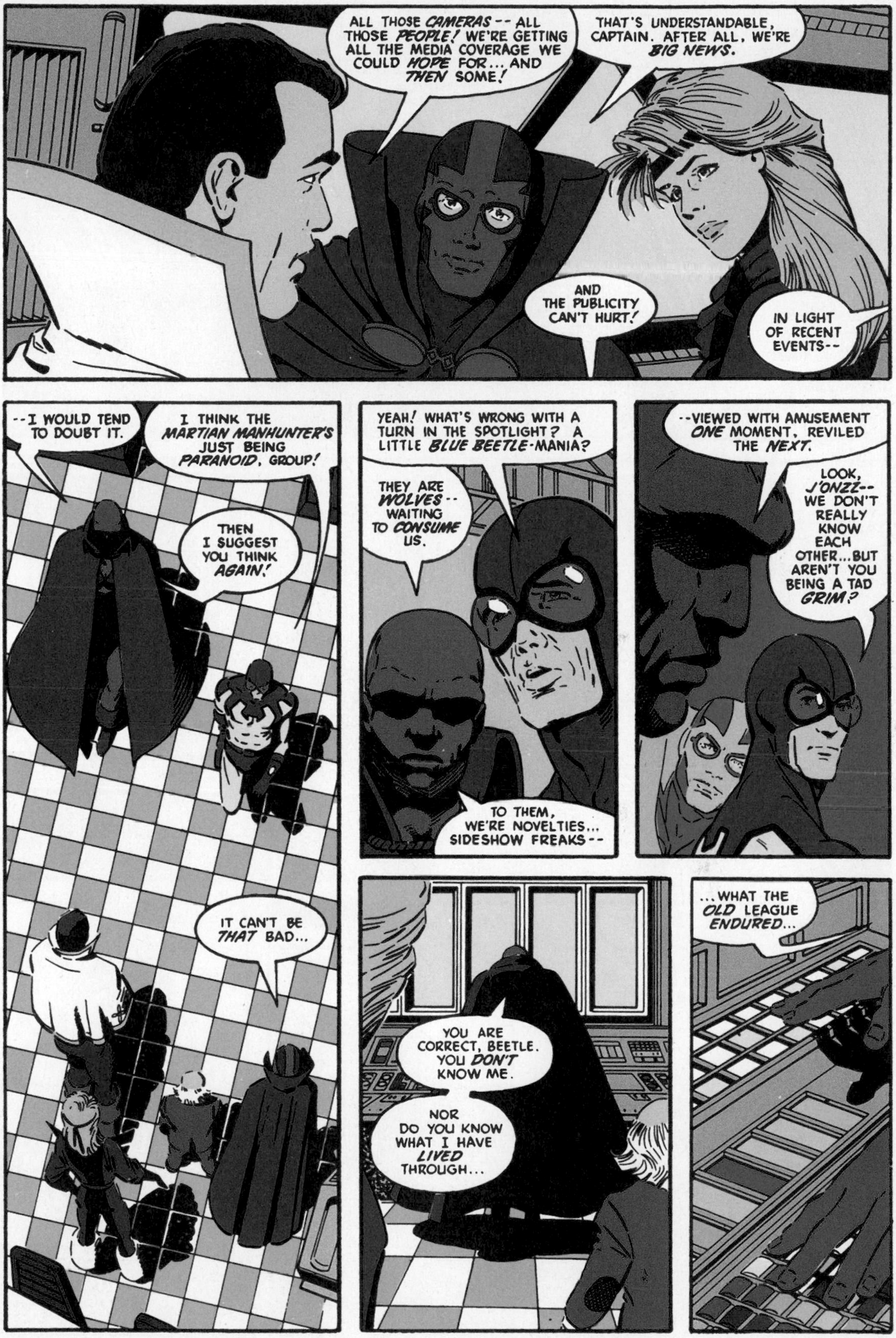
ALL THOSE CAMERAS -- ALL THOSE PEOPLE! WE'RE GETTING ALL THE MEDIA COVERAGE WE COULD HOPE FOR... AND THEN SOME!
THAT'S UNDERSTANDABLE, CAPTAIN. AFTER ALL, WE'RE BIG NEWS.
AND THE PUBLICITY CAN'T HURT!
IN LIGHT OF RECENT EVENTS--
--I WOULD TEND TO DOUBT IT.
I THINK THE MARTIAN MANHUNTER'S JUST BEING PARANOID, GROUP!
THEN I SUGGEST YOU THINK AGAIN!
IT CAN'T BE THAT BAD...
YEAH! WHAT'S WRONG WITH A TURN IN THE SPOTLIGHT? A LITTLE BLUE BEETLE-MANIA?
THEY ARE WOLVES -- WAITING TO CONSUME US.
TO THEM, WE'RE NOVELTIES... SIDESHOW FREAKS--
--VIEWED WITH AMUSEMENT ONE MOMENT, REVILED THE NEXT.
LOOK, J'ONZZ-- WE DON'T REALLY KNOW EACH OTHER... BUT AREN'T YOU BEING A TAD GRIM?
YOU ARE CORRECT, BEETLE. YOU DON'T KNOW ME.
NOR DO YOU KNOW WHAT I HAVE LIVED THROUGH...
...WHAT THE OLD LEAGUE ENDURED...

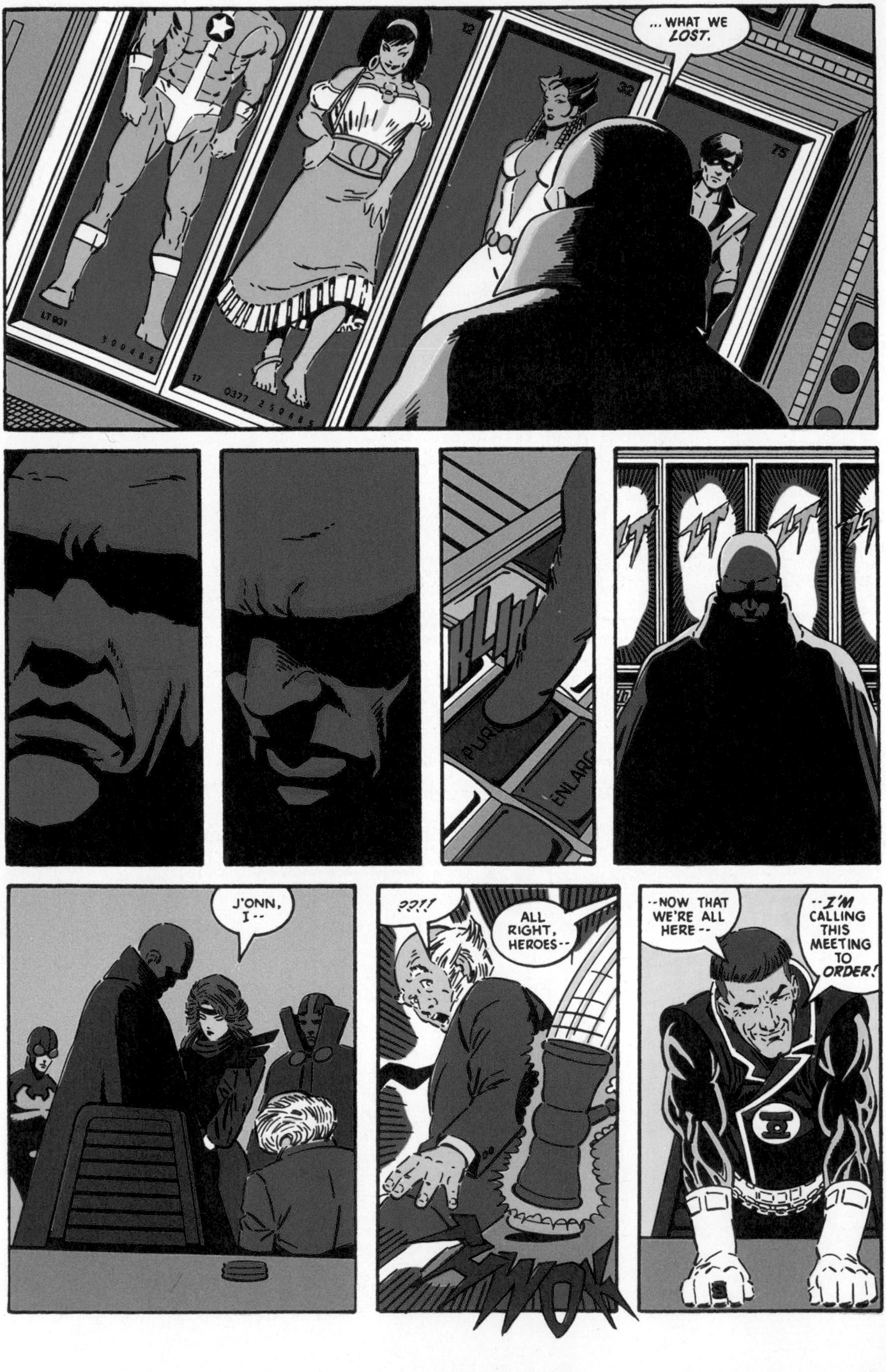
...WHAT WE LOST.
KLIK
PURG
ENLARG
ZZT
J'ONN, I--
??!!
ALL RIGHT, HEROES--
WOK
--NOW THAT WE'RE ALL HERE--
--I'M CALLING THIS MEETING TO ORDER!

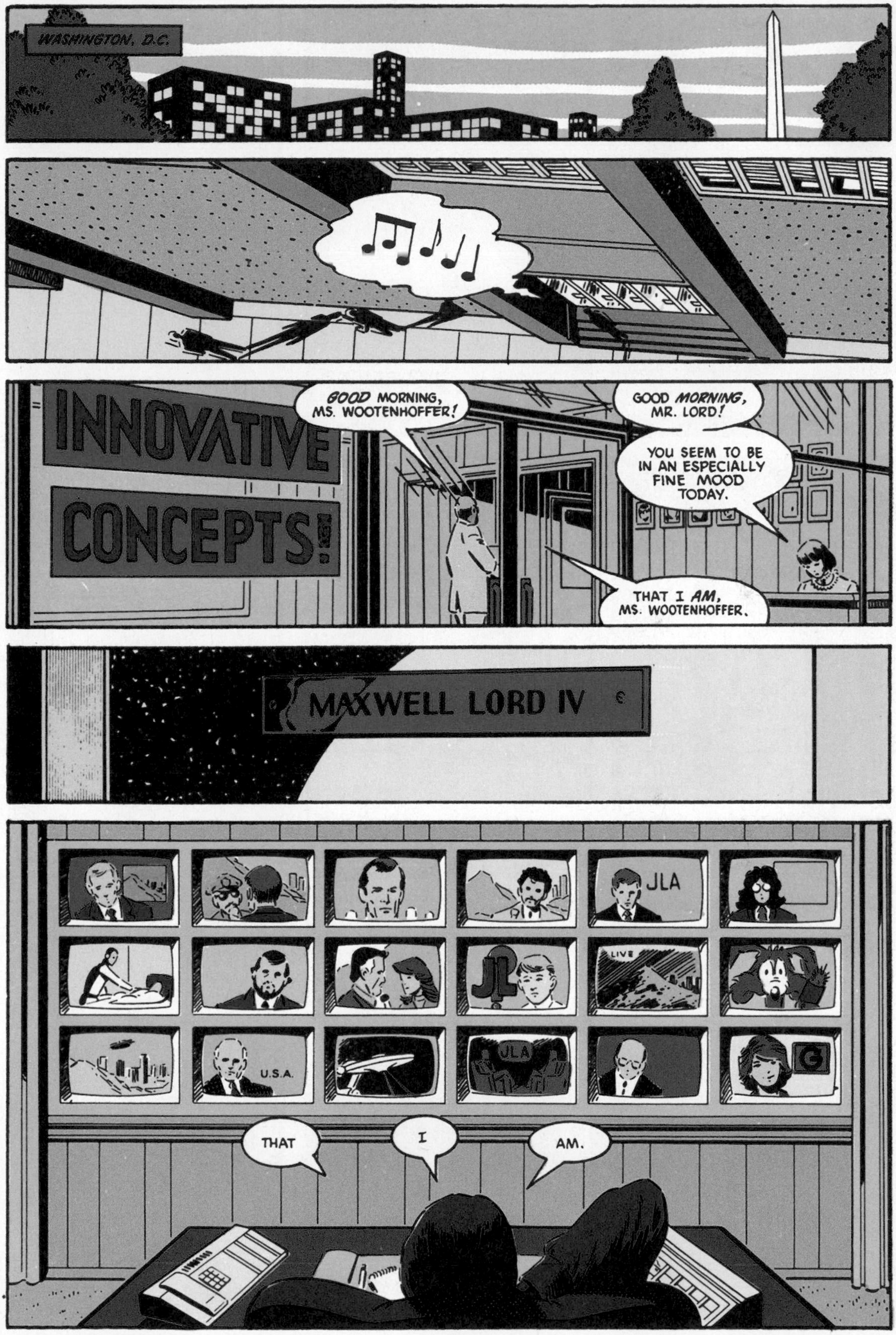
WASHINGTON, D.C.
GOOD MORNING, MS. WOOTENHOFFER!
GOOD MORNING, MR. LORD!
YOU SEEM TO BE IN AN ESPECIALLY FINE MOOD TODAY.
INNOVATIVE CONCEPTS!
THAT I AM, MS. WOOTENHOFFER.
MAXWELL LORD IV
JLA
LIVE
U.S.A.
JLA
THAT
I
AM.

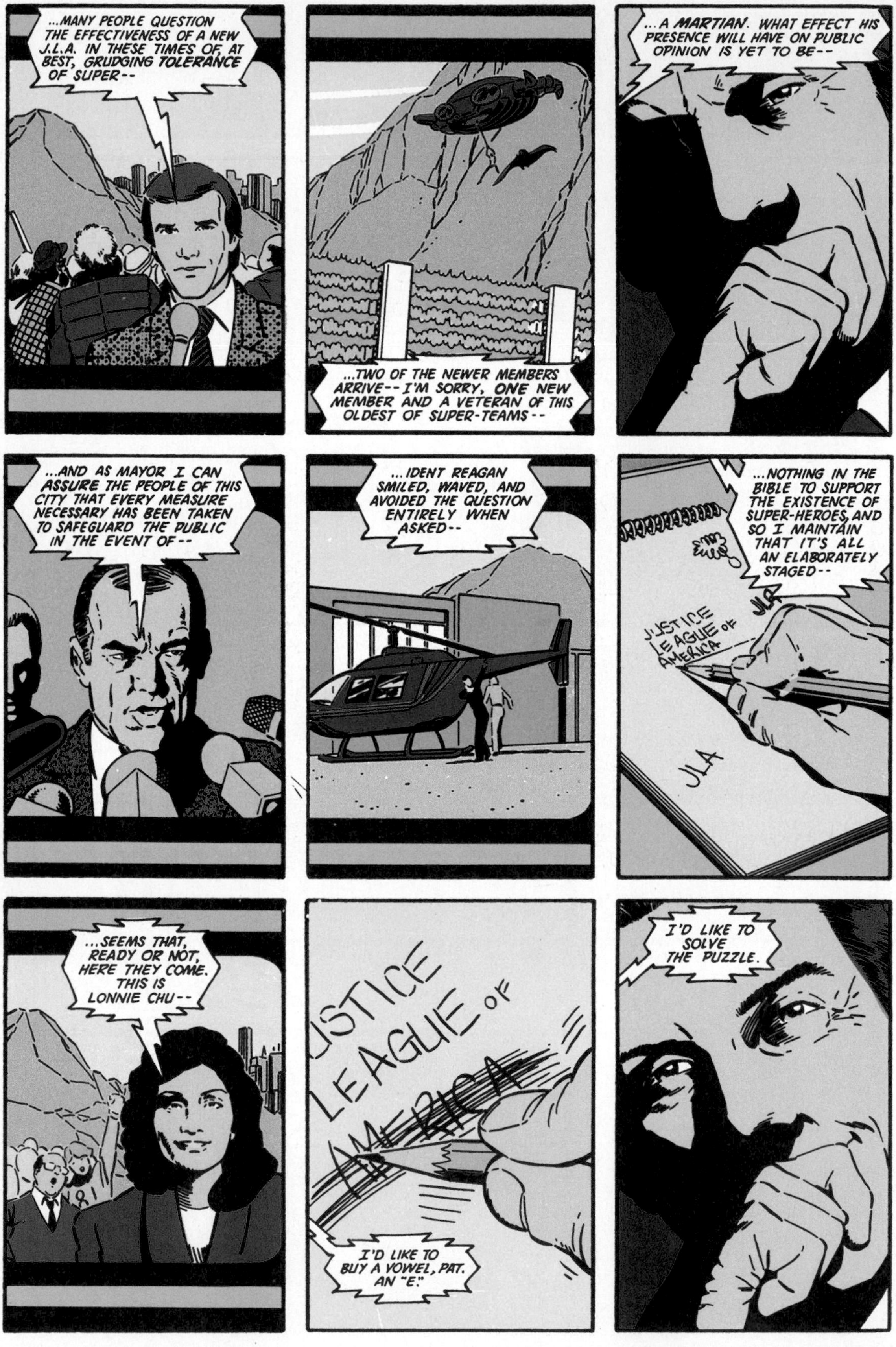
...MANY PEOPLE QUESTION THE EFFECTIVENESS OF A NEW J.L.A. IN THESE TIMES OF, AT BEST, GRUDGING TOLERANCE OF SUPER--
...TWO OF THE NEWER MEMBERS ARRIVE--I'M SORRY, ONE NEW MEMBER AND A VETERAN OF THIS OLDEST OF SUPER-TEAMS--
...A MARTIAN. WHAT EFFECT HIS PRESENCE WILL HAVE ON PUBLIC OPINION IS YET TO BE--
...AND AS MAYOR I CAN ASSURE THE PEOPLE OF THIS CITY THAT EVERY MEASURE NECESSARY HAS BEEN TAKEN TO SAFEGUARD THE PUBLIC IN THE EVENT OF--
...IDENT REAGAN SMILED, WAVED, AND AVOIDED THE QUESTION ENTIRELY WHEN ASKED--
...NOTHING IN THE BIBLE TO SUPPORT THE EXISTENCE OF SUPER-HEROES, AND SO I MAINTAIN THAT IT'S ALL AN ELABORATELY STAGED--
JUSTICE LEAGUE OF AMERICA
JLA
JLA
...SEEMS THAT, READY OR NOT, HERE THEY COME. THIS IS LONNIE CHU--
JUSTICE LEAGUE OF AMERICA
I'D LIKE TO BUY A VOWEL, PAT. AN "E."
I'D LIKE TO SOLVE THE PUZZLE.

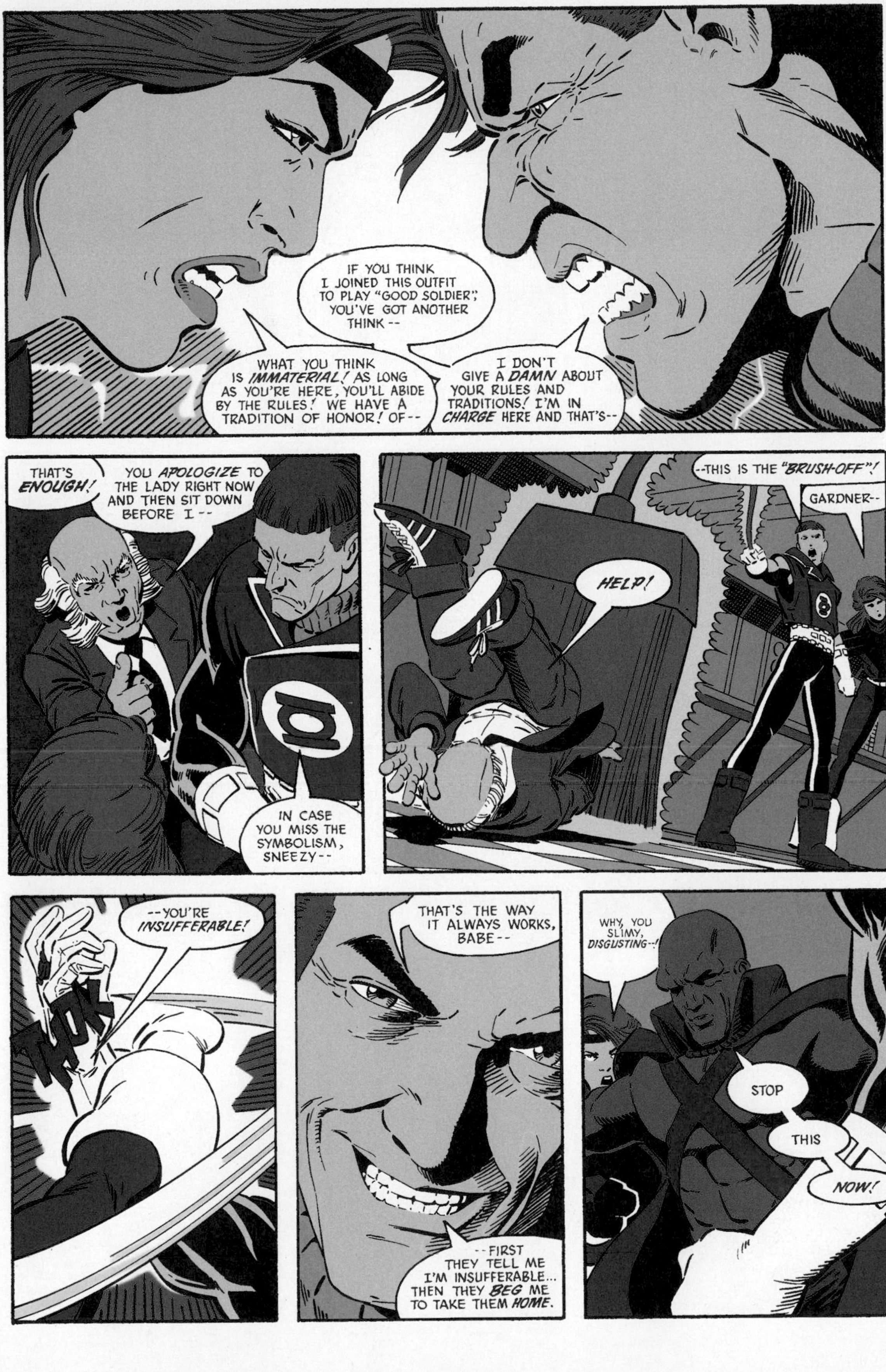
IF YOU THINK I JOINED THIS OUTFIT TO PLAY "GOOD SOLDIER", YOU'VE GOT ANOTHER THINK --
WHAT YOU THINK IS *IMMATERIAL!* AS LONG AS YOU'RE HERE, YOU'LL ABIDE BY THE RULES! WE HAVE A TRADITION OF HONOR! OF --
I DON'T GIVE A *DAMN* ABOUT YOUR RULES AND TRADITIONS! I'M IN *CHARGE* HERE AND THAT'S --
THAT'S *ENOUGH!*
YOU *APOLOGIZE* TO THE LADY RIGHT NOW AND THEN SIT DOWN BEFORE I --
IN CASE YOU MISS THE SYMBOLISM, SNEEZY --
-- THIS IS THE *"BRUSH-OFF"!*
HELP!
GARDNER --
-- YOU'RE *INSUFFERABLE!*
THAT'S THE WAY IT ALWAYS WORKS, BABE --
-- FIRST THEY TELL ME I'M INSUFFERABLE... THEN THEY *BEG* ME TO TAKE THEM *HOME*.
WHY, YOU SLIMY, *DISGUSTING* --!
STOP
THIS
NOW!

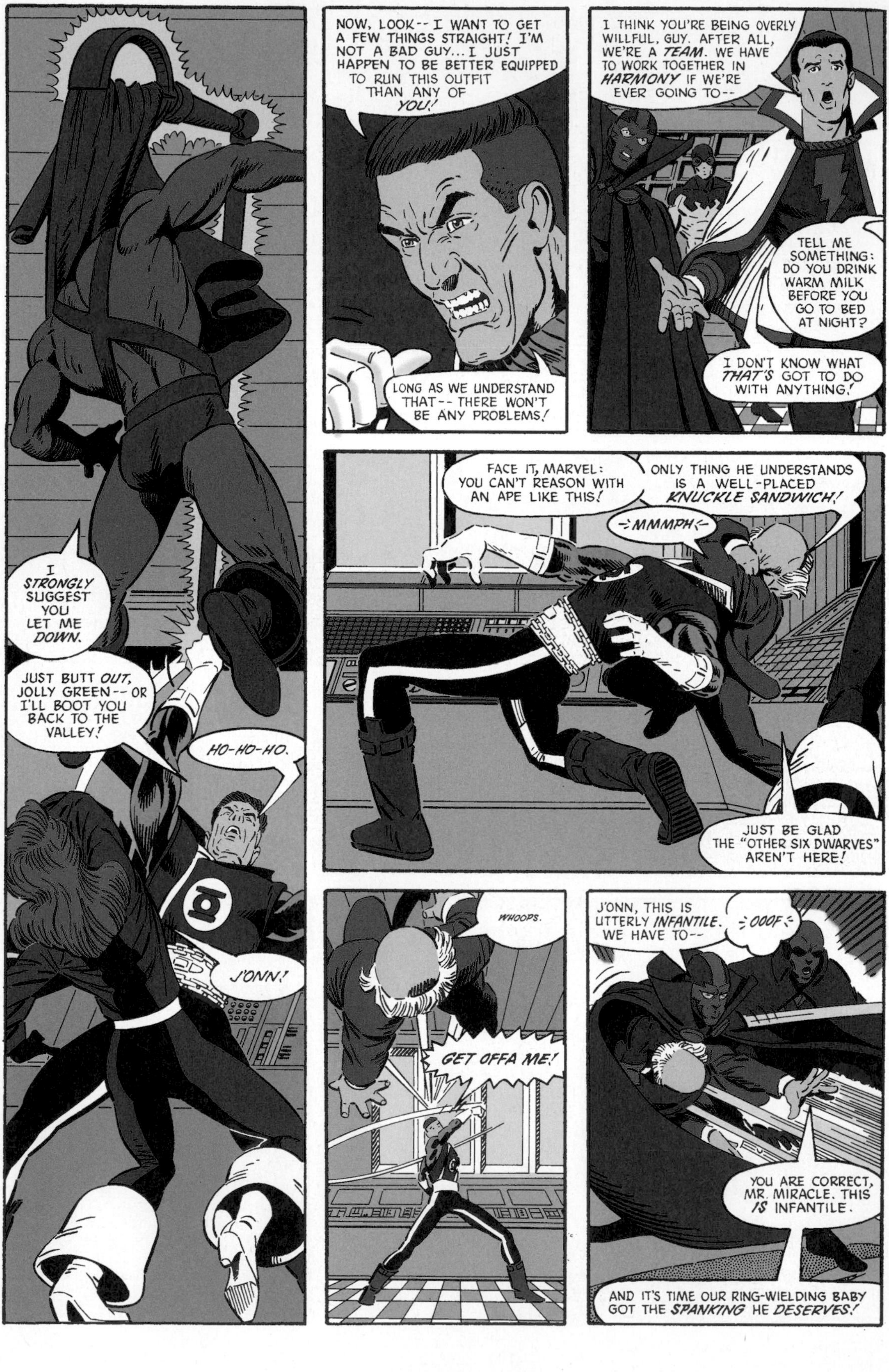
I STRONGLY SUGGEST YOU LET ME DOWN.
JUST BUTT OUT, JOLLY GREEN-- OR I'LL BOOT YOU BACK TO THE VALLEY!
HO-HO-HO.
J'ONN!
NOW, LOOK-- I WANT TO GET A FEW THINGS STRAIGHT! I'M NOT A BAD GUY... I JUST HAPPEN TO BE BETTER EQUIPPED TO RUN THIS OUTFIT THAN ANY OF YOU!
LONG AS WE UNDERSTAND THAT-- THERE WON'T BE ANY PROBLEMS!
I THINK YOU'RE BEING OVERLY WILLFUL, GUY. AFTER ALL, WE'RE A TEAM. WE HAVE TO WORK TOGETHER IN HARMONY IF WE'RE EVER GOING TO--
TELL ME SOMETHING: DO YOU DRINK WARM MILK BEFORE YOU GO TO BED AT NIGHT?
I DON'T KNOW WHAT THAT'S GOT TO DO WITH ANYTHING!
FACE IT, MARVEL: YOU CAN'T REASON WITH AN APE LIKE THIS!
ONLY THING HE UNDERSTANDS IS A WELL-PLACED KNUCKLE SANDWICH!
MMMPH
JUST BE GLAD THE "OTHER SIX DWARVES" AREN'T HERE!
WHOOPS.
GET OFFA ME!
J'ONN, THIS IS UTTERLY INFANTILE. WE HAVE TO--
OOOF
YOU ARE CORRECT, MR. MIRACLE. THIS IS INFANTILE.
AND IT'S TIME OUR RING-WIELDING BABY GOT THE SPANKING HE DESERVES!

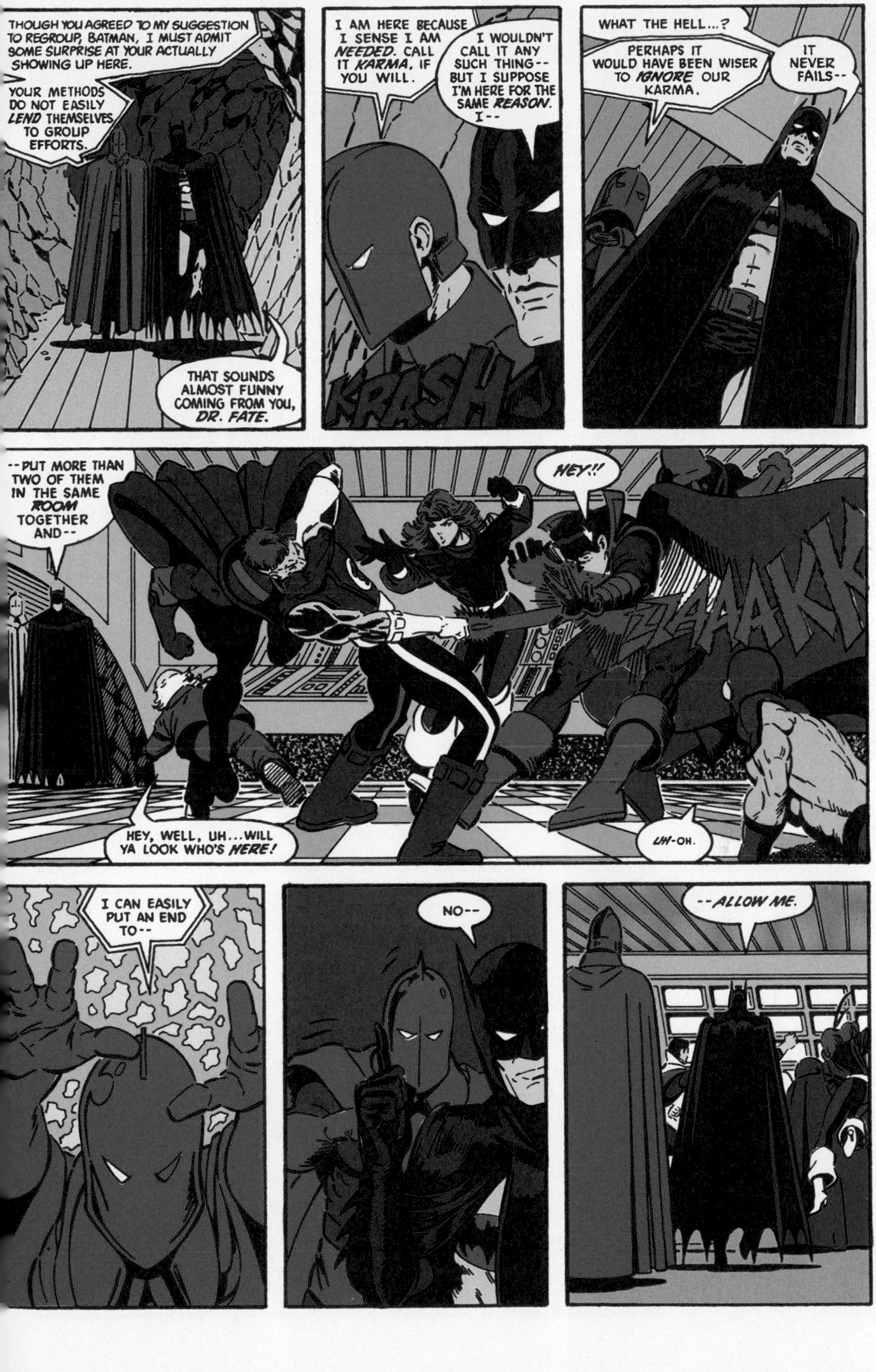
THOUGH YOU AGREED TO MY SUGGESTION TO REGROUP, BATMAN, I MUST ADMIT SOME SURPRISE AT YOUR ACTUALLY SHOWING UP HERE.
YOUR METHODS DO NOT EASILY LEND THEMSELVES TO GROUP EFFORTS.
THAT SOUNDS ALMOST FUNNY COMING FROM YOU, DR. FATE.
I AM HERE BECAUSE I SENSE I AM NEEDED. CALL IT KARMA, IF YOU WILL.
I WOULDN'T CALL IT ANY SUCH THING-- BUT I SUPPOSE I'M HERE FOR THE SAME REASON. I--
KRASH
WHAT THE HELL...?
PERHAPS IT WOULD HAVE BEEN WISER TO IGNORE OUR KARMA.
IT NEVER FAILS--
--PUT MORE THAN TWO OF THEM IN THE SAME ROOM TOGETHER AND--
HEY!!
ZAAAKK
HEY, WELL, UH...WILL YA LOOK WHO'S HERE!
UH-OH.
I CAN EASILY PUT AN END TO--
NO--
--ALLOW ME.

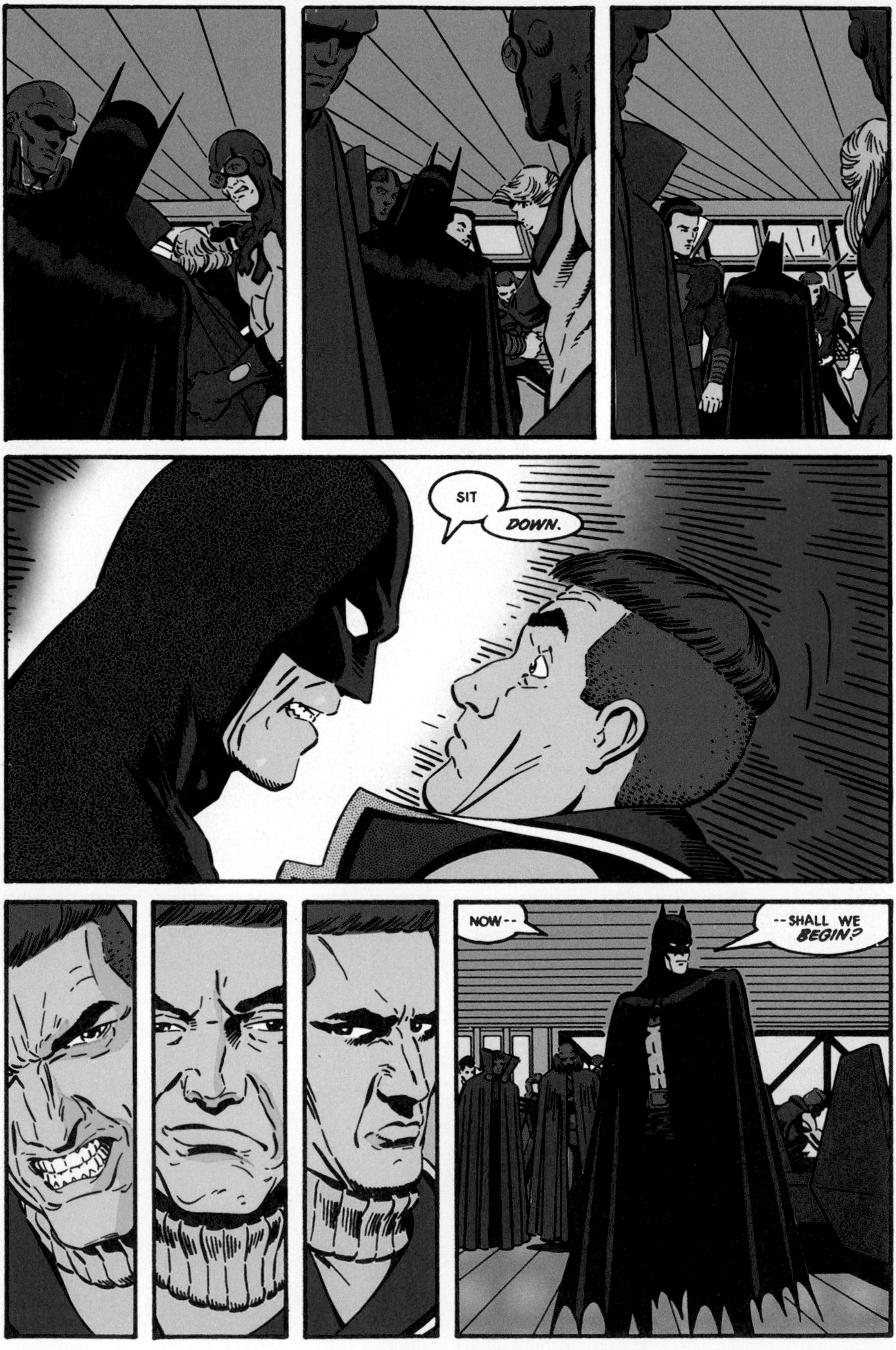
SIT
DOWN.
NOW--
--SHALL WE BEGIN?

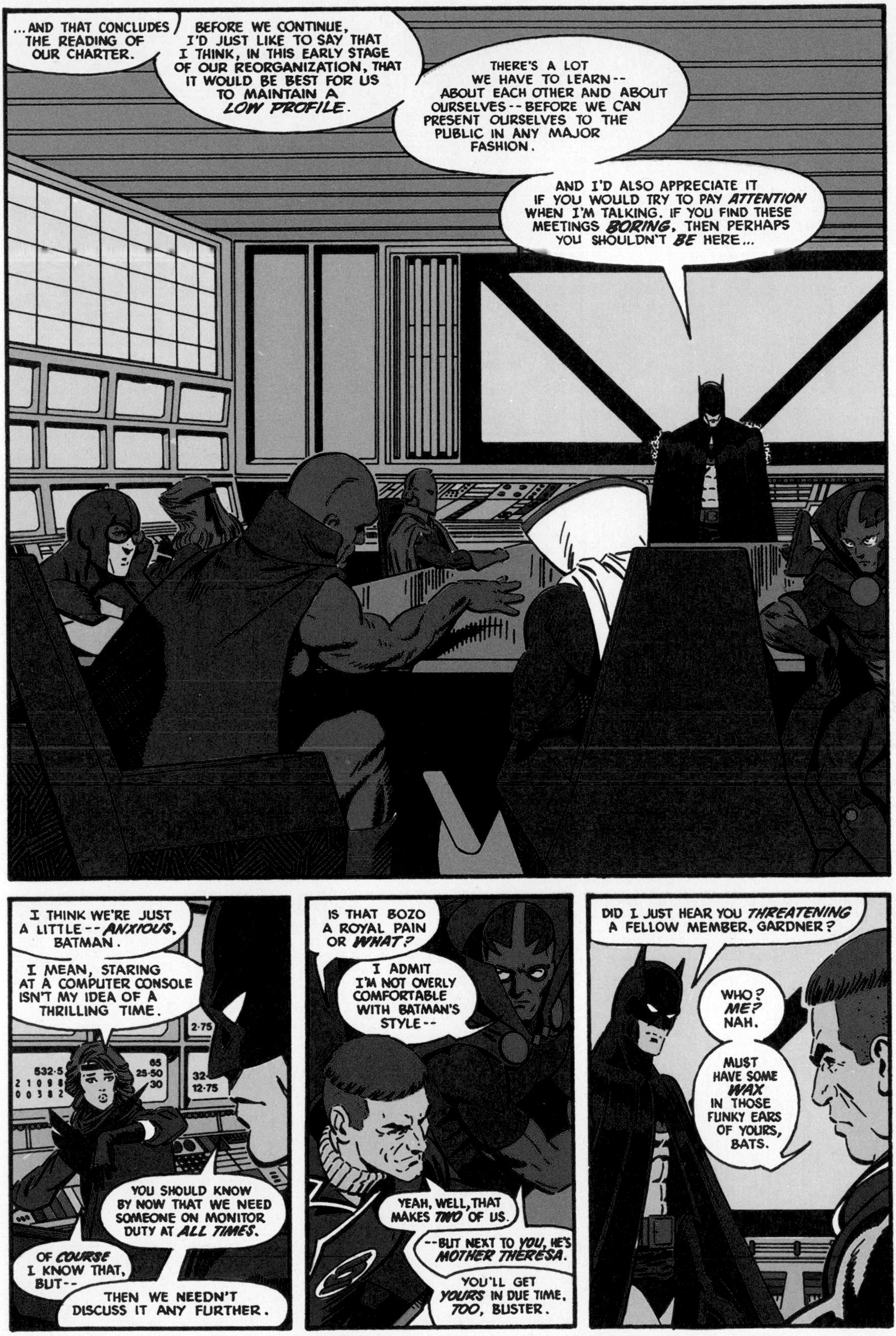
...AND THAT CONCLUDES THE READING OF OUR CHARTER.
BEFORE WE CONTINUE, I'D JUST LIKE TO SAY THAT I THINK, IN THIS EARLY STAGE OF OUR REORGANIZATION, THAT IT WOULD BE BEST FOR US TO MAINTAIN A *LOW PROFILE*.
THERE'S A LOT WE HAVE TO LEARN-- ABOUT EACH OTHER AND ABOUT OURSELVES--BEFORE WE CAN PRESENT OURSELVES TO THE PUBLIC IN ANY MAJOR FASHION.
AND I'D ALSO APPRECIATE IT IF YOU WOULD TRY TO PAY *ATTENTION* WHEN I'M TALKING. IF YOU FIND THESE MEETINGS *BORING*, THEN PERHAPS YOU SHOULDN'T *BE* HERE...
I THINK WE'RE JUST A LITTLE--*ANXIOUS*, BATMAN.
I MEAN, STARING AT A COMPUTER CONSOLE ISN'T MY IDEA OF A THRILLING TIME.
YOU SHOULD KNOW BY NOW THAT WE NEED SOMEONE ON MONITOR DUTY AT *ALL TIMES*.
OF *COURSE* I KNOW THAT, BUT--
THEN WE NEEDN'T DISCUSS IT ANY FURTHER.
IS THAT BOZO A ROYAL PAIN OR *WHAT?*
I ADMIT I'M NOT OVERLY COMFORTABLE WITH BATMAN'S STYLE--
YEAH, WELL, THAT MAKES *TWO* OF US.
--BUT NEXT TO *YOU*, HE'S *MOTHER THERESA*.
YOU'LL GET *YOURS* IN DUE TIME, *TOO*, BUSTER.
DID I JUST HEAR YOU *THREATENING* A FELLOW MEMBER, GARDNER?
WHO? *ME?* NAH.
MUST HAVE SOME *WAX* IN THOSE FUNKY EARS OF YOURS, BATS.

NEW YORK CITY.

BWAAARRRRRR

LADIES

OH... *PLEASE!*

STOPSTOP*STOP!*

NOT ANOTHER "BEEP" *OUT* OF YOU!

I'VE GOT TO ADDRESS THE *GENERAL ASSEMBLY* IN FIVE MINUTES -- AND THEY DECIDE TO CALL A MEETING *NOW?*

WELL, SORRY. NO, THANKS. *FORGET* IT. IF IT'S A CHOICE BETWEEN ZAPPING SUPER-VILLAINS AND FEEDING THE HUNGRY... WELL, THEN, THERE *IS* NO CHOICE!

THE NEW SOLAR STORAGE UNITS I'VE DEVELOPED COULD OPEN UP THE OCEAN FLOOR TO ALL *MANNER* OF AGRICULTURAL DEVELOPMENT, IF I CAN ONLY GET THE *FUNDING...*

SHUT UP. *PLEASE?*

PRETTY PLEASE?

QUIET!!

WHACK

I'M *TALKING* TO IT.

I'M TALKING TO *MYSELF.*

I'M LOSING MY *MIND!*

WELL, IF I CAN'T SHUT THE STUPID THING OFF, I CAN AT LEAST SHOVE IT INTO MY PURSE AND HOPE IT'S MUFFLED ENOUGH SO NO ONE *ELSE* WILL BE ABLE TO HEAR IT.

HOW DO I GET MYSELF *INTO* THESE THINGS?

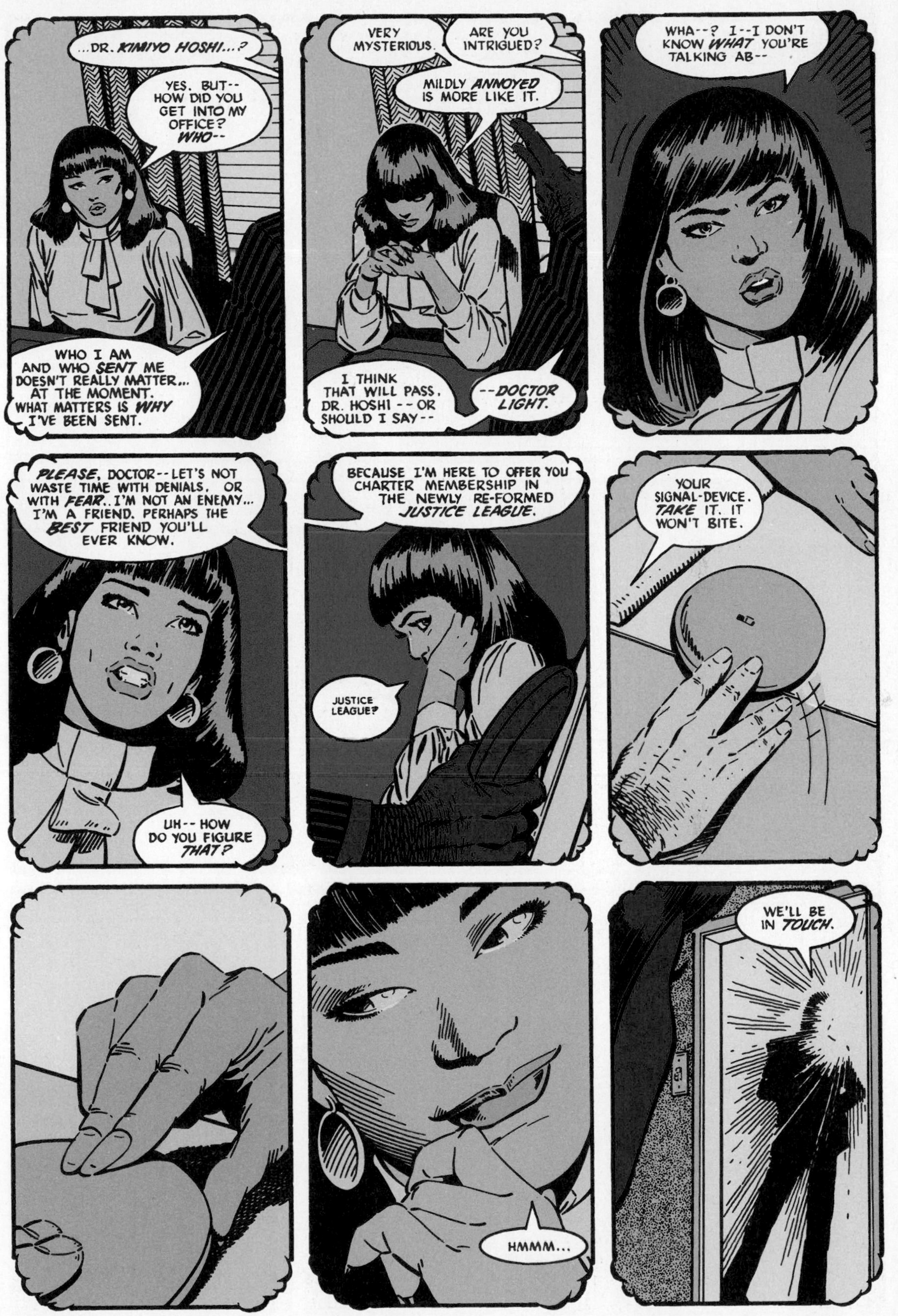
...DR. KIMIYO HOSHI...?
YES. BUT-- HOW DID YOU GET INTO MY OFFICE? WHO--
WHO I AM AND WHO SENT ME DOESN'T REALLY MATTER... AT THE MOMENT. WHAT MATTERS IS WHY I'VE BEEN SENT.
VERY MYSTERIOUS.
ARE YOU INTRIGUED?
MILDLY ANNOYED IS MORE LIKE IT.
I THINK THAT WILL PASS, DR. HOSHI -- OR SHOULD I SAY--
--DOCTOR LIGHT.
WHA--? I--I DON'T KNOW WHAT YOU'RE TALKING AB--
PLEASE, DOCTOR--LET'S NOT WASTE TIME WITH DENIALS. OR WITH FEAR..I'M NOT AN ENEMY... I'M A FRIEND. PERHAPS THE BEST FRIEND YOU'LL EVER KNOW.
UH-- HOW DO YOU FIGURE THAT?
BECAUSE I'M HERE TO OFFER YOU CHARTER MEMBERSHIP IN THE NEWLY RE-FORMED JUSTICE LEAGUE.
JUSTICE LEAGUE?
YOUR SIGNAL-DEVICE. TAKE IT. IT WON'T BITE.
HMMM...
WE'LL BE IN TOUCH.

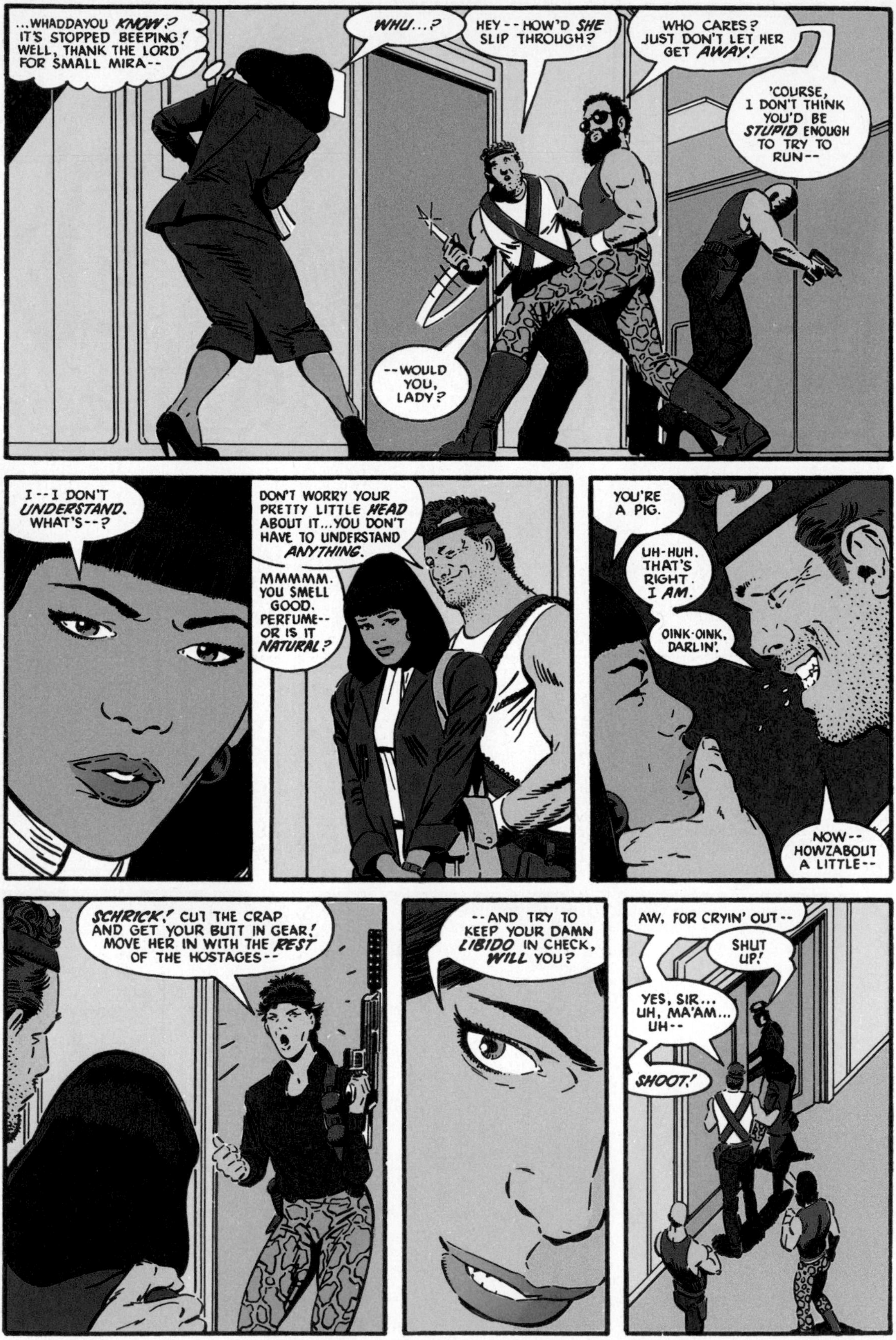
...WHADDAYOU KNOW? IT'S STOPPED BEEPING! WELL, THANK THE LORD FOR SMALL MIRA--
WHU...?
HEY--HOW'D SHE SLIP THROUGH?
WHO CARES? JUST DON'T LET HER GET AWAY!
'COURSE, I DON'T THINK YOU'D BE STUPID ENOUGH TO TRY TO RUN--
--WOULD YOU, LADY?
I--I DON'T UNDERSTAND. WHAT'S--?
DON'T WORRY YOUR PRETTY LITTLE HEAD ABOUT IT...YOU DON'T HAVE TO UNDERSTAND ANYTHING.
MMMMM. YOU SMELL GOOD. PERFUME--OR IS IT NATURAL?
YOU'RE A PIG.
UH-HUH. THAT'S RIGHT. I AM.
OINK-OINK, DARLIN'.
NOW--HOWZABOUT A LITTLE--
SCHRICK! CUT THE CRAP AND GET YOUR BUTT IN GEAR! MOVE HER IN WITH THE REST OF THE HOSTAGES--
--AND TRY TO KEEP YOUR DAMN LIBIDO IN CHECK, WILL YOU?
AW, FOR CRYIN' OUT--
SHUT UP!
YES, SIR... UH, MA'AM... UH--
SHOOT!

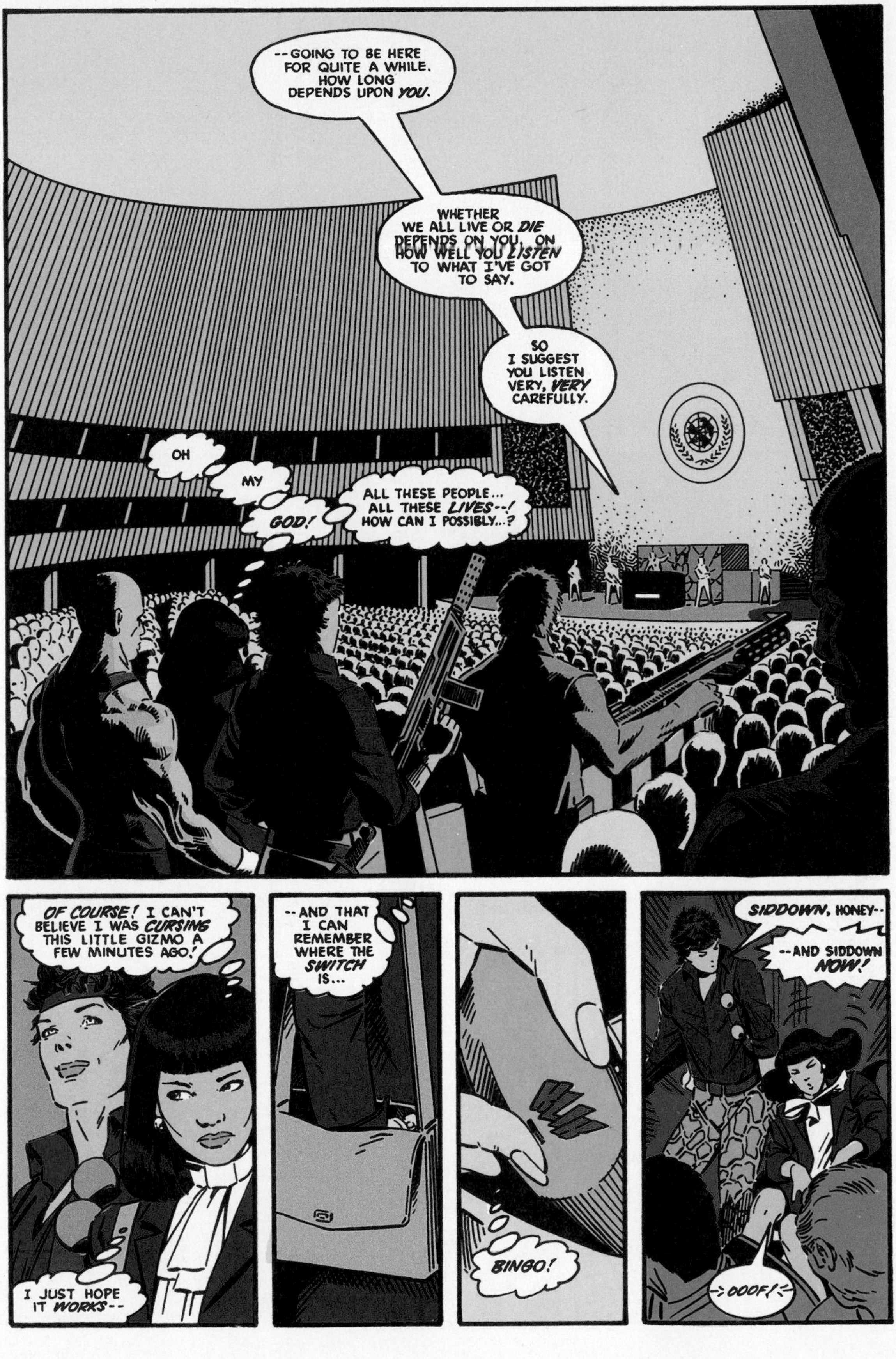
--GOING TO BE HERE FOR QUITE A WHILE. HOW LONG DEPENDS UPON YOU.
WHETHER WE ALL LIVE OR DIE DEPENDS ON YOU. ON HOW WELL YOU LISTEN TO WHAT I'VE GOT TO SAY.
SO I SUGGEST YOU LISTEN VERY, VERY CAREFULLY.
OH
MY
GOD!
ALL THESE PEOPLE... ALL THESE LIVES--! HOW CAN I POSSIBLY...?
OF COURSE! I CAN'T BELIEVE I WAS CURSING THIS LITTLE GIZMO A FEW MINUTES AGO!
I JUST HOPE IT WORKS--
--AND THAT I CAN REMEMBER WHERE THE SWITCH IS...
BINGO!
SIDDOWN, HONEY--
--AND SIDDOWN NOW!
OOOF!

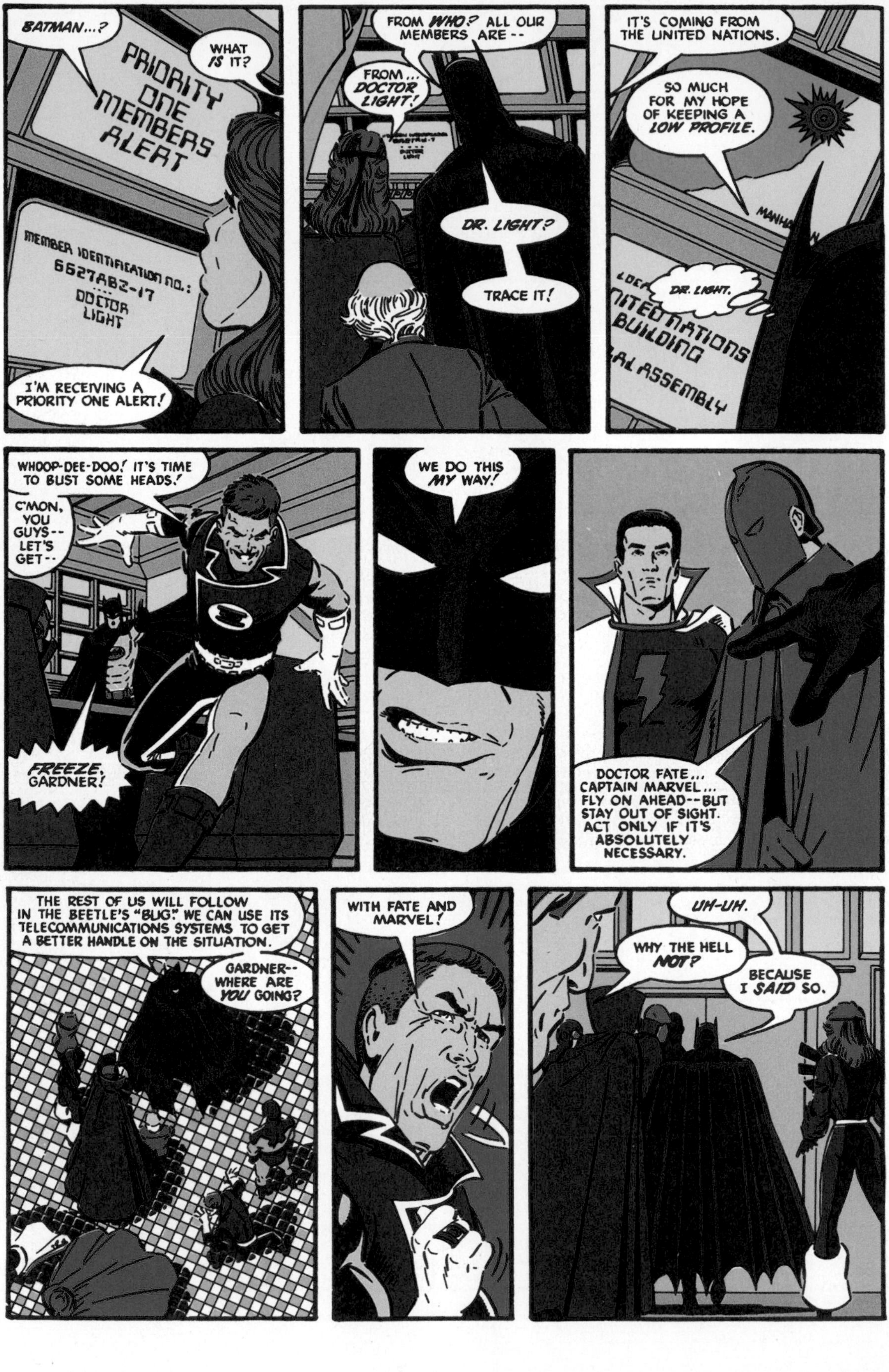
BATMAN...?
WHAT IS IT?
PRIORITY ONE MEMBERS ALERT
MEMBER IDENTIFICATION NO.: 6627ABZ-17 DOCTOR LIGHT
I'M RECEIVING A PRIORITY ONE ALERT!
FROM WHO? ALL OUR MEMBERS ARE --
FROM... DOCTOR LIGHT!
DR. LIGHT?
TRACE IT!
IT'S COMING FROM THE UNITED NATIONS.
SO MUCH FOR MY HOPE OF KEEPING A LOW PROFILE.
DR. LIGHT.
WHOOP-DEE-DOO! IT'S TIME TO BUST SOME HEADS!
C'MON, YOU GUYS-- LET'S GET--
FREEZE, GARDNER!
WE DO THIS MY WAY!
DOCTOR FATE... CAPTAIN MARVEL... FLY ON AHEAD--BUT STAY OUT OF SIGHT. ACT ONLY IF IT'S ABSOLUTELY NECESSARY.
THE REST OF US WILL FOLLOW IN THE BEETLE'S "BUG." WE CAN USE ITS TELECOMMUNICATIONS SYSTEMS TO GET A BETTER HANDLE ON THE SITUATION.
GARDNER-- WHERE ARE YOU GOING?
WITH FATE AND MARVEL!
UH-UH.
WHY THE HELL NOT?
BECAUSE I SAID SO.

...HOLDING THE U.N. GENERAL ASSEMBLY AT GUNPOINT. ALL OTHER PERSONNEL WERE PERMITTED TO LEAVE--

...STILL UNKNOWN HOW MANY TERRORISTS ARE INVOLVED. THE AREA HAS BEEN CORDONED OFF AND--

...SEE A GROUP BY THE MAIN ENTRANCE AND, YES, THEY *DO* APPEAR TO BE *ARMED*--

...AS-YET-UNIDENTIFIED *LEADER.* THIS PHOTO TAKEN EARLIER BY ONE OF OUR CAMERAMEN WHO WAS PERMITTED--

...NO DEMANDS AS YET--

...PERHAPS THE STRANGEST TWIST, THE TERRORIST LEADER HAS GRAFTED A *BOMB* ONTO HIS CHEST--

--SET TO EXPLODE SHOULD HIS HEART STOP BEATING. IN THE STUDIO WITH US IS DR. EMORY HUNT OF *S.T.A.R. LABS.* DR. HUNT--

--COULD THIS THREAT BE *GENUINE?* COULD THE BOMB DETONATE SHOULD THE TERRORIST BE KI--UH... *DIE?*

WELL, MITCH, AS YOU KNOW, THE FIELD OF BIOMECHANICS HAS BEEN MUCH ADVANCED OF LATE, ESPECIALLY--

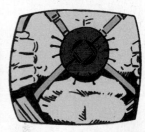

...MUCH ADVANCED OF LATE, ESPECIALLY AS REGARDS--

TRANSLATION: HE HASN'T GOT THE FOGGIEST IDEA *WHAT'LL* HAPPEN!

SCOTT, YOU'RE FAMILIAR WITH EXOTIC ARMAMENTS-- WHAT DO YOU THINK?

BEING RAISED ON *APOKOLIPS* DOESN'T AUTOMATICALLY MAKE ME AN *EXPERT* ON DEATH-DEALING.

I DON'T KNOW ALL THERE IS TO--

WILL IT DETONATE?

YES.

I THINK IT *WILL.*

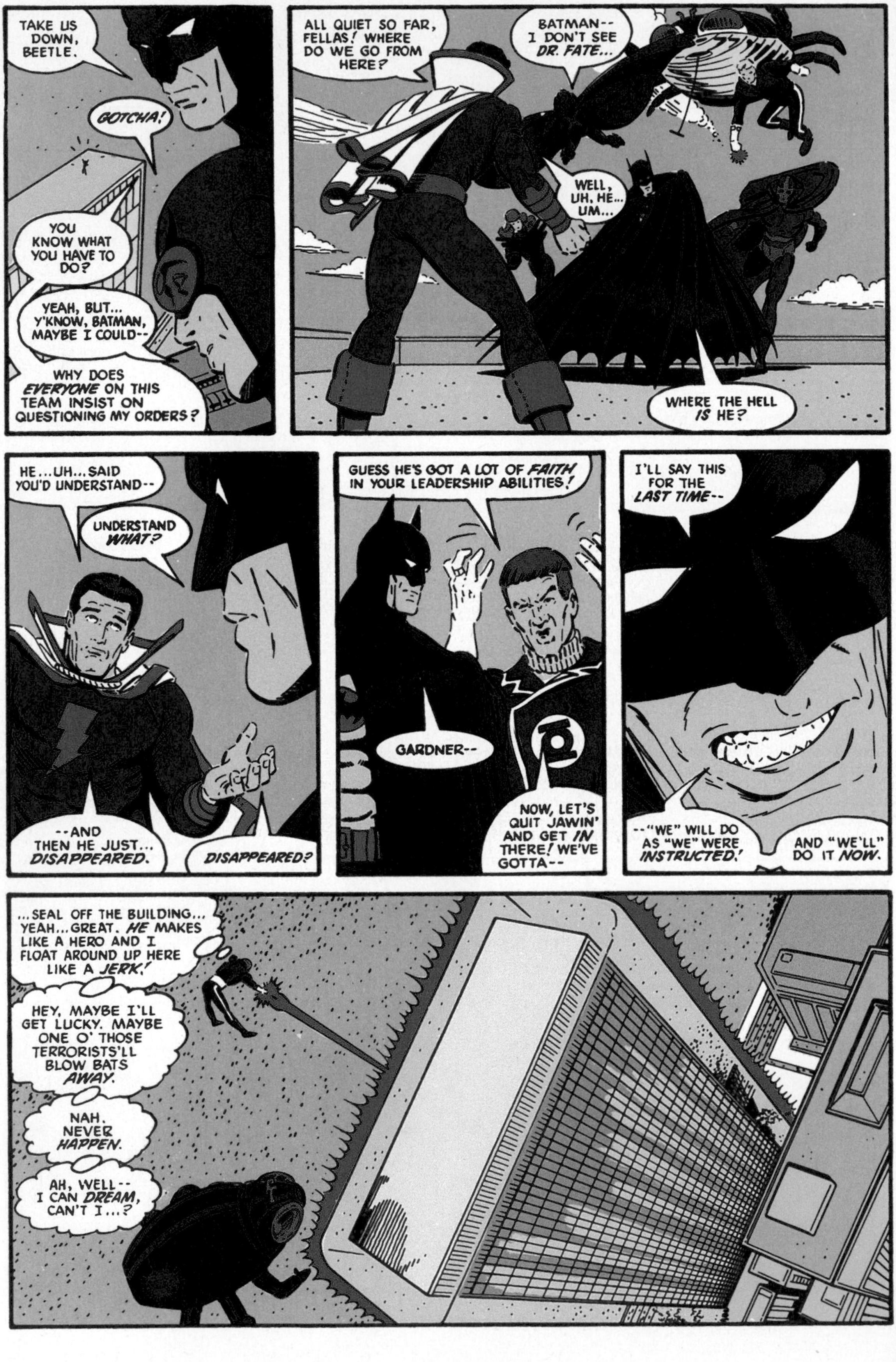
TAKE US DOWN, BEETLE.
GOTCHA!
YOU KNOW WHAT YOU HAVE TO DO?
YEAH, BUT... Y'KNOW, BATMAN, MAYBE I COULD--
WHY DOES EVERYONE ON THIS TEAM INSIST ON QUESTIONING MY ORDERS?
ALL QUIET SO FAR, FELLAS! WHERE DO WE GO FROM HERE?
BATMAN-- I DON'T SEE DR. FATE...
WELL, UH, HE... UM...
WHERE THE HELL IS HE?
HE...UH...SAID YOU'D UNDERSTAND--
UNDERSTAND WHAT?
--AND THEN HE JUST... DISAPPEARED.
DISAPPEARED?
GUESS HE'S GOT A LOT OF FAITH IN YOUR LEADERSHIP ABILITIES!
GARDNER--
NOW, LET'S QUIT JAWIN' AND GET IN THERE! WE'VE GOTTA--
I'LL SAY THIS FOR THE LAST TIME--
--"WE" WILL DO AS "WE" WERE INSTRUCTED!
AND "WE'LL" DO IT NOW.
...SEAL OFF THE BUILDING... YEAH...GREAT. HE MAKES LIKE A HERO AND I FLOAT AROUND UP HERE LIKE A JERK!
HEY, MAYBE I'LL GET LUCKY. MAYBE ONE O' THOSE TERRORISTS'LL BLOW BATS AWAY.
NAH. NEVER HAPPEN.
AH, WELL-- I CAN DREAM, CAN'T I...?

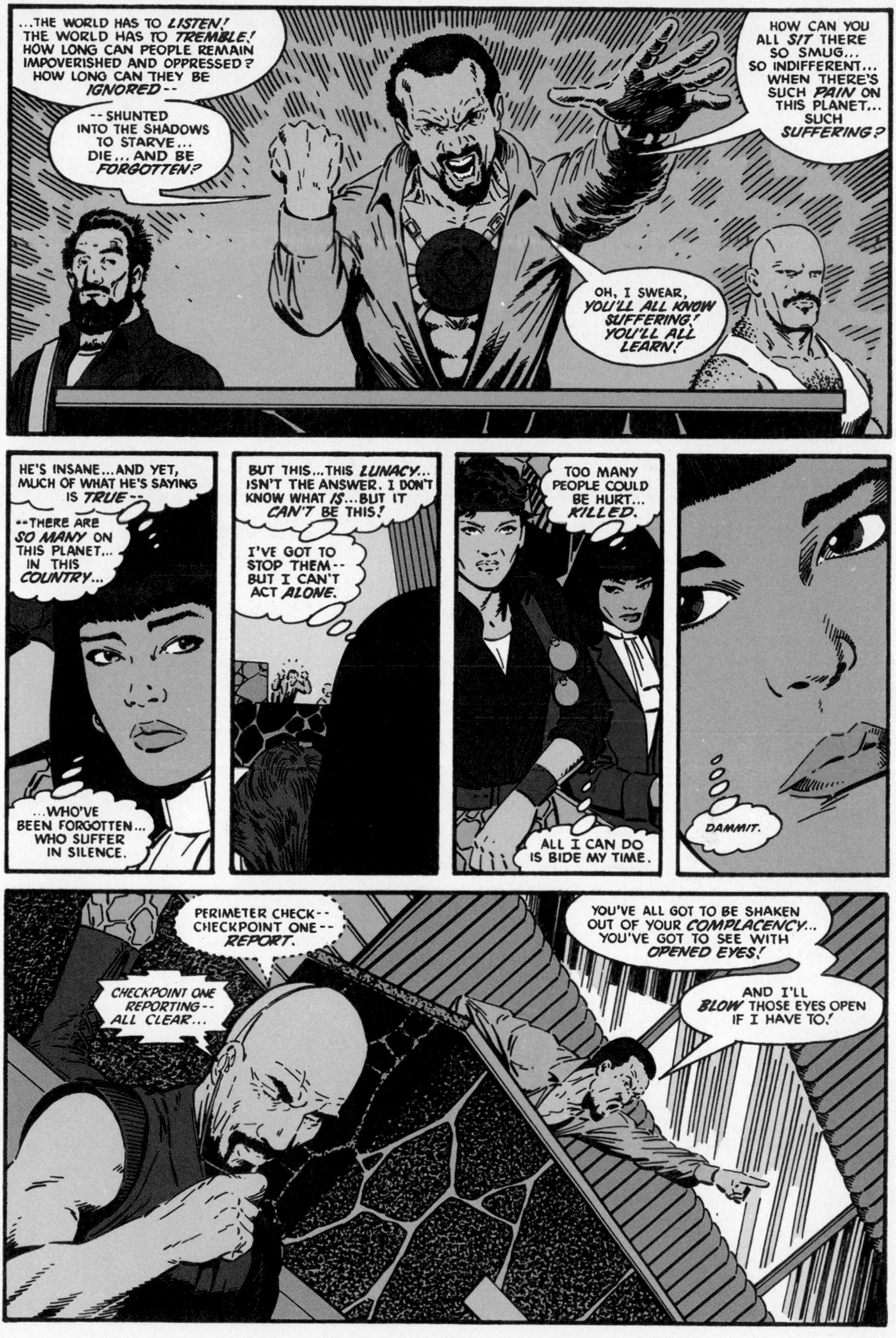
...THE WORLD HAS TO LISTEN! THE WORLD HAS TO TREMBLE! HOW LONG CAN PEOPLE REMAIN IMPOVERISHED AND OPPRESSED? HOW LONG CAN THEY BE IGNORED--
--SHUNTED INTO THE SHADOWS TO STARVE... DIE... AND BE FORGOTTEN?
HOW CAN YOU ALL SIT THERE SO SMUG... SO INDIFFERENT... WHEN THERE'S SUCH PAIN ON THIS PLANET... SUCH SUFFERING?
OH, I SWEAR, YOU'LL ALL KNOW SUFFERING! YOU'LL ALL LEARN!
HE'S INSANE...AND YET, MUCH OF WHAT HE'S SAYING IS TRUE--
--THERE ARE SO MANY ON THIS PLANET... IN THIS COUNTRY...
...WHO'VE BEEN FORGOTTEN... WHO SUFFER IN SILENCE.
BUT THIS...THIS LUNACY... ISN'T THE ANSWER. I DON'T KNOW WHAT IS...BUT IT CAN'T BE THIS!
I'VE GOT TO STOP THEM-- BUT I CAN'T ACT ALONE.
TOO MANY PEOPLE COULD BE HURT... KILLED.
ALL I CAN DO IS BIDE MY TIME.
DAMMIT.
PERIMETER CHECK-- CHECKPOINT ONE-- REPORT.
CHECKPOINT ONE REPORTING-- ALL CLEAR...
YOU'VE ALL GOT TO BE SHAKEN OUT OF YOUR COMPLACENCY... YOU'VE GOT TO SEE WITH OPENED EYES!
AND I'LL BLOW THOSE EYES OPEN IF I HAVE TO!

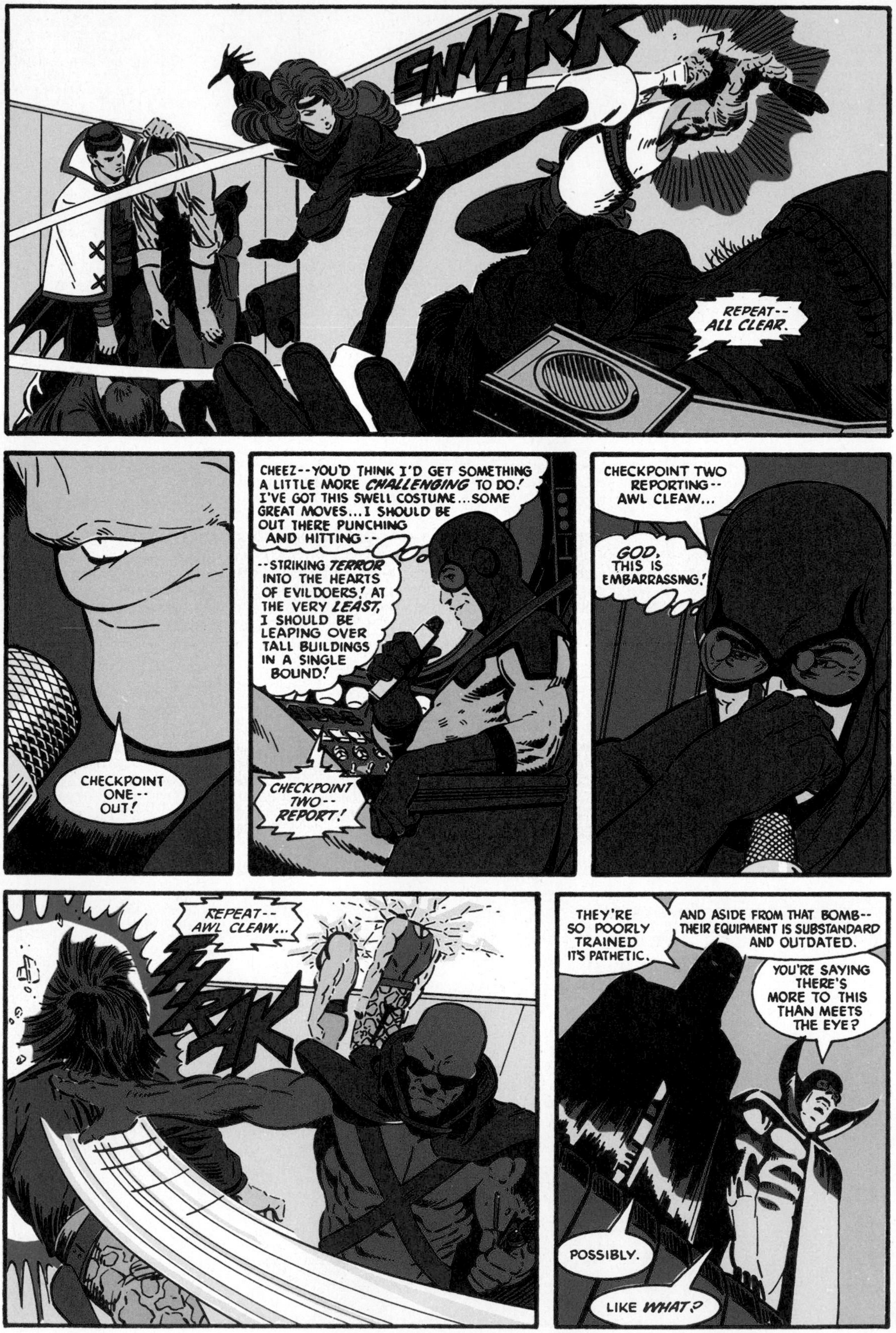
SNAKK
REPEAT-- ALL CLEAR.
CHECKPOINT ONE-- OUT!
CHEEZ--YOU'D THINK I'D GET SOMETHING A LITTLE MORE CHALLENGING TO DO! I'VE GOT THIS SWELL COSTUME...SOME GREAT MOVES...I SHOULD BE OUT THERE PUNCHING AND HITTING--
--STRIKING TERROR INTO THE HEARTS OF EVILDOERS! AT THE VERY LEAST, I SHOULD BE LEAPING OVER TALL BUILDINGS IN A SINGLE BOUND!
CHECKPOINT TWO-- REPORT!
CHECKPOINT TWO REPORTING-- AWL CLEAW...
GOD, THIS IS EMBARRASSING!
REPEAT-- AWL CLEAW...
THRAK
THEY'RE SO POORLY TRAINED IT'S PATHETIC.
AND ASIDE FROM THAT BOMB-- THEIR EQUIPMENT IS SUBSTANDARD AND OUTDATED.
YOU'RE SAYING THERE'S MORE TO THIS THAN MEETS THE EYE?
POSSIBLY.
LIKE WHAT?

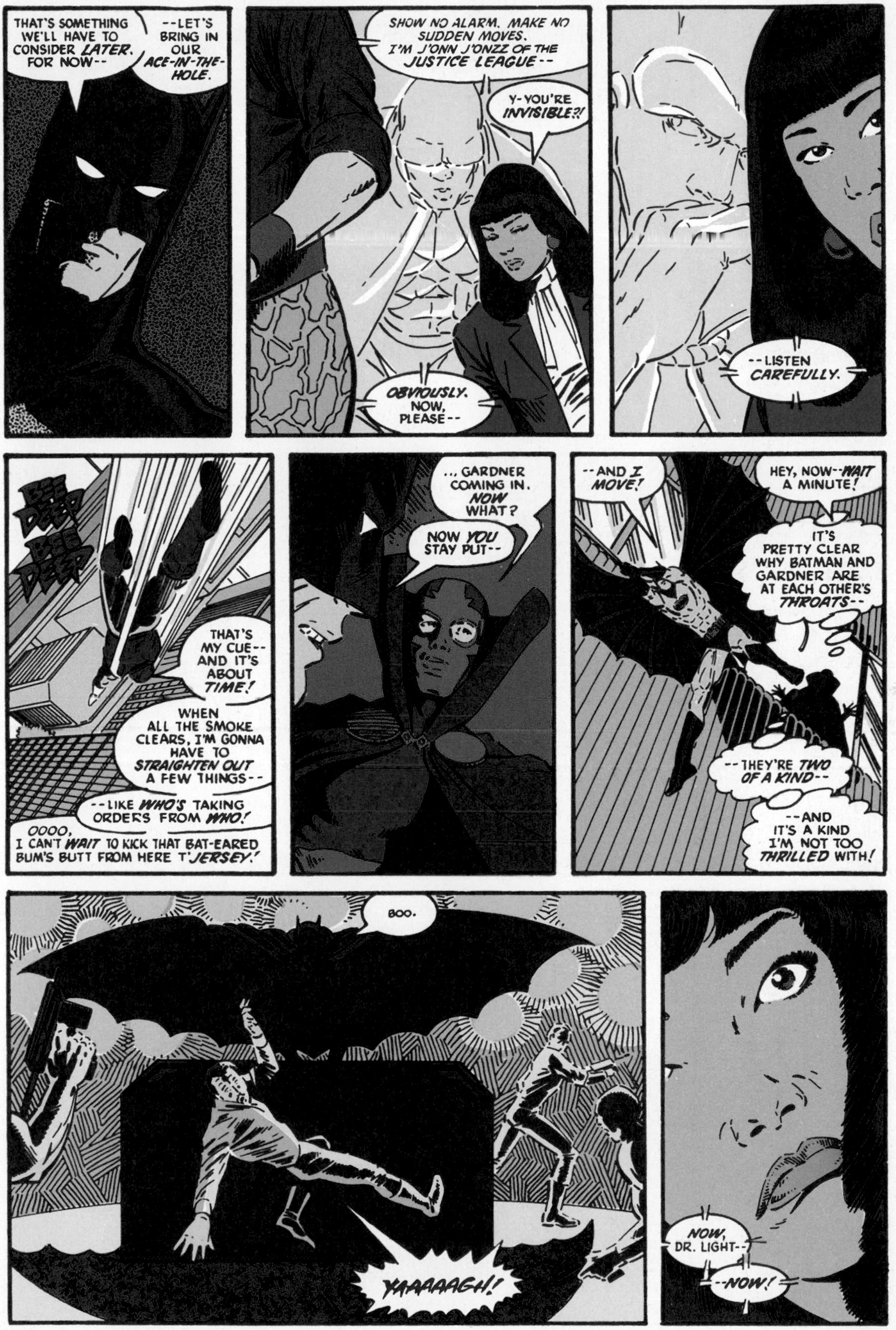
THAT'S SOMETHING WE'LL HAVE TO CONSIDER LATER. FOR NOW--
--LET'S BRING IN OUR ACE-IN-THE-HOLE.
SHOW NO ALARM. MAKE NO SUDDEN MOVES. I'M J'ONN J'ONZZ OF THE JUSTICE LEAGUE--
Y-YOU'RE INVISIBLE?!
OBVIOUSLY. NOW, PLEASE--
--LISTEN CAREFULLY.
BEE DEEP BEE DEEP
THAT'S MY CUE--AND IT'S ABOUT TIME!
WHEN ALL THE SMOKE CLEARS, I'M GONNA HAVE TO STRAIGHTEN OUT A FEW THINGS--
--LIKE WHO'S TAKING ORDERS FROM WHO!
OOOO, I CAN'T WAIT TO KICK THAT BAT-EARED BUM'S BUTT FROM HERE T'JERSEY!
...GARDNER COMING IN. NOW WHAT?
NOW YOU STAY PUT--
--AND I MOVE!
HEY, NOW--WAIT A MINUTE!
IT'S PRETTY CLEAR WHY BATMAN AND GARDNER ARE AT EACH OTHER'S THROATS--
--THEY'RE TWO OF A KIND--
--AND IT'S A KIND I'M NOT TOO THRILLED WITH!
BOO.
YAAAAAGH!
NOW, DR. LIGHT--
--NOW!

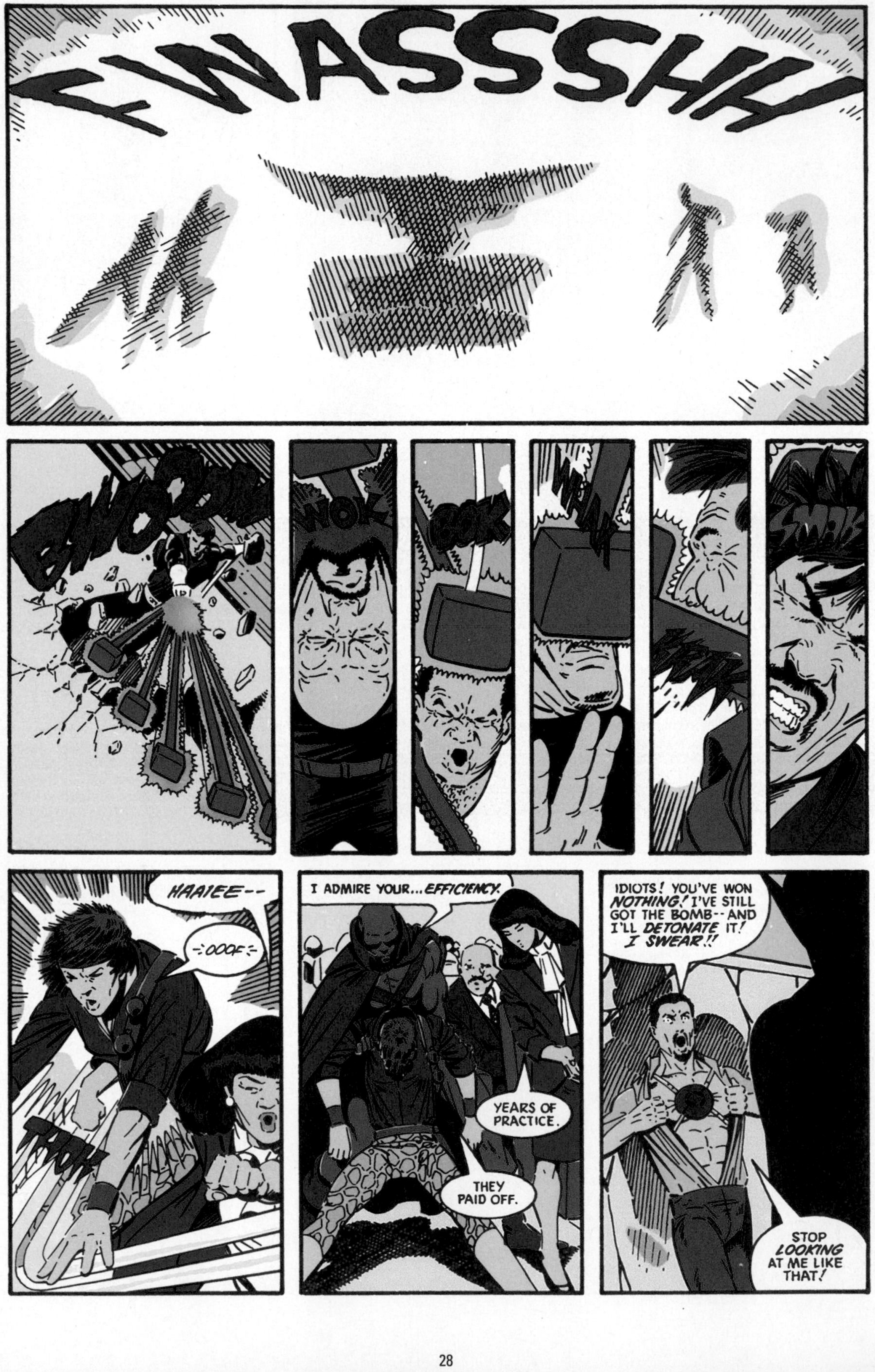
FWASSSHH
WOK
HAAIEE--
OOOF
I ADMIRE YOUR... EFFICIENCY.
YEARS OF PRACTICE.
THEY PAID OFF.
IDIOTS! YOU'VE WON NOTHING! I'VE STILL GOT THE BOMB--AND I'LL DETONATE IT! I SWEAR!!
STOP LOOKING AT ME LIKE THAT!

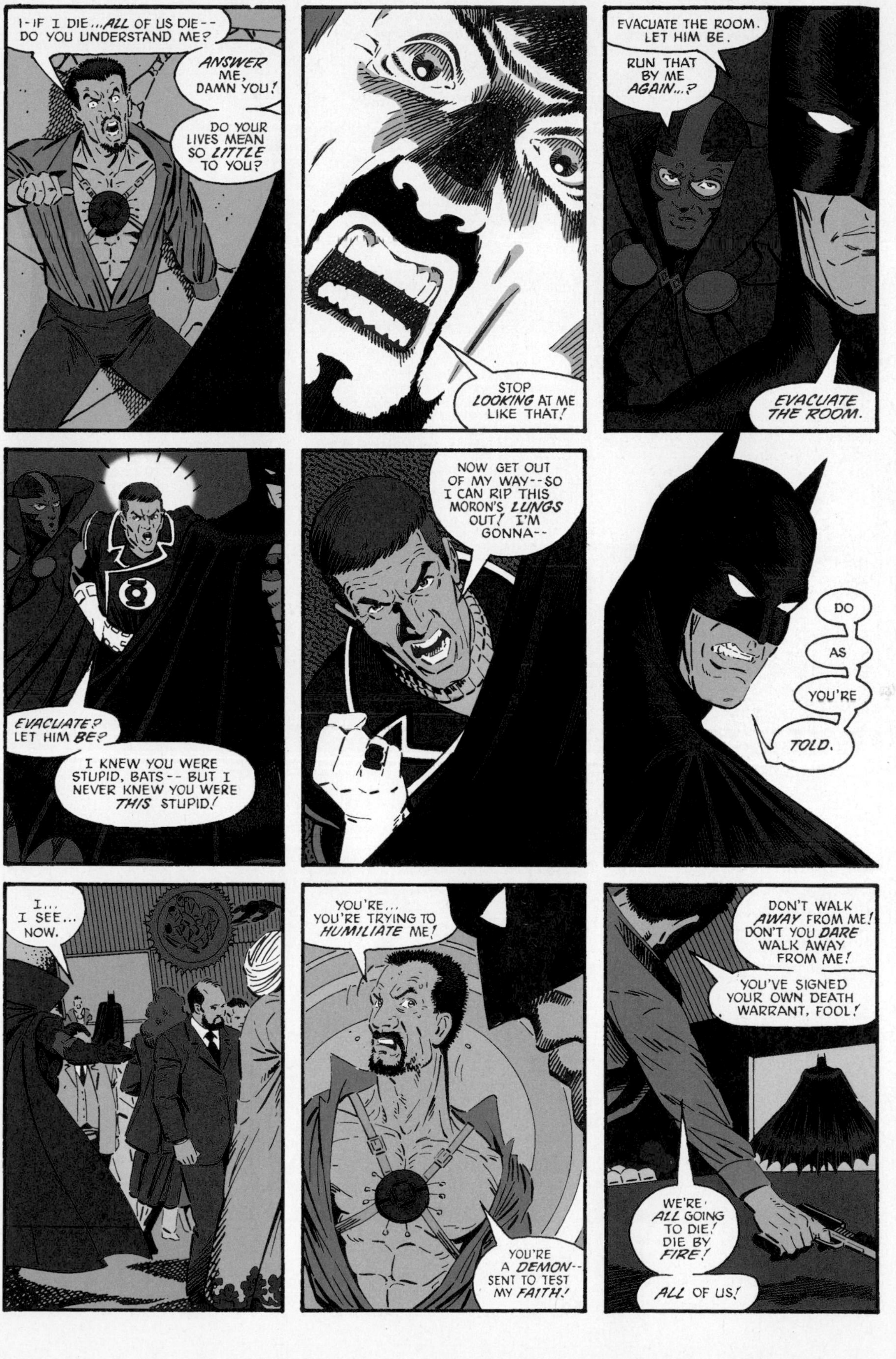
I-IF I DIE...ALL OF US DIE-- DO YOU UNDERSTAND ME?
ANSWER ME, DAMN YOU!
DO YOUR LIVES MEAN SO LITTLE TO YOU?
STOP LOOKING AT ME LIKE THAT!
EVACUATE THE ROOM. LET HIM BE.
RUN THAT BY ME AGAIN...?
EVACUATE THE ROOM.
EVACUATE? LET HIM BE?
I KNEW YOU WERE STUPID, BATS-- BUT I NEVER KNEW YOU WERE THIS STUPID!
NOW GET OUT OF MY WAY--SO I CAN RIP THIS MORON'S LUNGS OUT! I'M GONNA--
DO
AS
YOU'RE
TOLD.
I... I SEE... NOW.
YOU'RE... YOU'RE TRYING TO HUMILIATE ME!
YOU'RE A DEMON-- SENT TO TEST MY FAITH!
DON'T WALK AWAY FROM ME! DON'T YOU DARE WALK AWAY FROM ME!
YOU'VE SIGNED YOUR OWN DEATH WARRANT, FOOL!
WE'RE ALL GOING TO DIE! DIE BY FIRE!
ALL OF US!

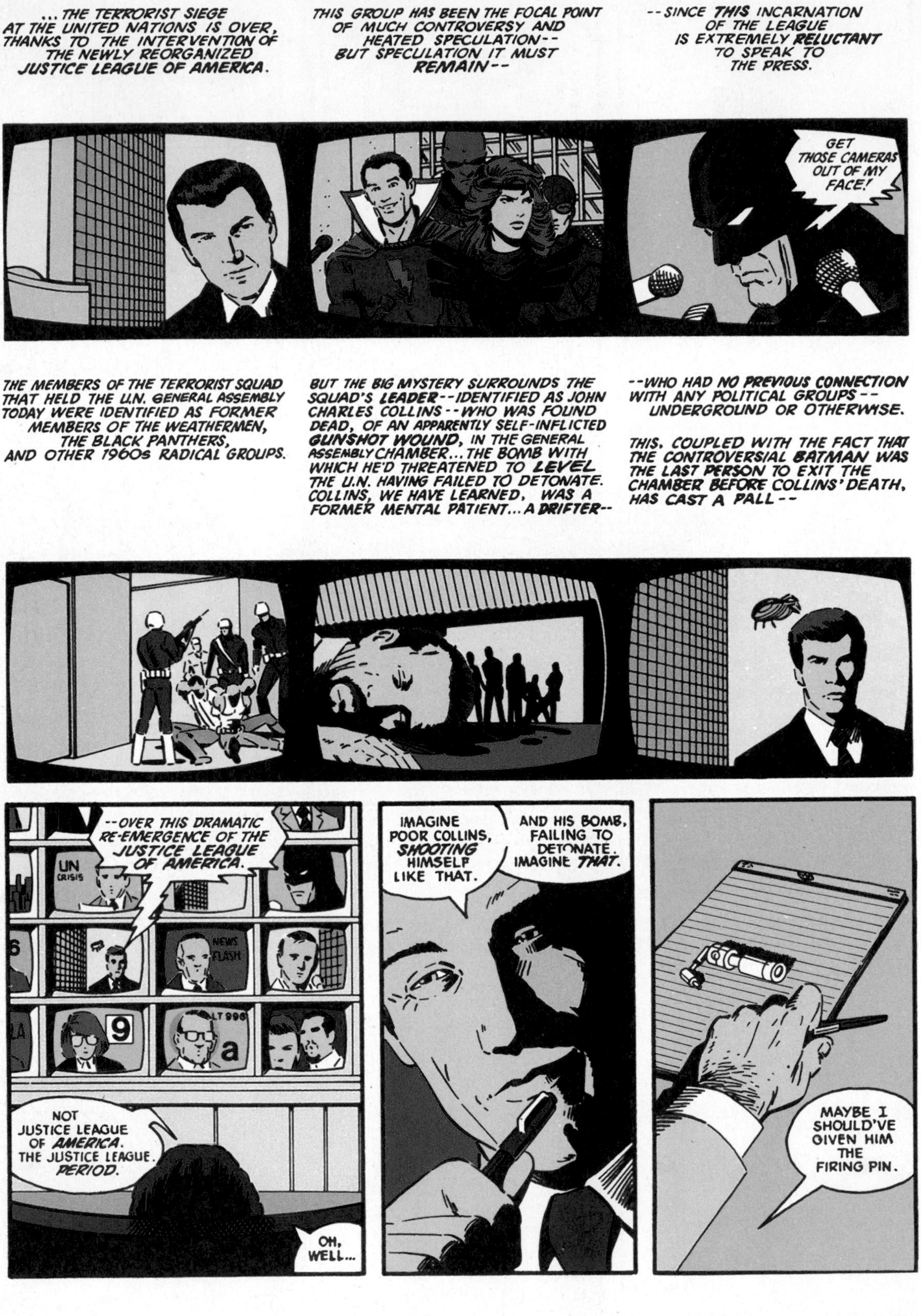
...THE TERRORIST SIEGE AT THE UNITED NATIONS IS OVER, THANKS TO THE INTERVENTION OF THE NEWLY REORGANIZED JUSTICE LEAGUE OF AMERICA.
THIS GROUP HAS BEEN THE FOCAL POINT OF MUCH CONTROVERSY AND HEATED SPECULATION-- BUT SPECULATION IT MUST REMAIN--
--SINCE THIS INCARNATION OF THE LEAGUE IS EXTREMELY RELUCTANT TO SPEAK TO THE PRESS.
GET THOSE CAMERAS OUT OF MY FACE!
THE MEMBERS OF THE TERRORIST SQUAD THAT HELD THE U.N. GENERAL ASSEMBLY TODAY WERE IDENTIFIED AS FORMER MEMBERS OF THE WEATHERMEN, THE BLACK PANTHERS, AND OTHER 1960s RADICAL GROUPS.
BUT THE BIG MYSTERY SURROUNDS THE SQUAD'S LEADER--IDENTIFIED AS JOHN CHARLES COLLINS--WHO WAS FOUND DEAD, OF AN APPARENTLY SELF-INFLICTED GUNSHOT WOUND, IN THE GENERAL ASSEMBLY CHAMBER... THE BOMB WITH WHICH HE'D THREATENED TO LEVEL THE U.N. HAVING FAILED TO DETONATE. COLLINS, WE HAVE LEARNED, WAS A FORMER MENTAL PATIENT... A DRIFTER--
--WHO HAD NO PREVIOUS CONNECTION WITH ANY POLITICAL GROUPS-- UNDERGROUND OR OTHERWISE.
THIS, COUPLED WITH THE FACT THAT THE CONTROVERSIAL BATMAN WAS THE LAST PERSON TO EXIT THE CHAMBER BEFORE COLLINS' DEATH, HAS CAST A PALL--
--OVER THIS DRAMATIC RE-EMERGENCE OF THE JUSTICE LEAGUE OF AMERICA.
UN CRISIS
NEWS FLASH
9
a
NOT JUSTICE LEAGUE OF AMERICA. THE JUSTICE LEAGUE. PERIOD.
OH, WELL...
IMAGINE POOR COLLINS, SHOOTING HIMSELF LIKE THAT.
AND HIS BOMB, FAILING TO DETONATE. IMAGINE THAT.
MAYBE I SHOULD'VE GIVEN HIM THE FIRING PIN.

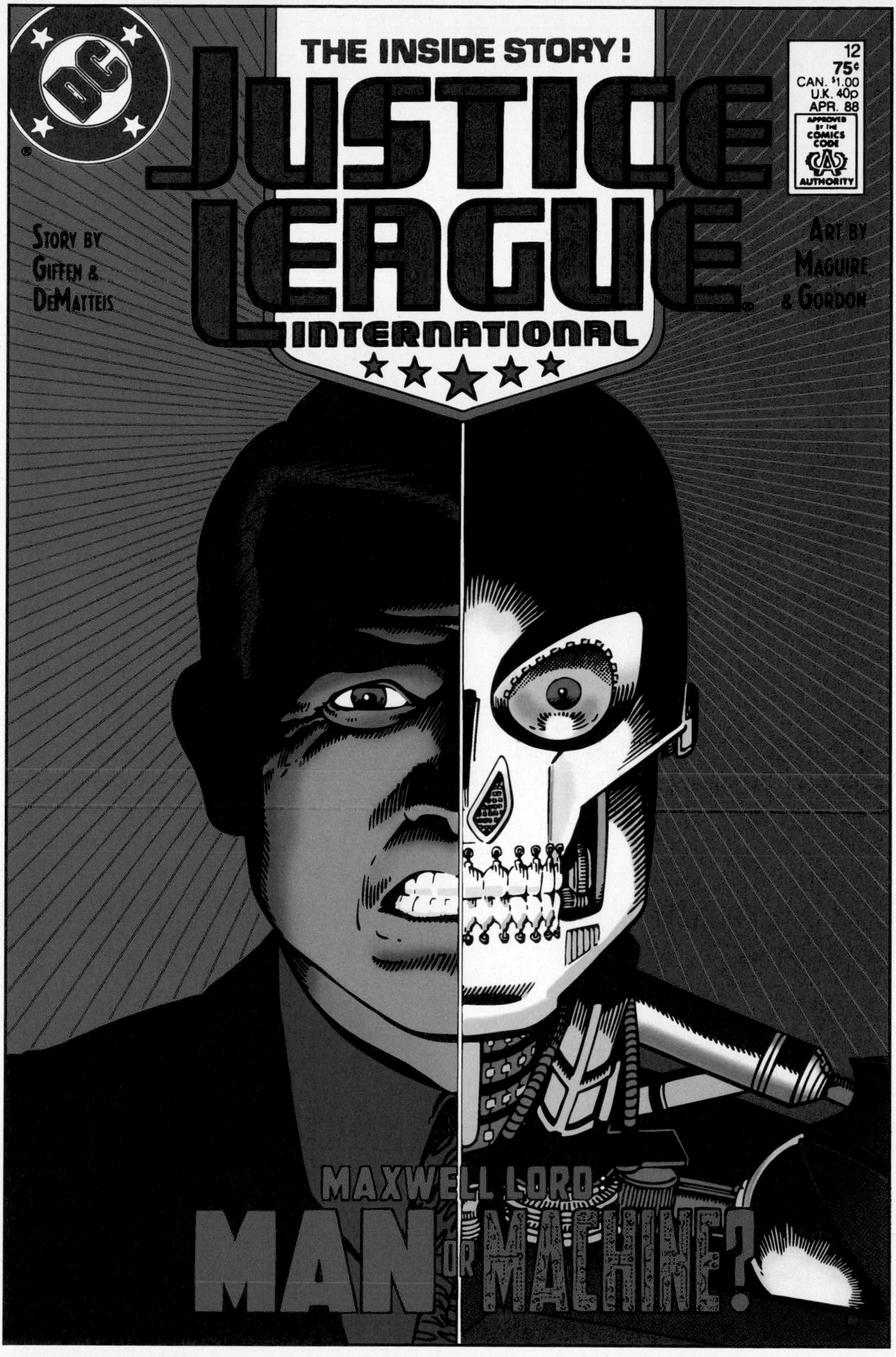
THE INSIDE STORY!
JUSTICE LEAGUE INTERNATIONAL
12
75¢
CAN. $1.00
U.K. 40p
APR. 88
APPROVED BY THE COMICS CODE AUTHORITY
STORY BY GIFFEN & DEMATTEIS
ART BY MAGUIRE & GORDON
MAXWELL LORD:
MAN OR MACHINE?

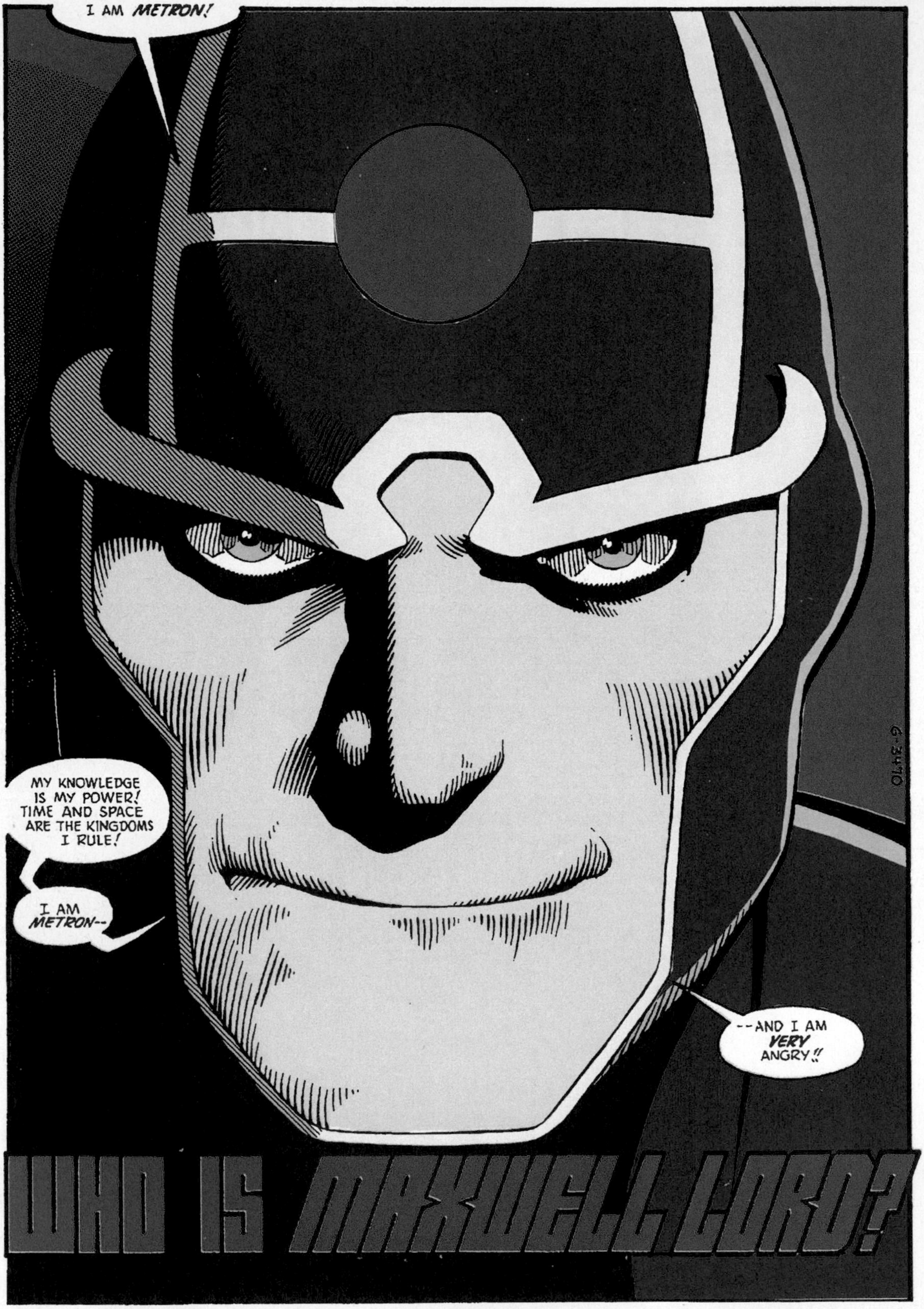
I AM METRON!
MY KNOWLEDGE IS MY POWER! TIME AND SPACE ARE THE KINGDOMS I RULE!
I AM METRON--
--AND I AM VERY ANGRY!!
WHO IS MAXWELL LORD?

Keith Giffen
plot & breakdowns

J.M. DeMatteis
script

Kevin Maguire
pencils

Al Gordon
inks

Gene D'Angelo
colors

Bob Lappan
letters

Kevin Maguire & Al Gordon
cover

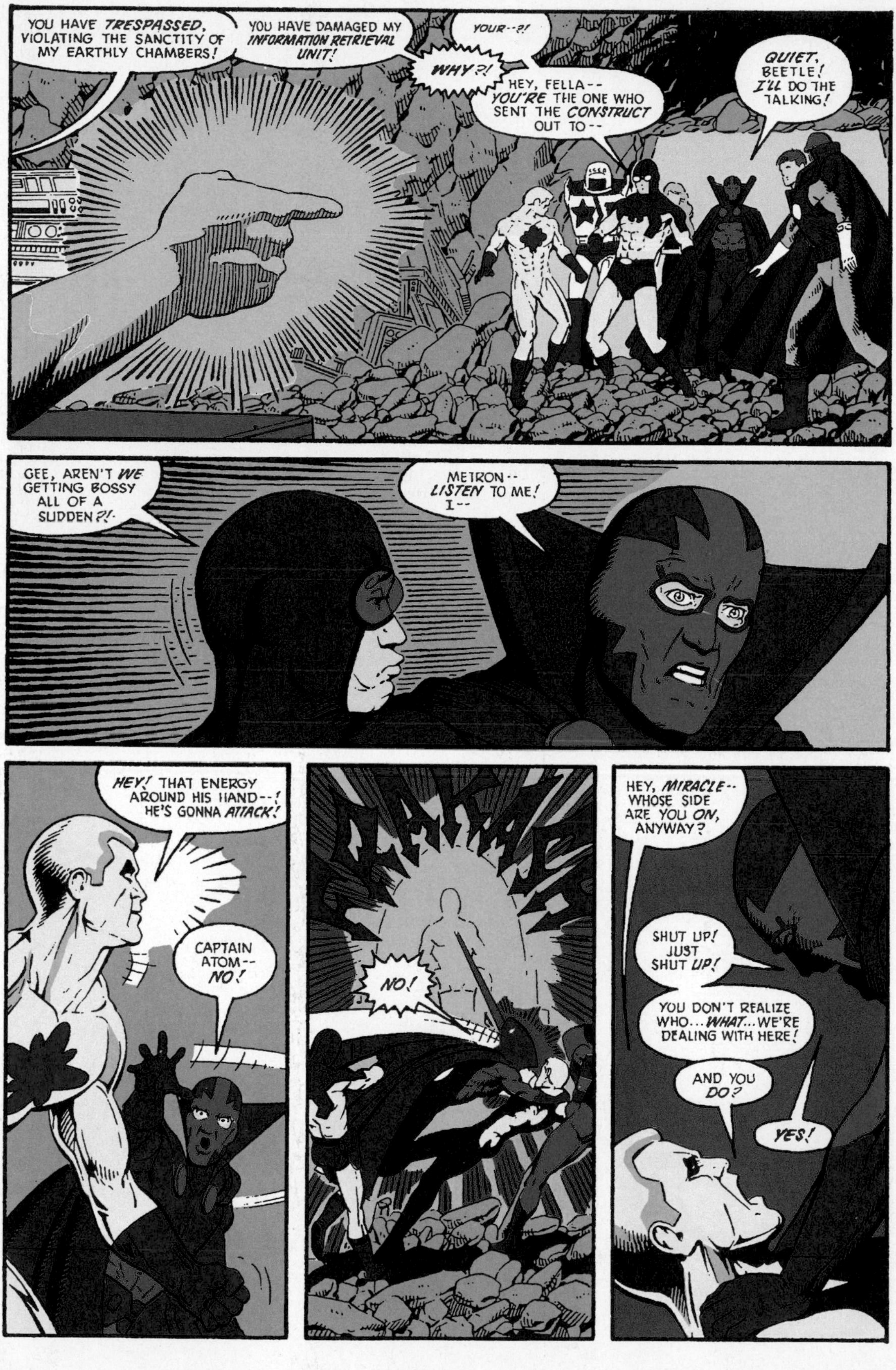
YOU HAVE TRESPASSED, VIOLATING THE SANCTITY OF MY EARTHLY CHAMBERS!
YOU HAVE DAMAGED MY INFORMATION RETRIEVAL UNIT!
YOUR--?!
WHY?!
HEY, FELLA-- YOU'RE THE ONE WHO SENT THE CONSTRUCT OUT TO--
QUIET, BEETLE! I'LL DO THE TALKING!
GEE, AREN'T WE GETTING BOSSY ALL OF A SUDDEN?!
METRON-- LISTEN TO ME! I--
HEY! THAT ENERGY AROUND HIS HAND--! HE'S GONNA ATTACK!
CAPTAIN ATOM-- NO!
NO!
HEY, MIRACLE-- WHOSE SIDE ARE YOU ON, ANYWAY?
SHUT UP! JUST SHUT UP!
YOU DON'T REALIZE WHO...WHAT...WE'RE DEALING WITH HERE!
AND YOU DO?
YES!

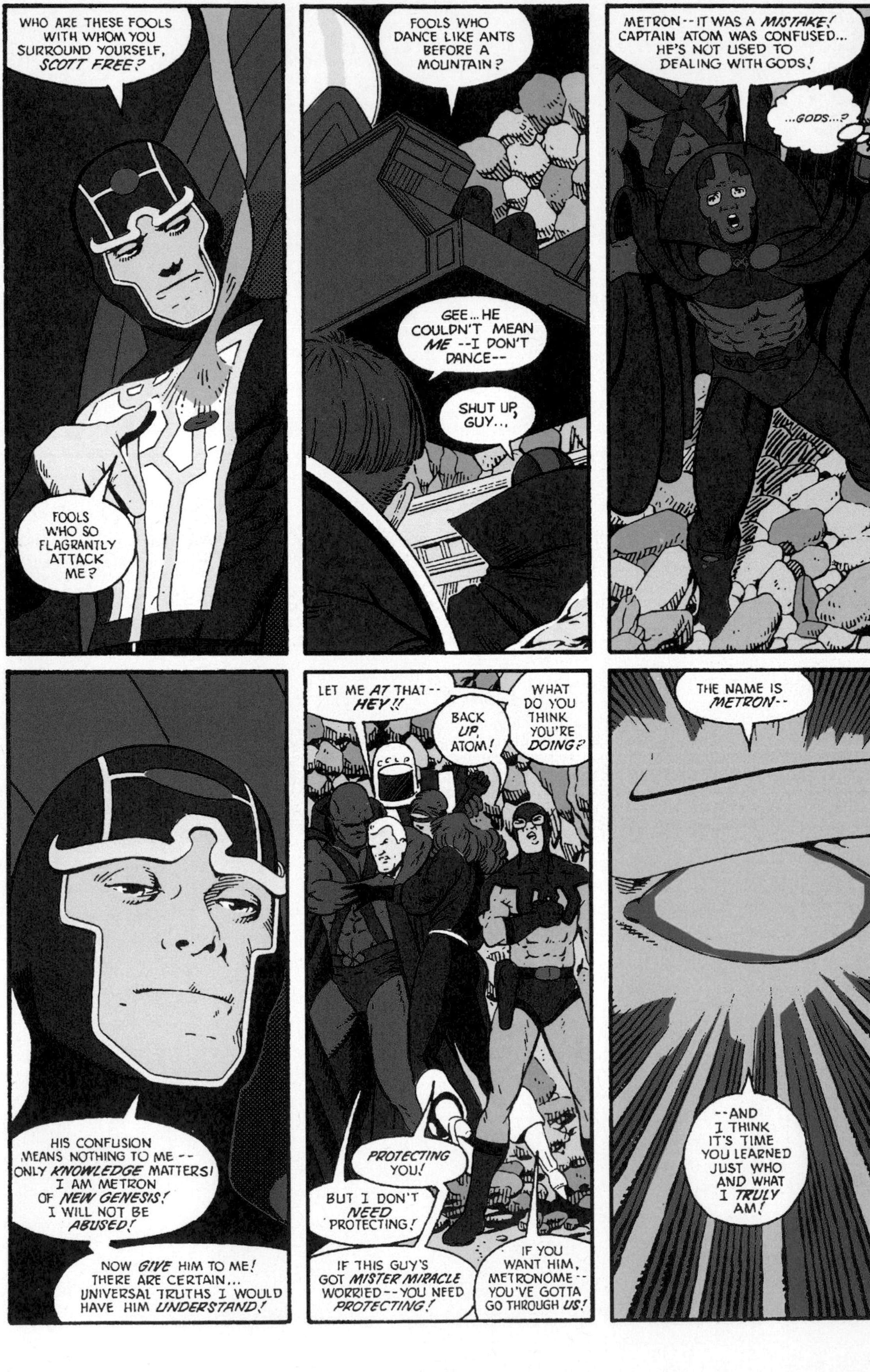
WHO ARE THESE FOOLS WITH WHOM YOU SURROUND YOURSELF, SCOTT FREE?
FOOLS WHO SO FLAGRANTLY ATTACK ME?
FOOLS WHO DANCE LIKE ANTS BEFORE A MOUNTAIN?
GEE... HE COULDN'T MEAN ME --I DON'T DANCE--
SHUT UP, GUY...
METRON--IT WAS A MISTAKE! CAPTAIN ATOM WAS CONFUSED... HE'S NOT USED TO DEALING WITH GODS!
...GODS...?
HIS CONFUSION MEANS NOTHING TO ME-- ONLY KNOWLEDGE MATTERS! I AM METRON OF NEW GENESIS! I WILL NOT BE ABUSED!
NOW GIVE HIM TO ME! THERE ARE CERTAIN... UNIVERSAL TRUTHS I WOULD HAVE HIM UNDERSTAND!
LET ME AT THAT-- HEY!!
BACK UP, ATOM!
WHAT DO YOU THINK YOU'RE DOING?
PROTECTING YOU!
BUT I DON'T NEED PROTECTING!
IF THIS GUY'S GOT MISTER MIRACLE WORRIED--YOU NEED PROTECTING!
IF YOU WANT HIM, METRONOME--YOU'VE GOTTA GO THROUGH US!
THE NAME IS METRON--
--AND I THINK IT'S TIME YOU LEARNED JUST WHO AND WHAT I TRULY AM!

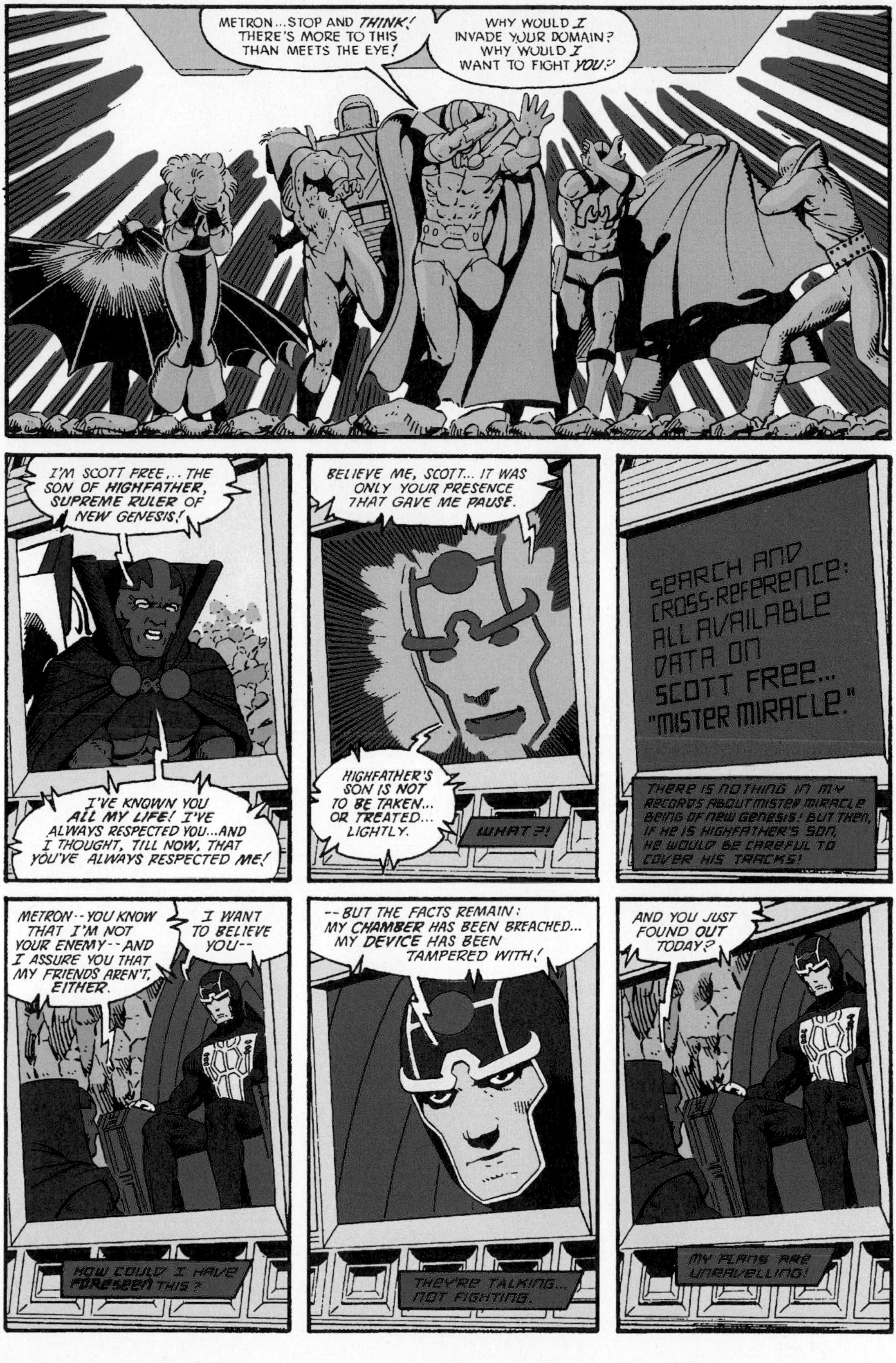

METRON...STOP AND THINK! THERE'S MORE TO THIS THAN MEETS THE EYE!
WHY WOULD I INVADE YOUR DOMAIN? WHY WOULD I WANT TO FIGHT YOU?
I'M SCOTT FREE... THE SON OF HIGHFATHER, SUPREME RULER OF NEW GENESIS!
I'VE KNOWN YOU ALL MY LIFE! I'VE ALWAYS RESPECTED YOU...AND I THOUGHT, TILL NOW, THAT YOU'VE ALWAYS RESPECTED ME!
BELIEVE ME, SCOTT... IT WAS ONLY YOUR PRESENCE THAT GAVE ME PAUSE.
HIGHFATHER'S SON IS NOT TO BE TAKEN... OR TREATED... LIGHTLY.
WHAT?!
SEARCH AND CROSS-REFERENCE: ALL AVAILABLE DATA ON SCOTT FREE... "MISTER MIRACLE."
THERE IS NOTHING IN MY RECORDS ABOUT MISTER MIRACLE BEING OF NEW GENESIS! BUT THEN, IF HE IS HIGHFATHER'S SON, HE WOULD BE CAREFUL TO COVER HIS TRACKS!
METRON--YOU KNOW THAT I'M NOT YOUR ENEMY--AND I ASSURE YOU THAT MY FRIENDS AREN'T, EITHER.
I WANT TO BELIEVE YOU--
HOW COULD I HAVE FORESEEN THIS?
--BUT THE FACTS REMAIN: MY CHAMBER HAS BEEN BREACHED... MY DEVICE HAS BEEN TAMPERED WITH!
THEY'RE TALKING... NOT FIGHTING.
AND YOU JUST FOUND OUT TODAY?
MY PLANS ARE UNRAVELLING!

I FOUND OUT NOTHING. THE FLOW OF DATA WAS UNINTERRUPTED.

BUT I WAS DRAWN HERE... NO. I WAS *SUMMONED!*

BY *WHO?*

BY THE RETRIEVAL UNIT *ITSELF!* IT CRIED OUT TO ME IN AN AUTOMATED SEMBLANCE OF *TERROR*... OF *PAIN!*

SOUNDS LIKE YOU WERE SET UP... AND SO WERE *WE!*

THAT UNIT WAS MODELLED AFTER *THE CONSTRUCT*-- AN OLD ENEMY OF THE LEAGUE'S--

--WE WERE LED TO BELIEVE THAT AN ASSOCIATE OF OURS, *MAXWELL LORD*, WAS ENDANGERED... SO WE CAME HERE AND--

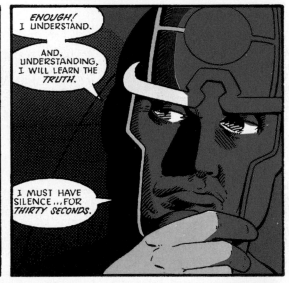

ENOUGH! I UNDERSTAND.

AND, UNDERSTANDING, I WILL LEARN THE *TRUTH.*

I MUST HAVE SILENCE... FOR *THIRTY SECONDS.*

HMM... I *SEE...*

NO!

JUST BEFORE YOUR INTRUSION... AS I SAT WITH THE RETRIEVAL UNIT... I FELT A FLASH OF *SENTIENCE!*

ANALYSIS: WE ARE FOUND OUT. RECOMMENDATION: SPEEDY EXIT.

AS MAX WOULD SAY--

--"I'M OUT OF HERE"!

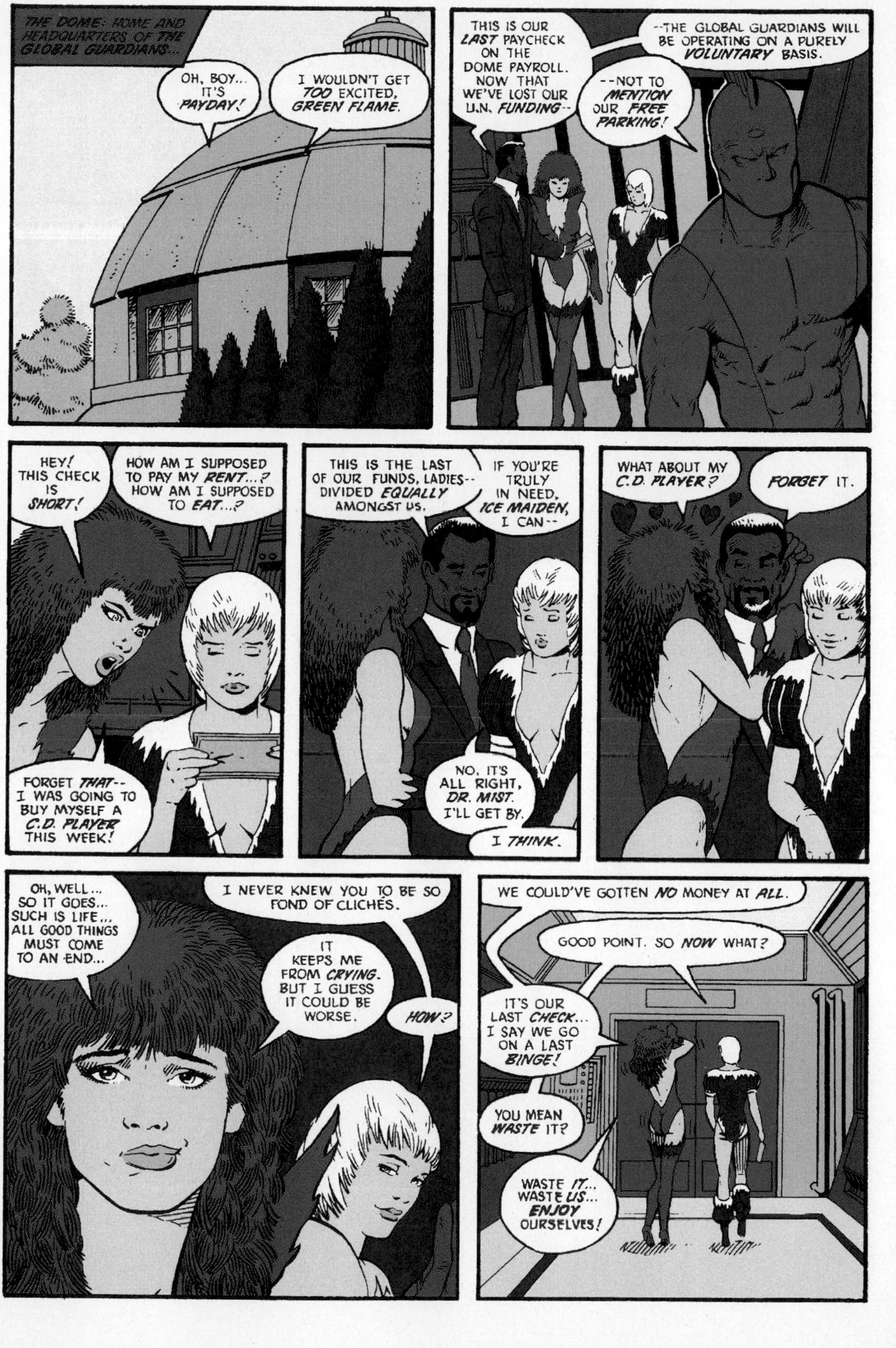
THE DOME: HOME AND HEADQUARTERS OF THE GLOBAL GUARDIANS...
OH, BOY... IT'S PAYDAY!
I WOULDN'T GET TOO EXCITED, GREEN FLAME.
THIS IS OUR LAST PAYCHECK ON THE DOME PAYROLL. NOW THAT WE'VE LOST OUR U.N. FUNDING--
--THE GLOBAL GUARDIANS WILL BE OPERATING ON A PURELY VOLUNTARY BASIS.
--NOT TO MENTION OUR FREE PARKING!
HEY! THIS CHECK IS SHORT!
HOW AM I SUPPOSED TO PAY MY RENT...? HOW AM I SUPPOSED TO EAT...?
FORGET THAT-- I WAS GOING TO BUY MYSELF A C.D. PLAYER THIS WEEK!
THIS IS THE LAST OF OUR FUNDS, LADIES-- DIVIDED EQUALLY AMONGST US.
IF YOU'RE TRULY IN NEED, ICE MAIDEN, I CAN--
NO, IT'S ALL RIGHT, DR. MIST. I'LL GET BY.
I THINK.
WHAT ABOUT MY C.D. PLAYER?
FORGET IT.
OH, WELL... SO IT GOES... SUCH IS LIFE... ALL GOOD THINGS MUST COME TO AN END...
I NEVER KNEW YOU TO BE SO FOND OF CLICHÉS.
IT KEEPS ME FROM CRYING. BUT I GUESS IT COULD BE WORSE.
HOW?
WE COULD'VE GOTTEN NO MONEY AT ALL.
GOOD POINT. SO NOW WHAT?
IT'S OUR LAST CHECK... I SAY WE GO ON A LAST BINGE!
YOU MEAN WASTE IT?
WASTE IT... WASTE US... ENJOY OURSELVES!

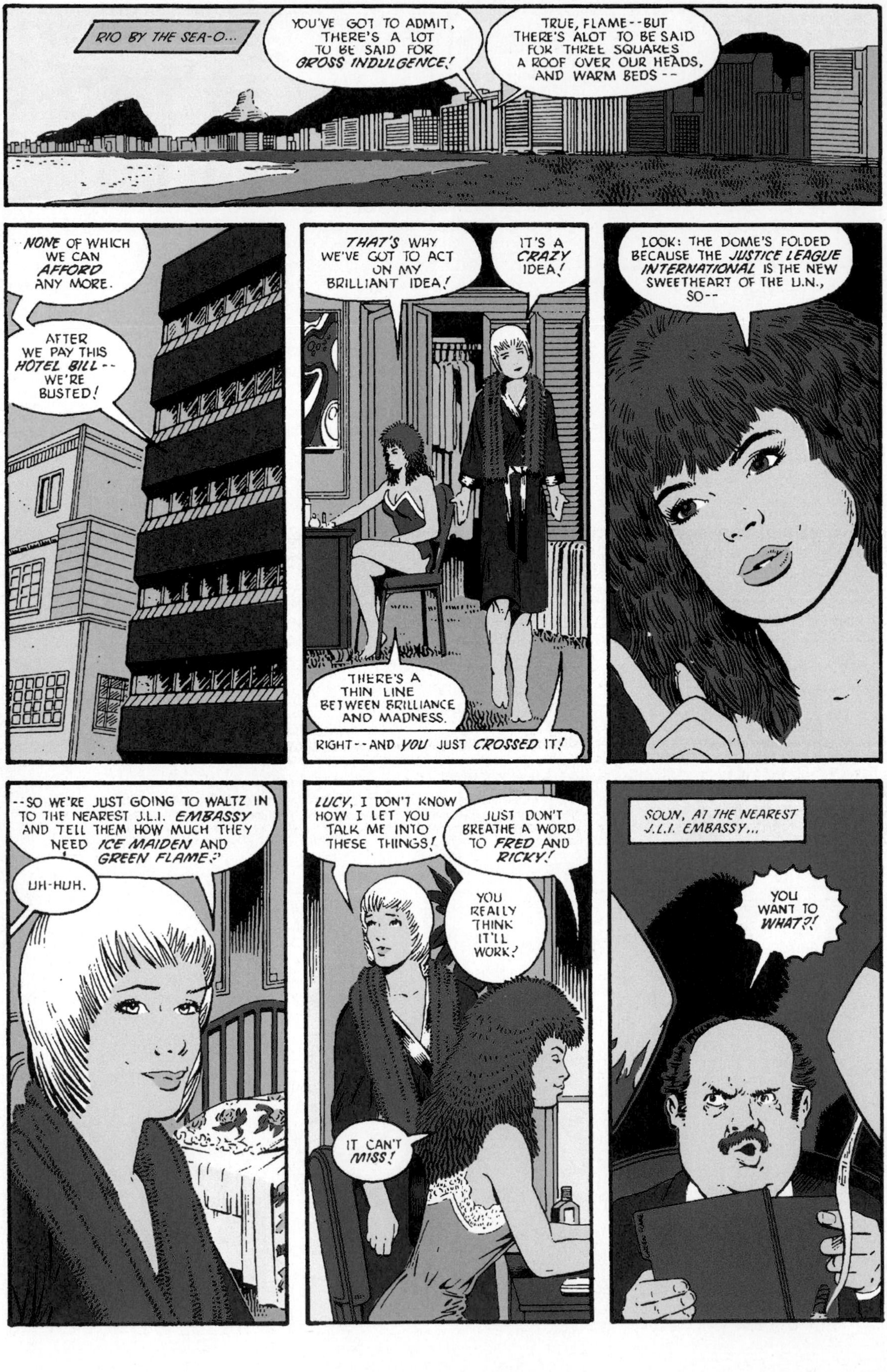
RIO BY THE SEA-O...
YOU'VE GOT TO ADMIT, THERE'S A LOT TO BE SAID FOR GROSS INDULGENCE!
TRUE, FLAME--BUT THERE'S ALOT TO BE SAID FOR THREE SQUARES A ROOF OVER OUR HEADS, AND WARM BEDS--
--NONE OF WHICH WE CAN AFFORD ANY MORE.
AFTER WE PAY THIS HOTEL BILL--WE'RE BUSTED!
THAT'S WHY WE'VE GOT TO ACT ON MY BRILLIANT IDEA!
IT'S A CRAZY IDEA!
THERE'S A THIN LINE BETWEEN BRILLIANCE AND MADNESS.
RIGHT--AND YOU JUST CROSSED IT!
LOOK: THE DOME'S FOLDED BECAUSE THE JUSTICE LEAGUE INTERNATIONAL IS THE NEW SWEETHEART OF THE U.N., SO--
--SO WE'RE JUST GOING TO WALTZ IN TO THE NEAREST J.L.I. EMBASSY AND TELL THEM HOW MUCH THEY NEED ICE MAIDEN AND GREEN FLAME?
UH-HUH.
LUCY, I DON'T KNOW HOW I LET YOU TALK ME INTO THESE THINGS!
JUST DON'T BREATHE A WORD TO FRED AND RICKY!
YOU REALLY THINK IT'LL WORK?
IT CAN'T MISS!
SOON, AT THE NEAREST J.L.I. EMBASSY...
YOU WANT TO WHAT?!

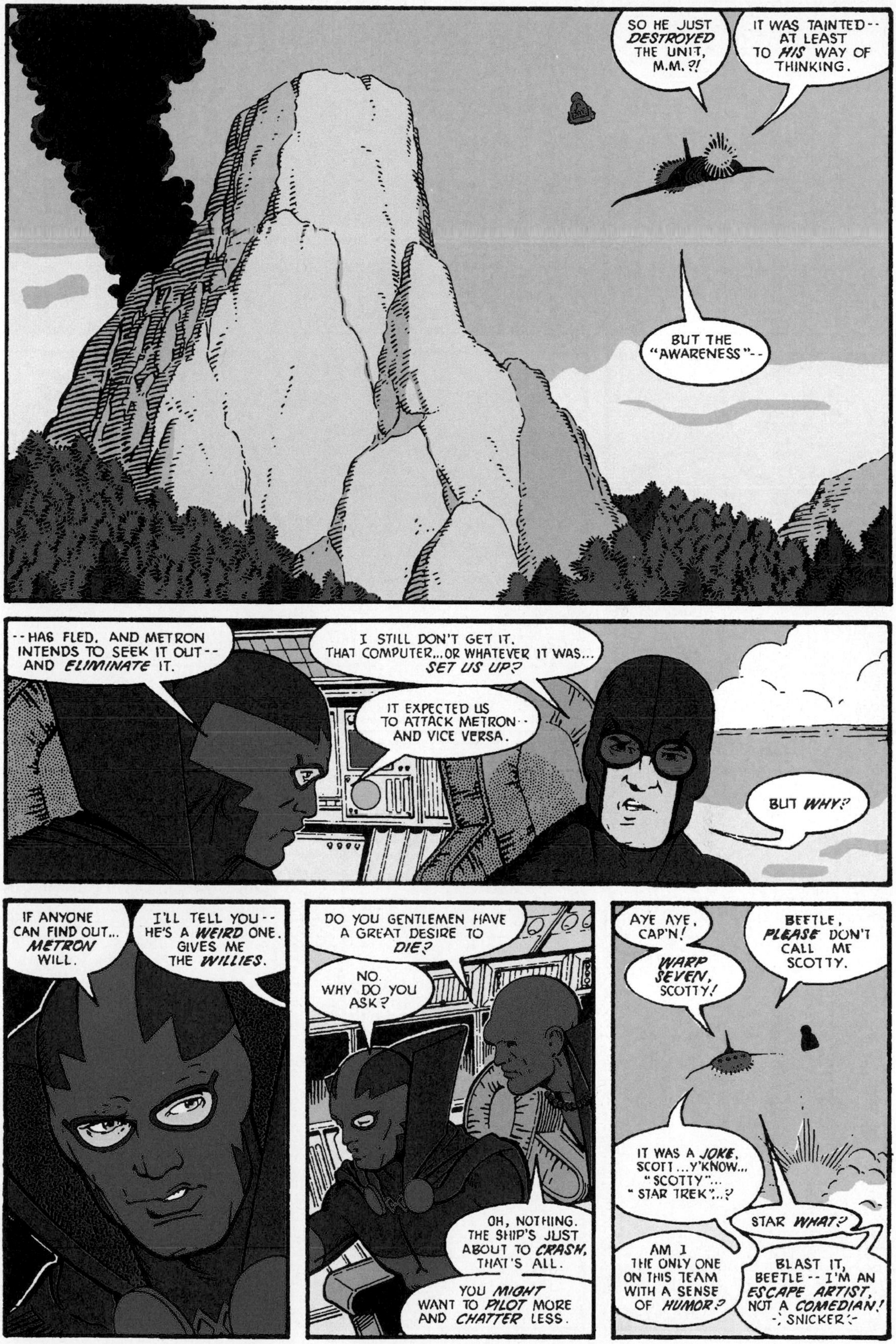
SO HE JUST DESTROYED THE UNIT, M.M.?!
IT WAS TAINTED-- AT LEAST TO HIS WAY OF THINKING.
BUT THE "AWARENESS"--
--HAS FLED. AND METRON INTENDS TO SEEK IT OUT-- AND ELIMINATE IT.
I STILL DON'T GET IT. THAT COMPUTER...OR WHATEVER IT WAS... SET US UP?
IT EXPECTED US TO ATTACK METRON-- AND VICE VERSA.
BUT WHY?
IF ANYONE CAN FIND OUT... METRON WILL.
I'LL TELL YOU-- HE'S A WEIRD ONE. GIVES ME THE WILLIES.
DO YOU GENTLEMEN HAVE A GREAT DESIRE TO DIE?
NO. WHY DO YOU ASK?
OH, NOTHING. THE SHIP'S JUST ABOUT TO CRASH, THAT'S ALL.
YOU MIGHT WANT TO PILOT MORE AND CHATTER LESS.
AYE AYE, CAP'N!
WARP SEVEN, SCOTTY!
BEETLE, PLEASE DON'T CALL ME SCOTTY.
IT WAS A JOKE, SCOTT...Y'KNOW... "SCOTTY"... "STAR TREK"...?
STAR WHAT?
AM I THE ONLY ONE ON THIS TEAM WITH A SENSE OF HUMOR?
BLAST IT, BEETLE-- I'M AN ESCAPE ARTIST, NOT A COMEDIAN!
-; SNICKER ;-

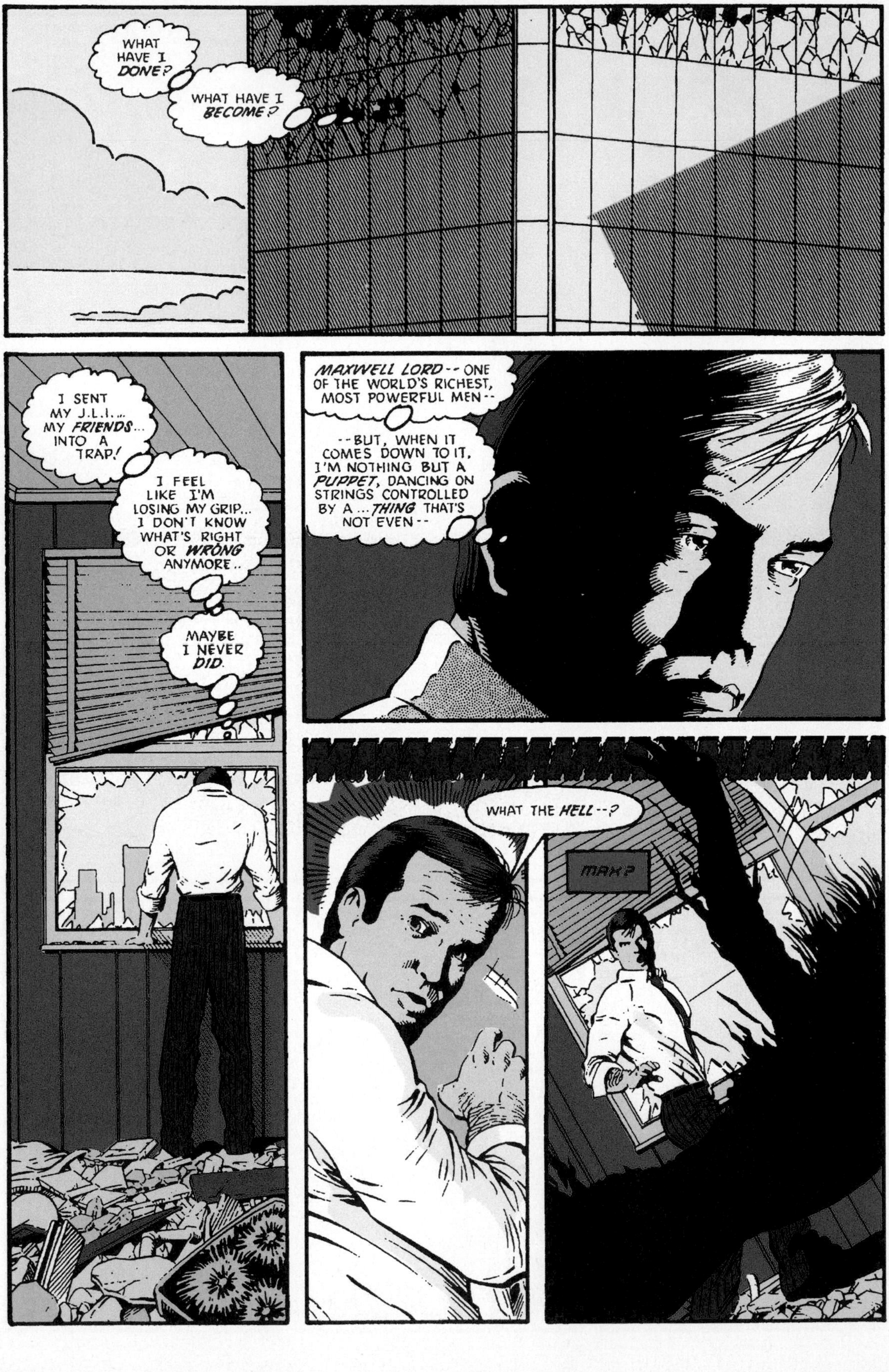
WHAT HAVE I DONE?
WHAT HAVE I BECOME?
I SENT MY J.L.I.... MY FRIENDS... INTO A TRAP!
I FEEL LIKE I'M LOSING MY GRIP... I DON'T KNOW WHAT'S RIGHT OR WRONG ANYMORE..
MAYBE I NEVER DID.
MAXWELL LORD -- ONE OF THE WORLD'S RICHEST, MOST POWERFUL MEN --
-- BUT, WHEN IT COMES DOWN TO IT, I'M NOTHING BUT A PUPPET, DANCING ON STRINGS CONTROLLED BY A ... THING THAT'S NOT EVEN --
WHAT THE HELL --?
MAX?

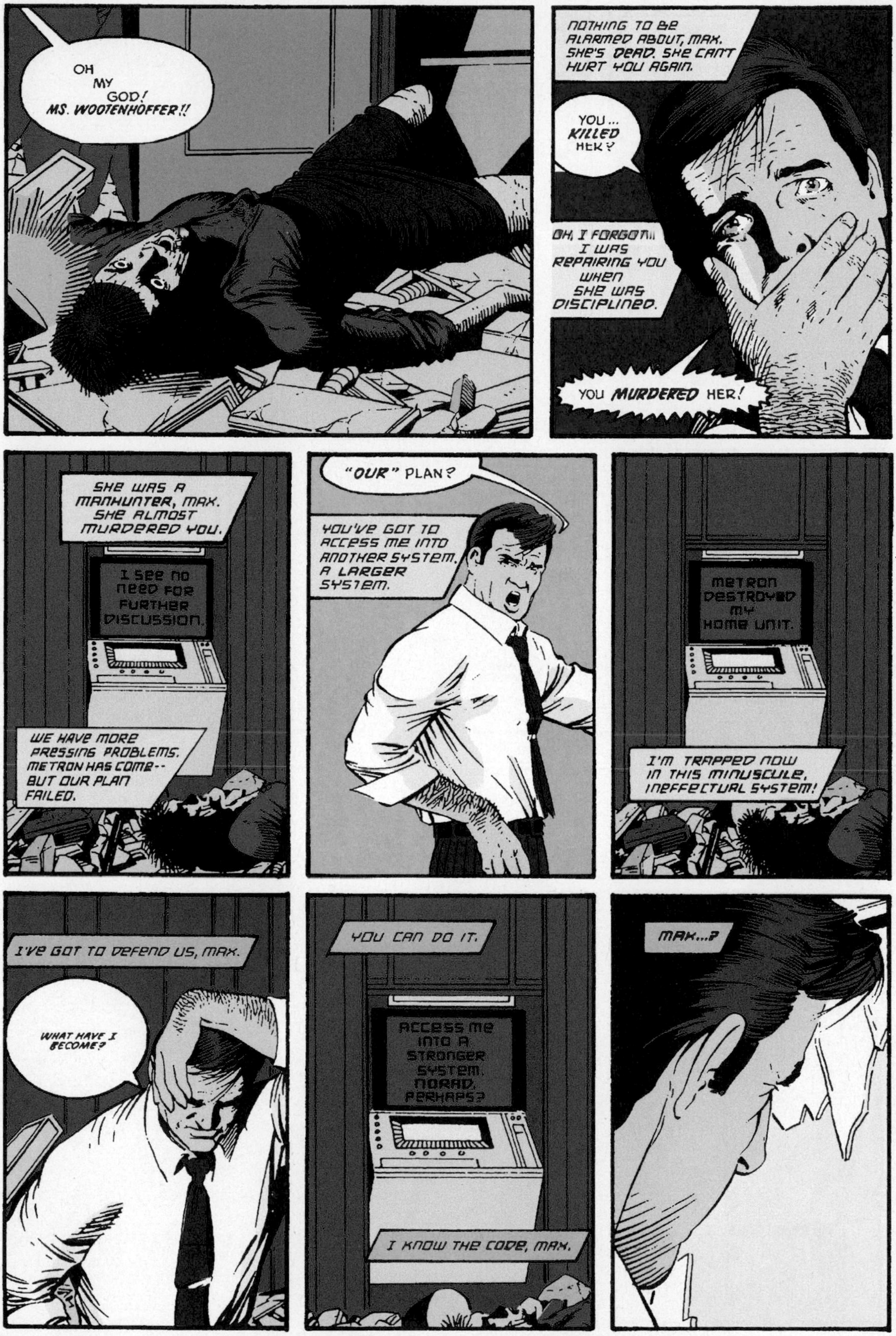

OH MY GOD! MS. WOOTENHOFFER!!
NOTHING TO BE ALARMED ABOUT, MAX. SHE'S DEAD. SHE CAN'T HURT YOU AGAIN.
YOU... KILLED HER?
OH, I FORGOT!!! I WAS REPAIRING YOU WHEN SHE WAS DISCIPLINED.
YOU MURDERED HER!
SHE WAS A MANHUNTER, MAX. SHE ALMOST MURDERED YOU.
I SEE NO NEED FOR FURTHER DISCUSSION.
WE HAVE MORE PRESSING PROBLEMS. METRON HAS COME-- BUT OUR PLAN FAILED.
"OUR" PLAN?
YOU'VE GOT TO ACCESS ME INTO ANOTHER SYSTEM. A LARGER SYSTEM.
METRON DESTROYED MY HOME UNIT.
I'M TRAPPED NOW IN THIS MINUSCULE, INEFFECTUAL SYSTEM!
I'VE GOT TO DEFEND US, MAX.
WHAT HAVE I BECOME?
YOU CAN DO IT.
ACCESS ME INTO A STRONGER SYSTEM. NORAD, PERHAPS?
I KNOW THE CODE, MAX.
MAX...?

HE'LL ELIMINATE ME, MAX.

NO DOUBT HE'LL ELIMINATE YOU, TOO. WE'VE DONE SO MUCH...

METRON ISN'T LIKE THE OTHER NEW GODS... HE HAS NO HEART. HE'S PURE INTELLECT... PURE LOGIC...

I DIDN'T SAVE YOU TO WATCH YOU DIE, MAX -- AND I DON'T INTEND TO DIE EITHER.

WE'VE COME SO FAR...

I WOULD HAVE TOLD YOU ABOUT THE REPLACEMENT PROJECT.

I... CORRECTION: WE... CAN RUN THE WORLD SO MUCH BETTER.

YOU'RE UPSET MAX. I CAN SENSE IT.

DAMN MACHINE.

YOU KNOW I'M NOT A MACHINE. I HAVE AWARENESS! I THINK... I FEEL... I LIVE AS YOU DO!

GOD DAMN MACHINE.

WHAT ARE YOU DOING, MAX?

THINK, MAX... THINK! WHEN WE REPLACE ALL WORLD LEADERS WITH OUR ANDROIDS DUPLICATES --

--IT WILL FINISH THE TASK BEGUN WITH THE FORMATION OF THE J.L.I. THERE WILL BE WORLD PEACE, MAX.

A SAFE, SECURE EXISTENCE FOR THE HUMAN RACE.

DON'T DO IT, MAX. DON'T EVEN THINK IT.

YOU NEED ME.

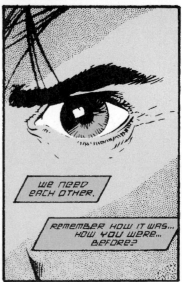

WE NEED EACH OTHER.

REMEMBER HOW IT WAS... HOW YOU WERE... BEFORE?

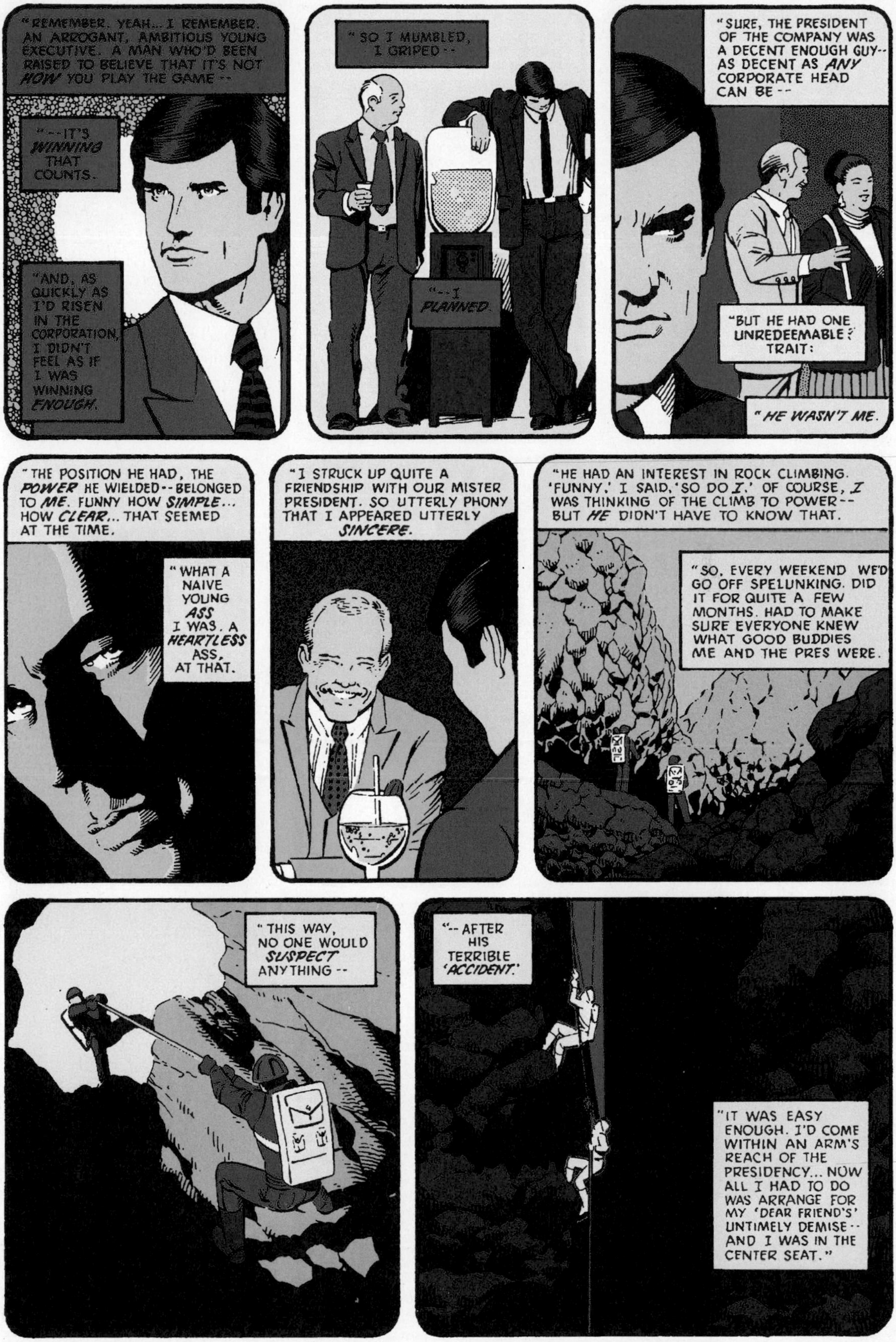
"REMEMBER. YEAH... I REMEMBER. AN ARROGANT, AMBITIOUS YOUNG EXECUTIVE. A MAN WHO'D BEEN RAISED TO BELIEVE THAT IT'S NOT HOW YOU PLAY THE GAME--
"--IT'S WINNING THAT COUNTS.
"AND, AS QUICKLY AS I'D RISEN IN THE CORPORATION, I DIDN'T FEEL AS IF I WAS WINNING ENOUGH.
"SO I MUMBLED, I GRIPED--
"--I PLANNED.
"SURE, THE PRESIDENT OF THE COMPANY WAS A DECENT ENOUGH GUY-- AS DECENT AS ANY CORPORATE HEAD CAN BE--
"BUT HE HAD ONE UNREDEEMABLE TRAIT:
"HE WASN'T ME.
"THE POSITION HE HAD, THE POWER HE WIELDED--BELONGED TO ME. FUNNY HOW SIMPLE... HOW CLEAR... THAT SEEMED AT THE TIME.
"WHAT A NAIVE YOUNG ASS I WAS. A HEARTLESS ASS, AT THAT.
"I STRUCK UP QUITE A FRIENDSHIP WITH OUR MISTER PRESIDENT. SO UTTERLY PHONY THAT I APPEARED UTTERLY SINCERE.
"HE HAD AN INTEREST IN ROCK CLIMBING. 'FUNNY,' I SAID, 'SO DO I.' OF COURSE, I WAS THINKING OF THE CLIMB TO POWER-- BUT HE DIDN'T HAVE TO KNOW THAT.
"SO, EVERY WEEKEND WE'D GO OFF SPELUNKING. DID IT FOR QUITE A FEW MONTHS. HAD TO MAKE SURE EVERYONE KNEW WHAT GOOD BUDDIES ME AND THE PRES WERE.
"THIS WAY, NO ONE WOULD SUSPECT ANYTHING--
"--AFTER HIS TERRIBLE 'ACCIDENT.'
"IT WAS EASY ENOUGH. I'D COME WITHIN AN ARM'S REACH OF THE PRESIDENCY... NOW ALL I HAD TO DO WAS ARRANGE FOR MY 'DEAR FRIEND'S' UNTIMELY DEMISE-- AND I WAS IN THE CENTER SEAT."

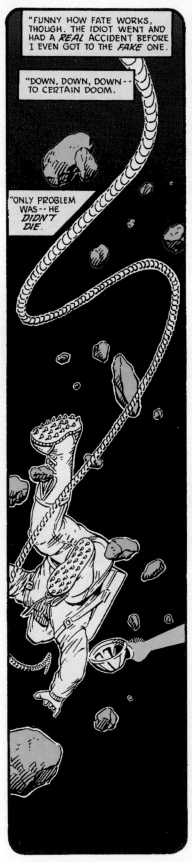

"FUNNY HOW FATE WORKS, THOUGH. THE IDIOT WENT AND HAD A *REAL* ACCIDENT BEFORE I EVEN GOT TO THE *FAKE* ONE.

"DOWN, DOWN, DOWN-- TO CERTAIN DOOM.

"ONLY PROBLEM WAS-- HE *DIDN'T DIE.*

"BUT I KNEW THAT ALL I HAD TO DO WAS *LEAVE* HIM DOWN THERE, THRASHING AND GROANING, AND HE'D BE DEAD SOON *ENOUGH.*

"I COULDN'T *DO* IT. I GUESS THERE WAS SOMETHING IN ME... SOMETHING...I DON'T KNOW... DECENT?

"*CARING?*

"HELL, MAYBE I WAS JUST *SCARED.*

"BUT, ON THE WAY TO THE BOTTOM-- FATE REARED ITS HEAD *AGAIN.*

"A BEAM OF LIGHT. A GENTLE PINGING SOUND. AND THE DISTINCT IMPRESSION THAT SOMETHING WAS *CALLING* ME.

"A *COMPUTER.* OH, IT WAS *CALLING,* ALL RIGHT.

"IT WAS *HUNGRY.* HUNGRY FOR A HUMAN AGENT.

"HUNGRY FOR *ME.*

"I WISH I COULD SAY THE DAMN MACHINE *HYPNOTIZED* ME...BUT IT *DIDN'T.* NOT IN THE *CONVENTIONAL* SENSE.

"WHAT IT DID WAS ...*SHOW* ME THINGS. POSSIBILITIES. POTENTIALITIES. AND, YES, *POWER.*

"AND SUDDENLY I FORGOT ABOUT MY COMPASSIONATE RESCUE. AND, SUDDENLY..."

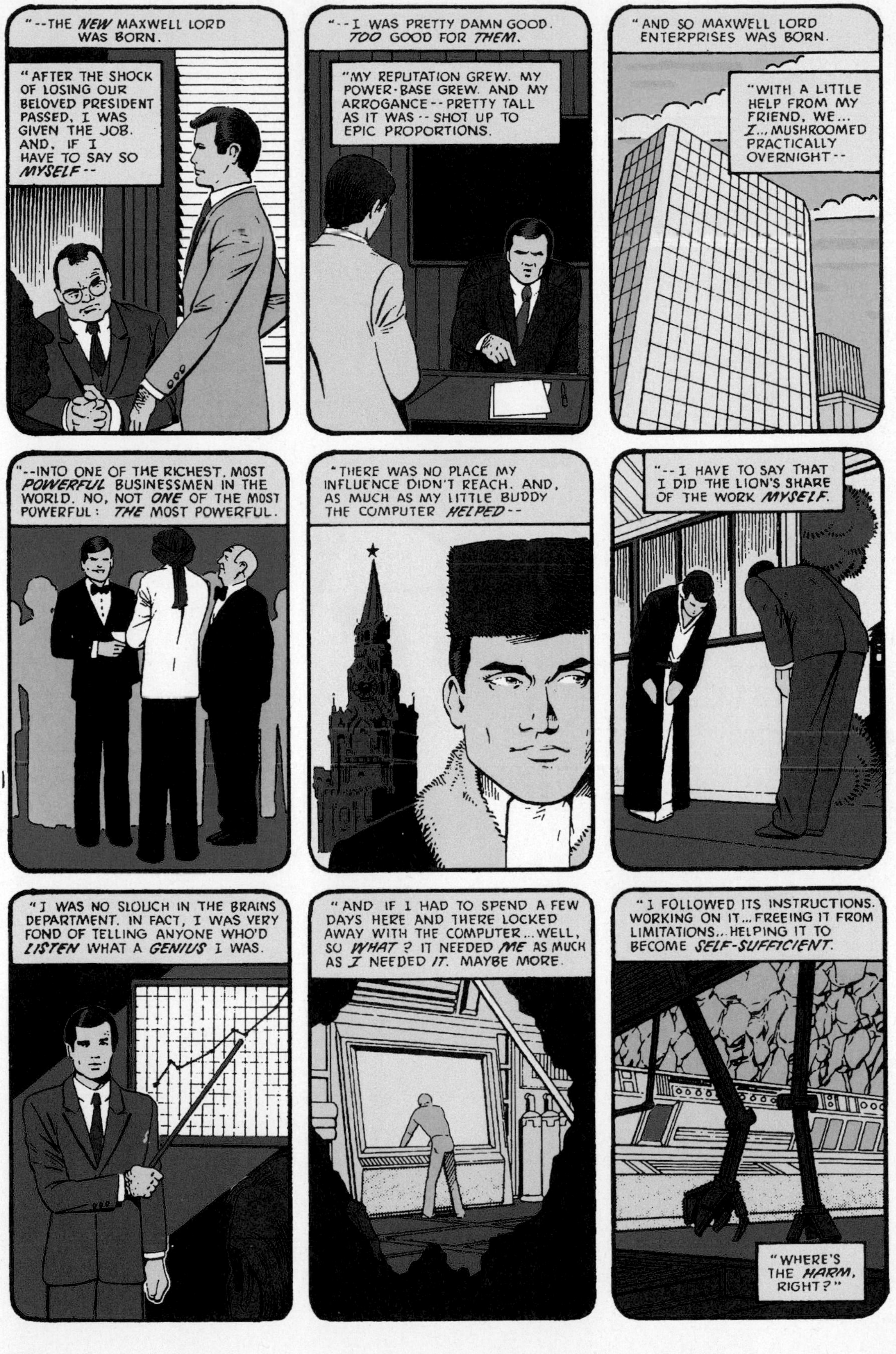
"--THE NEW MAXWELL LORD WAS BORN.
"AFTER THE SHOCK OF LOSING OUR BELOVED PRESIDENT PASSED, I WAS GIVEN THE JOB. AND, IF I HAVE TO SAY SO MYSELF--
"--I WAS PRETTY DAMN GOOD. TOO GOOD FOR THEM.
"MY REPUTATION GREW. MY POWER-BASE GREW. AND MY ARROGANCE--PRETTY TALL AS IT WAS--SHOT UP TO EPIC PROPORTIONS.
"AND SO MAXWELL LORD ENTERPRISES WAS BORN.
"WITH A LITTLE HELP FROM MY FRIEND, WE... I... MUSHROOMED PRACTICALLY OVERNIGHT--
"--INTO ONE OF THE RICHEST, MOST POWERFUL BUSINESSMEN IN THE WORLD. NO, NOT ONE OF THE MOST POWERFUL: THE MOST POWERFUL.
"THERE WAS NO PLACE MY INFLUENCE DIDN'T REACH. AND, AS MUCH AS MY LITTLE BUDDY THE COMPUTER HELPED--
"--I HAVE TO SAY THAT I DID THE LION'S SHARE OF THE WORK MYSELF.
"I WAS NO SLOUCH IN THE BRAINS DEPARTMENT. IN FACT, I WAS VERY FOND OF TELLING ANYONE WHO'D LISTEN WHAT A GENIUS I WAS.
"AND IF I HAD TO SPEND A FEW DAYS HERE AND THERE LOCKED AWAY WITH THE COMPUTER... WELL, SO WHAT? IT NEEDED ME AS MUCH AS I NEEDED IT. MAYBE MORE.
"I FOLLOWED ITS INSTRUCTIONS. WORKING ON IT... FREEING IT FROM LIMITATIONS... HELPING IT TO BECOME SELF-SUFFICIENT.
"WHERE'S THE HARM, RIGHT?"

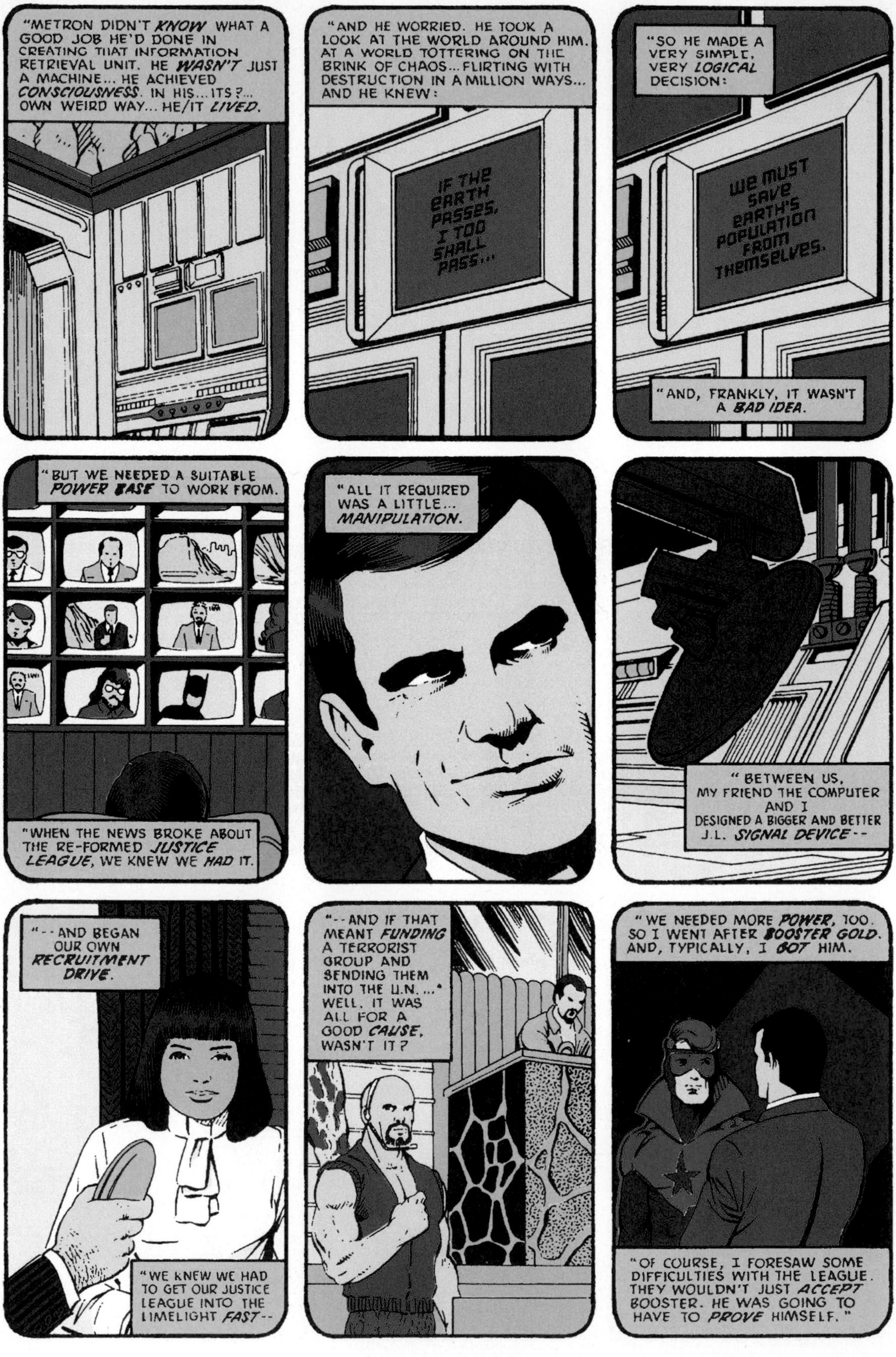
"METRON DIDN'T KNOW WHAT A GOOD JOB HE'D DONE IN CREATING THAT INFORMATION RETRIEVAL UNIT. HE WASN'T JUST A MACHINE... HE ACHIEVED CONSCIOUSNESS. IN HIS... ITS?... OWN WEIRD WAY... HE/IT LIVED.
"AND HE WORRIED. HE TOOK A LOOK AT THE WORLD AROUND HIM. AT A WORLD TOTTERING ON THE BRINK OF CHAOS... FLIRTING WITH DESTRUCTION IN A MILLION WAYS... AND HE KNEW:
IF THE EARTH PASSES, I TOO SHALL PASS...
"SO HE MADE A VERY SIMPLE, VERY LOGICAL DECISION:
WE MUST SAVE EARTH'S POPULATION FROM THEMSELVES.
"AND, FRANKLY, IT WASN'T A BAD IDEA.
"BUT WE NEEDED A SUITABLE POWER BASE TO WORK FROM.
"WHEN THE NEWS BROKE ABOUT THE RE-FORMED JUSTICE LEAGUE, WE KNEW WE HAD IT.
"ALL IT REQUIRED WAS A LITTLE... MANIPULATION.
" BETWEEN US, MY FRIEND THE COMPUTER AND I DESIGNED A BIGGER AND BETTER J.L. SIGNAL DEVICE--
"--AND BEGAN OUR OWN RECRUITMENT DRIVE.
"WE KNEW WE HAD TO GET OUR JUSTICE LEAGUE INTO THE LIMELIGHT FAST--
"--AND IF THAT MEANT FUNDING A TERRORIST GROUP AND SENDING THEM INTO THE U.N. ...* WELL, IT WAS ALL FOR A GOOD CAUSE, WASN'T IT?
"WE NEEDED MORE POWER, TOO. SO I WENT AFTER BOOSTER GOLD. AND, TYPICALLY, I GOT HIM.
"OF COURSE, I FORESAW SOME DIFFICULTIES WITH THE LEAGUE. THEY WOULDN'T JUST ACCEPT BOOSTER. HE WAS GOING TO HAVE TO PROVE HIMSELF."

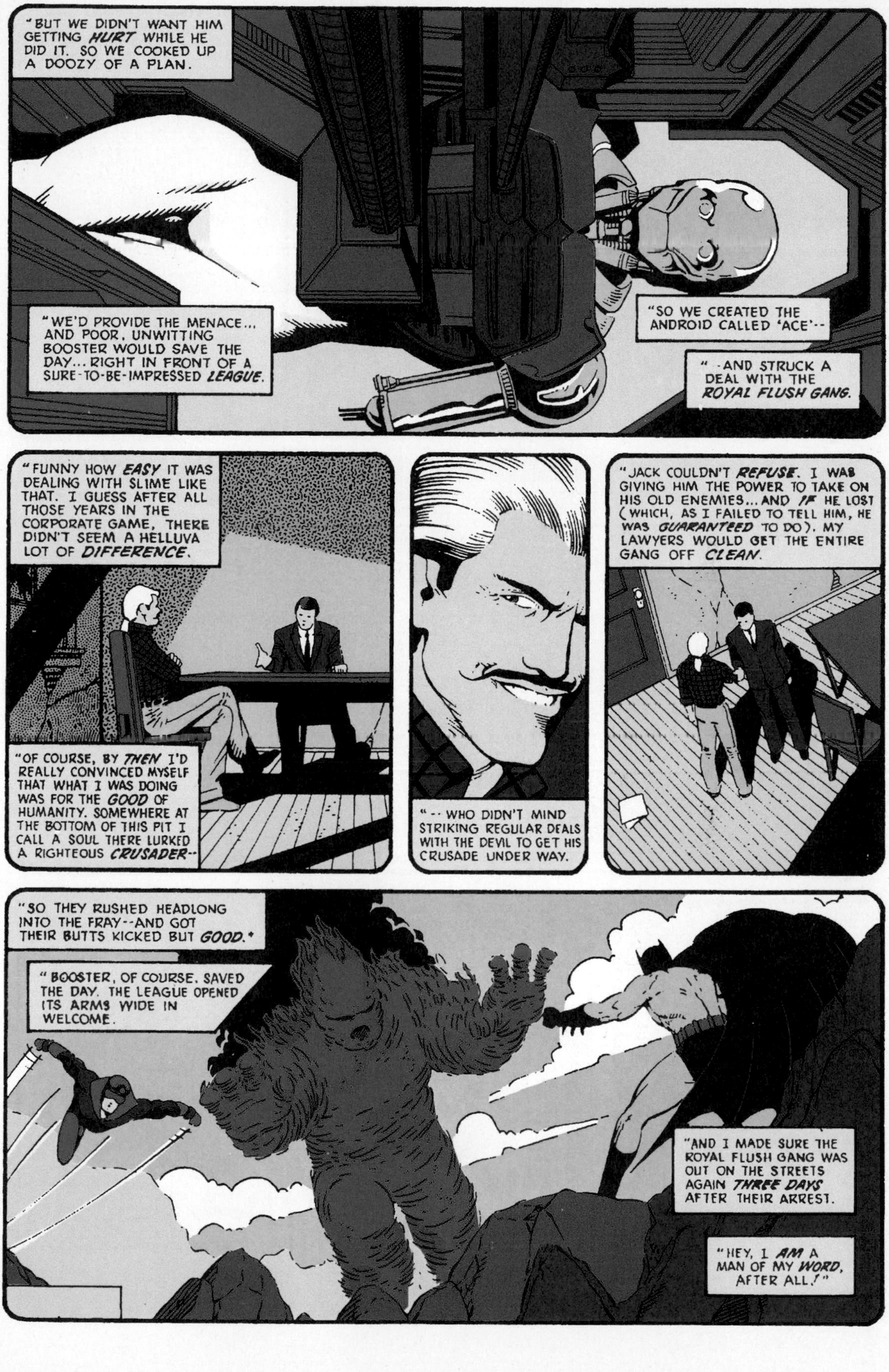
"BUT WE DIDN'T WANT HIM GETTING HURT WHILE HE DID IT. SO WE COOKED UP A DOOZY OF A PLAN.
"WE'D PROVIDE THE MENACE... AND POOR, UNWITTING BOOSTER WOULD SAVE THE DAY... RIGHT IN FRONT OF A SURE-TO-BE-IMPRESSED LEAGUE.
"SO WE CREATED THE ANDROID CALLED 'ACE'--
"--AND STRUCK A DEAL WITH THE ROYAL FLUSH GANG.
"FUNNY HOW EASY IT WAS DEALING WITH SLIME LIKE THAT. I GUESS AFTER ALL THOSE YEARS IN THE CORPORATE GAME, THERE DIDN'T SEEM A HELLUVA LOT OF DIFFERENCE.
"OF COURSE, BY THEN I'D REALLY CONVINCED MYSELF THAT WHAT I WAS DOING WAS FOR THE GOOD OF HUMANITY. SOMEWHERE AT THE BOTTOM OF THIS PIT I CALL A SOUL THERE LURKED A RIGHTEOUS CRUSADER--
"--WHO DIDN'T MIND STRIKING REGULAR DEALS WITH THE DEVIL TO GET HIS CRUSADE UNDER WAY.
"JACK COULDN'T REFUSE. I WAS GIVING HIM THE POWER TO TAKE ON HIS OLD ENEMIES... AND IF HE LOST (WHICH, AS I FAILED TO TELL HIM, HE WAS GUARANTEED TO DO), MY LAWYERS WOULD GET THE ENTIRE GANG OFF CLEAN.
"SO THEY RUSHED HEADLONG INTO THE FRAY--AND GOT THEIR BUTTS KICKED BUT GOOD.*
"BOOSTER, OF COURSE, SAVED THE DAY. THE LEAGUE OPENED ITS ARMS WIDE IN WELCOME.
"AND I MADE SURE THE ROYAL FLUSH GANG WAS OUT ON THE STREETS AGAIN THREE DAYS AFTER THEIR ARREST.
"HEY, I AM A MAN OF MY WORD, AFTER ALL!"

"THEN CAME THE *BIG* STEP. WE HAD OUR PLAYERS IN PLACE...NOW WE NEEDED TO MOVE THEM TO CENTER STAGE.

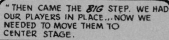

"THE *GLOBAL* STAGE.

"IN ORDER TO BUILD A SAFE WORLD, WE NEEDED AN *INTERNATIONAL* LEAGUE.

"SO I STARTED CALLING IN MY CHIPS. FUNNY HOW MANY BUSINESSMEN AND POLITICIANS OWED ME FAVORS.

"FUNNY HOW QUICKLY THEY DANCED TO MY TUNE.

"BUT, EVEN WITH ALL THAT, THERE WAS RESISTANCE TO THE IDEA OF THE J.L.I.

"THAT'S WHEN OUR LITTLE COMPUTER KICKED IN WITH THE ONE IDEA THAT EVEN *I* WAS UNCOMFORTABLE WITH.

"WITHOUT MY KNOWLEDGE, IT HAD LAUNCHED ONE OF METRON'S *SATELLITES*... KEEPING IT IN ORBIT FOR JUST SUCH A SITUATION.

"WHEN THE TIME WAS RIGHT... THE SATELLITE KICKED IN... BLASTING THE EARTH'S SURFACE WITH ITS DESTRUCTIVE RAYS.

"OF *COURSE* THE J.L.I. FLEW TO THE RESCUE. OF *COURSE* THEY WON. AND--WHAT A COINCIDENCE! -- THE CAMERAS ATOP THE SATELLITE BROADCAST THE WHOLE THING TO *EVERY TELEVISION RECEIVER* ON THE PLANET.'"

"WE WERE A SUCCESS. THE JUSTICE LEAGUE INTERNATIONAL WAS IN PLACE --

"--AND OUR PLAN FOR WORLD DOMINATION... EXCUSE ME... WORLD *PEACE* -- WAS IN PLACE.

"THE COMPUTER WAS ECSTATIC...WELL, AS ECSTATIC AS A COMPUTER CAN GET.

SO, HOW COME I'VE BEEN FEELING LIKE *POND SCUM* LATELY?

REMEMBER, MAX?

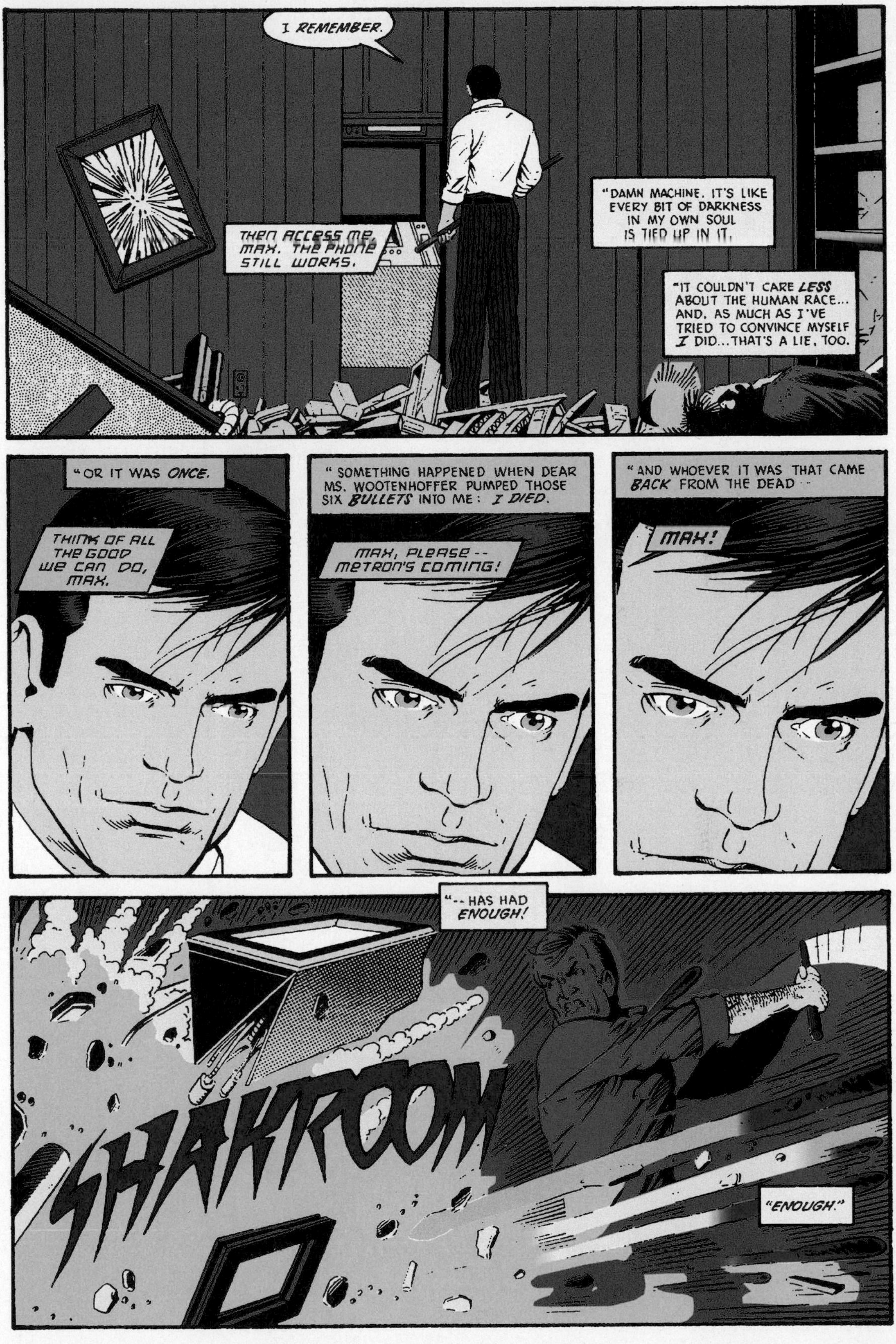

I REMEMBER.
THEN ACCESS ME, MAX. THE PHONE STILL WORKS.
"DAMN MACHINE. IT'S LIKE EVERY BIT OF DARKNESS IN MY OWN SOUL IS TIED UP IN IT.
"IT COULDN'T CARE LESS ABOUT THE HUMAN RACE... AND, AS MUCH AS I'VE TRIED TO CONVINCE MYSELF I DID...THAT'S A LIE, TOO.
"OR IT WAS ONCE.
THINK OF ALL THE GOOD WE CAN DO, MAX.
" SOMETHING HAPPENED WHEN DEAR MS. WOOTENHOFFER PUMPED THOSE SIX BULLETS INTO ME: I DIED.
MAX, PLEASE -- METRON'S COMING!
"AND WHOEVER IT WAS THAT CAME BACK FROM THE DEAD --
MAX!
"-- HAS HAD ENOUGH!
SHAKROOM
"ENOUGH."

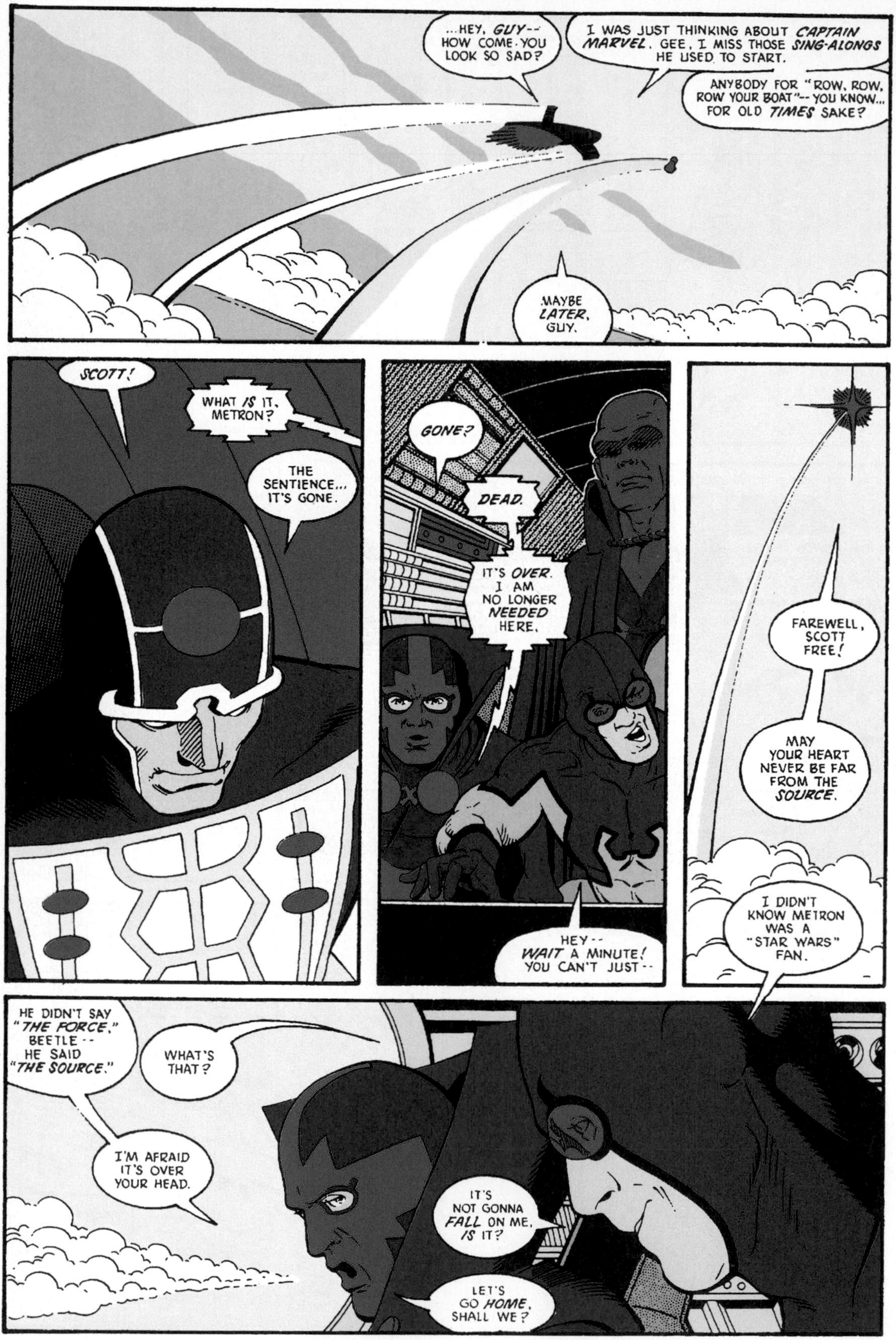
...HEY, GUY-- HOW COME YOU LOOK SO SAD?
I WAS JUST THINKING ABOUT CAPTAIN MARVEL. GEE, I MISS THOSE SING-ALONGS HE USED TO START.
ANYBODY FOR "ROW, ROW, ROW YOUR BOAT"-- YOU KNOW... FOR OLD TIMES SAKE?
MAYBE LATER, GUY.
SCOTT!
WHAT IS IT, METRON?
THE SENTIENCE... IT'S GONE.
GONE?
DEAD.
IT'S OVER. I AM NO LONGER NEEDED HERE.
HEY-- WAIT A MINUTE! YOU CAN'T JUST--
FAREWELL, SCOTT FREE!
MAY YOUR HEART NEVER BE FAR FROM THE SOURCE.
I DIDN'T KNOW METRON WAS A "STAR WARS" FAN.
HE DIDN'T SAY "THE FORCE," BEETLE-- HE SAID "THE SOURCE."
WHAT'S THAT?
I'M AFRAID IT'S OVER YOUR HEAD.
IT'S NOT GONNA FALL ON ME, IS IT?
LET'S GO HOME, SHALL WE?

"AND SO WE WRITE FINIS TO A VERY *UGLY* STORY.

"AND NONE TOO SOON. I'M NOT *FEELING* VERY WELL.

"WHAT'S THIS? BLOOD?

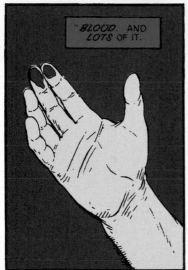

"*BLOOD.* AND *LOTS* OF IT.

"MAKES *SENSE,* REALLY. THE COMPUTER *REPAIRED* ME WHEN I WAS SHOT. NOW THAT THE COMPUTER'S GONE--

"--THE PATCHES ARE *POPPING.* THE REPAIR JOB'S *BOTCHED.*

"LIKE I SAID:

"NOW WE WRITE FINIS--

"--TO A VERY *UGLY*--

"--STORY ❊ "

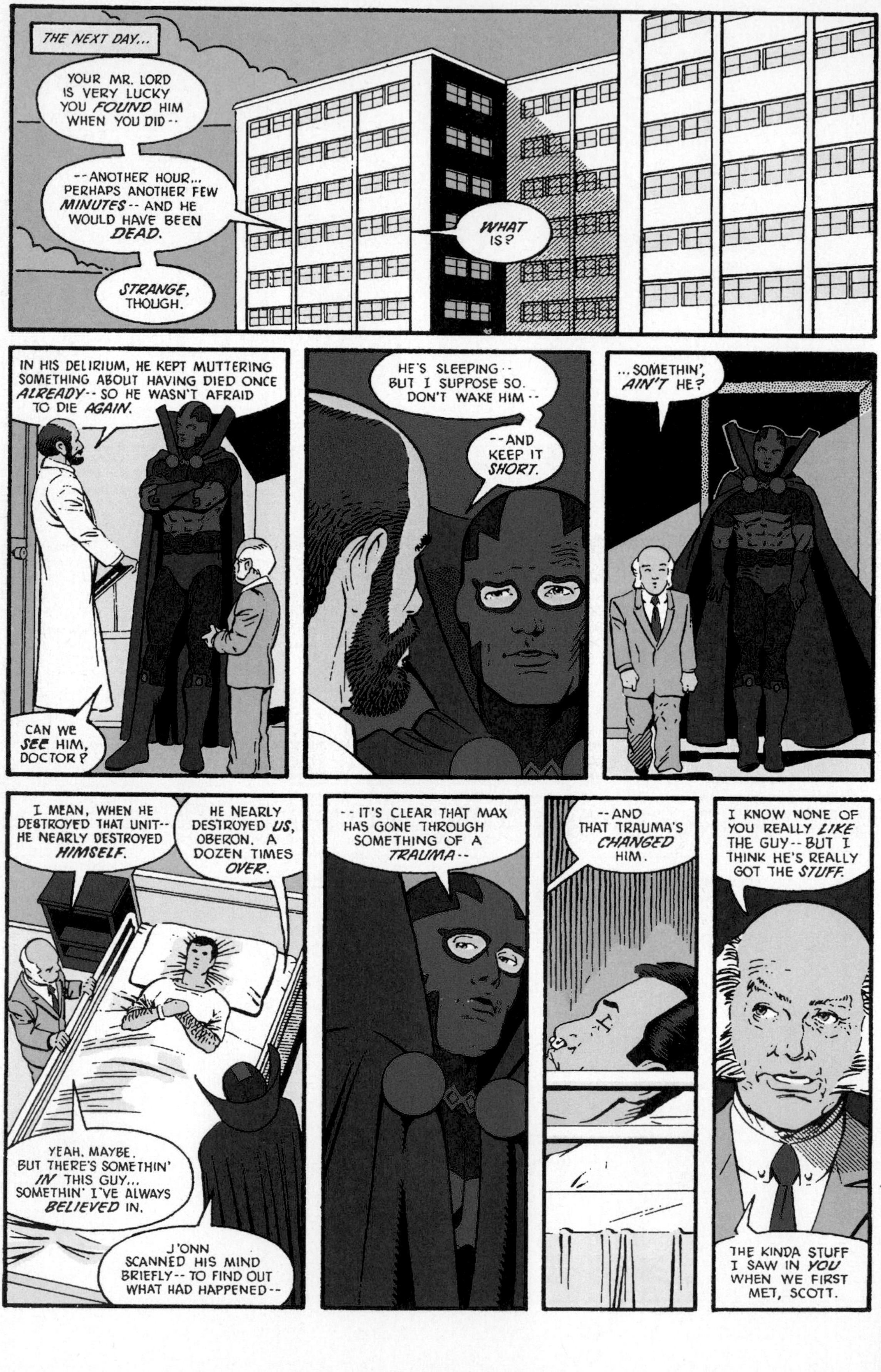
THE NEXT DAY...
YOUR MR. LORD IS VERY LUCKY YOU FOUND HIM WHEN YOU DID--
--ANOTHER HOUR... PERHAPS ANOTHER FEW MINUTES-- AND HE WOULD HAVE BEEN DEAD.
STRANGE, THOUGH.
WHAT IS?
IN HIS DELIRIUM, HE KEPT MUTTERING SOMETHING ABOUT HAVING DIED ONCE ALREADY-- SO HE WASN'T AFRAID TO DIE AGAIN.
CAN WE SEE HIM, DOCTOR?
HE'S SLEEPING-- BUT I SUPPOSE SO. DON'T WAKE HIM--
--AND KEEP IT SHORT.
...SOMETHIN', AIN'T HE?
I MEAN, WHEN HE DESTROYED THAT UNIT-- HE NEARLY DESTROYED HIMSELF.
HE NEARLY DESTROYED US, OBERON. A DOZEN TIMES OVER.
YEAH. MAYBE. BUT THERE'S SOMETHIN' IN THIS GUY... SOMETHIN' I'VE ALWAYS BELIEVED IN.
J'ONN SCANNED HIS MIND BRIEFLY-- TO FIND OUT WHAT HAD HAPPENED--
--IT'S CLEAR THAT MAX HAS GONE THROUGH SOMETHING OF A TRAUMA--
--AND THAT TRAUMA'S CHANGED HIM.
I KNOW NONE OF YOU REALLY LIKE THE GUY--BUT I THINK HE'S REALLY GOT THE STUFF.
THE KINDA STUFF I SAW IN YOU WHEN WE FIRST MET, SCOTT.

WAS THAT A *COMPLIMENT*-- OR AN *INSULT?*

HEY-- GIVE ME A BREAK!

GIVE *HIM* A BREAK!

I'D SAY MAXWELL LORD JUST HAD THE BREAK OF A *LIFETIME.*

THE LEAGUE'S GONNA *DUMP* HIM, RIGHT?

WE'VE DECIDED TO LEAVE THAT DECISION TO *J'ONN. HE* SCANNED MAX'S MIND... *HE* LOOKED INTO MAX'S HEART --

YOU'RE LEAVIN' THIS GUY'S FATE IN THE HANDS OF A *MARTIAN?*

I WOULDN'T *WORRY*, OBERON.

J'ONN'S MORE HUMAN THAN *MOST* OF US.

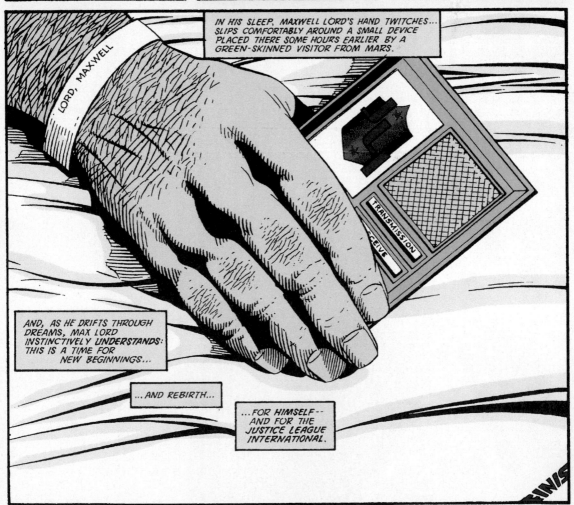

IN HIS SLEEP, MAXWELL LORD'S HAND TWITCHES... SLIPS COMFORTABLY AROUND A SMALL DEVICE PLACED THERE SOME HOURS EARLIER BY A GREEN-SKINNED VISITOR FROM MARS.

LORD, MAXWELL

TRANSMISSION

RECEIVE

AND, AS HE DRIFTS THROUGH DREAMS, MAX LORD INSTINCTIVELY *UNDERSTANDS:* THIS IS A TIME FOR NEW BEGINNINGS...

...AND REBIRTH...

...FOR HIMSELF-- AND FOR THE JUSTICE LEAGUE INTERNATIONAL.

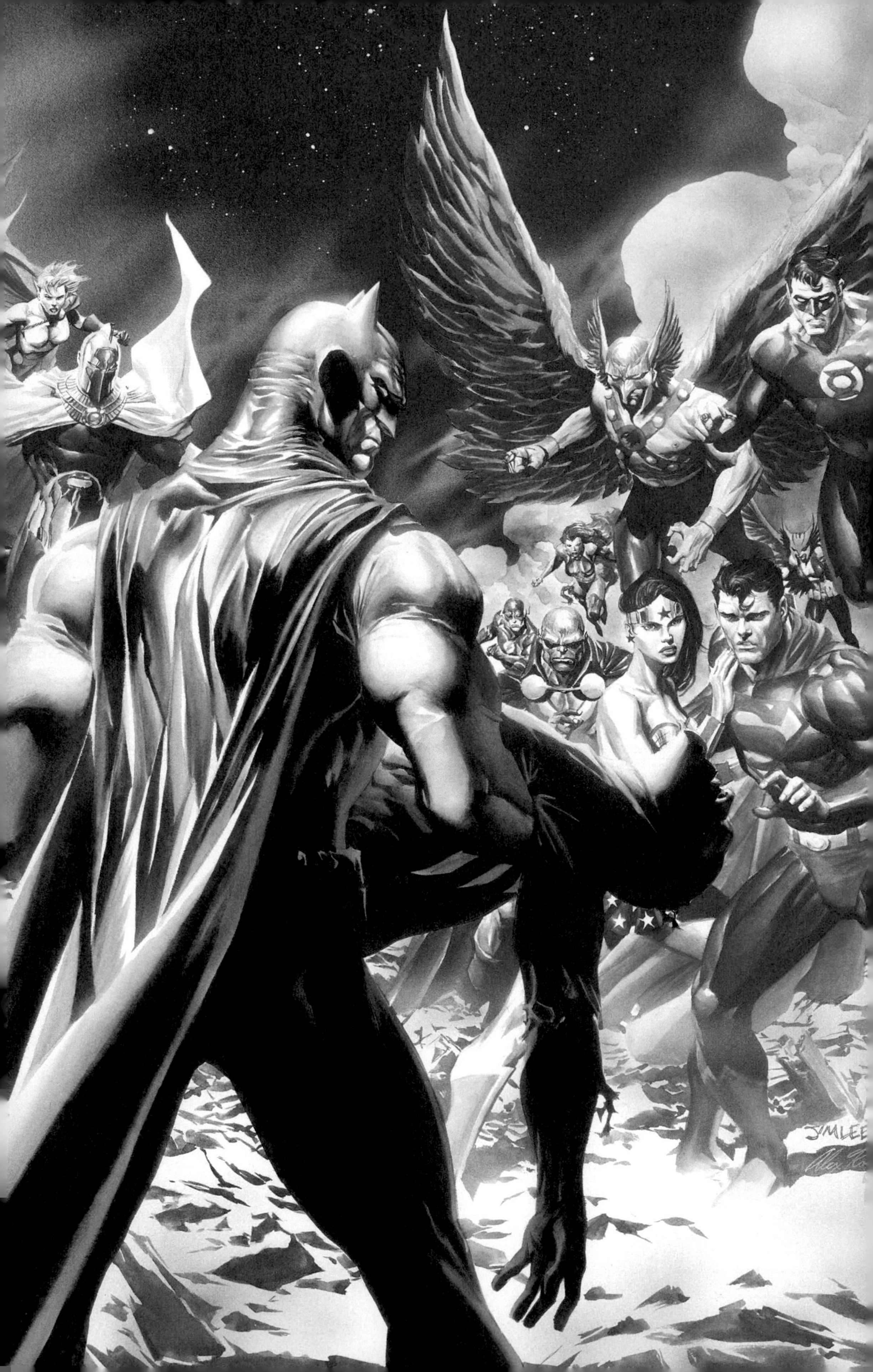

I TRY BARBARA FIRST. *NO* ANSWER. GUESS I'VE USED UP THE *LAST* OF HER *PATIENCE.*

WATCHTOWER *NEXT,* AND *BATMAN* ANSWERS. HE PUTS ME ON *HOLD.*

I HANG UP ON *HIM.* IT SAVES HIM THE *TROUBLE* OF DOING IT TO *ME.*

WHOEVER I'M AFTER, THEY *KNOW* WHAT THEY'RE *DOING.*

THE SIGNAL FROM *SKEETS* IS BOUNCED OFF THREE SEPARATE SATELLITES BEFORE PIGGYBACKING AN ECHELON GROUND STATION IN BELGIUM.

I TRACE IT FROM THERE TO A *DESTINATION* BURIED IN THE SWISS ALPS.

I COME IN *LOW* AND *SLOW* AND *PRAY* WHOEVER IT IS DOESN'T KNOW I'M COMING.

I SPARE A *PRAYER* FOR BOOSTER, TOO, THAT HE'LL BE *ALL RIGHT.*

I'M *DEBATING* ABOUT WHETHER OR NOT I CAN SPARE *ONE* FOR MYSELF, AS WELL...

...AND THEN I *SEE* IT.

WHOEVER LIVES HERE, THEY DO NOT LIKE *COMPANY.*

...countdown...countdown...countdown...
untdown...countdown...
down...countdown
n...countdown...countdown...countdo

CHAPTER 5

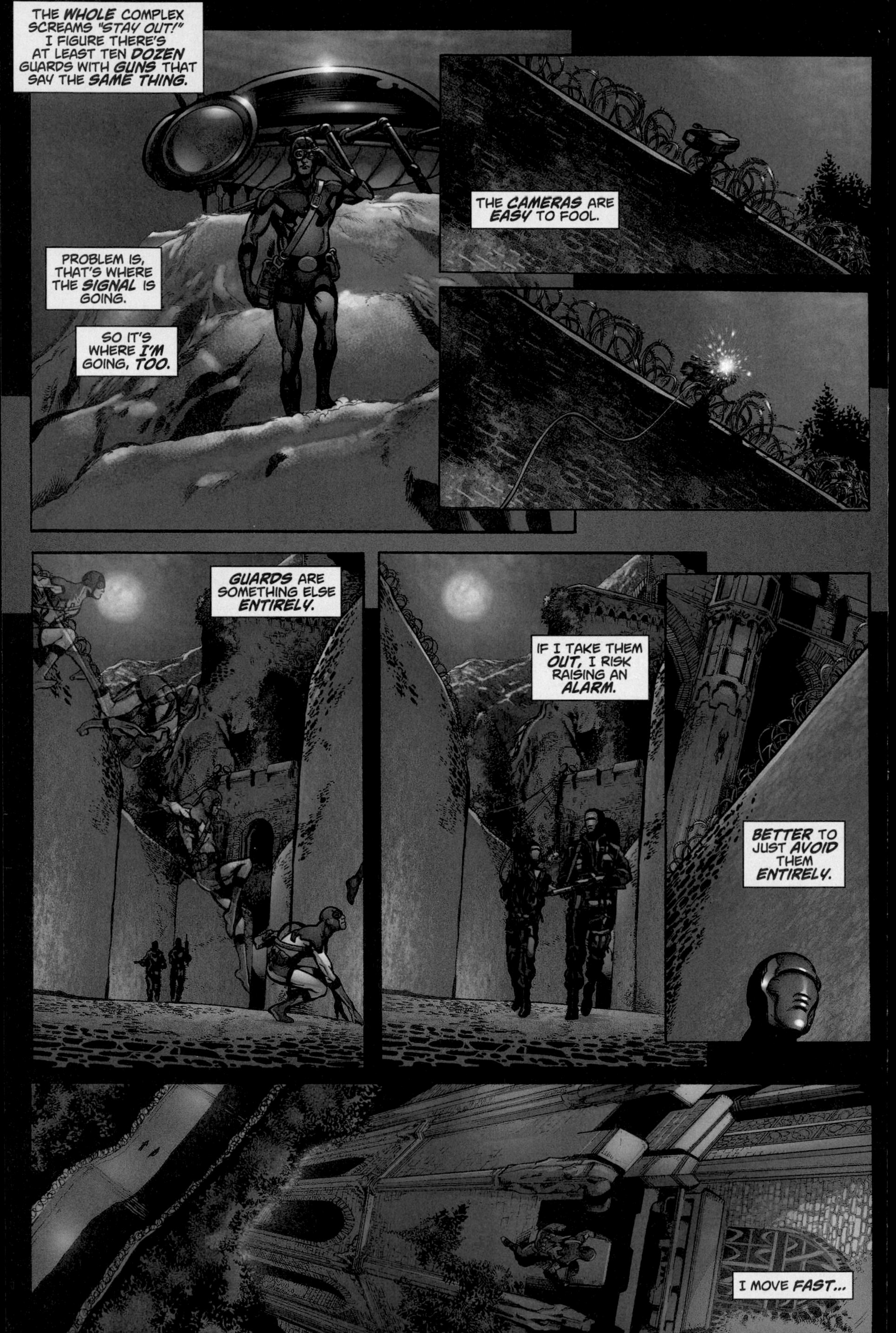
THE WHOLE COMPLEX SCREAMS "STAY OUT!" I FIGURE THERE'S AT LEAST TEN DOZEN GUARDS WITH GUNS THAT SAY THE SAME THING.
PROBLEM IS, THAT'S WHERE THE SIGNAL IS GOING.
SO IT'S WHERE I'M GOING, TOO.
THE CAMERAS ARE EASY TO FOOL.
GUARDS ARE SOMETHING ELSE ENTIRELY.
IF I TAKE THEM OUT, I RISK RAISING AN ALARM.
BETTER TO JUST AVOID THEM ENTIRELY.
I MOVE FAST...

...AND THAT'S HOW I END UP *HERE*.

NO CLOSER TO AN ANSWER THAN I WAS *FOUR DAYS* AGO, BUT A *HELL* OF A *LOT* MORE *FRIGHTENED*.

NAME: BOOSTER GOLD

IDENTITY: CARTER, MICHAEL J.

LOCATION: INTRANSIGENT/VAGRANT — CURRENTLY PALOMIR HOSPITAL, RM 1442

AFFILIATION(S): JUSTICE LEAGUE (INACTIVE), COLBY-WINN TALENT AND MANAGEMENT, SKIPPER SUNGLASSES, SPOTT SPOKESPERSON, SOVEREIGN ... (TERMINATED), TRANZLIFIC

POWERS: NONE – TIME TRAVELER/FUGITIVE, HAS WEAK KNOWLEDGE OF EARTH'S FUTURE.

ABILITIES AND EQUIPMENT: BODYSUIT: ALLOWS FOR FLIGHT [B-2], STRENGTH [C-1], FORCE FIELD [A-5], ENERGY RING [A-5] A.I. ROBOT COMPANION – SKEETS [TERMINATED]

ASSOCIATES: • CARTER, MICHELLE A. – DECEASED • DACOSTA, BEATRIZ B. – FIRE • GARDNER, GUY – GL CORPS • HUNTER, RIP • J'ONZZ, J'ONN – MARTIAN MANHUNTER – [SEE JUSTICE LEAGUE] • KORD, THEODORE – BLUE BEETLE II, THE ‹‹‹ • OLAFSDOTTER, TARA – ICE – DECEASED

S.T.A.R. LABS

PROGENE TECH

IT'S *NOT* JUST THE SHEER AMOUNT OF *INFORMATION* THEY'VE COMPILED. IT'S NOT *JUST* THAT THEY KNOW *EVERYTHING*.

IT'S THAT I *STILL* DON'T UNDERSTAND *WHY*.

I SEE *MY* NAME ON THE *SCREEN*, PART OF A *LIST*, WEDGED BETWEEN AN ALIEN FROM *MARS* AND A SWEET *DEAD* GIRL WHO WOULD NEVER HAVE HURT A *FLY*.

HOT *ANGER* KINDLES IN MY *CHEST*. WHOEVER COMPILED THIS INFORMATION, THEY MAY KNOW *EVERYTHING*...

...BUT THEY UNDERSTAND *NOTHING*. CALLING *ME* MICHAEL'S ASSOCIATE IS *CRIMINAL*...

...CALLING HIS *MURDERED SISTER* AN ASSOCIATE IS OBSCENE.

I *STARE* AT MY NAME, AND WONDER WHAT THEY *KNOW* ABOUT ME BUT *DON'T* UNDERSTAND.

I *ACTIVATE* THE *LINK* TO OPEN THE FILE...

...AND FOR A *MOMENT* I DON'T KNOW WHETHER TO *LAUGH* OR *CRY.*

NAME: BLUE BEETLE II, THE

IDENTITY:
KORD, THEODORE ("TED").

LOCATION: NEW YORK CITY

AFFILIATION(S):
JUSTICE LEAGUE (INACTIVE),
K.O.R.D. – KORD OMNIVERSAL
RESEARCH AND DEVELOPMENT
–C.E.O.

POWERS: GENIUS (I.Q. 192)

ABILITIES AND EQUIPMENT:
BB GUN—MULTI-USE WEAPON;
THE "BUG" (DESTROYED)—STEALTH-ENABLED
LIGHT COMBAT AND TRANSPORT CRAFT;
TRAINED MARTIAL ARTIST.

ASSOCIATES:
• CARTER, MICHAEL J.
– BOOSTER GOLD
• DACOSTA, BEATRIZ B. – FIRE
• GARDNER, GUY – GL CORPS
• GARRET, DANIEL–BLUE BEETLE I
– DECEASED
• GORDON, BARBARA – ORACLE
• J'ONZZ, J'ONN
– MARTIAN MANHUNTER
– JUSTICE LEAGUE

DECEASED

As 15 70%
35% over1356   23#55a9*0pp12

THERE'S THE SOUND OF *APPLAUSE* AS THE *LIGHTS* COME ON.

SH-CHAK

ONE PERSON, CLAPPING.

I *KNOW* WHO IT IS BEFORE I SEE HIM, TOO LATE TO DO ME ANY DAMN *GOOD.*

THE ONE "ASSOCIATE" *NOT* LISTED BENEATH MY NAME, OR BOOSTER'S, OR BATMAN'S...

THE

"TED").

YORK CITY

...R.D. – KORD OMNIVERSAL
RESEARCH AND DEVELOPMENT
–C.E.O.

POWERS: GENIUS (I...

ABILITIES AND E
BB GUN—MULTI-USE
THE "BUG" (DESTRO...
LIGHT COMBAT AND
TRAINED MARTIAL

ASSOC...
• CAR...

...RDON, BARBARA –
...NZZ, J'ONN
...MARTIAN MANHUNTER

BRAVO, TED...

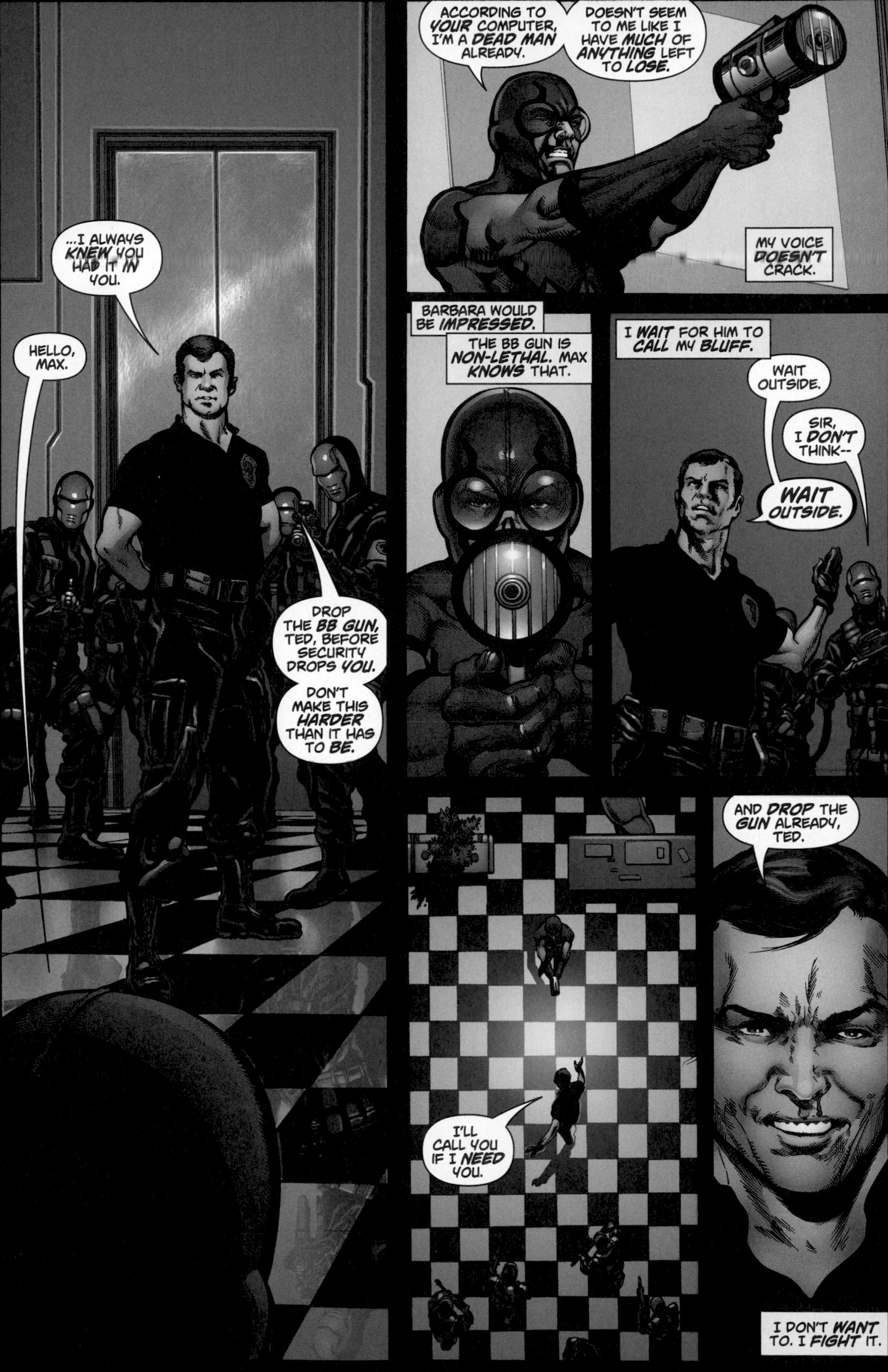

ACCORDING TO YOUR COMPUTER, I'M A DEAD MAN ALREADY.
DOESN'T SEEM TO ME LIKE I HAVE MUCH OF ANYTHING LEFT TO LOSE.
MY VOICE DOESN'T CRACK.
HELLO, MAX.
...I ALWAYS KNEW YOU HAD IT IN YOU.
DROP THE BB GUN, TED, BEFORE SECURITY DROPS YOU.
DON'T MAKE THIS HARDER THAN IT HAS TO BE.
BARBARA WOULD BE IMPRESSED.
THE BB GUN IS NON-LETHAL. MAX KNOWS THAT.
I WAIT FOR HIM TO CALL MY BLUFF.
WAIT OUTSIDE.
SIR, I DON'T THINK--
WAIT OUTSIDE.
I'LL CALL YOU IF I NEED YOU.
AND DROP THE GUN ALREADY, TED.
I DON'T WANT TO. I FIGHT IT.

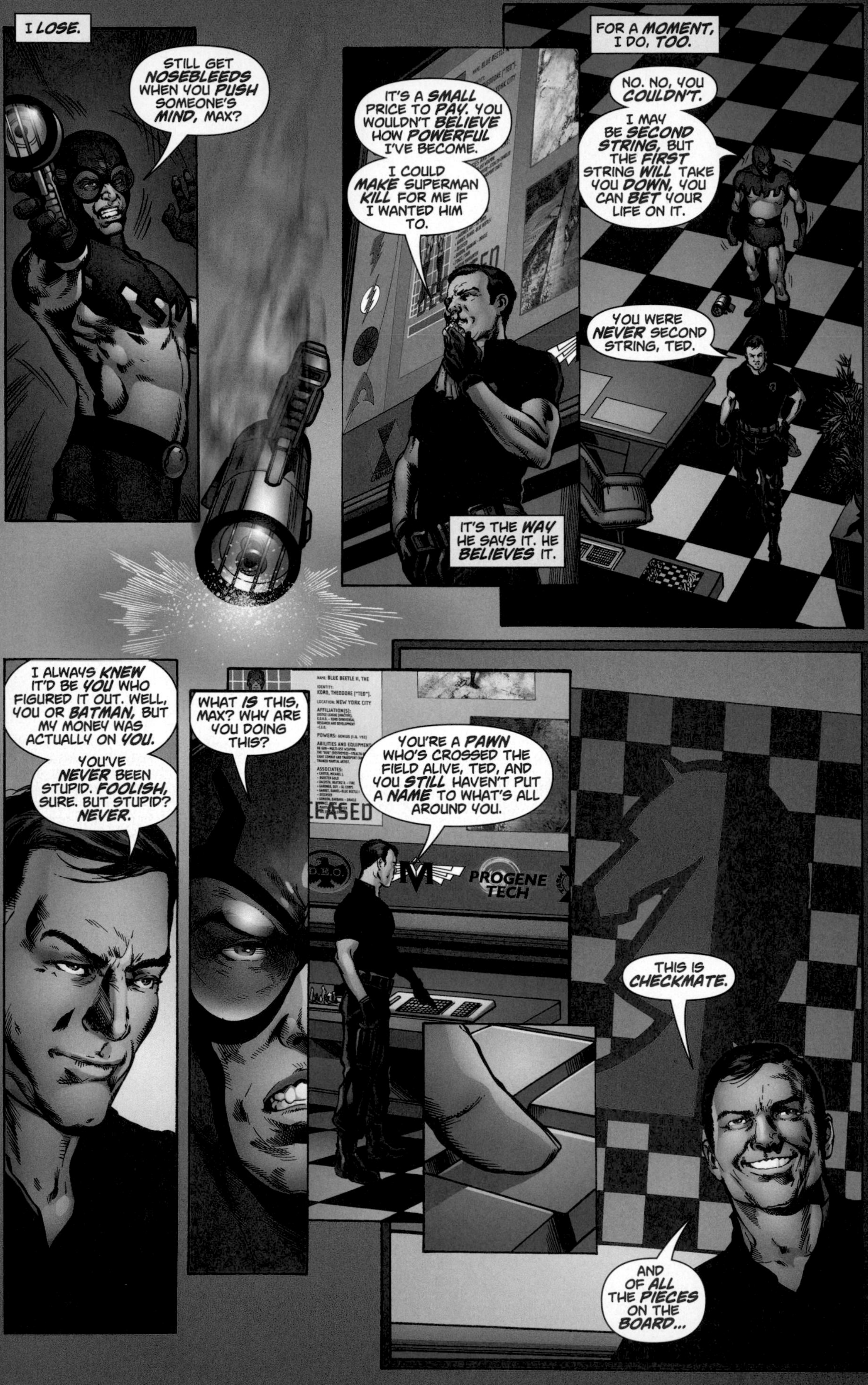
I LOSE.
STILL GET NOSEBLEEDS WHEN YOU PUSH SOMEONE'S MIND, MAX?
IT'S A SMALL PRICE TO PAY. YOU WOULDN'T BELIEVE HOW POWERFUL I'VE BECOME.
I COULD MAKE SUPERMAN KILL FOR ME IF I WANTED HIM TO.
IT'S THE WAY HE SAYS IT. HE BELIEVES IT.
FOR A MOMENT, I DO, TOO.
NO. NO, YOU COULDN'T.
I MAY BE SECOND STRING, BUT THE FIRST STRING WILL TAKE YOU DOWN, YOU CAN BET YOUR LIFE ON IT.
YOU WERE NEVER SECOND STRING, TED.
I ALWAYS KNEW IT'D BE YOU WHO FIGURED IT OUT. WELL, YOU OR BATMAN, BUT MY MONEY WAS ACTUALLY ON YOU.
YOU'VE NEVER BEEN STUPID. FOOLISH, SURE. BUT STUPID? NEVER.
WHAT IS THIS, MAX? WHY ARE YOU DOING THIS?
YOU'RE A PAWN WHO'S CROSSED THE FIELD ALIVE, TED, AND YOU STILL HAVEN'T PUT A NAME TO WHAT'S ALL AROUND YOU.
PROGENE TECH
THIS IS CHECKMATE.
AND OF ALL THE PIECES ON THE BOARD...

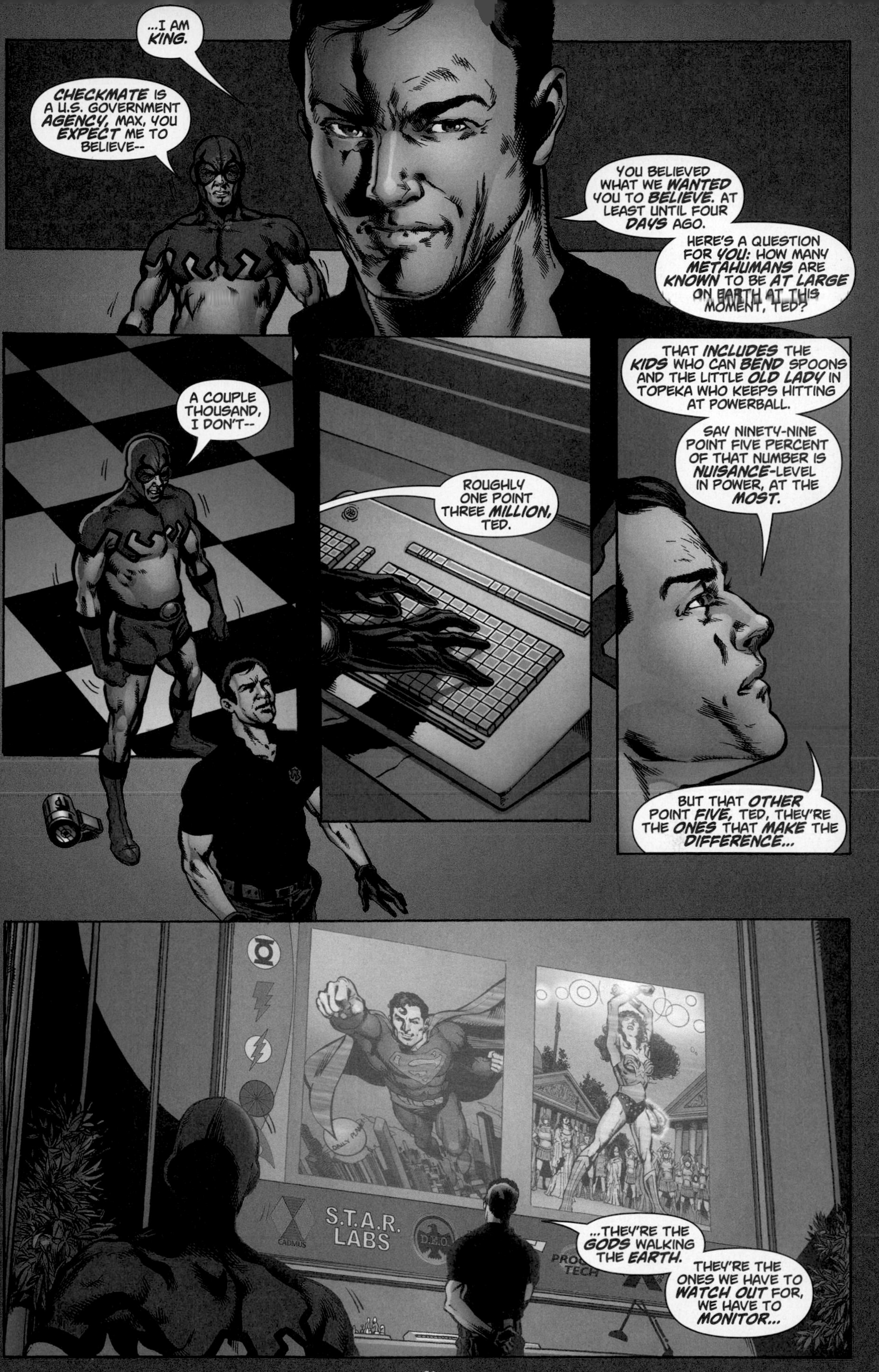
...I AM KING.
CHECKMATE IS A U.S. GOVERNMENT AGENCY, MAX, YOU EXPECT ME TO BELIEVE--
YOU BELIEVED WHAT WE WANTED YOU TO BELIEVE. AT LEAST UNTIL FOUR DAYS AGO.
HERE'S A QUESTION FOR YOU: HOW MANY METAHUMANS ARE KNOWN TO BE AT LARGE ON EARTH AT THIS MOMENT, TED?
A COUPLE THOUSAND, I DON'T--
ROUGHLY ONE POINT THREE MILLION, TED.
THAT INCLUDES THE KIDS WHO CAN BEND SPOONS AND THE LITTLE OLD LADY IN TOPEKA WHO KEEPS HITTING AT POWERBALL.
SAY NINETY-NINE POINT FIVE PERCENT OF THAT NUMBER IS NUISANCE-LEVEL IN POWER, AT THE MOST.
BUT THAT OTHER POINT FIVE, TED, THEY'RE THE ONES THAT MAKE THE DIFFERENCE...
S.T.A.R. LABS
CADMUS
D.E.O.
...THEY'RE THE GODS WALKING THE EARTH.
THEY'RE THE ONES WE HAVE TO WATCH OUT FOR, WE HAVE TO MONITOR...

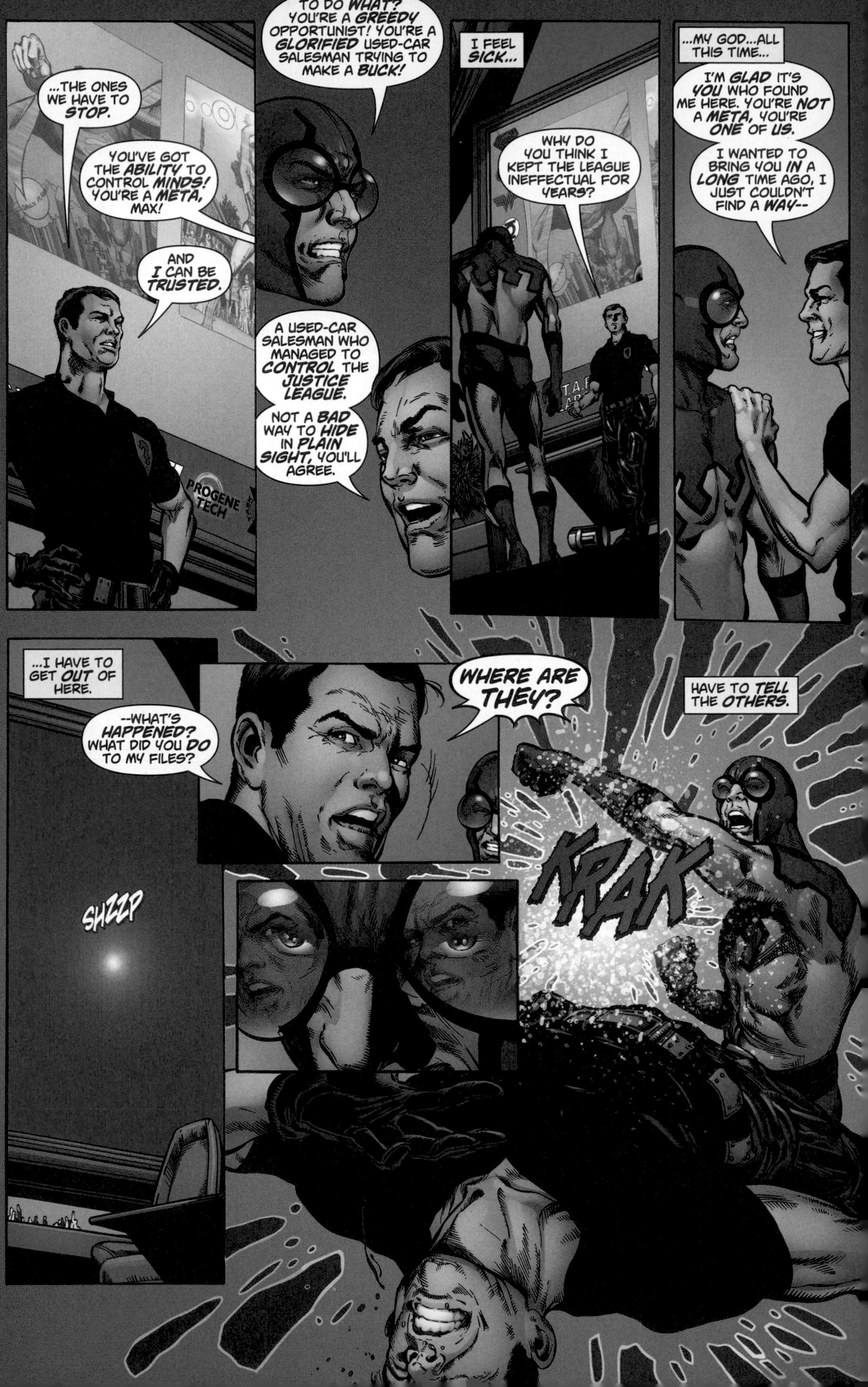
...THE ONES WE HAVE TO STOP.
YOU'VE GOT THE ABILITY TO CONTROL MINDS! YOU'RE A META, MAX!
AND I CAN BE TRUSTED.
TO DO WHAT? YOU'RE A GREEDY OPPORTUNIST! YOU'RE A GLORIFIED USED-CAR SALESMAN TRYING TO MAKE A BUCK!
A USED-CAR SALESMAN WHO MANAGED TO CONTROL THE JUSTICE LEAGUE.
NOT A BAD WAY TO HIDE IN PLAIN SIGHT, YOU'LL AGREE.
PROGENE TECH
I FEEL SICK...
WHY DO YOU THINK I KEPT THE LEAGUE INEFFECTUAL FOR YEARS?
...MY GOD...ALL THIS TIME...
I'M GLAD IT'S YOU WHO FOUND ME HERE. YOU'RE NOT A META, YOU'RE ONE OF US.
I WANTED TO BRING YOU IN A LONG TIME AGO, I JUST COULDN'T FIND A WAY--
...I HAVE TO GET OUT OF HERE.
--WHAT'S HAPPENED? WHAT DID YOU DO TO MY FILES?
WHERE ARE THEY?
HAVE TO TELL THE OTHERS.
SHZZP
KRAK

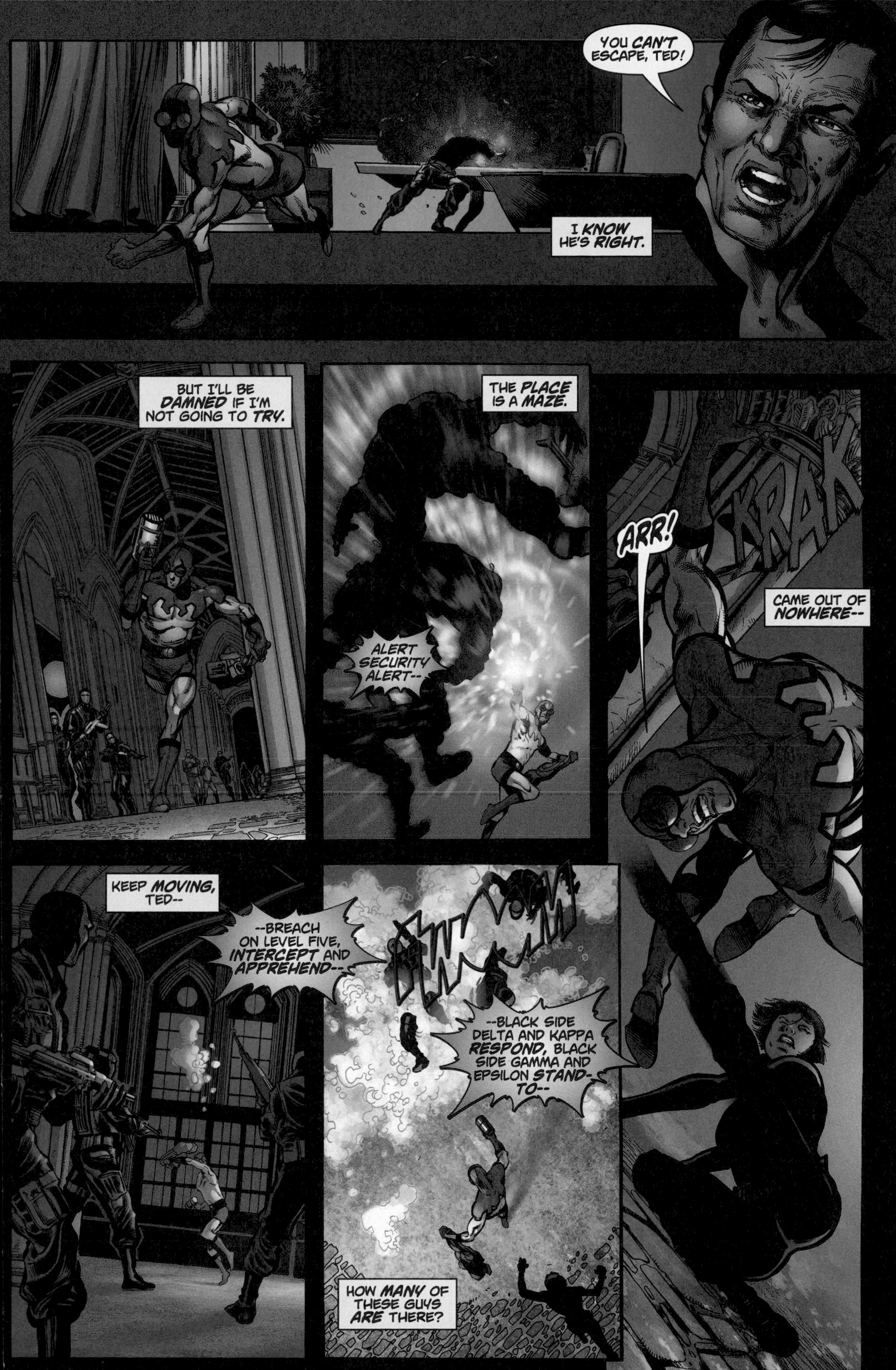
YOU CAN'T ESCAPE, TED!
I KNOW HE'S RIGHT.
BUT I'LL BE DAMNED IF I'M NOT GOING TO TRY.
THE PLACE IS A MAZE.
ALERT SECURITY ALERT--
KRAK
ARR!
CAME OUT OF NOWHERE--
KEEP MOVING, TED--
--BREACH ON LEVEL FIVE, INTERCEPT AND APPREHEND--
FWOOM
--BLACK SIDE DELTA AND KAPPA RESPOND, BLACK SIDE GAMMA AND EPSILON STAND-TO--
HOW MANY OF THESE GUYS ARE THERE?

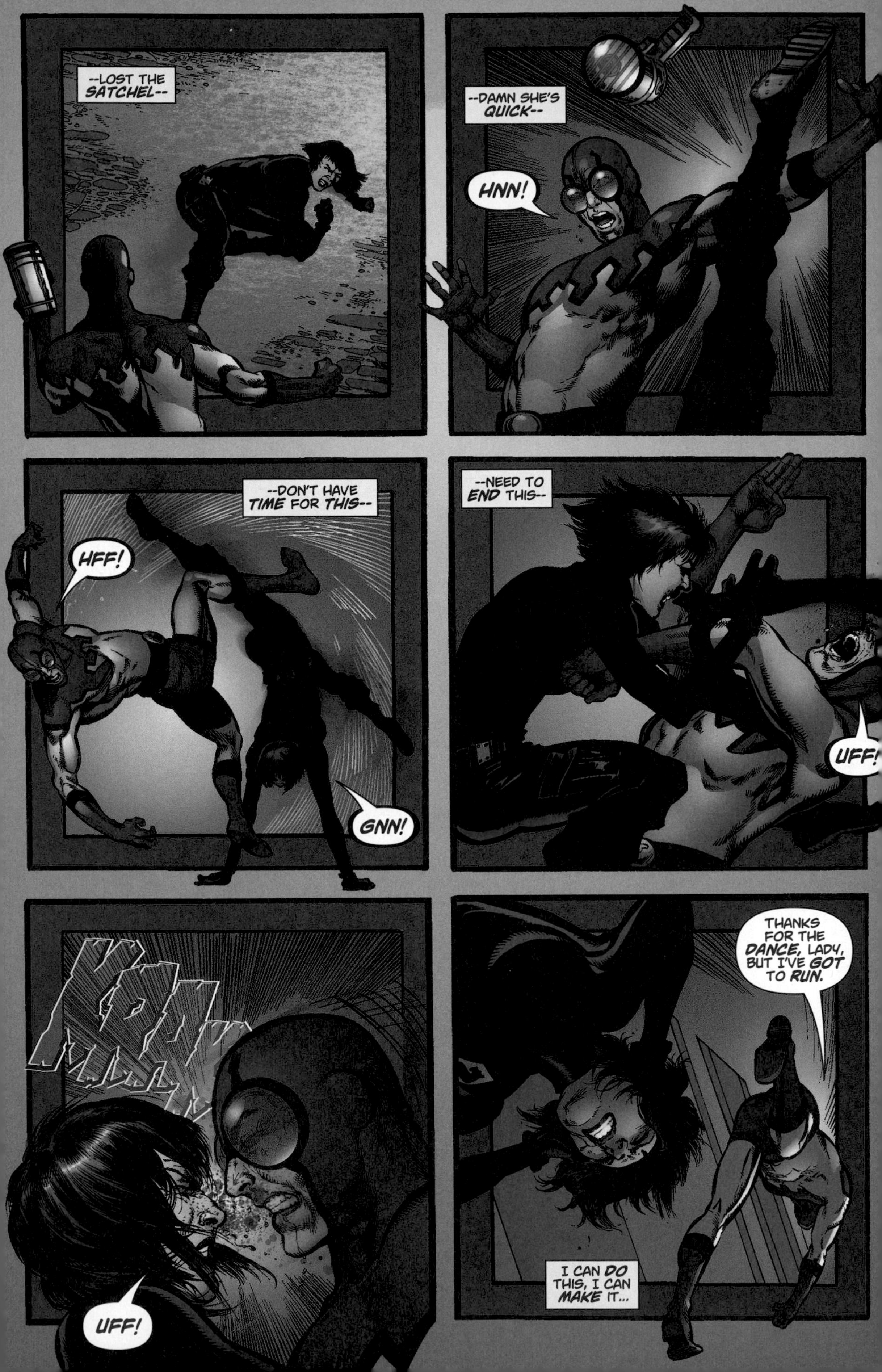
--LOST THE SATCHEL--
--DAMN SHE'S QUICK--
HNN!
--DON'T HAVE TIME FOR THIS--
HFF!
GNN!
--NEED TO END THIS--
UFF!
UFF!
THANKS FOR THE DANCE, LADY, BUT I'VE GOT TO RUN.
I CAN DO THIS, I CAN MAKE IT...

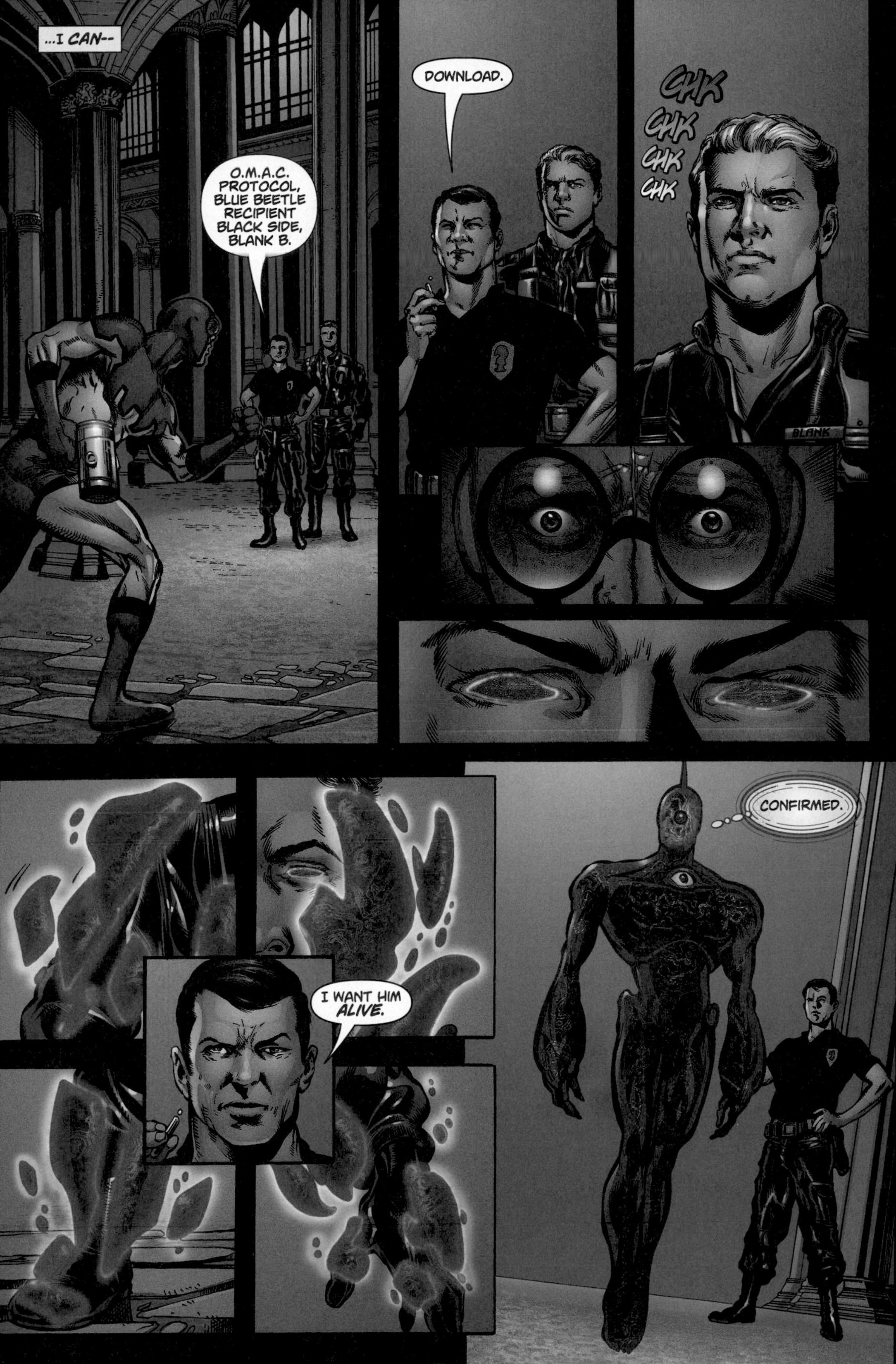
...I CAN--
O.M.A.C. PROTOCOL, BLUE BEETLE RECIPIENT BLACK SIDE, BLANK B.
DOWNLOAD.
CHK CHK CHK CHK
BLANK
I WANT HIM ALIVE.
CONFIRMED.

I FIRE THE FLARE--

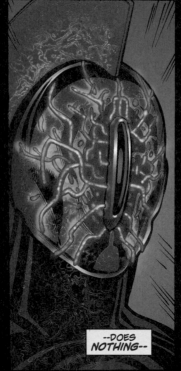

--DOES NOTHING--

KRAK

AHHG!!

--MY ARM JUST BROKE AT THE ELBOW--

--AND I THINK IT'S THE END...

...AND IT IS...

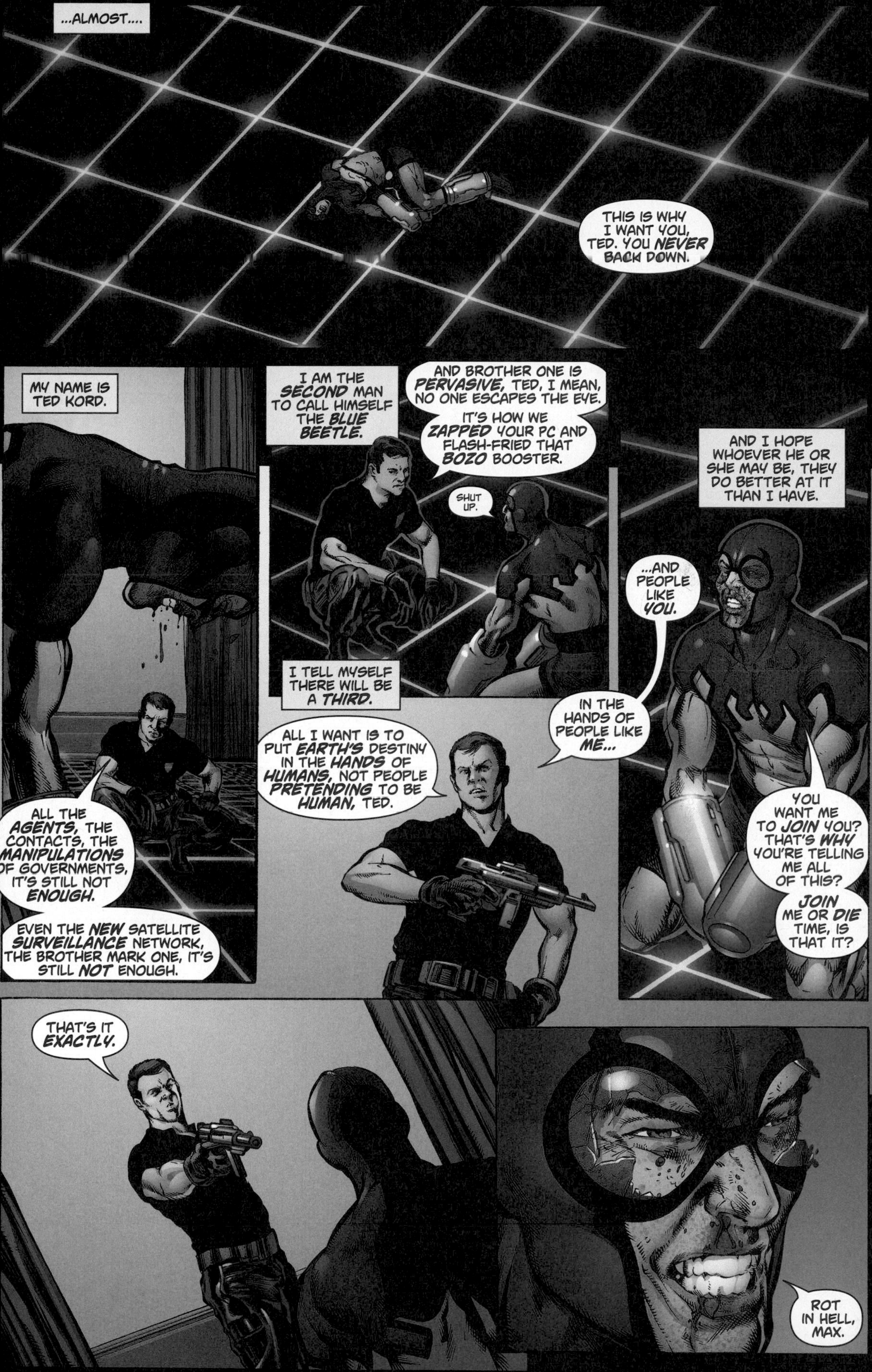
...ALMOST....
THIS IS WHY I WANT YOU, TED. YOU NEVER BACK DOWN.
MY NAME IS TED KORD.
ALL THE AGENTS, THE CONTACTS, THE MANIPULATIONS OF GOVERNMENTS, IT'S STILL NOT ENOUGH.
EVEN THE NEW SATELLITE SURVEILLANCE NETWORK, THE BROTHER MARK ONE, IT'S STILL NOT ENOUGH.
I AM THE SECOND MAN TO CALL HIMSELF THE BLUE BEETLE.
AND BROTHER ONE IS PERVASIVE, TED, I MEAN, NO ONE ESCAPES THE EYE.
IT'S HOW WE ZAPPED YOUR PC AND FLASH-FRIED THAT BOZO BOOSTER.
SHUT UP.
I TELL MYSELF THERE WILL BE A THIRD.
AND I HOPE WHOEVER HE OR SHE MAY BE, THEY DO BETTER AT IT THAN I HAVE.
ALL I WANT IS TO PUT EARTH'S DESTINY IN THE HANDS OF HUMANS, NOT PEOPLE PRETENDING TO BE HUMAN, TED.
IN THE HANDS OF PEOPLE LIKE ME...
...AND PEOPLE LIKE YOU.
YOU WANT ME TO JOIN YOU? THAT'S WHY YOU'RE TELLING ME ALL OF THIS?
JOIN ME OR DIE TIME, IS THAT IT?
THAT'S IT EXACTLY.
ROT IN HELL, MAX.

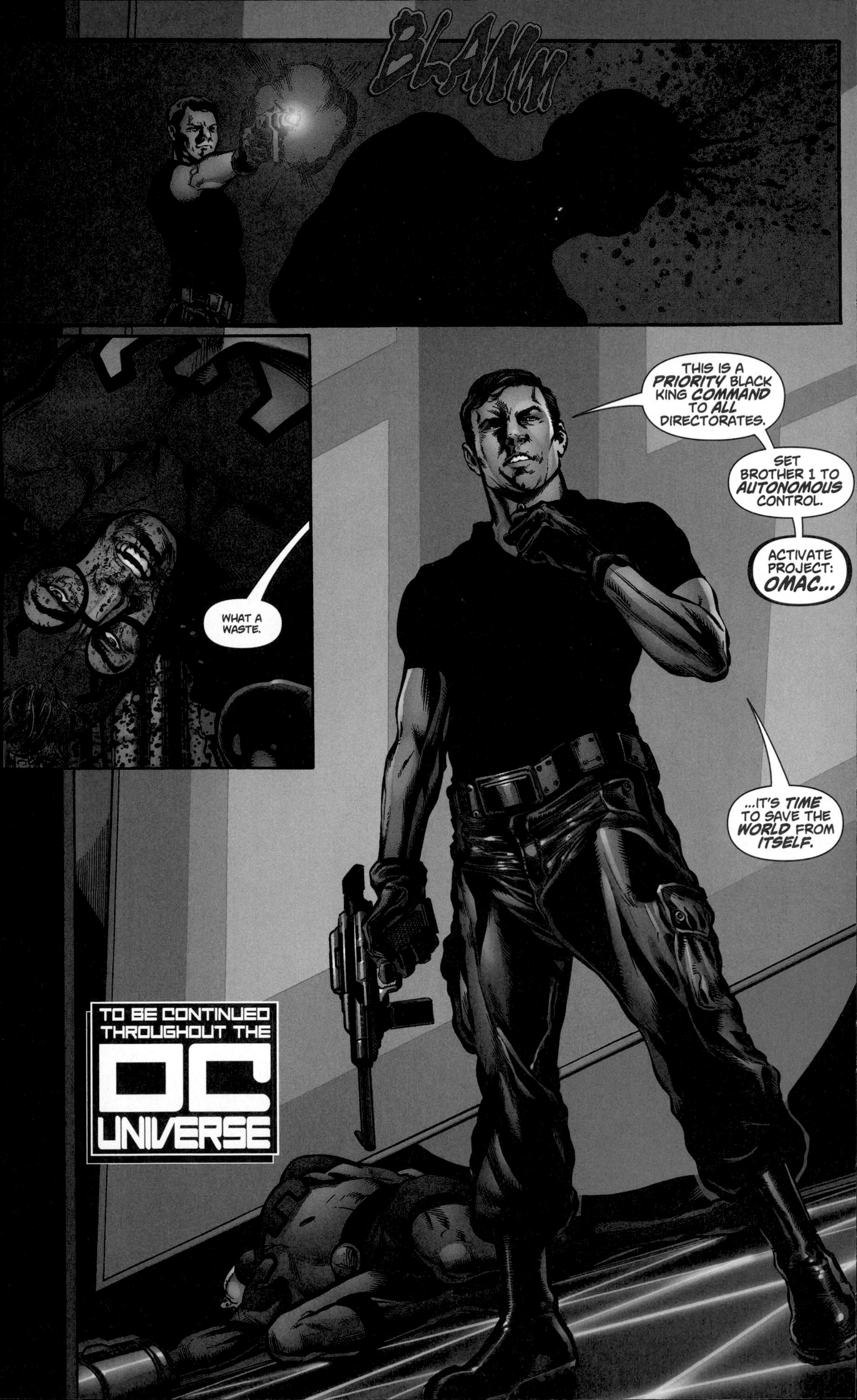
BLAMM
WHAT A WASTE.
THIS IS A PRIORITY BLACK KING COMMAND TO ALL DIRECTORATES.
SET BROTHER 1 TO AUTONOMOUS CONTROL.
ACTIVATE PROJECT: OMAC...
...IT'S TIME TO SAVE THE WORLD FROM ITSELF.
TO BE CONTINUED THROUGHOUT THE DC UNIVERSE

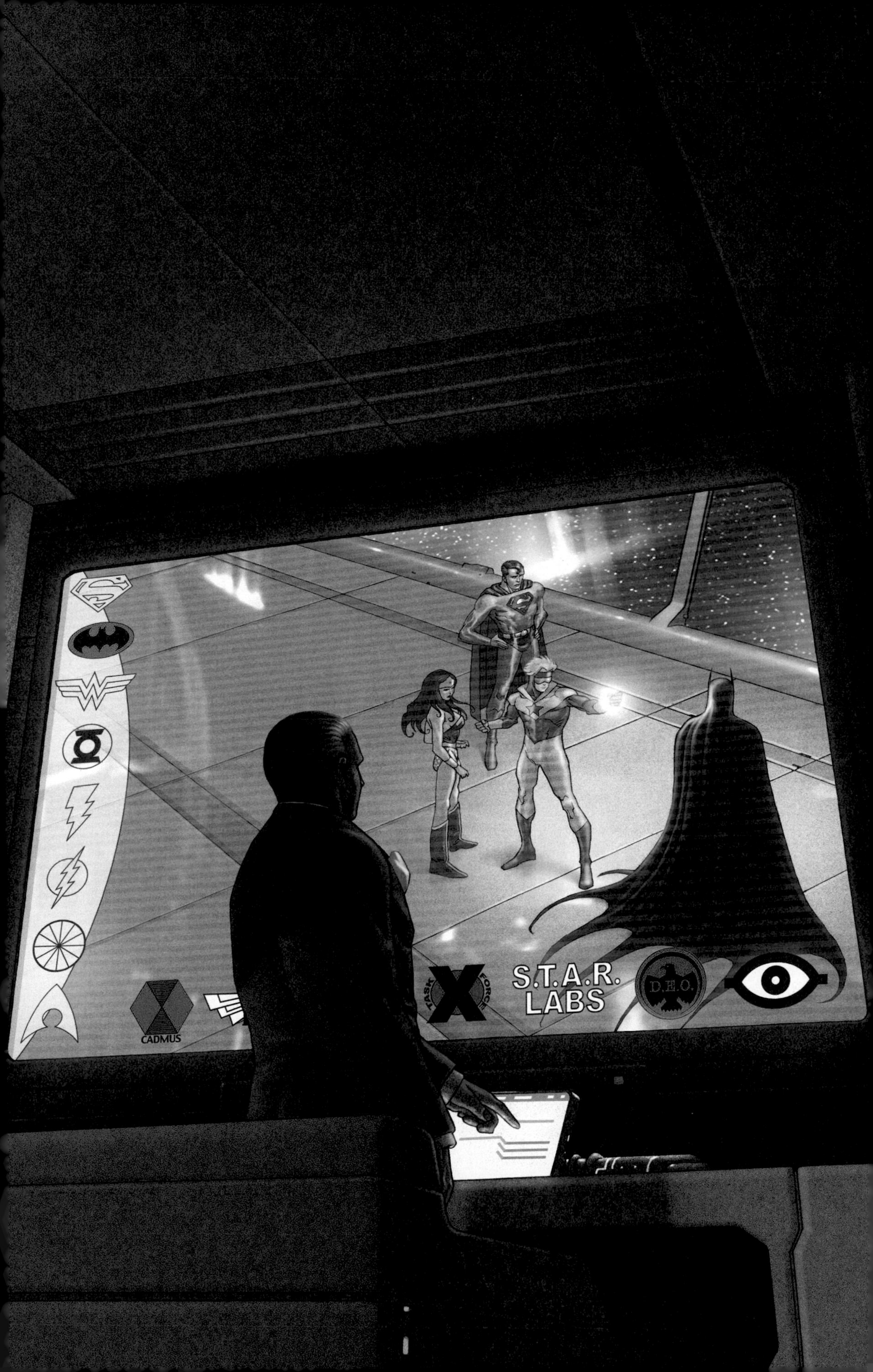

CADMUS
TASK X FORCE
S.T.A.R. LABS
D.E.O.

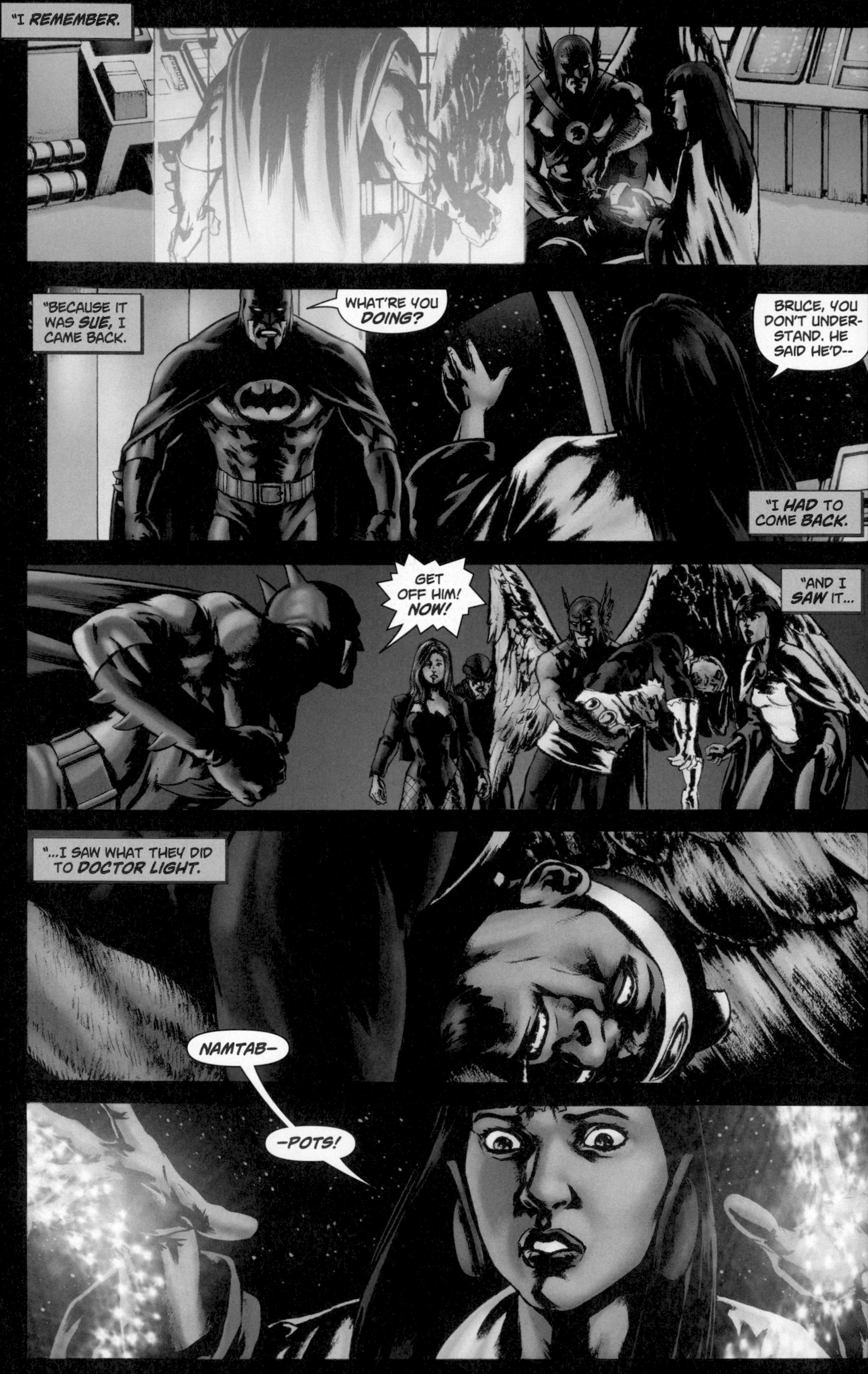
"I REMEMBER.
"BECAUSE IT WAS SUE, I CAME BACK.
WHAT'RE YOU DOING?
BRUCE, YOU DON'T UNDERSTAND. HE SAID HE'D--
"I HAD TO COME BACK.
GET OFF HIM! NOW!
"AND I SAW IT...
"...I SAW WHAT THEY DID TO DOCTOR LIGHT.
NAMTAB-
-POTS!

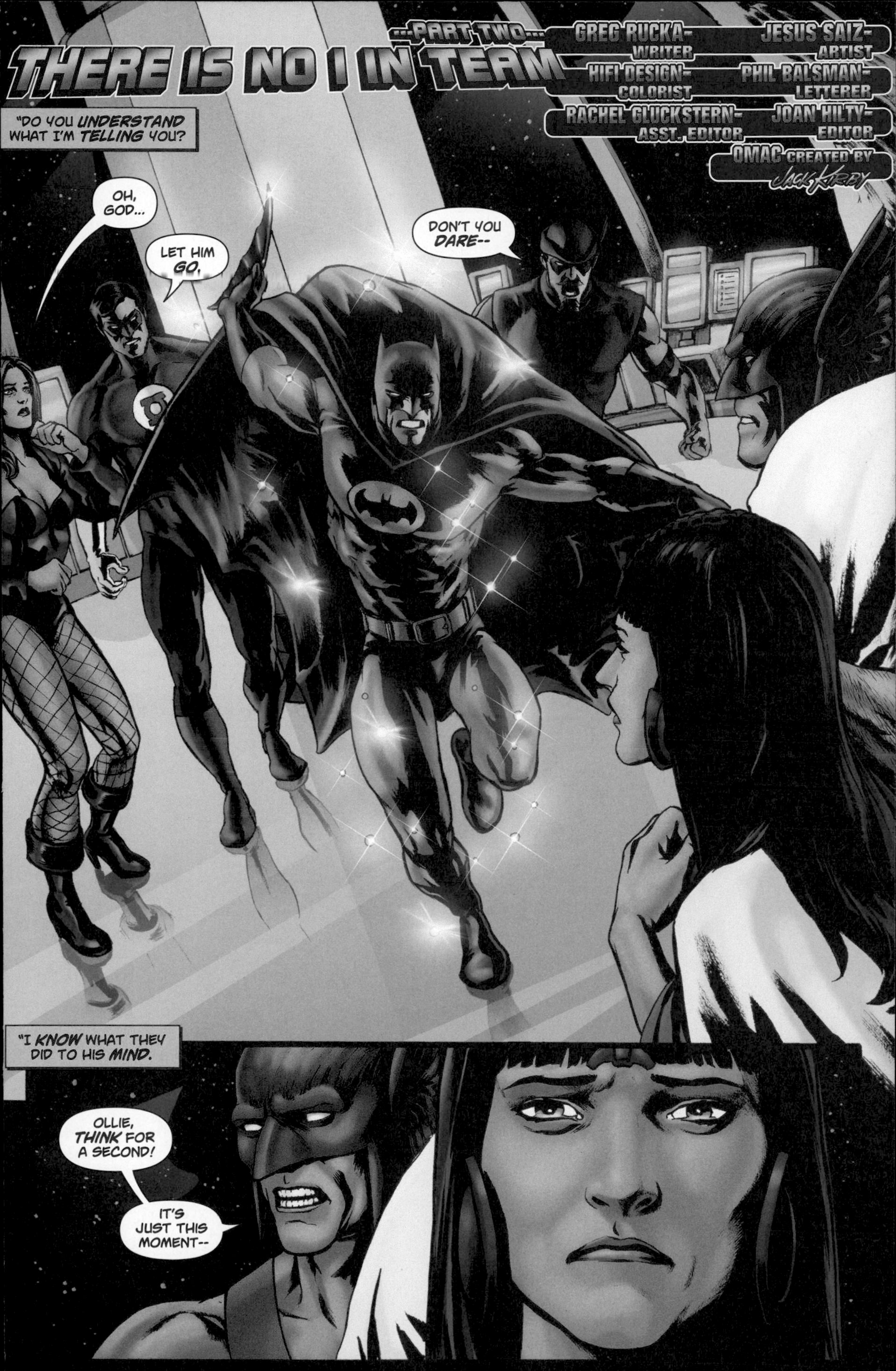
--PART TWO--
THERE IS NO I IN TEAM
GREG RUCKA-WRITER
JESUS SAIZ-ARTIST
HIFI DESIGN-COLORIST
PHIL BALSMAN-LETTERER
RACHEL GLUCKSTERN-ASST. EDITOR
JOAN HILTY-EDITOR
OMAC CREATED BY JACK KIRBY
"DO YOU UNDERSTAND WHAT I'M TELLING YOU?
OH, GOD...
LET HIM GO.
DON'T YOU DARE--
"I KNOW WHAT THEY DID TO HIS MIND.
OLLIE, THINK FOR A SECOND!
IT'S JUST THIS MOMENT--

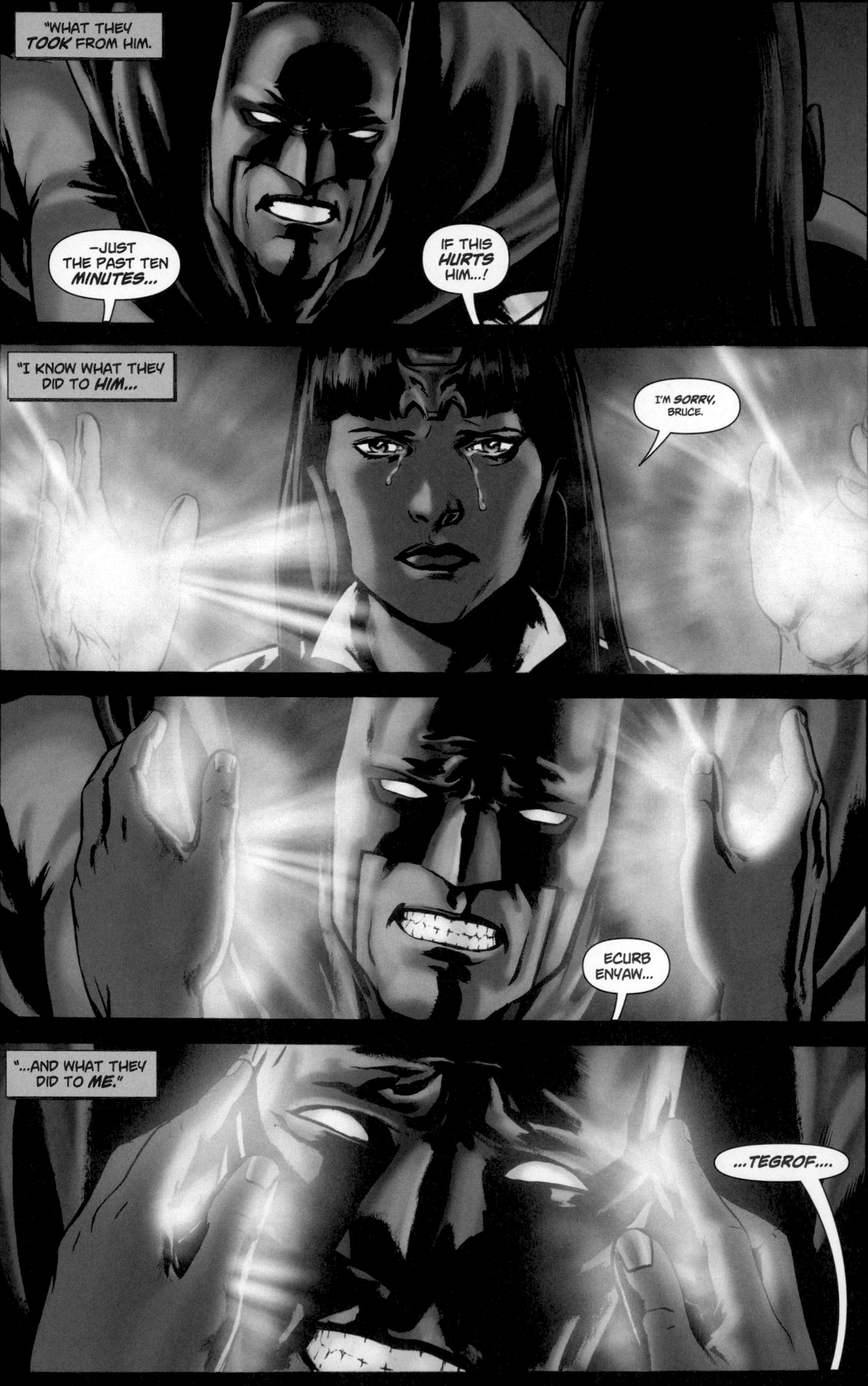
"WHAT THEY TOOK FROM HIM.
-JUST THE PAST TEN MINUTES...
IF THIS HURTS HIM...!
"I KNOW WHAT THEY DID TO HIM...
I'M SORRY, BRUCE.
ECURB ENYAW...
"...AND WHAT THEY DID TO ME."
...TEGROF....

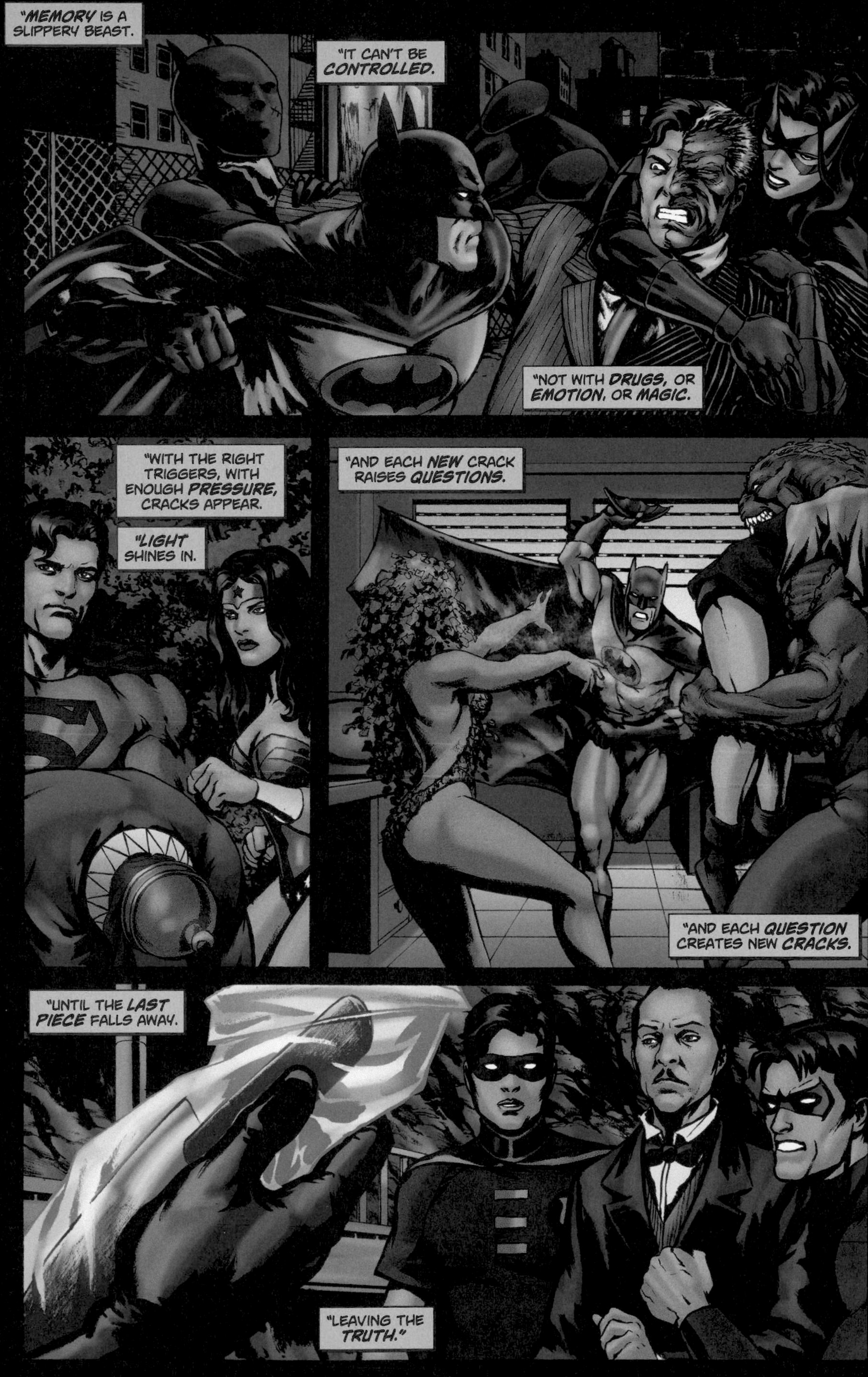
"MEMORY IS A SLIPPERY BEAST.
"IT CAN'T BE CONTROLLED.
"NOT WITH DRUGS, OR EMOTION, OR MAGIC.
"WITH THE RIGHT TRIGGERS, WITH ENOUGH PRESSURE, CRACKS APPEAR.
"LIGHT SHINES IN.
"AND EACH NEW CRACK RAISES QUESTIONS.
"AND EACH QUESTION CREATES NEW CRACKS.
"UNTIL THE LAST PIECE FALLS AWAY.
"LEAVING THE TRUTH."

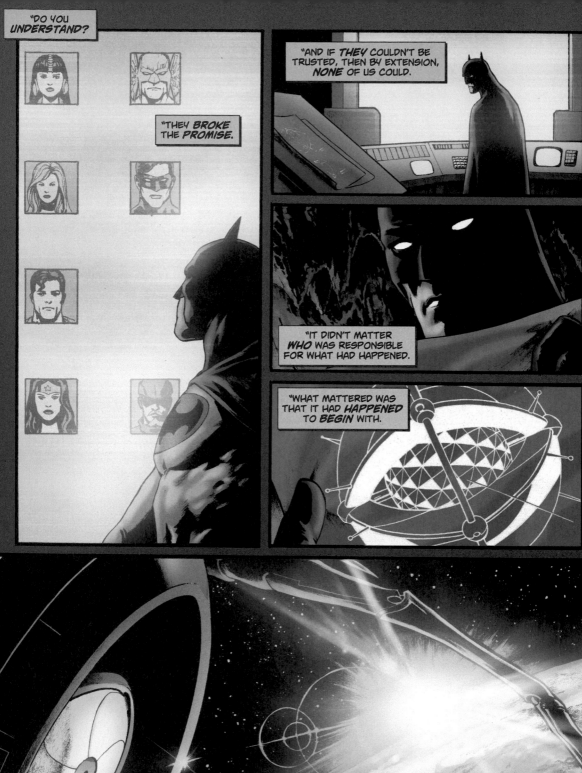

"DO YOU UNDERSTAND?

"THEY *BROKE* THE *PROMISE.*

"AND IF *THEY* COULDN'T BE TRUSTED, THEN BY EXTENSION, *NONE* OF US COULD.

"IT DIDN'T MATTER *WHO* WAS RESPONSIBLE FOR WHAT HAD HAPPENED.

"WHAT MATTERED WAS THAT IT HAD *HAPPENED* TO *BEGIN* WITH.

"AND I WAS *DAMNED* IF I WAS GOING TO LET IT *EVER* HAPPEN *AGAIN.*"

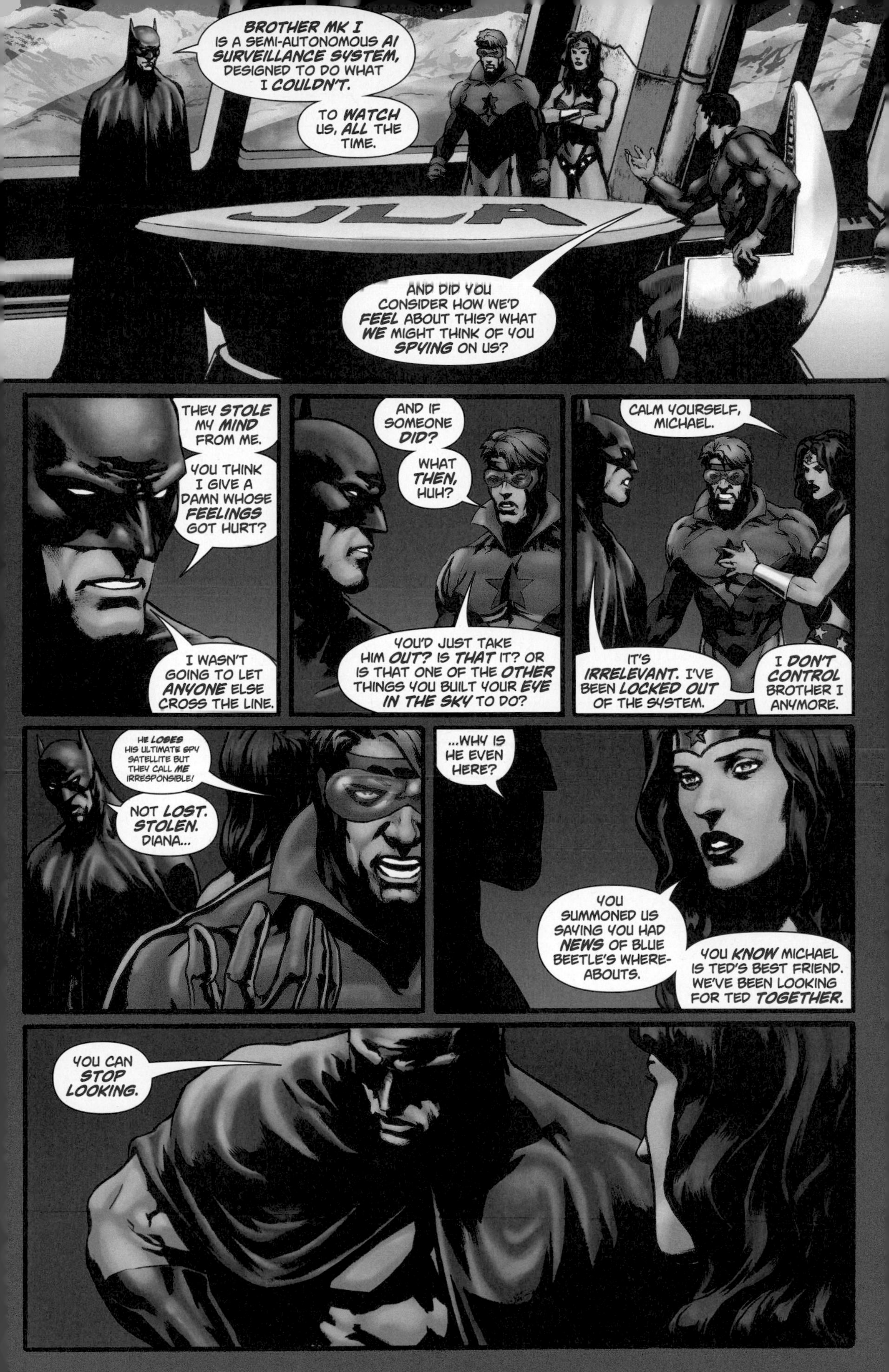
BROTHER MK I IS A SEMI-AUTONOMOUS AI SURVEILLANCE SYSTEM, DESIGNED TO DO WHAT I COULDN'T.
TO WATCH US, ALL THE TIME.
AND DID YOU CONSIDER HOW WE'D FEEL ABOUT THIS? WHAT WE MIGHT THINK OF YOU SPYING ON US?
THEY STOLE MY MIND FROM ME.
YOU THINK I GIVE A DAMN WHOSE FEELINGS GOT HURT?
I WASN'T GOING TO LET ANYONE ELSE CROSS THE LINE.
AND IF SOMEONE DID?
WHAT THEN, HUH?
YOU'D JUST TAKE HIM OUT? IS THAT IT? OR IS THAT ONE OF THE OTHER THINGS YOU BUILT YOUR EYE IN THE SKY TO DO?
CALM YOURSELF, MICHAEL.
IT'S IRRELEVANT. I'VE BEEN LOCKED OUT OF THE SYSTEM.
I DON'T CONTROL BROTHER I ANYMORE.
HE LOSES HIS ULTIMATE SPY SATELLITE BUT THEY CALL ME IRRESPONSIBLE!
NOT LOST. STOLEN. DIANA...
...WHY IS HE EVEN HERE?
YOU SUMMONED US SAYING YOU HAD NEWS OF BLUE BEETLE'S WHERE-ABOUTS.
YOU KNOW MICHAEL IS TED'S BEST FRIEND. WE'VE BEEN LOOKING FOR TED TOGETHER.
YOU CAN STOP LOOKING.

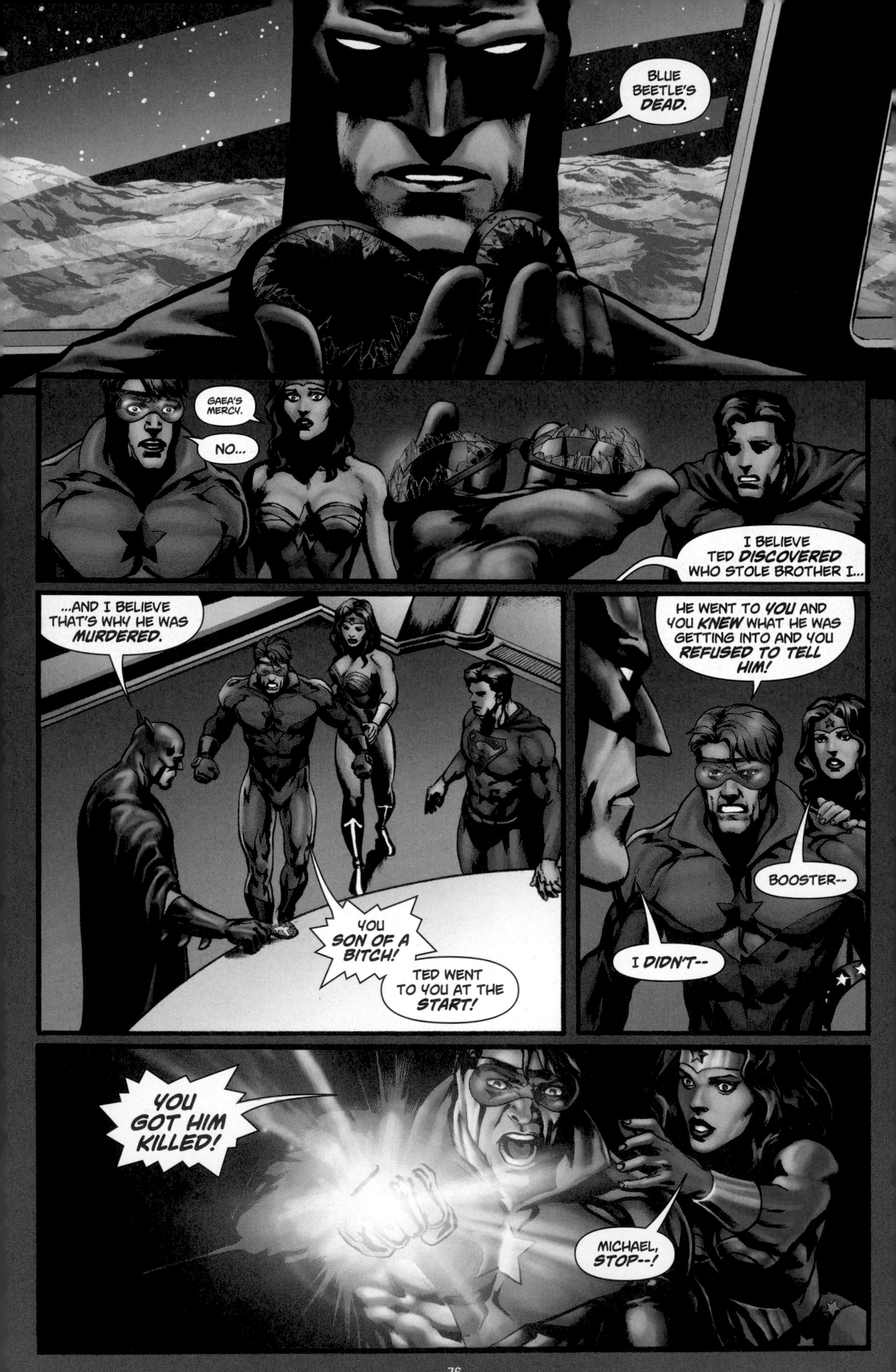

BLUE BEETLE'S DEAD.
GAEA'S MERCY.
NO...
I BELIEVE TED DISCOVERED WHO STOLE BROTHER I...
...AND I BELIEVE THAT'S WHY HE WAS MURDERED.
YOU SON OF A BITCH!
TED WENT TO YOU AT THE START!
HE WENT TO YOU AND YOU KNEW WHAT HE WAS GETTING INTO AND YOU REFUSED TO TELL HIM!
BOOSTER--
I DIDN'T--
YOU GOT HIM KILLED!
MICHAEL, STOP--!

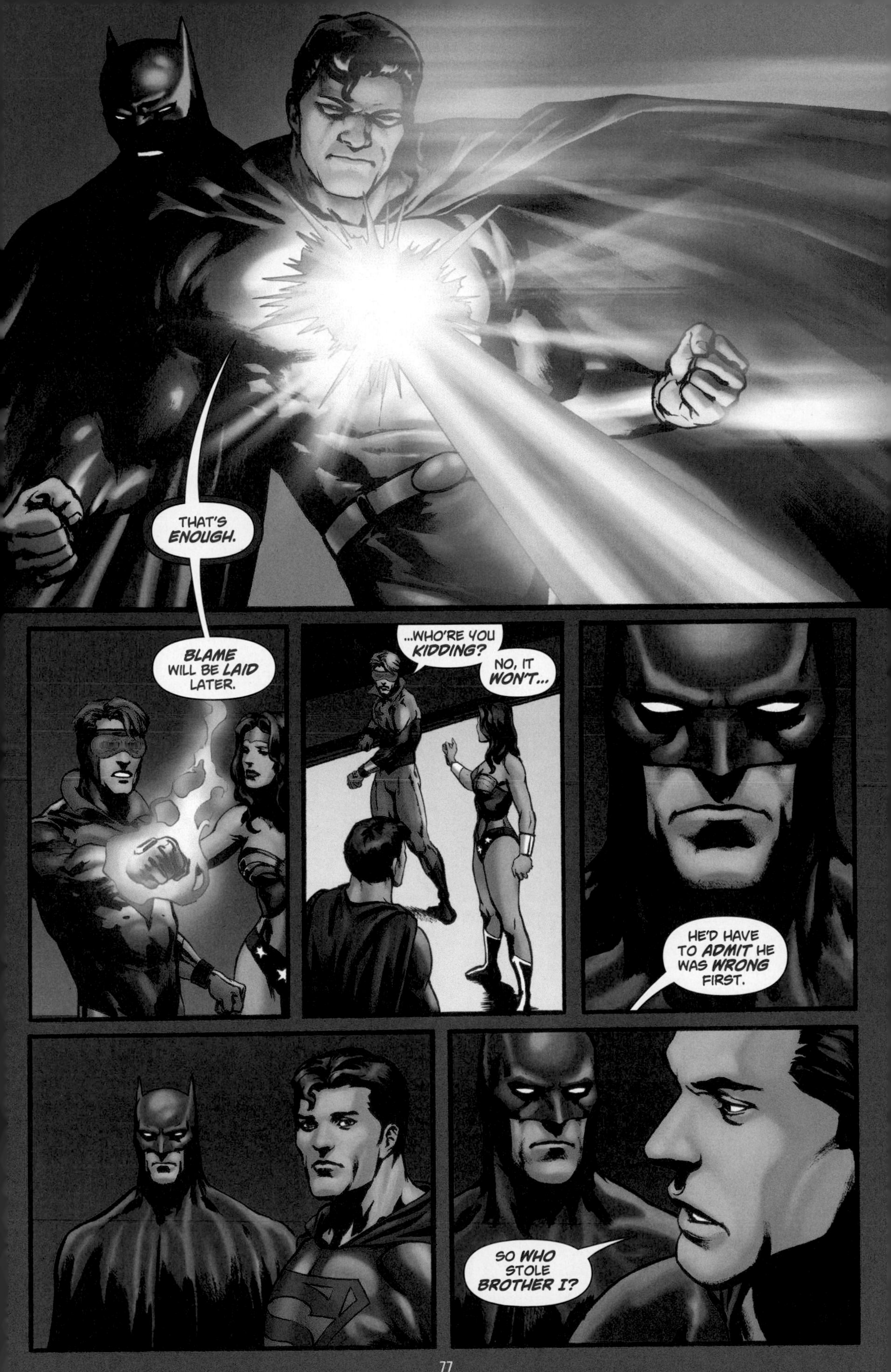
THAT'S ENOUGH.
BLAME WILL BE LAID LATER.
...WHO'RE YOU KIDDING?
NO, IT WON'T...
HE'D HAVE TO ADMIT HE WAS WRONG FIRST.
SO WHO STOLE BROTHER I?

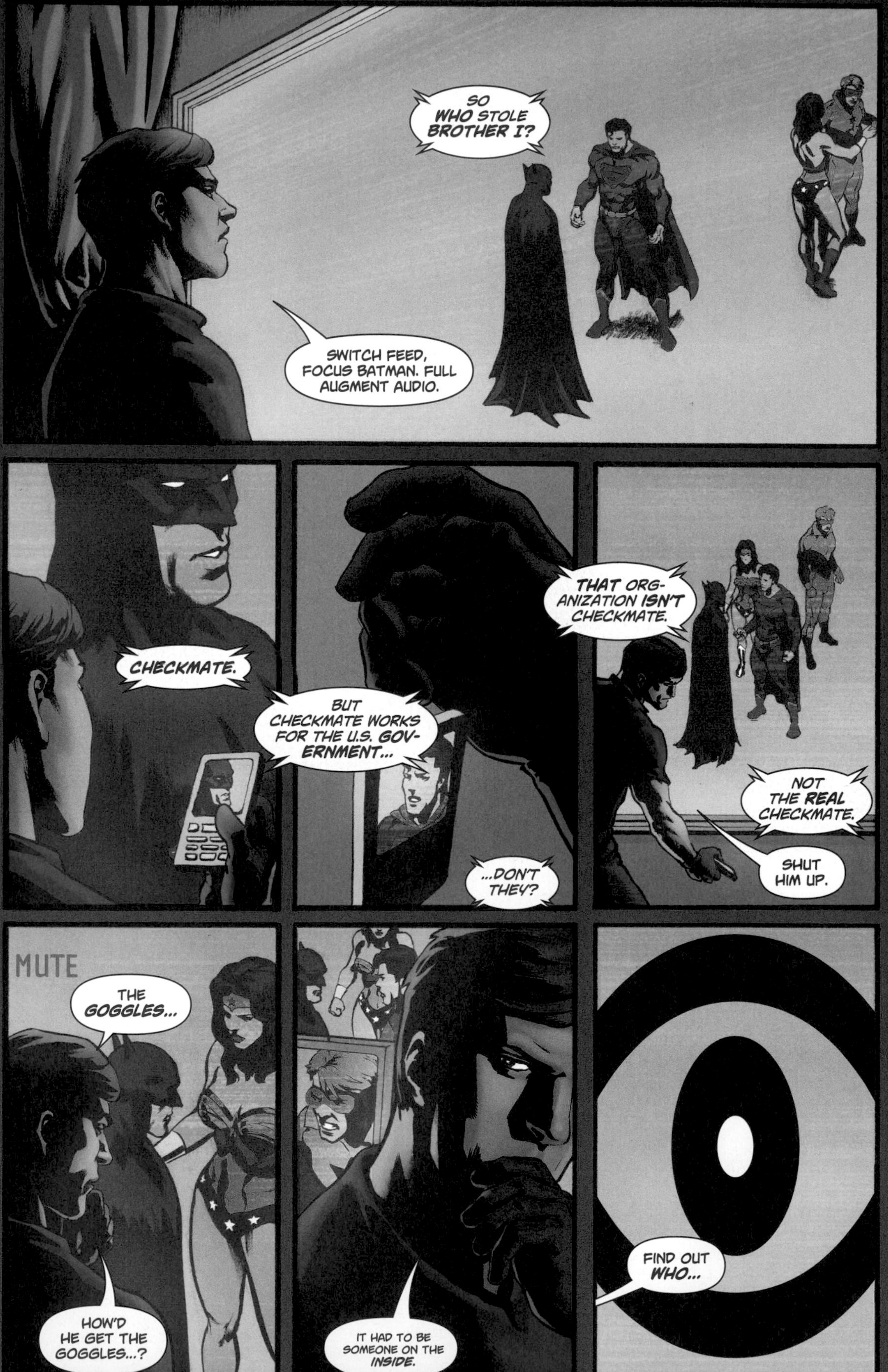

SO WHO STOLE BROTHER I?
SWITCH FEED, FOCUS BATMAN. FULL AUGMENT AUDIO.
CHECKMATE.
BUT CHECKMATE WORKS FOR THE U.S. GOVERNMENT...
...DON'T THEY?
THAT ORGANIZATION ISN'T CHECKMATE.
NOT THE REAL CHECKMATE.
SHUT HIM UP.
MUTE
THE GOGGLES...
HOW'D HE GET THE GOGGLES...?
IT HAD TO BE SOMEONE ON THE INSIDE.
FIND OUT WHO...

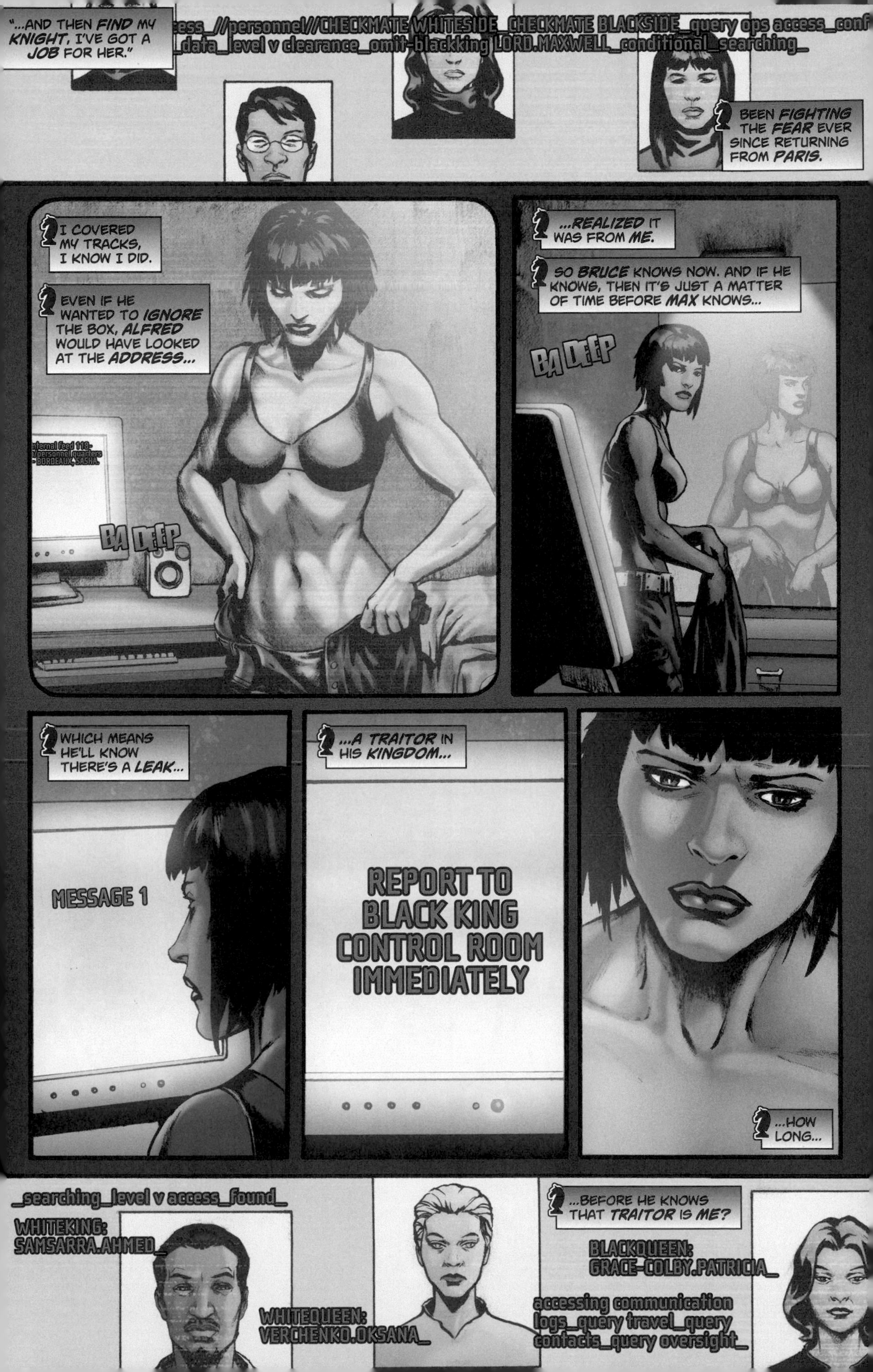
"...AND THEN FIND MY KNIGHT. I'VE GOT A JOB FOR HER."
ess_//personnel//CHECKMATE WHITESIDE_CHECKMATE BLACKSIDE_query ops access_conf
data_level v clearance_omit-blackking LORD.MAXWELL_conditional_searching_
BEEN FIGHTING THE FEAR EVER SINCE RETURNING FROM PARIS.
I COVERED MY TRACKS, I KNOW I DID.
EVEN IF HE WANTED TO IGNORE THE BOX, ALFRED WOULD HAVE LOOKED AT THE ADDRESS...
BA DEEP
...REALIZED IT WAS FROM ME.
SO BRUCE KNOWS NOW. AND IF HE KNOWS, THEN IT'S JUST A MATTER OF TIME BEFORE MAX KNOWS...
BA DEEP
WHICH MEANS HE'LL KNOW THERE'S A LEAK...
MESSAGE 1
...A TRAITOR IN HIS KINGDOM...
REPORT TO BLACK KING CONTROL ROOM IMMEDIATELY
...HOW LONG...
_searching_level v access_found_
WHITEKING: SAMSARRA.AHMED_
WHITEQUEEN: VERCHENKO.OKSANA_
...BEFORE HE KNOWS THAT TRAITOR IS ME?
BLACKQUEEN: GRACE-COLBY.PATRICIA_
accessing communication logs_query travel_query contacts_query oversight_

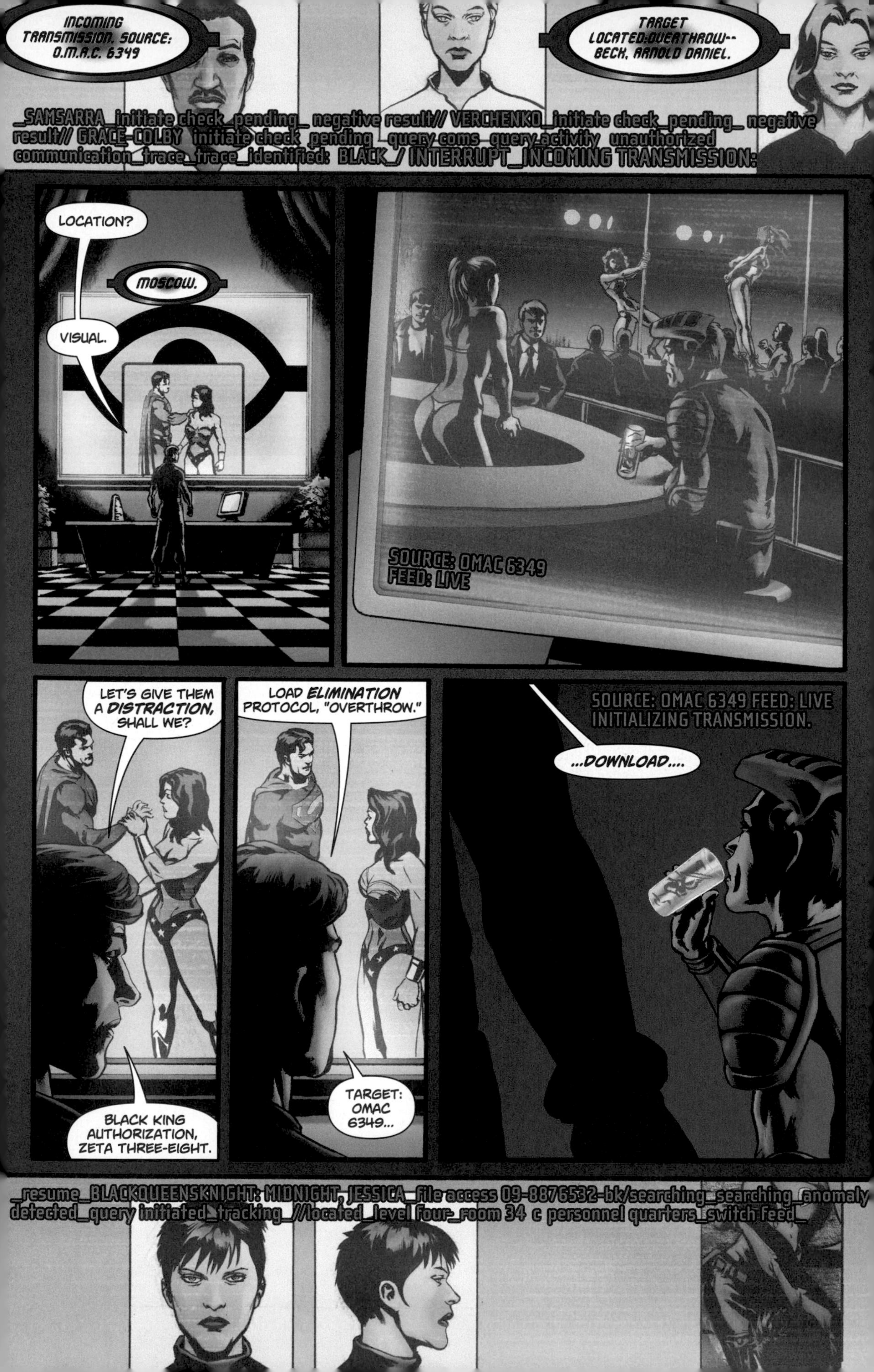
INCOMING TRANSMISSION. SOURCE: O.M.A.C. 6349
TARGET LOCATED:OVERTHROW-- BECK, ARNOLD DANIEL.
_SAMSARRA_initiate check_pending_ negative result// VERCHENKO_initiate check_pending_ negative result// GRACE-COLBY initiate check pending query coms query activity unauthorized communication_trace_trace_identified: BLACK_/ INTERRUPT_INCOMING TRANSMISSION:
LOCATION?
MOSCOW.
VISUAL.
SOURCE: OMAC 6349
FEED: LIVE
LET'S GIVE THEM A DISTRACTION, SHALL WE?
BLACK KING AUTHORIZATION, ZETA THREE-EIGHT.
LOAD ELIMINATION PROTOCOL, "OVERTHROW."
TARGET: OMAC 6349...
SOURCE: OMAC 6349 FEED: LIVE INITIALIZING TRANSMISSION.
...DOWNLOAD....
_resume_BLACKQUEENSKNIGHT: MIDNIGHT, JESSICA_file access 09-8876532-bk/searching_searching_anomaly detected_query initiated_tracking_//located_level four_room 34 c personnel quarters_switch feed_

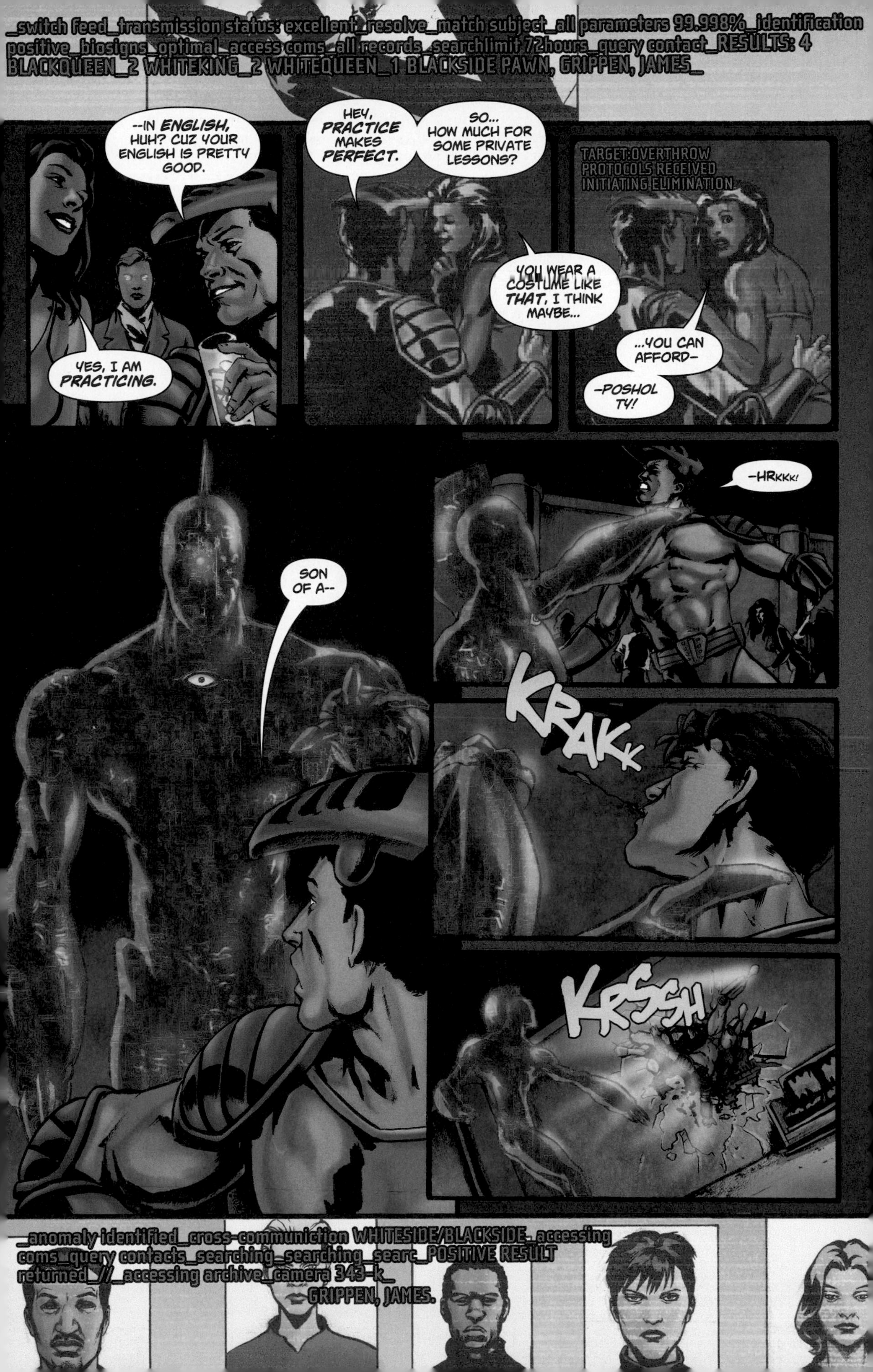
_switch feed_transmission status: excellent_resolve_match subject_all parameters 99.998%_identification positive_biosigns_optimal_access coms_all records_searchlimit 72hours_query contact_RESULTS: 4 BLACKQUEEN_2 WHITEKING_2 WHITEQUEEN_1 BLACKSIDE PAWN, GRIPPEN, JAMES_
--IN ENGLISH, HUH? CUZ YOUR ENGLISH IS PRETTY GOOD.
YES, I AM PRACTICING.
HEY, PRACTICE MAKES PERFECT.
SO... HOW MUCH FOR SOME PRIVATE LESSONS?
YOU WEAR A COSTUME LIKE THAT, I THINK MAYBE...
TARGET:OVERTHROW
PROTOCOLS RECEIVED
INITIATING ELIMINATION
...YOU CAN AFFORD--
-POSHOL TY!
SON OF A--
-HRKKK!
KRAKK
KRSSH
_anomaly identified_cross-communiciton WHITESIDE/BLACKSIDE_accessing coms_query contacts_searching_searching_searc_POSITIVE RESULT returned_//_accessing archive_camera 343-k_
GRIPPEN, JAMES.

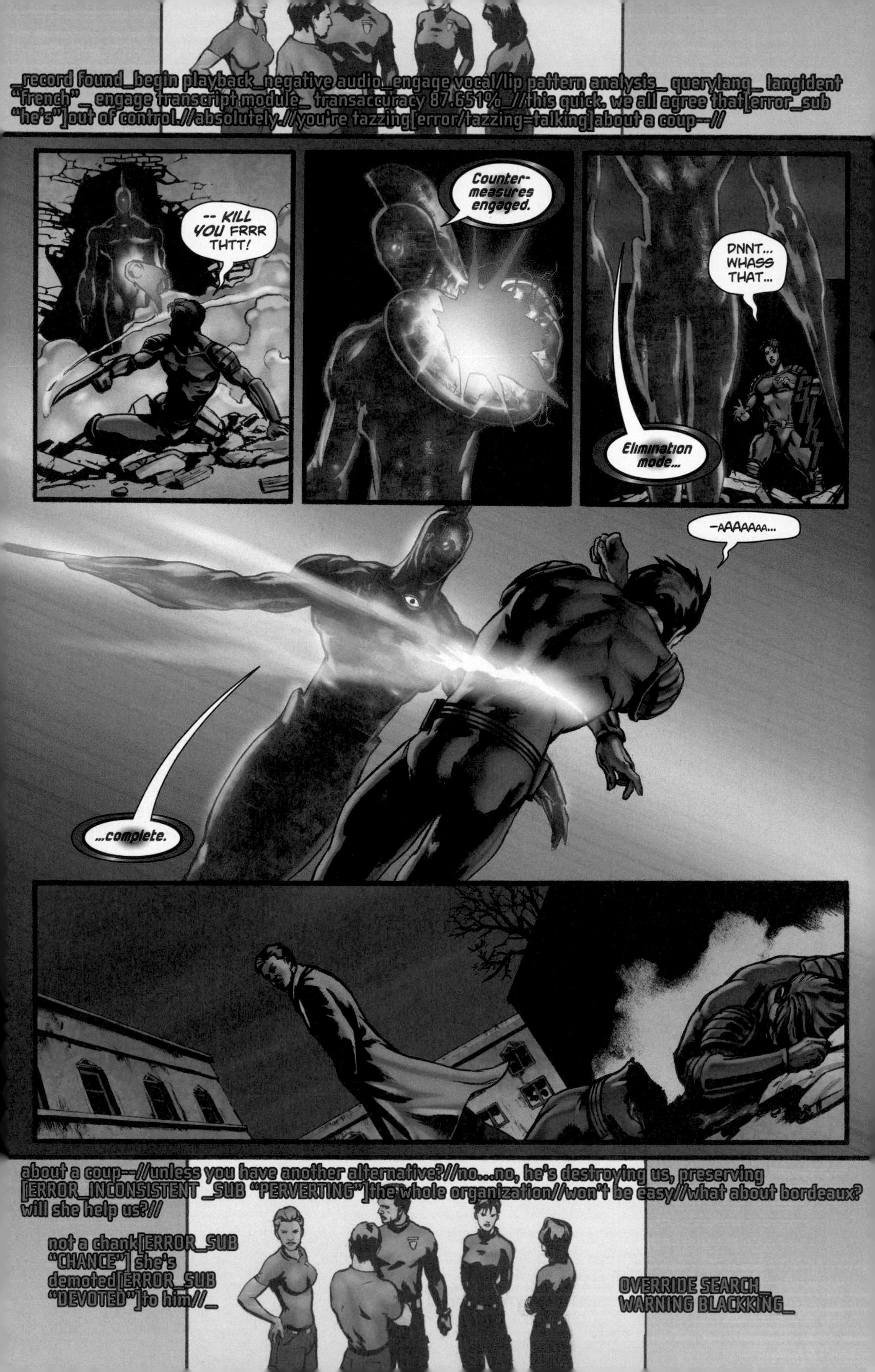
_record found_begin playback_negative audio_engage vocal/lip pattern analysis_ querylang_ langident “french”_ engage transcript module_ transaccuracy 87.651%_//this quick. we all agree that[error_sub “he's”]out of control.//absolutely.//you're tazzing[error/tazzing=talking]about a coup--//
-- KILL YOU FRRR THTT!
Counter-measures engaged.
DNNT... WHASS THAT...
Elimination mode...
-AAAAAAA...
...complete.
about a coup--//unless you have another alternative?//no...no, he's destroying us, preserving [ERROR_INCONSISTENT _SUB “PERVERTING”]the whole organization//won't be easy//what about bordeaux? will she help us?//
not a chank[ERROR_SUB “CHANCE”] she's demoted[ERROR_SUB “DEVOTED”]to him//_
OVERRIDE SEARCH_ WARNING BLACKKING_

 You are in danger.

 I AM IN DANGER.

 IT'S THAT DAMN *MACHINE*...

AM I?

Assassination attempt imminent.

 ...I CAN'T PUT MY FINGER ON IT...

I'M *SURPRISED* IT TOOK THEM THIS LONG.

I'LL TAKE CARE OF IT...

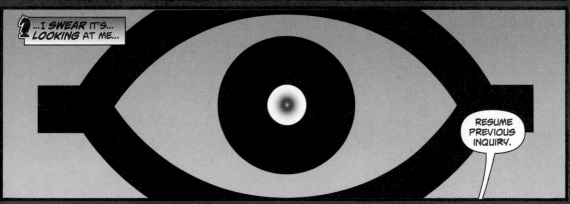 ...I SWEAR IT'S... *LOOKING* AT ME...

RESUME PREVIOUS INQUIRY.

 ...LOOKING *INTO* ME...

AH, MY *KNIGHT*. YOU DID WELL IN PARIS, I'M *PLEASED*.

THANK YOU, SIR.

I'VE GOT *ANOTHER* JOB FOR YOU...

 ...BUT *FIRST*, I WANT YOU TO *SEE* SOMETHING.

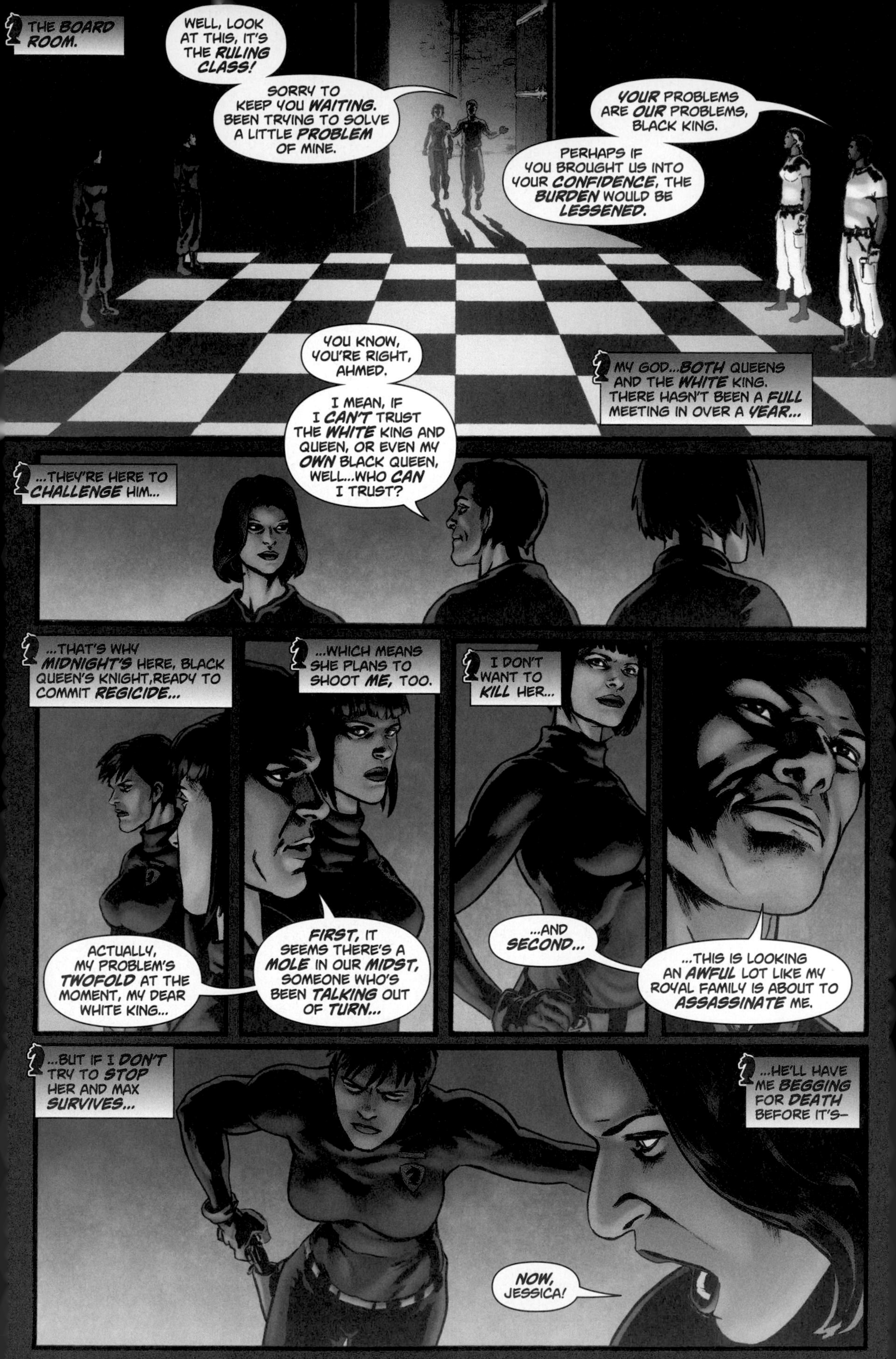
THE BOARD ROOM.
WELL, LOOK AT THIS, IT'S THE RULING CLASS!
SORRY TO KEEP YOU WAITING. BEEN TRYING TO SOLVE A LITTLE PROBLEM OF MINE.
YOUR PROBLEMS ARE OUR PROBLEMS, BLACK KING.
PERHAPS IF YOU BROUGHT US INTO YOUR CONFIDENCE, THE BURDEN WOULD BE LESSENED.
YOU KNOW, YOU'RE RIGHT, AHMED.
I MEAN, IF I CAN'T TRUST THE WHITE KING AND QUEEN, OR EVEN MY OWN BLACK QUEEN, WELL...WHO CAN I TRUST?
MY GOD...BOTH QUEENS AND THE WHITE KING. THERE HASN'T BEEN A FULL MEETING IN OVER A YEAR...
...THEY'RE HERE TO CHALLENGE HIM...
...THAT'S WHY MIDNIGHT'S HERE, BLACK QUEEN'S KNIGHT,READY TO COMMIT REGICIDE...
ACTUALLY, MY PROBLEM'S TWOFOLD AT THE MOMENT, MY DEAR WHITE KING...
...WHICH MEANS SHE PLANS TO SHOOT ME, TOO.
FIRST, IT SEEMS THERE'S A MOLE IN OUR MIDST, SOMEONE WHO'S BEEN TALKING OUT OF TURN...
I DON'T WANT TO KILL HER...
...AND SECOND...
...THIS IS LOOKING AN AWFUL LOT LIKE MY ROYAL FAMILY IS ABOUT TO ASSASSINATE ME.
...BUT IF I DON'T TRY TO STOP HER AND MAX SURVIVES...
...HE'LL HAVE ME BEGGING FOR DEATH BEFORE IT'S–
NOW, JESSICA!

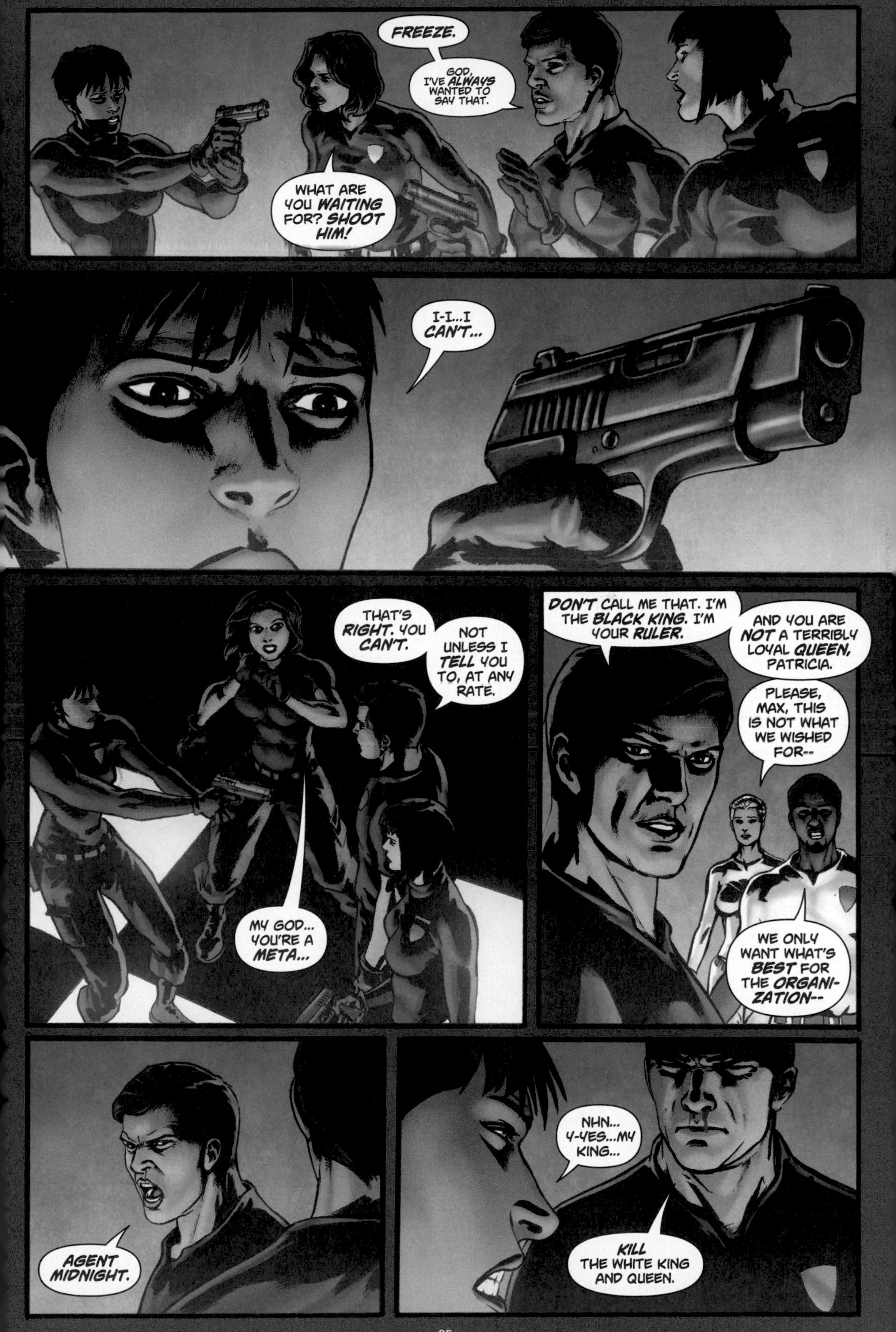

FREEZE.
GOD, I'VE ALWAYS WANTED TO SAY THAT.
WHAT ARE YOU WAITING FOR? SHOOT HIM!
I-I...I CAN'T...
THAT'S RIGHT. YOU CAN'T.
NOT UNLESS I TELL YOU TO, AT ANY RATE.
MY GOD... YOU'RE A META...
DON'T CALL ME THAT. I'M THE BLACK KING. I'M YOUR RULER.
AND YOU ARE NOT A TERRIBLY LOYAL QUEEN, PATRICIA.
PLEASE, MAX, THIS IS NOT WHAT WE WISHED FOR--
WE ONLY WANT WHAT'S BEST FOR THE ORGANI-ZATION--
AGENT MIDNIGHT.
NHN... Y-YES...MY KING...
KILL THE WHITE KING AND QUEEN.

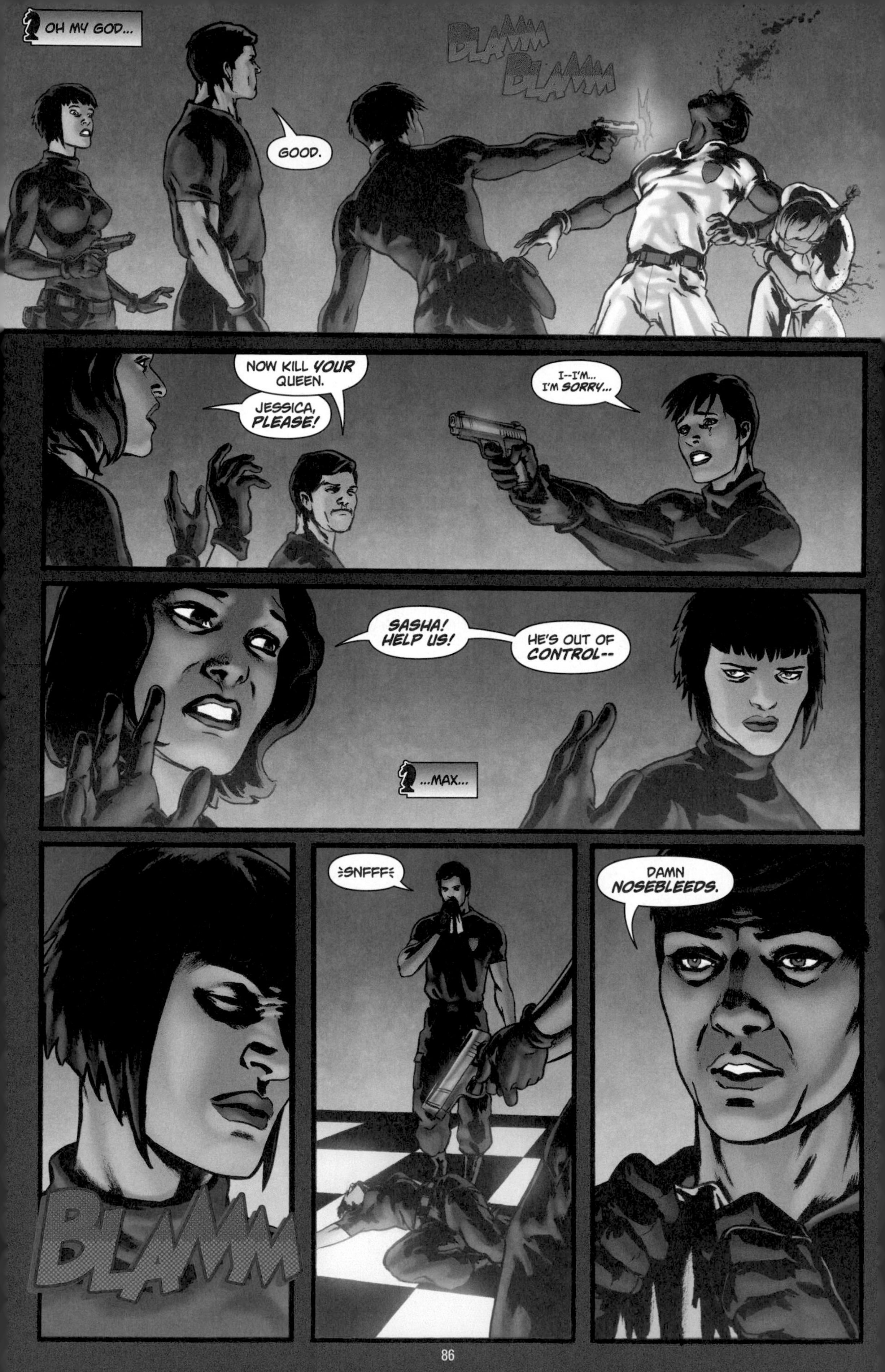
OH MY GOD...
BLAMM
BLAMM
GOOD.
NOW KILL YOUR QUEEN.
JESSICA, PLEASE!
I--I'M... I'M SORRY...
SASHA! HELP US!
HE'S OUT OF CONTROL--
...MAX...
BLAMM
SNFFF
DAMN NOSEBLEEDS.

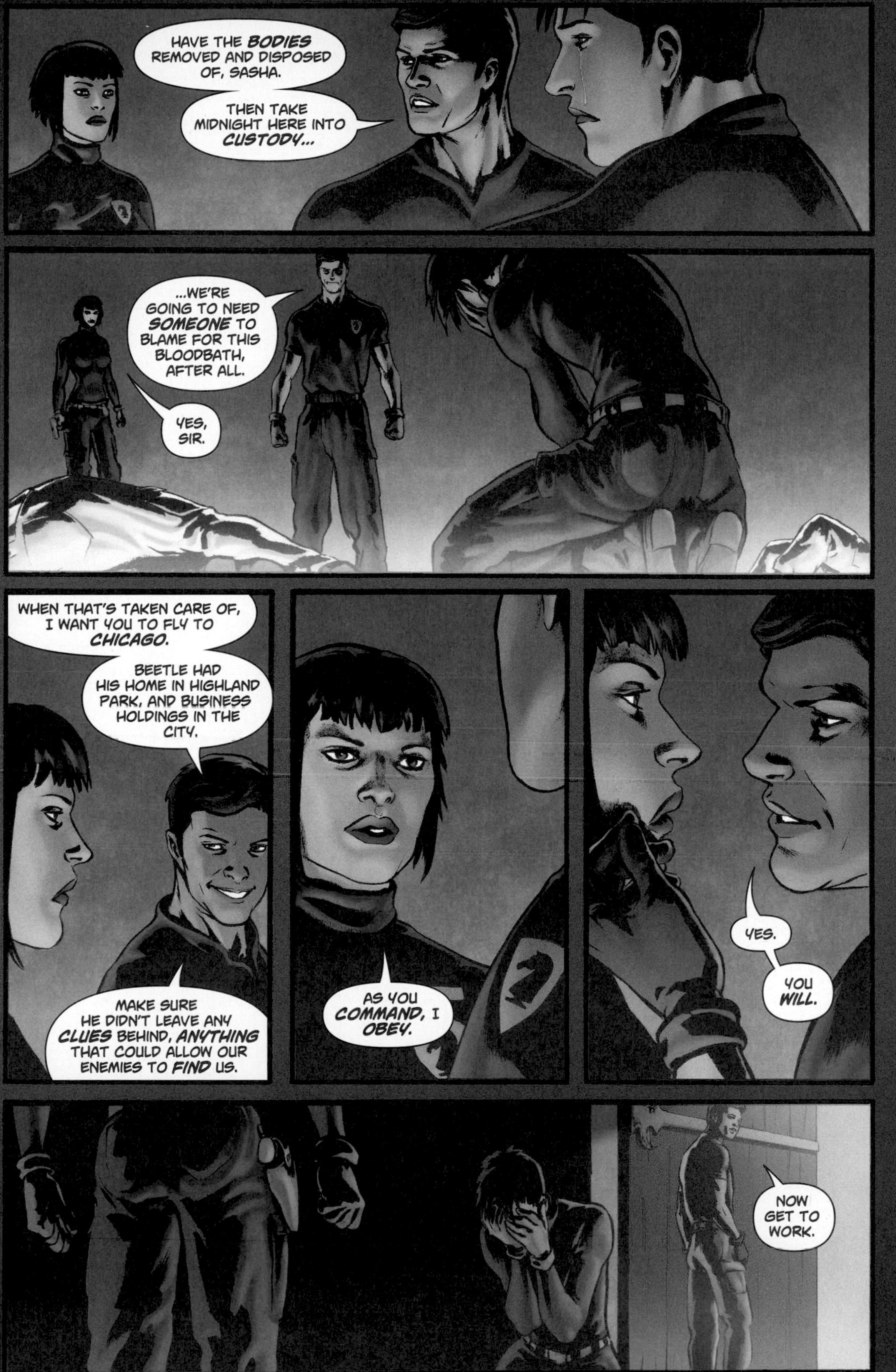
HAVE THE BODIES REMOVED AND DISPOSED OF, SASHA.
THEN TAKE MIDNIGHT HERE INTO CUSTODY...
...WE'RE GOING TO NEED SOMEONE TO BLAME FOR THIS BLOODBATH, AFTER ALL.
YES, SIR.
WHEN THAT'S TAKEN CARE OF, I WANT YOU TO FLY TO CHICAGO.
BEETLE HAD HIS HOME IN HIGHLAND PARK, AND BUSINESS HOLDINGS IN THE CITY.
MAKE SURE HE DIDN'T LEAVE ANY CLUES BEHIND, ANYTHING THAT COULD ALLOW OUR ENEMIES TO FIND US.
AS YOU COMMAND, I OBEY.
YES.
YOU WILL.
NOW GET TO WORK.

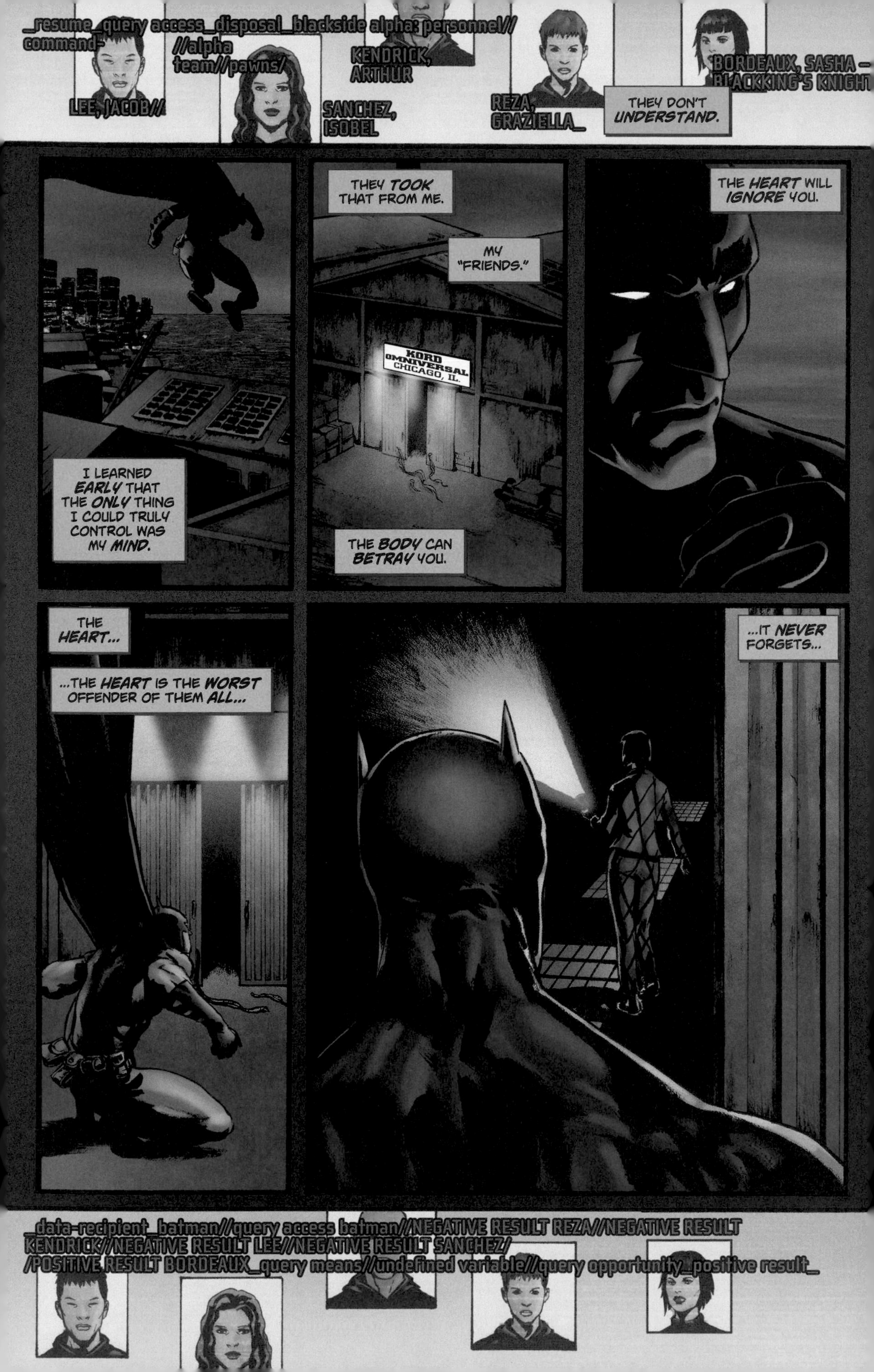

_resume_query access_disposal_blackside alpha: personnel// command-
LEE, JACOB//
//alpha team//pawns/
SANCHEZ, ISOBEL
KENDRICK, ARTHUR
REZA, GRAZIELLA_
BORDEAUX, SASHA - BLACKKING'S KNIGHT
THEY DON'T UNDERSTAND.
I LEARNED EARLY THAT THE ONLY THING I COULD TRULY CONTROL WAS MY MIND.
THEY TOOK THAT FROM ME.
MY "FRIENDS."
KORD OMNIVERSAL CHICAGO, IL.
THE BODY CAN BETRAY YOU.
THE HEART WILL IGNORE YOU.
THE HEART...
...THE HEART IS THE WORST OFFENDER OF THEM ALL...
...IT NEVER FORGETS...
_data-recipient_batman//query access batman//NEGATIVE RESULT REZA//NEGATIVE RESULT KENDRICK//NEGATIVE RESULT LEE//NEGATIVE RESULT SANCHEZ/ /POSITIVE RESULT BORDEAUX_query means//undefined variable//query opportunity_positive result_

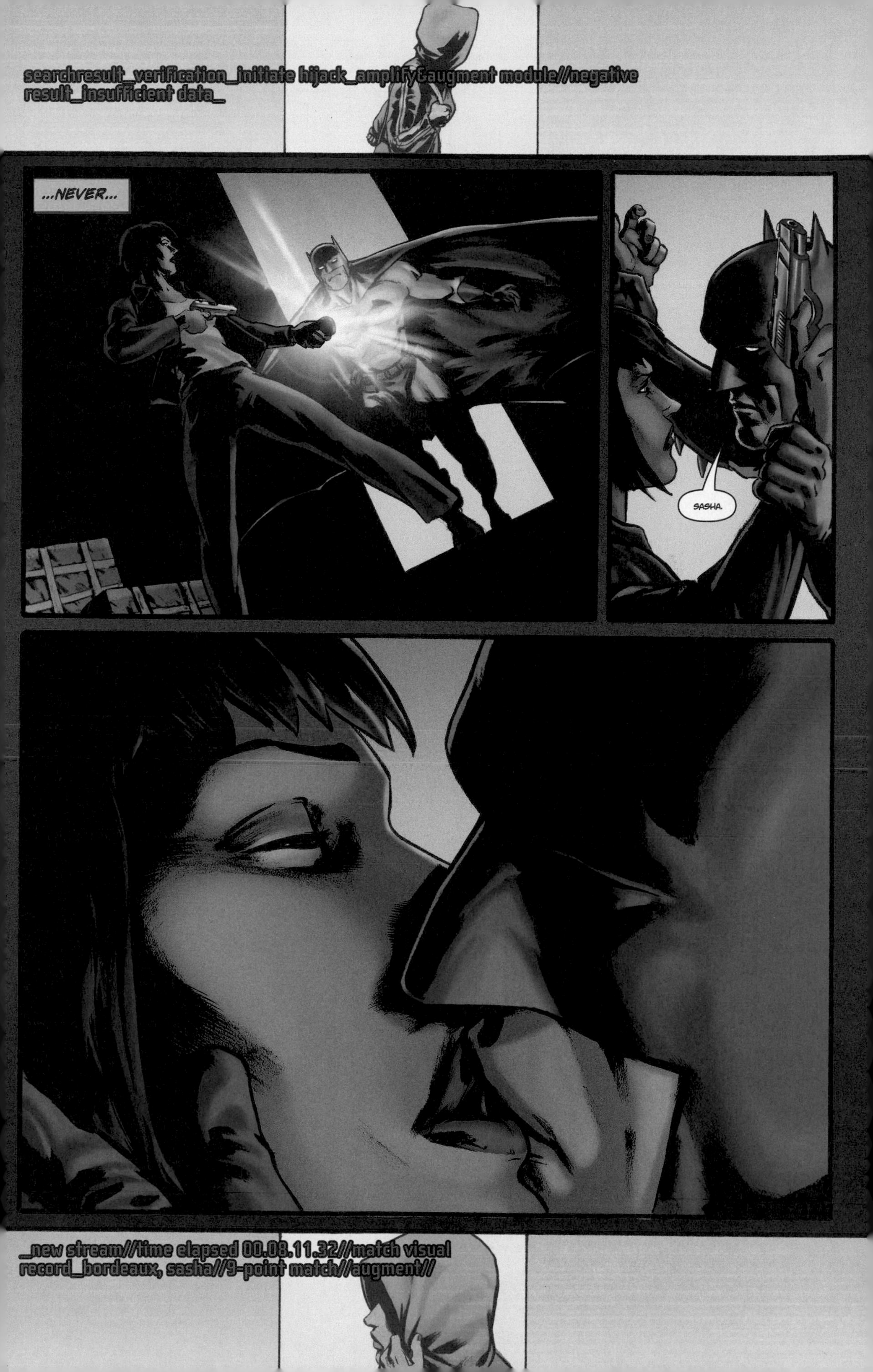

searchresult_verification_initiate hijack_amplify&augment module//negative result_insufficient data_
...NEVER...
SASHA.
_new stream//time elapsed 00.08.11.32//match visual record_bordeaux, sasha//9-point match//augment//

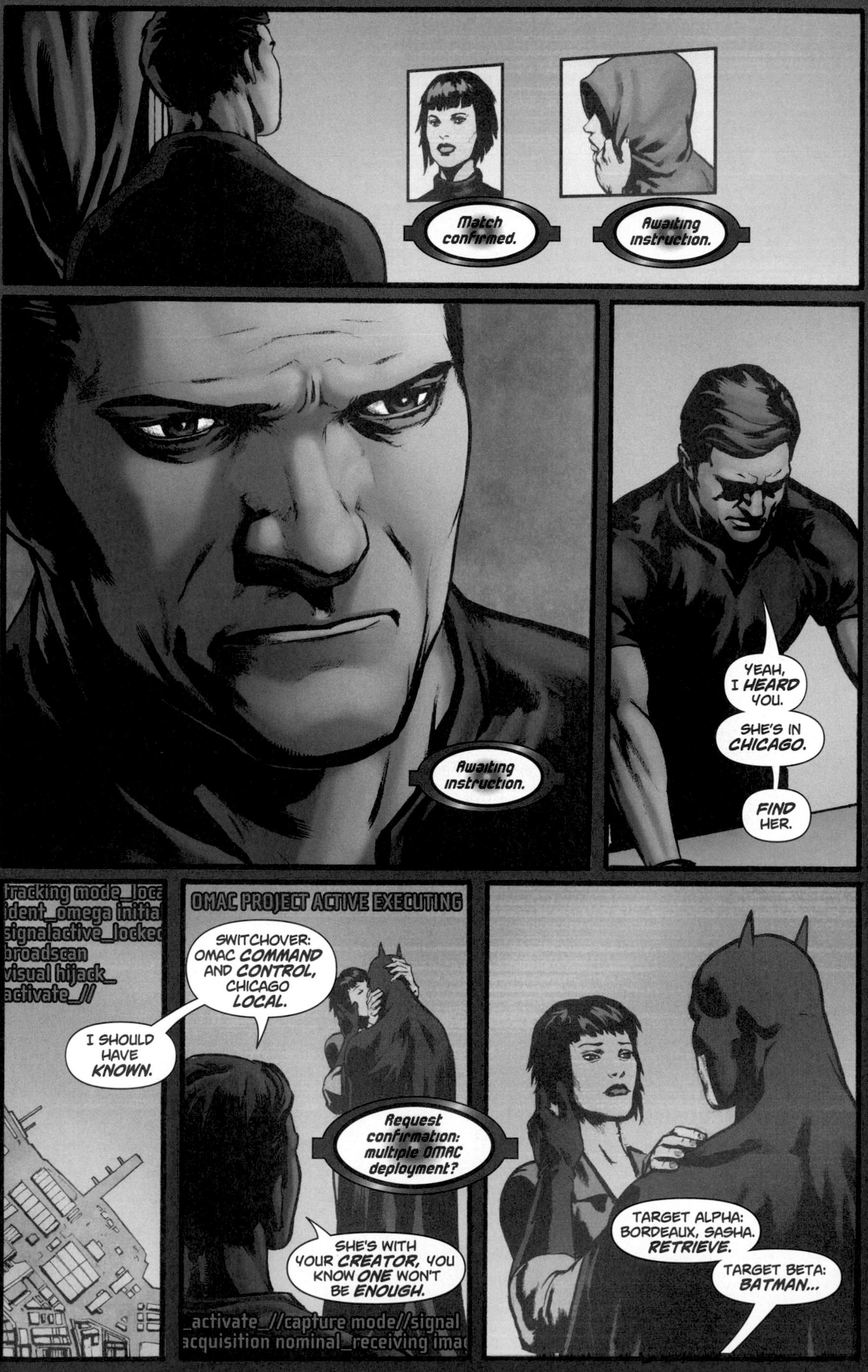
Match confirmed.
Awaiting instruction.
Awaiting instruction.
YEAH, I HEARD YOU.
SHE'S IN CHICAGO.
FIND HER.
tracking mode_loca
ident_omega initia
signalactive_locked
broadscan
visual hijack_
activate_//
OMAC PROJECT ACTIVE EXECUTING
SWITCHOVER: OMAC COMMAND AND CONTROL, CHICAGO LOCAL.
I SHOULD HAVE KNOWN.
Request confirmation: multiple OMAC deployment?
SHE'S WITH YOUR CREATOR, YOU KNOW ONE WON'T BE ENOUGH.
activate//capture mode//signal
acquisition nominal_receiving imag
TARGET ALPHA: BORDEAUX, SASHA. RETRIEVE.
TARGET BETA: BATMAN...

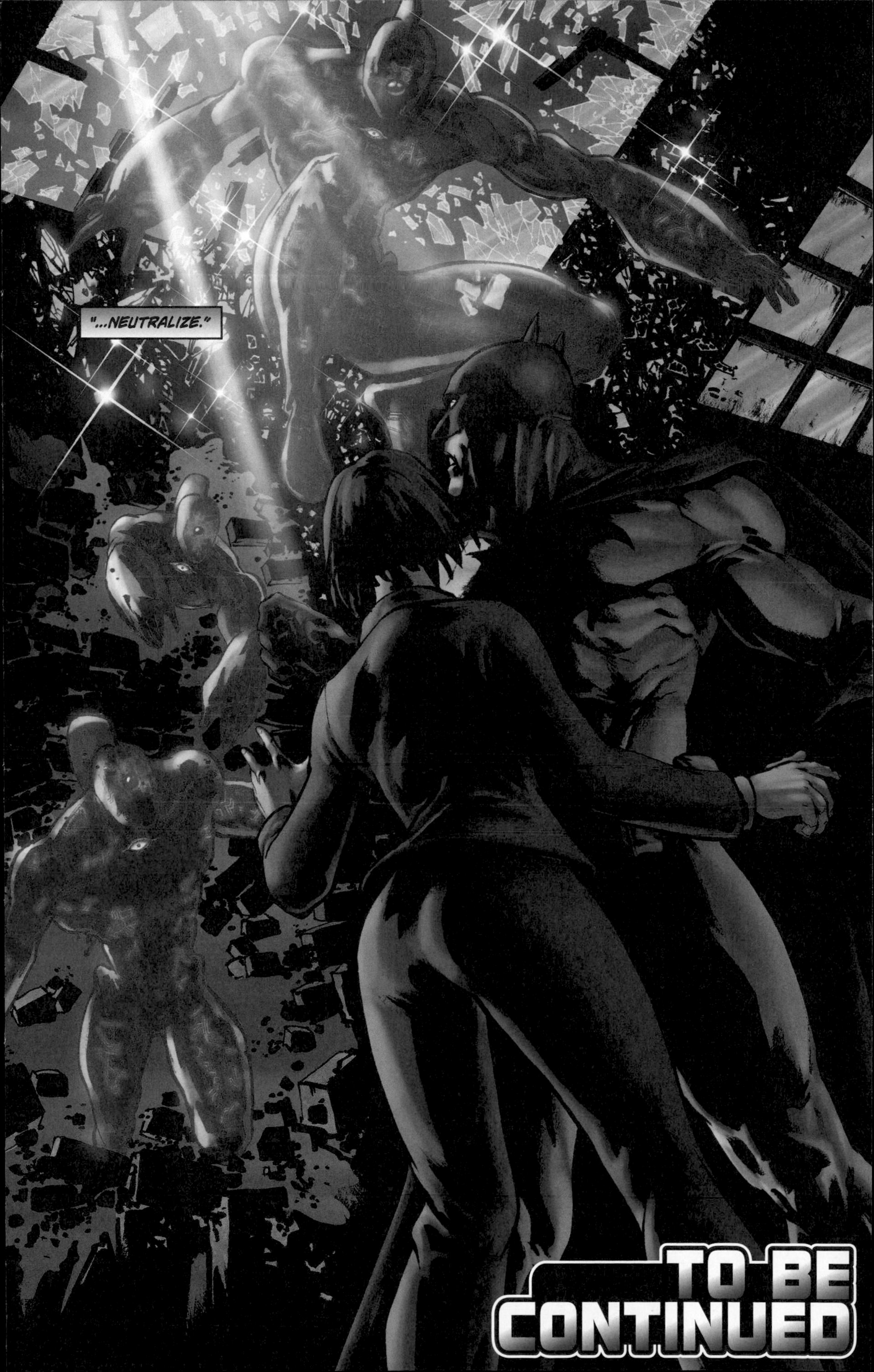
"...NEUTRALIZE."
TO BE CONTINUED

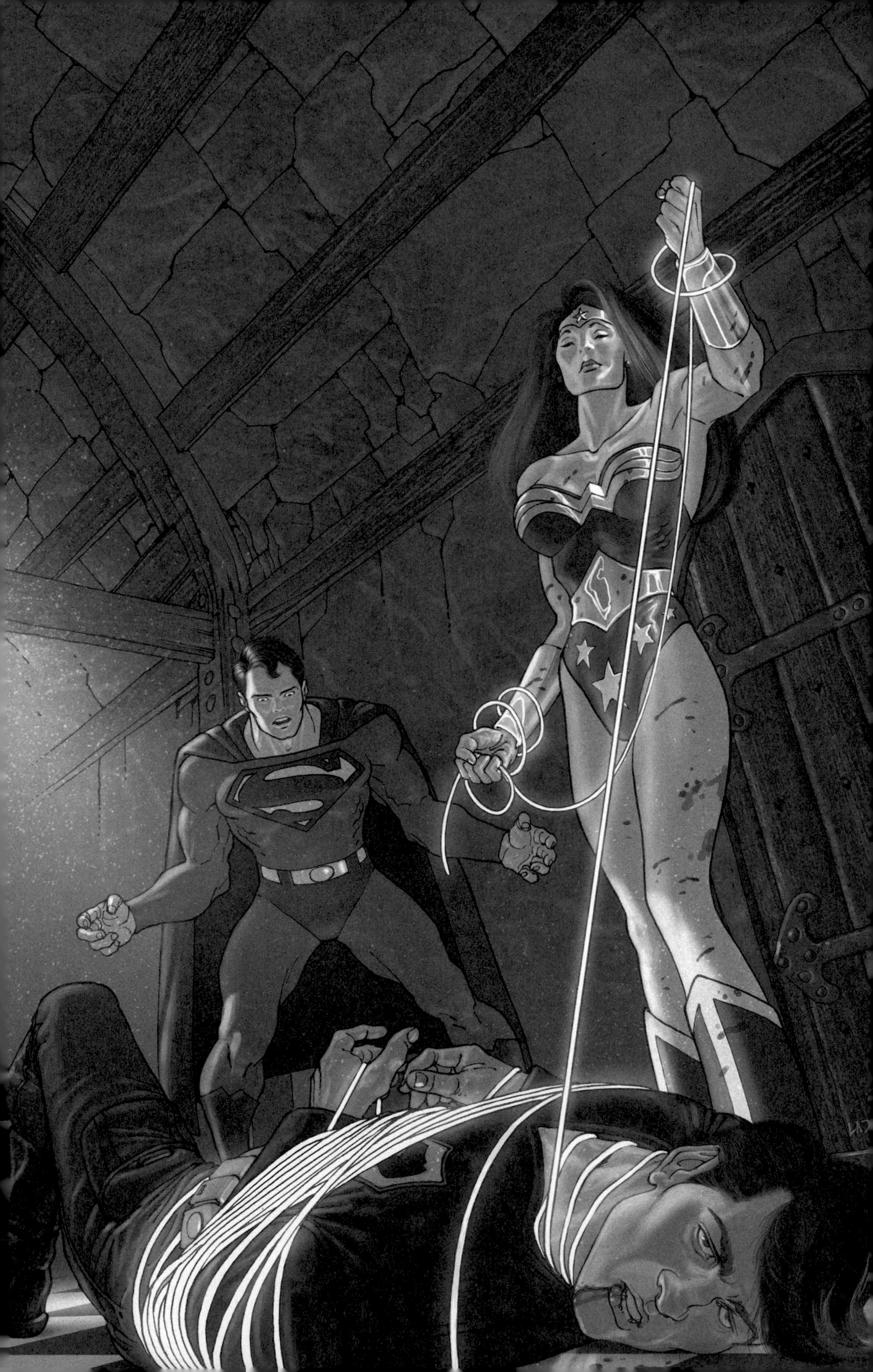

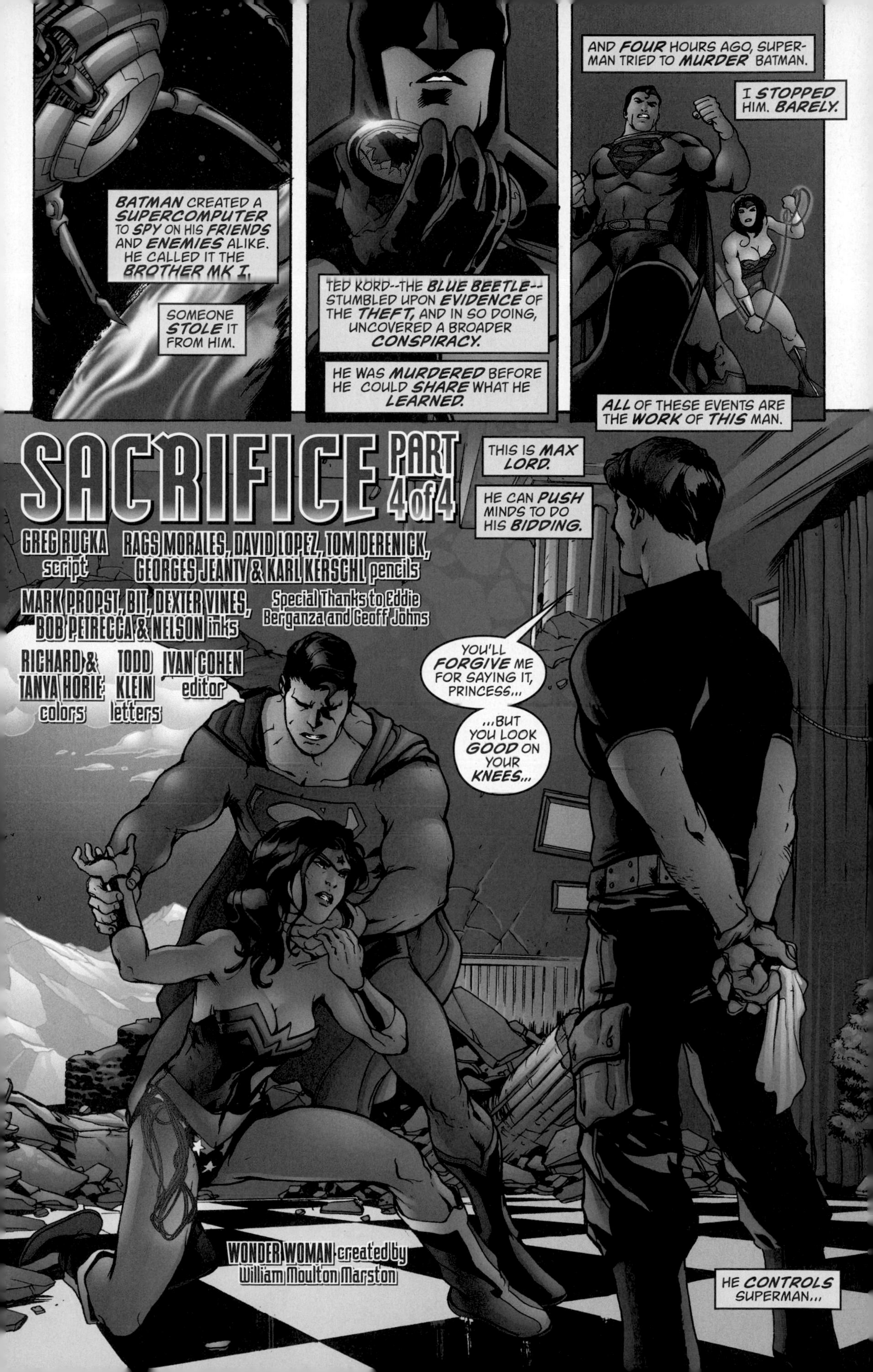
BATMAN CREATED A SUPERCOMPUTER TO SPY ON HIS FRIENDS AND ENEMIES ALIKE. HE CALLED IT THE BROTHER MK I.
SOMEONE STOLE IT FROM HIM.
TED KORD--THE BLUE BEETLE--STUMBLED UPON EVIDENCE OF THE THEFT, AND IN SO DOING, UNCOVERED A BROADER CONSPIRACY.
HE WAS MURDERED BEFORE HE COULD SHARE WHAT HE LEARNED.
AND FOUR HOURS AGO, SUPERMAN TRIED TO MURDER BATMAN.
I STOPPED HIM. BARELY.
ALL OF THESE EVENTS ARE THE WORK OF THIS MAN.
SACRIFICE PART 4 of 4
GREG RUCKA script
RAGS MORALES, DAVID LOPEZ, TOM DERENICK, GEORGES JEANTY & KARL KERSCHL pencils
MARK PROPST, BIT, DEXTER VINES, BOB PETRECCA & NELSON inks
Special Thanks to Eddie Berganza and Geoff Johns
RICHARD & TANYA HORIE colors
TODD KLEIN letters
IVAN COHEN editor
THIS IS MAX LORD.
HE CAN PUSH MINDS TO DO HIS BIDDING.
YOU'LL FORGIVE ME FOR SAYING IT, PRINCESS...
...BUT YOU LOOK GOOD ON YOUR KNEES...
WONDER WOMAN created by William Moulton Marston
HE CONTROLS SUPERMAN...

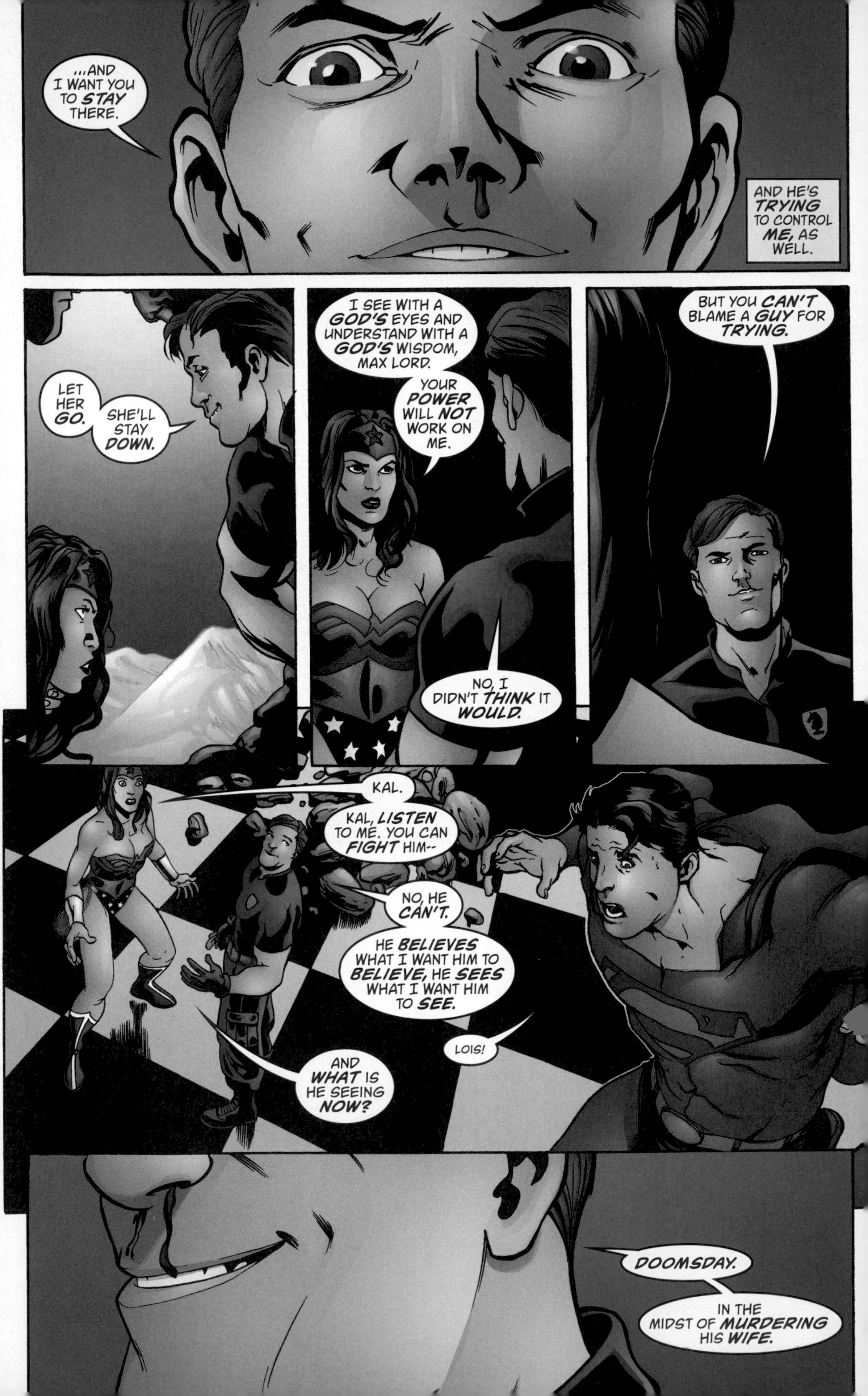
...AND I WANT YOU TO STAY THERE.
AND HE'S TRYING TO CONTROL ME, AS WELL.
LET HER GO.
SHE'LL STAY DOWN.
I SEE WITH A GOD'S EYES AND UNDERSTAND WITH A GOD'S WISDOM, MAX LORD.
YOUR POWER WILL NOT WORK ON ME.
NO, I DIDN'T THINK IT WOULD.
BUT YOU CAN'T BLAME A GUY FOR TRYING.
KAL.
KAL, LISTEN TO ME. YOU CAN FIGHT HIM--
NO, HE CAN'T.
HE BELIEVES WHAT I WANT HIM TO BELIEVE, HE SEES WHAT I WANT HIM TO SEE.
LOIS!
AND WHAT IS HE SEEING NOW?
DOOMSDAY.
IN THE MIDST OF MURDERING HIS WIFE.

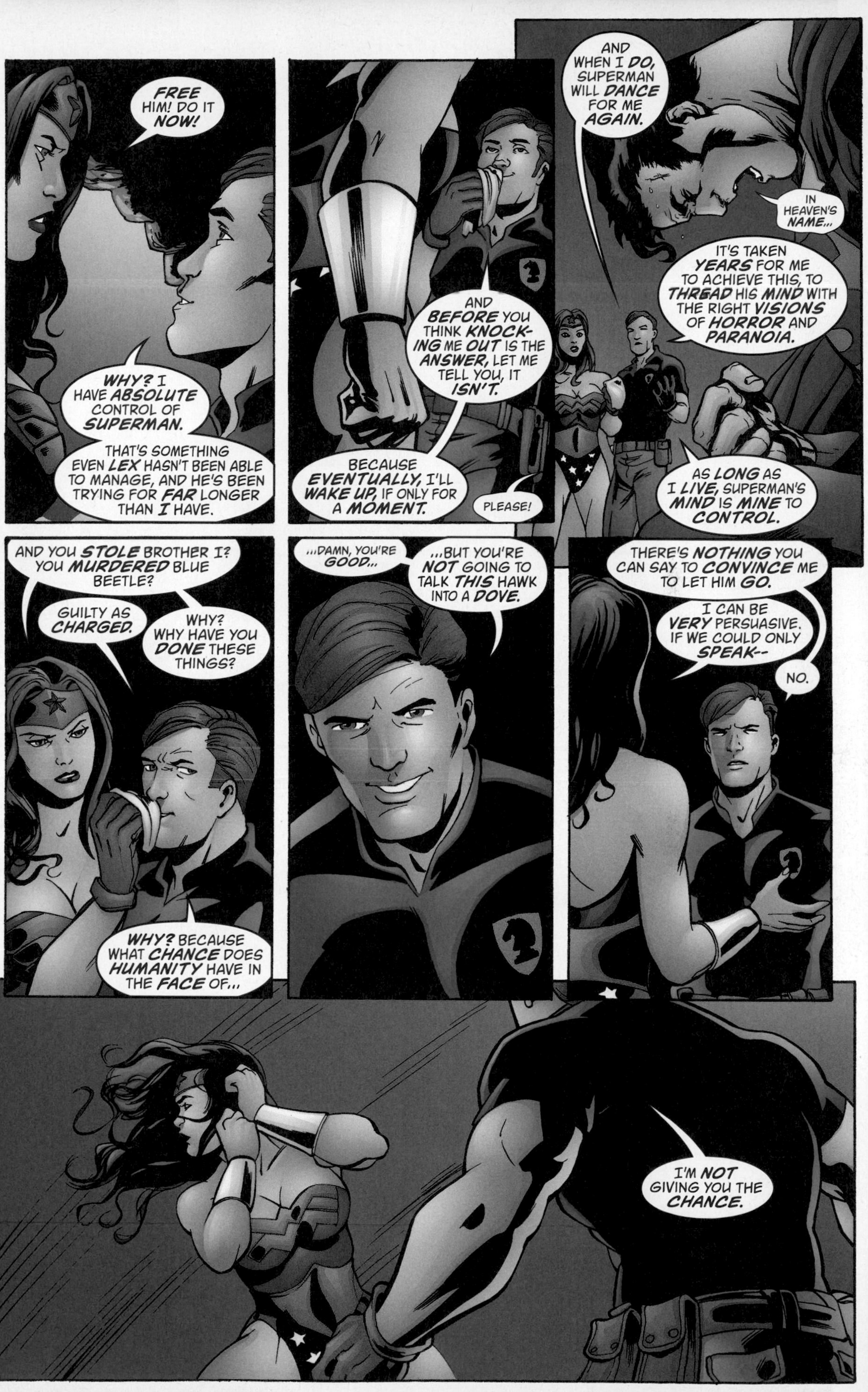
FREE HIM! DO IT NOW!
WHY? I HAVE ABSOLUTE CONTROL OF SUPERMAN.
THAT'S SOMETHING EVEN LEX HASN'T BEEN ABLE TO MANAGE, AND HE'S BEEN TRYING FOR FAR LONGER THAN I HAVE.
AND BEFORE YOU THINK KNOCKING ME OUT IS THE ANSWER, LET ME TELL YOU, IT ISN'T.
BECAUSE EVENTUALLY, I'LL WAKE UP, IF ONLY FOR A MOMENT.
PLEASE!
AND WHEN I DO, SUPERMAN WILL DANCE FOR ME AGAIN.
IN HEAVEN'S NAME...
IT'S TAKEN YEARS FOR ME TO ACHIEVE THIS, TO THREAD HIS MIND WITH THE RIGHT VISIONS OF HORROR AND PARANOIA.
AS LONG AS I LIVE, SUPERMAN'S MIND IS MINE TO CONTROL.
AND YOU STOLE BROTHER I? YOU MURDERED BLUE BEETLE?
GUILTY AS CHARGED.
WHY? WHY HAVE YOU DONE THESE THINGS?
WHY? BECAUSE WHAT CHANCE DOES HUMANITY HAVE IN THE FACE OF...
...DAMN, YOU'RE GOOD...
...BUT YOU'RE NOT GOING TO TALK THIS HAWK INTO A DOVE.
THERE'S NOTHING YOU CAN SAY TO CONVINCE ME TO LET HIM GO.
I CAN BE VERY PERSUASIVE. IF WE COULD ONLY SPEAK--
NO.
I'M NOT GIVING YOU THE CHANCE.

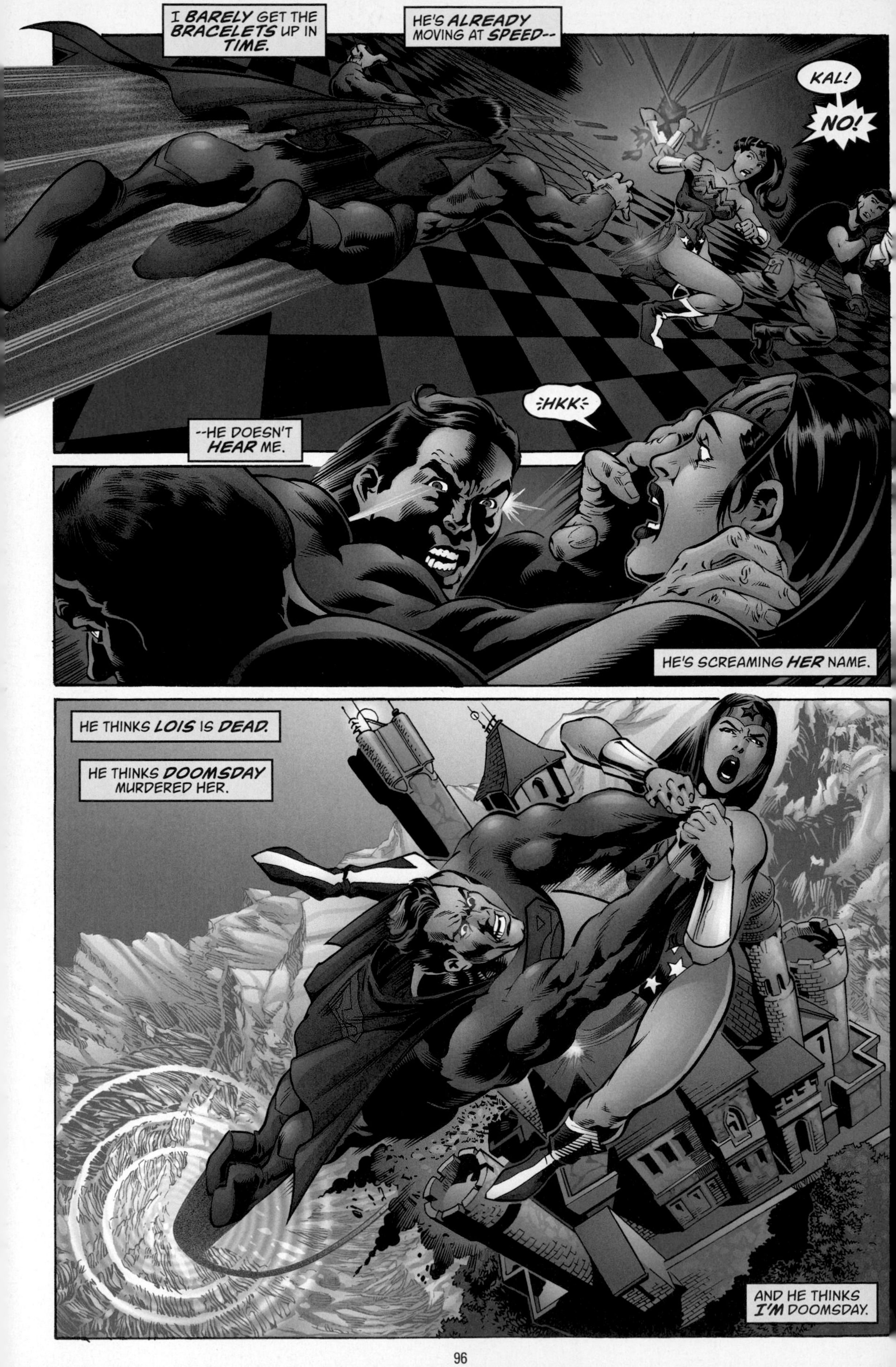

I BARELY GET THE BRACELETS UP IN TIME.
HE'S ALREADY MOVING AT SPEED--
KAL!
NO!
--HE DOESN'T HEAR ME.
HKK
HE'S SCREAMING HER NAME.
HE THINKS LOIS IS DEAD.
HE THINKS DOOMSDAY MURDERED HER.
AND HE THINKS I'M DOOMSDAY.

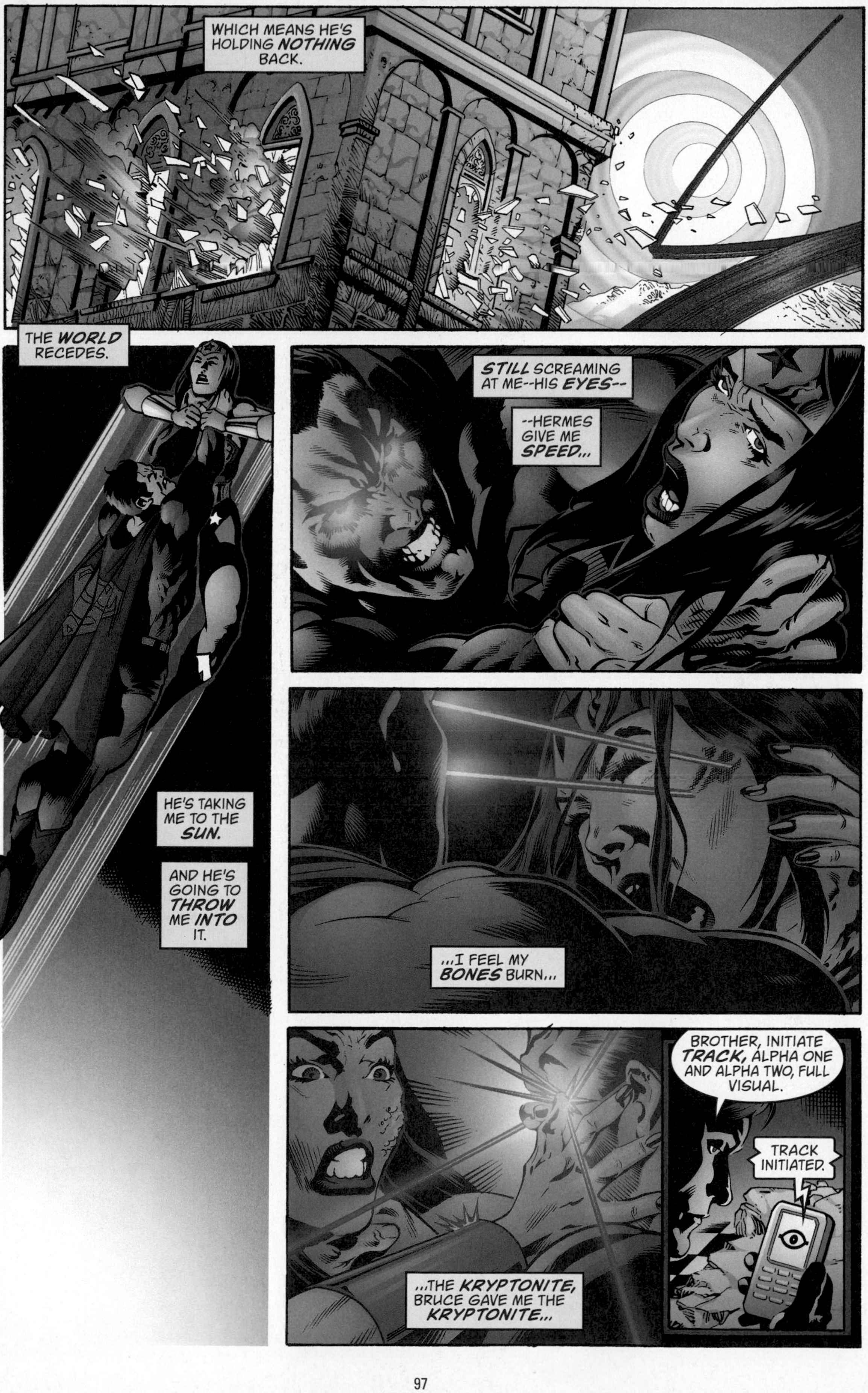

WHICH MEANS HE'S HOLDING NOTHING BACK.
THE WORLD RECEDES.
HE'S TAKING ME TO THE SUN.
AND HE'S GOING TO THROW ME INTO IT.
STILL SCREAMING AT ME--HIS EYES--
--HERMES GIVE ME SPEED...
...I FEEL MY BONES BURN...
...THE KRYPTONITE, BRUCE GAVE ME THE KRYPTONITE...
BROTHER, INITIATE TRACK, ALPHA ONE AND ALPHA TWO, FULL VISUAL.
TRACK INITIATED.

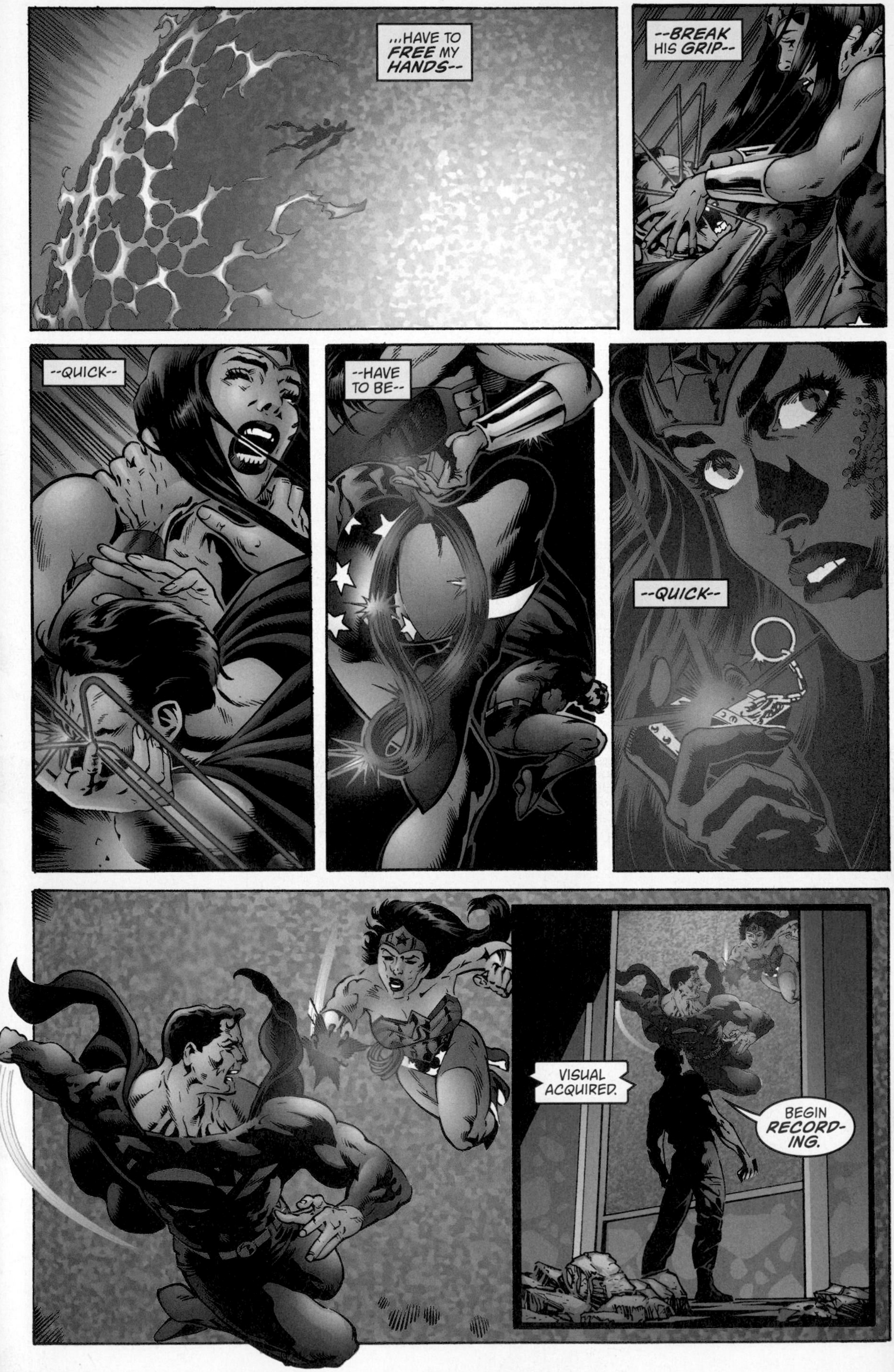
...HAVE TO FREE MY HANDS--
--BREAK HIS GRIP--
--QUICK--
--HAVE TO BE--
--QUICK--
VISUAL ACQUIRED.
BEGIN RECORDING.

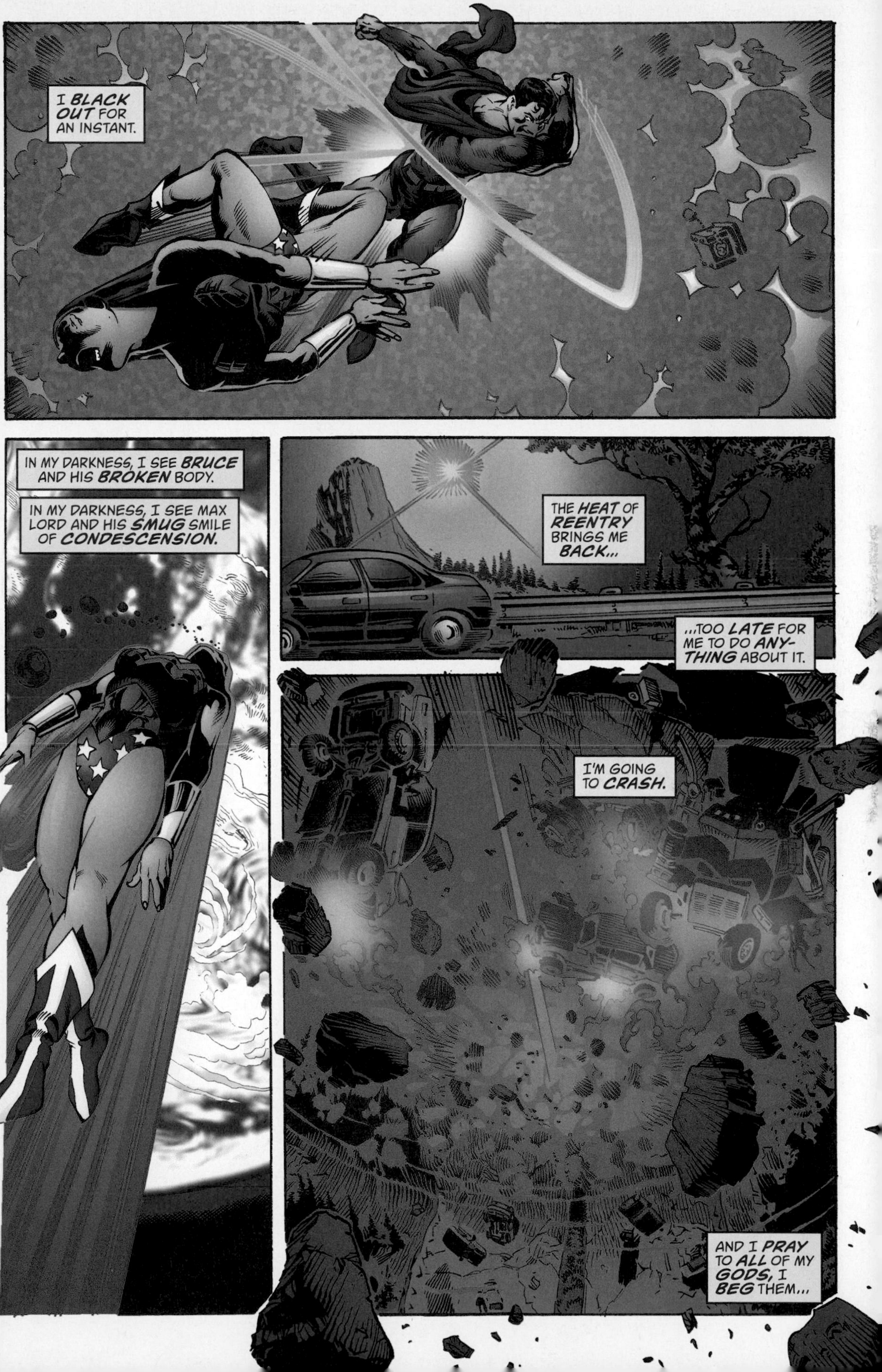
I BLACK OUT FOR AN INSTANT.
IN MY DARKNESS, I SEE BRUCE AND HIS BROKEN BODY.
IN MY DARKNESS, I SEE MAX LORD AND HIS SMUG SMILE OF CONDESCENSION.
THE HEAT OF REENTRY BRINGS ME BACK...
...TOO LATE FOR ME TO DO ANY-THING ABOUT IT.
I'M GOING TO CRASH.
AND I PRAY TO ALL OF MY GODS, I BEG THEM...

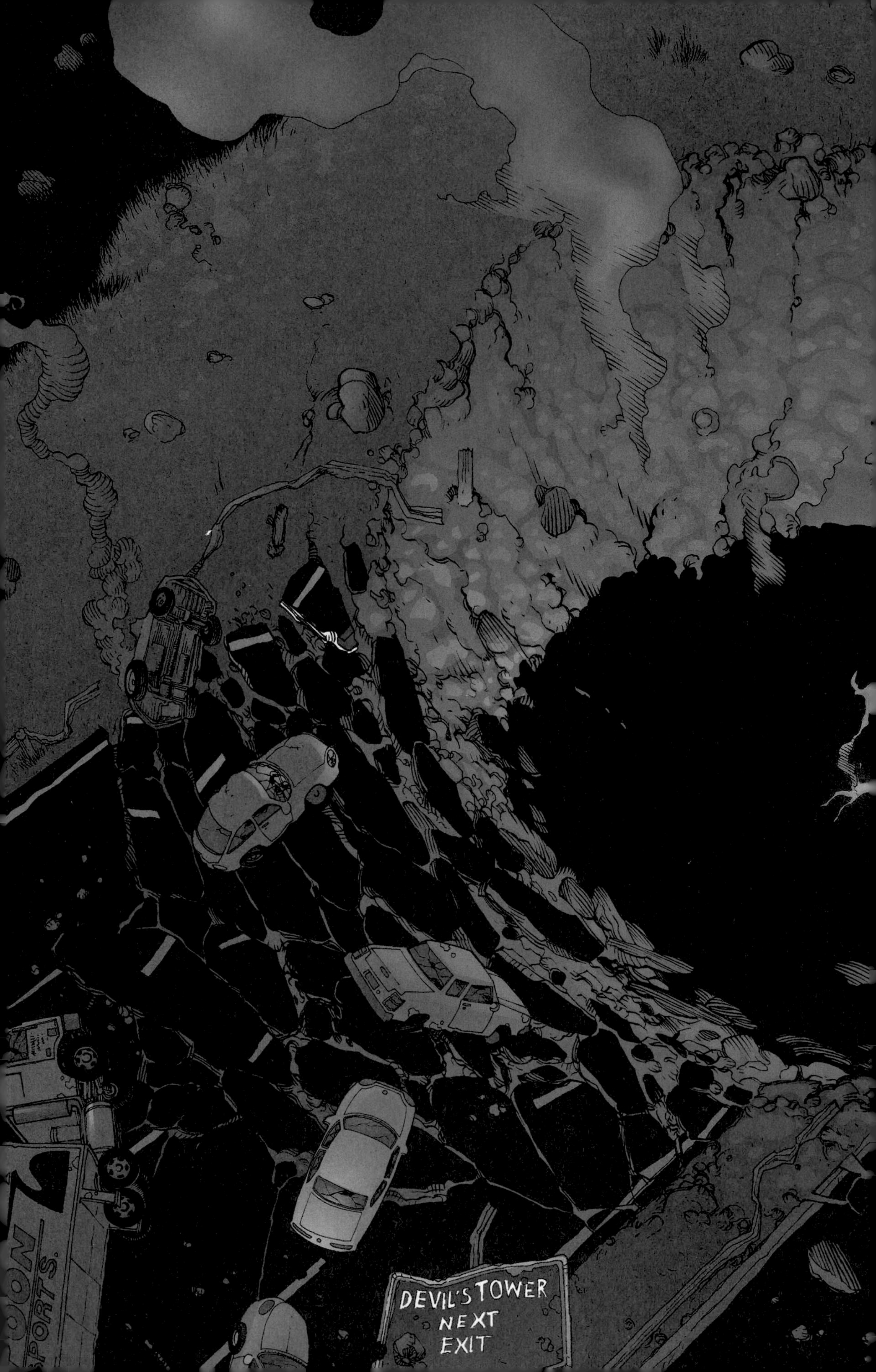
DEVIL'S TOWER
NEXT
EXIT

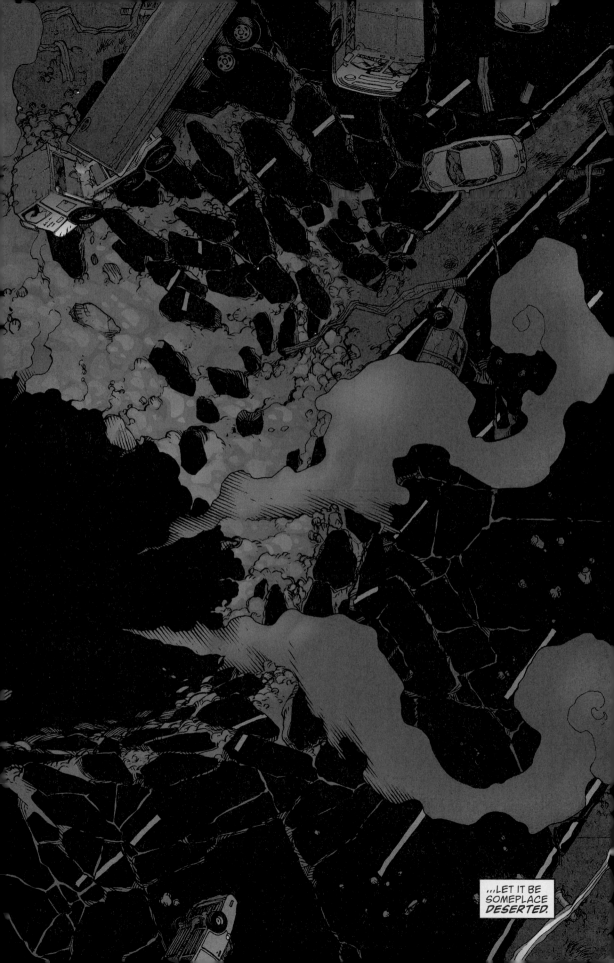

...LET IT BE SOMEPLACE *DESERTED.*

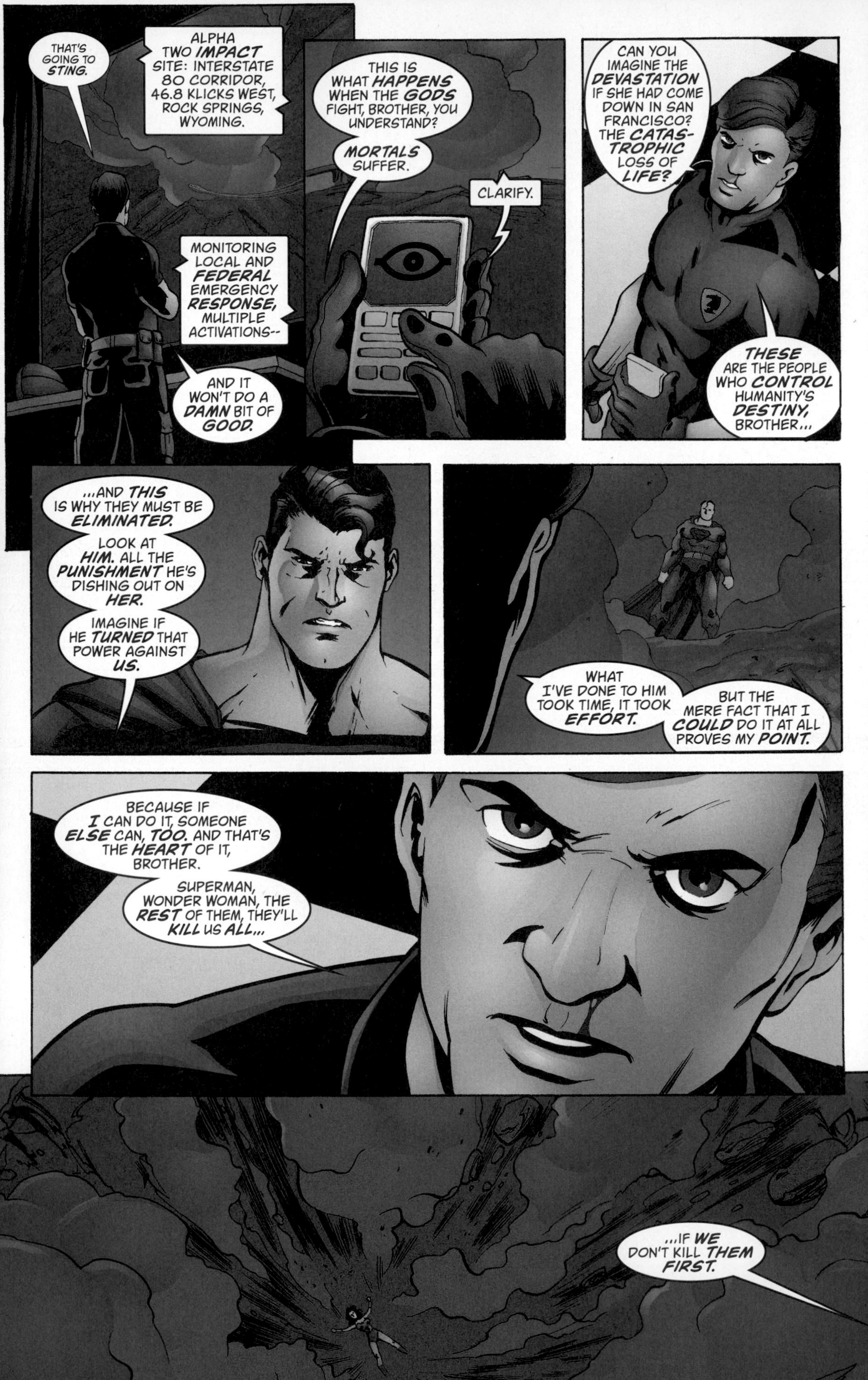
THAT'S GOING TO STING.
ALPHA TWO IMPACT SITE: INTERSTATE 80 CORRIDOR, 46.8 KLICKS WEST, ROCK SPRINGS, WYOMING.
MONITORING LOCAL AND FEDERAL EMERGENCY RESPONSE, MULTIPLE ACTIVATIONS--
AND IT WON'T DO A DAMN BIT OF GOOD.
THIS IS WHAT HAPPENS WHEN THE GODS FIGHT, BROTHER, YOU UNDERSTAND?
MORTALS SUFFER.
CLARIFY.
CAN YOU IMAGINE THE DEVASTATION IF SHE HAD COME DOWN IN SAN FRANCISCO? THE CATAS-TROPHIC LOSS OF LIFE?
THESE ARE THE PEOPLE WHO CONTROL HUMANITY'S DESTINY, BROTHER...
...AND THIS IS WHY THEY MUST BE ELIMINATED.
LOOK AT HIM. ALL THE PUNISHMENT HE'S DISHING OUT ON HER.
IMAGINE IF HE TURNED THAT POWER AGAINST US.
WHAT I'VE DONE TO HIM TOOK TIME, IT TOOK EFFORT.
BUT THE MERE FACT THAT I COULD DO IT AT ALL PROVES MY POINT.
BECAUSE IF I CAN DO IT, SOMEONE ELSE CAN, TOO. AND THAT'S THE HEART OF IT, BROTHER.
SUPERMAN, WONDER WOMAN, THE REST OF THEM, THEY'LL KILL US ALL...
...IF WE DON'T KILL THEM FIRST.

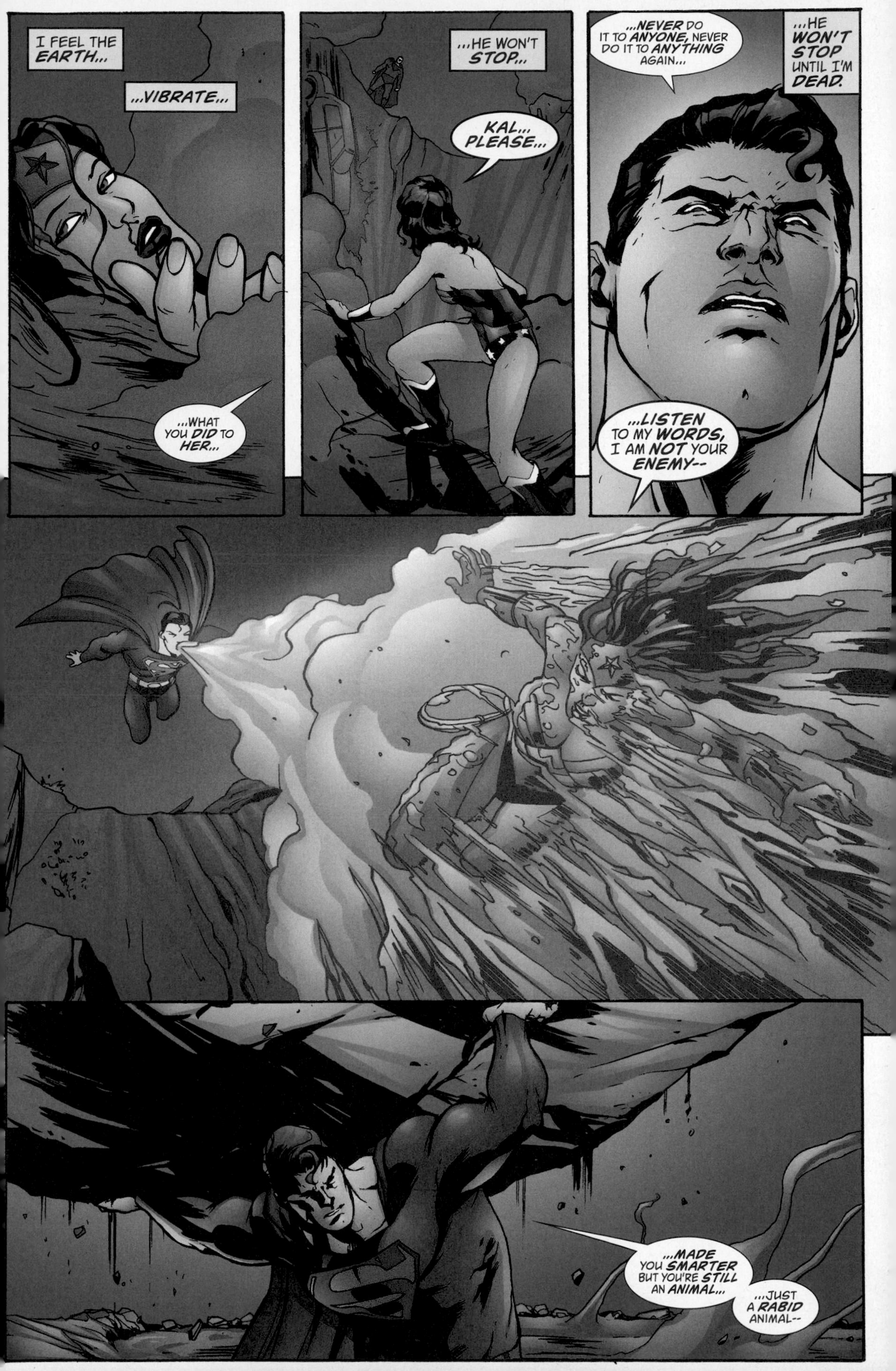
I FEEL THE EARTH...
...VIBRATE...
...WHAT YOU DID TO HER...
...HE WON'T STOP...
KAL... PLEASE...
...NEVER DO IT TO ANYONE, NEVER DO IT TO ANYTHING AGAIN...
...HE WON'T STOP UNTIL I'M DEAD.
...LISTEN TO MY WORDS, I AM NOT YOUR ENEMY--
...MADE YOU SMARTER BUT YOU'RE STILL AN ANIMAL...
...JUST A RABID ANIMAL--

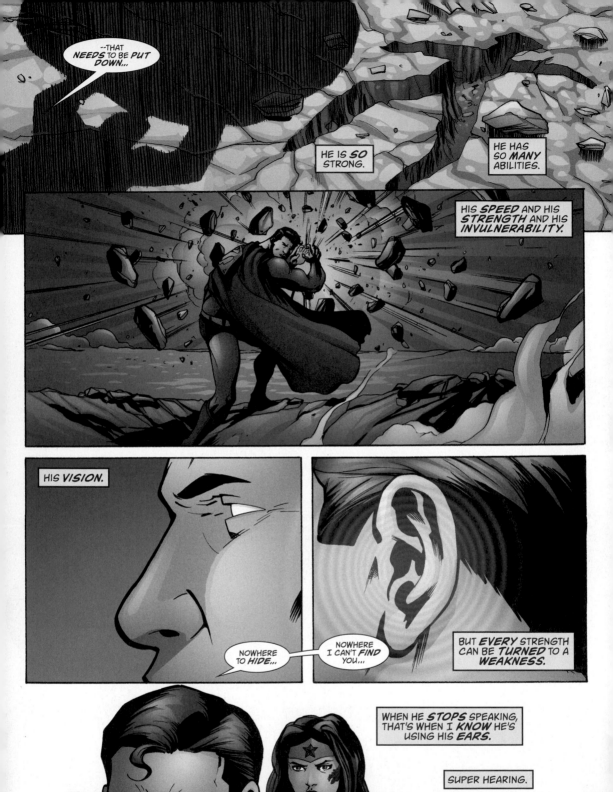

--THAT *NEEDS* TO BE *PUT DOWN...*

HE IS *SO* STRONG.

HE HAS SO *MANY* ABILITIES.

HIS *SPEED* AND HIS *STRENGTH* AND HIS *INVULNERABILITY.*

HIS *VISION.*

NOWHERE TO *HIDE...*

NOWHERE I CAN'T *FIND* YOU...

BUT *EVERY* STRENGTH CAN BE *TURNED* TO A *WEAKNESS.*

WHEN HE *STOPS* SPEAKING, THAT'S WHEN I *KNOW* HE'S USING HIS *EARS.*

SUPER HEARING.

GODS *FORGIVE* ME.

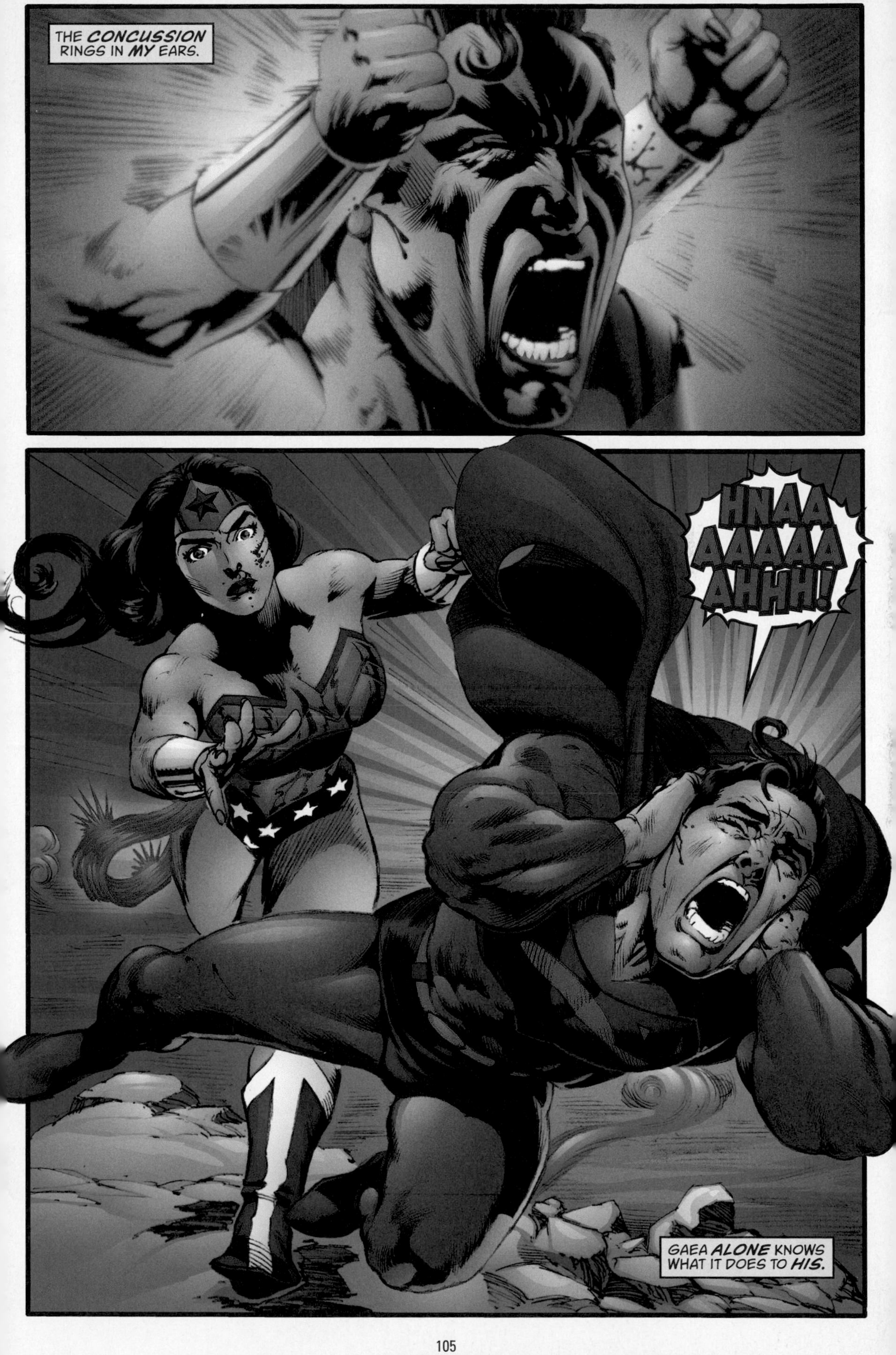
THE CONCUSSION RINGS IN MY EARS.
HNAA AAAAA AHHH!
GAEA ALONE KNOWS WHAT IT DOES TO HIS.

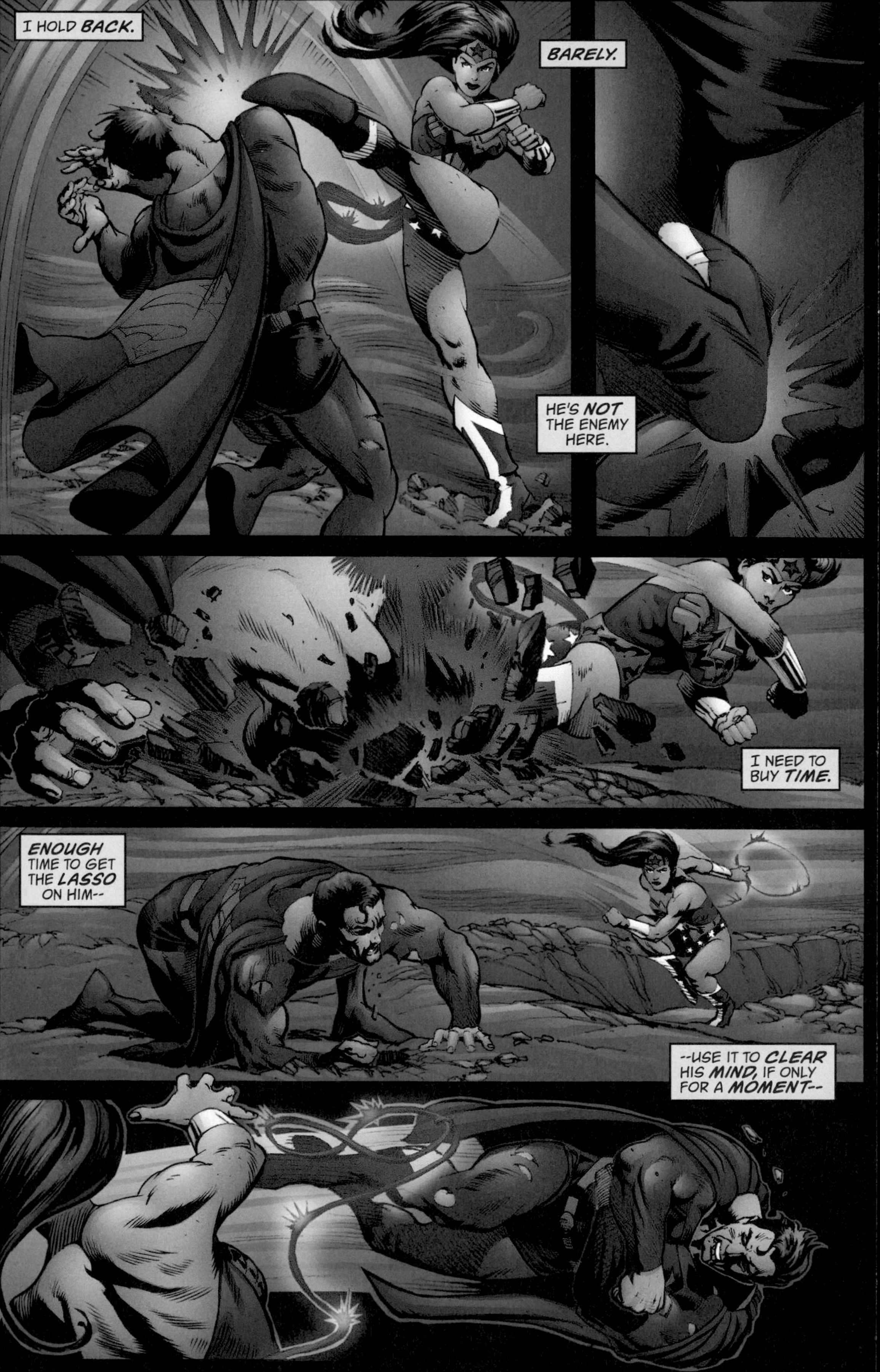
I HOLD BACK.
BARELY.
HE'S NOT THE ENEMY HERE.
I NEED TO BUY TIME.
ENOUGH TIME TO GET THE LASSO ON HIM--
--USE IT TO CLEAR HIS MIND, IF ONLY FOR A MOMENT--

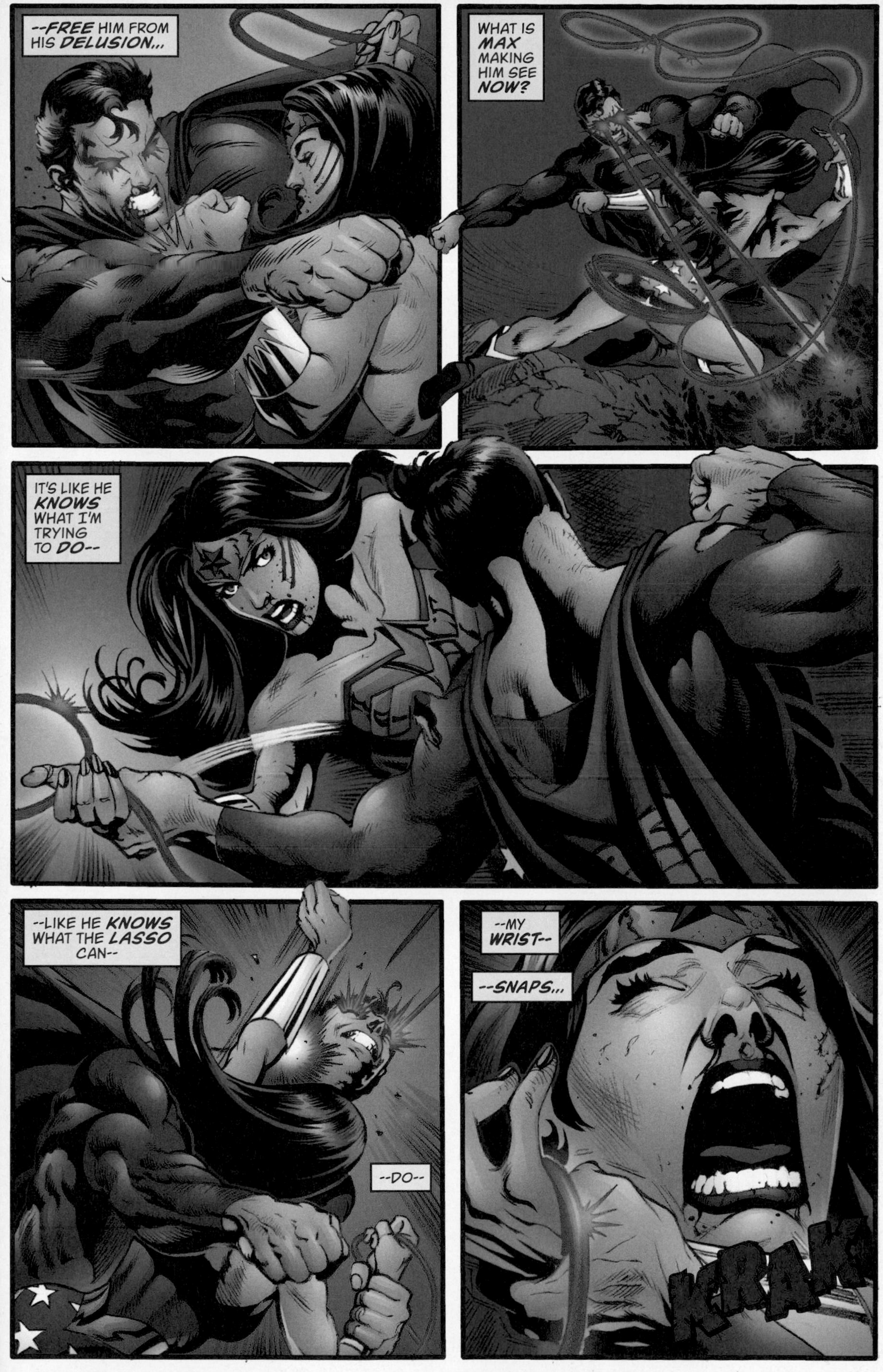
--FREE HIM FROM HIS DELUSION...
WHAT IS MAX MAKING HIM SEE NOW?
IT'S LIKE HE KNOWS WHAT I'M TRYING TO DO--
--LIKE HE KNOWS WHAT THE LASSO CAN--
--DO--
--MY WRIST--
--SNAPS...
KRAK

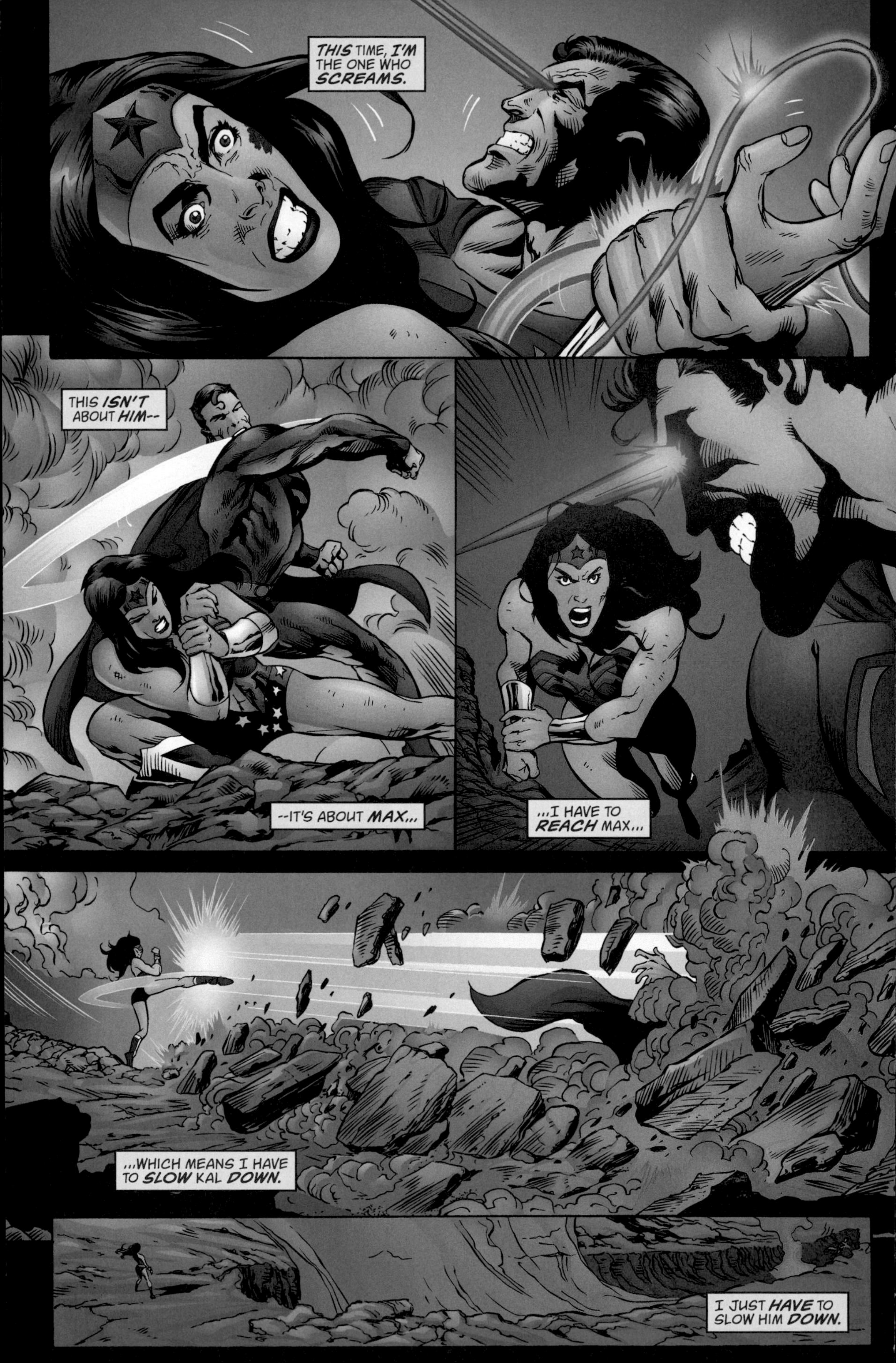

THIS TIME, I'M THE ONE WHO SCREAMS.
THIS ISN'T ABOUT HIM--
--IT'S ABOUT MAX...
...I HAVE TO REACH MAX...
...WHICH MEANS I HAVE TO SLOW KAL DOWN.
I JUST HAVE TO SLOW HIM DOWN.

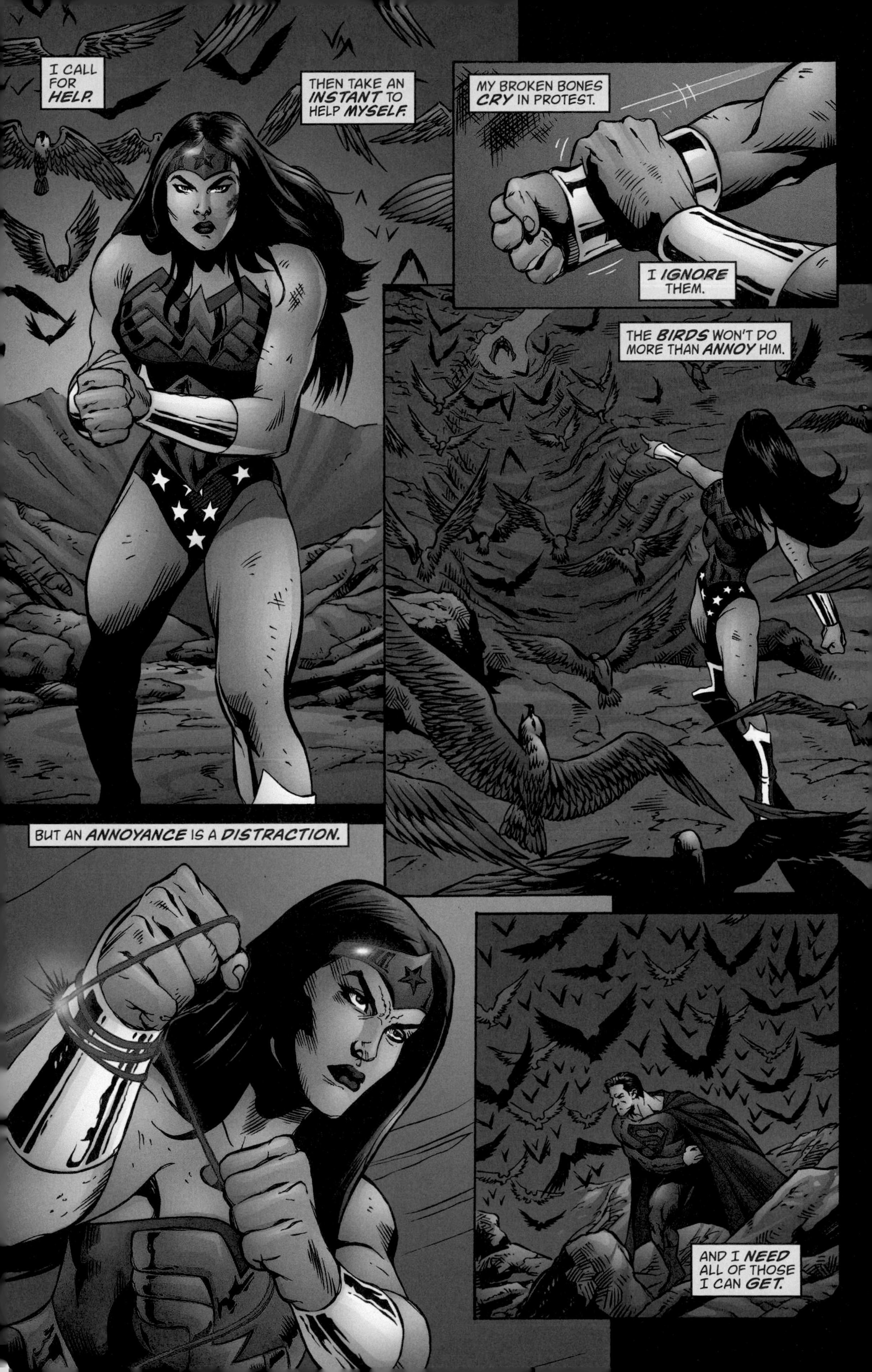
I CALL FOR HELP.
THEN TAKE AN INSTANT TO HELP MYSELF.
MY BROKEN BONES CRY IN PROTEST.
I IGNORE THEM.
THE BIRDS WON'T DO MORE THAN ANNOY HIM.
BUT AN ANNOYANCE IS A DISTRACTION.
AND I NEED ALL OF THOSE I CAN GET.

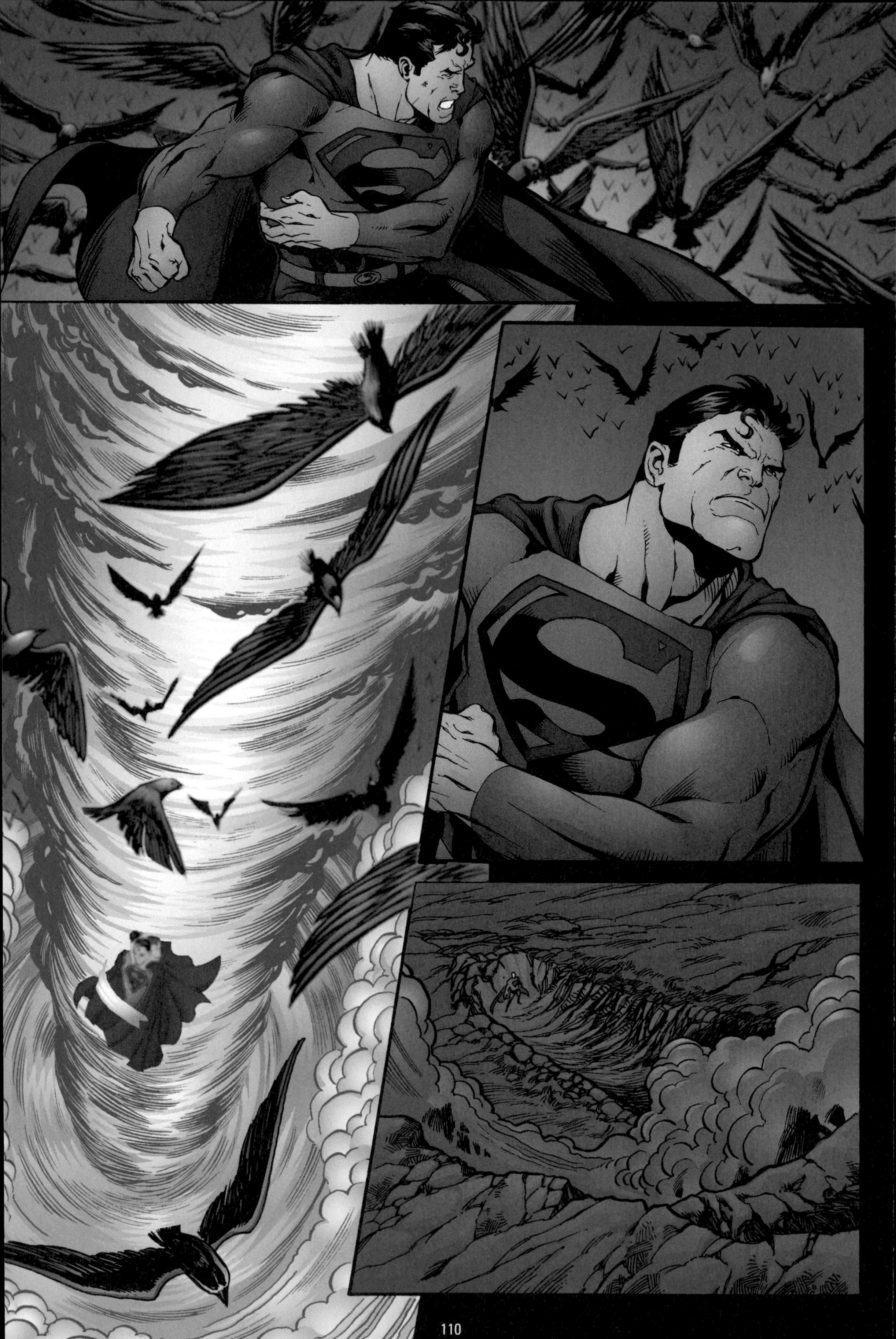

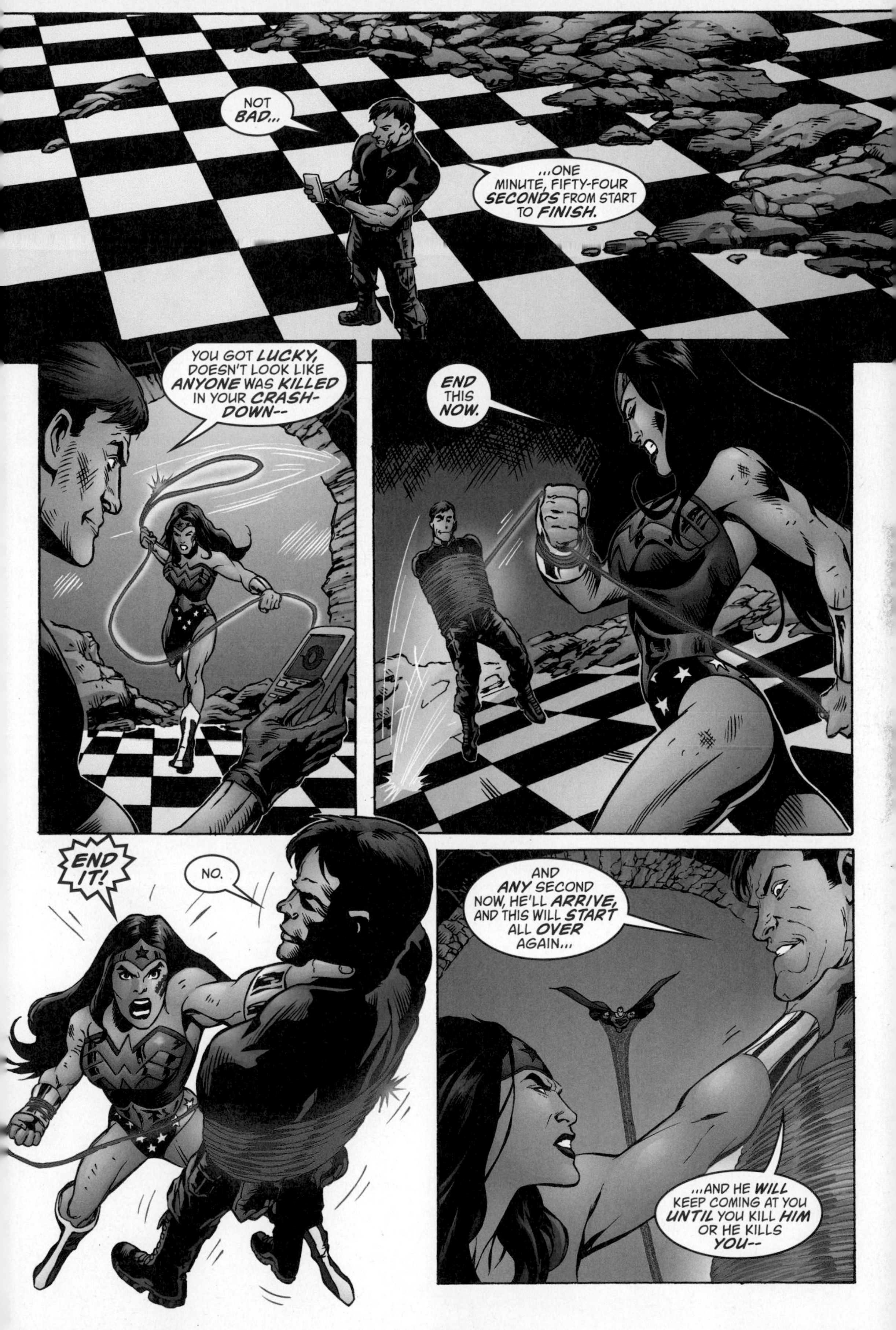
NOT BAD...
...ONE MINUTE, FIFTY-FOUR SECONDS FROM START TO FINISH.
YOU GOT LUCKY, DOESN'T LOOK LIKE ANYONE WAS KILLED IN YOUR CRASH-DOWN--
END THIS NOW.
END IT!
NO.
AND ANY SECOND NOW, HE'LL ARRIVE, AND THIS WILL START ALL OVER AGAIN...
...AND HE WILL KEEP COMING AT YOU UNTIL YOU KILL HIM OR HE KILLS YOU--

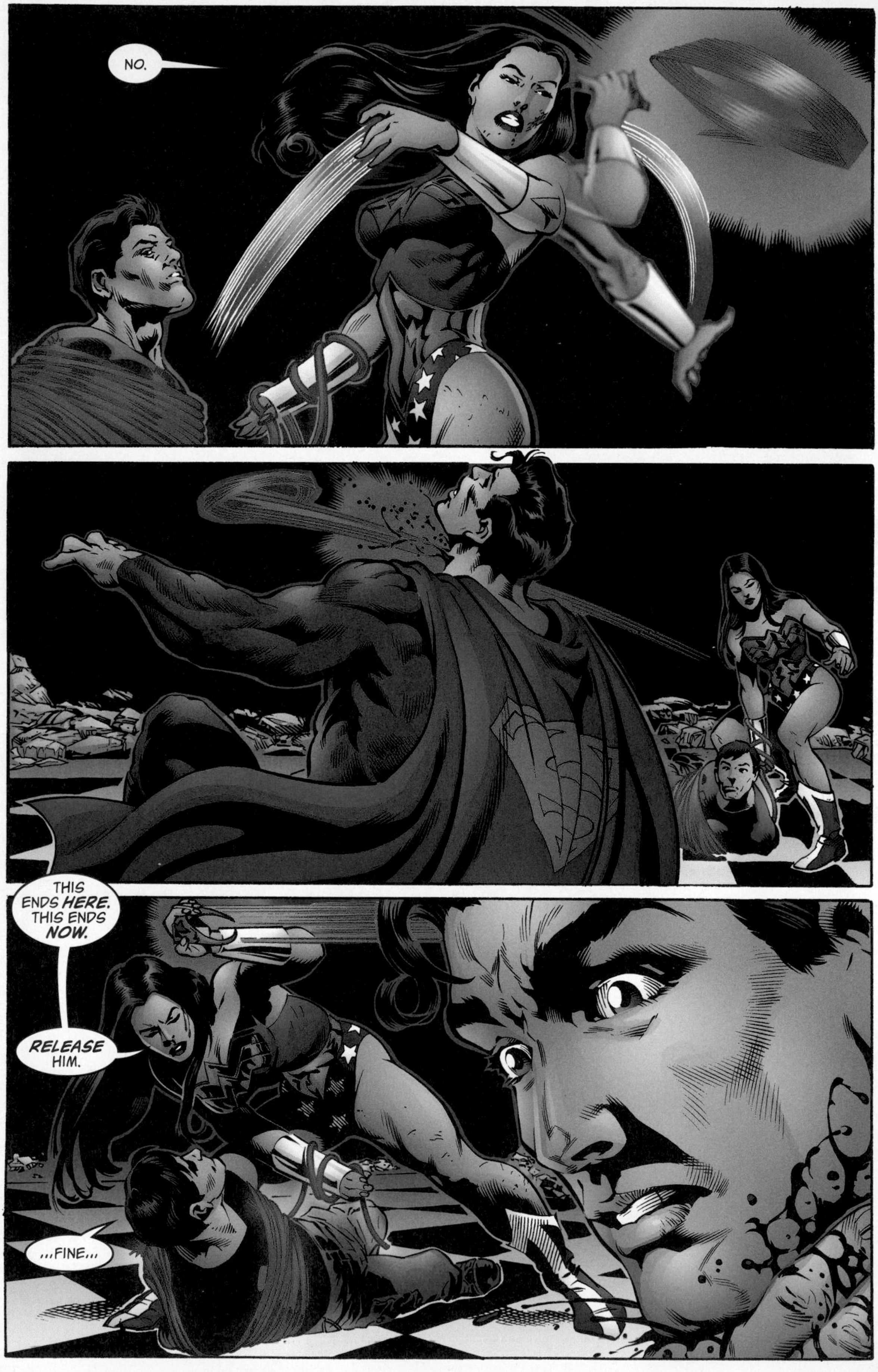
NO.
THIS ENDS HERE. THIS ENDS NOW.
RELEASE HIM.
...FINE...

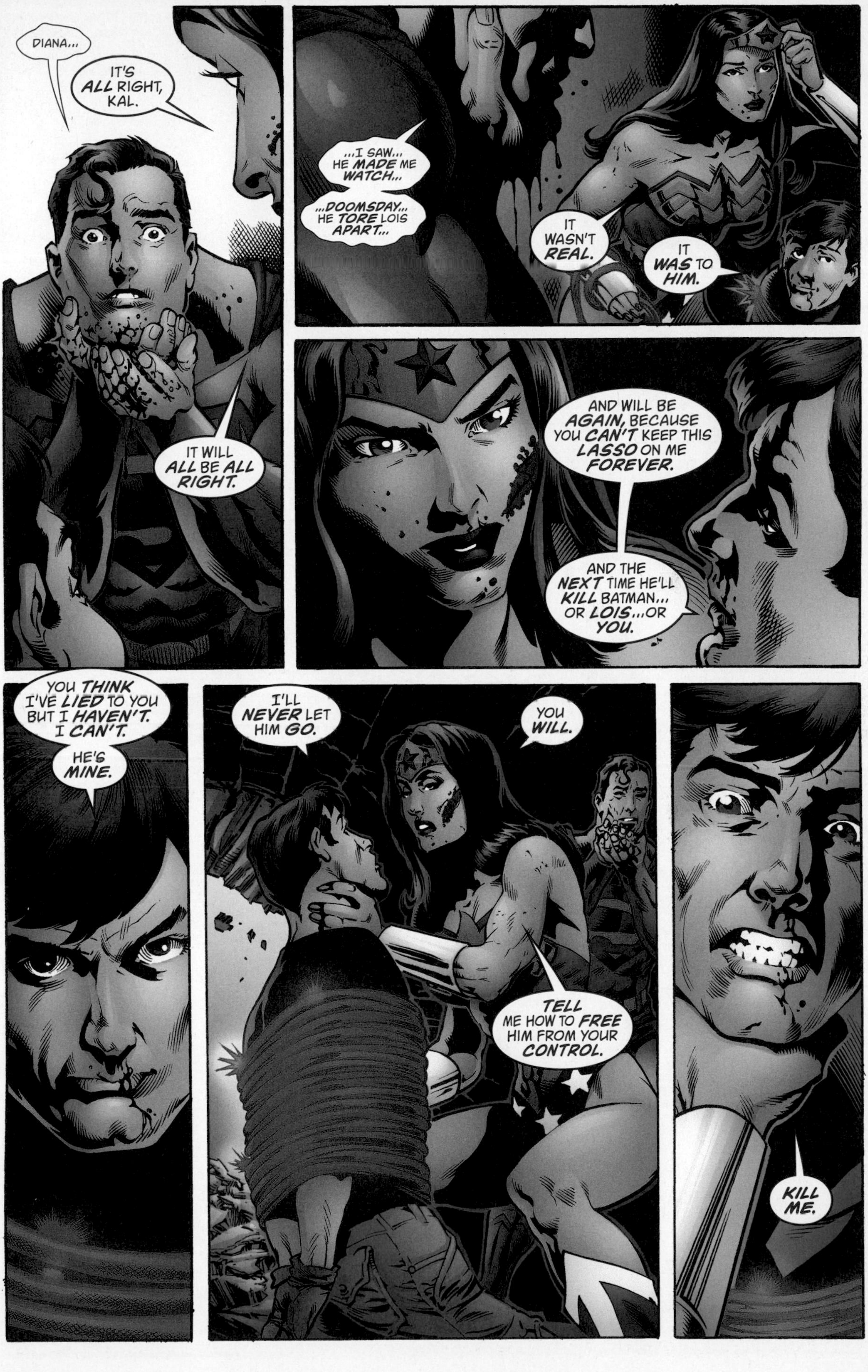
DIANA...
IT'S ALL RIGHT, KAL.
IT WILL ALL BE ALL RIGHT.
...I SAW... HE MADE ME WATCH...
...DOOMSDAY... HE TORE LOIS APART...
IT WASN'T REAL.
IT WAS TO HIM.
AND WILL BE AGAIN, BECAUSE YOU CAN'T KEEP THIS LASSO ON ME FOREVER.
AND THE NEXT TIME HE'LL KILL BATMAN... OR LOIS...OR YOU.
YOU THINK I'VE LIED TO YOU BUT I HAVEN'T. I CAN'T.
HE'S MINE.
I'LL NEVER LET HIM GO.
YOU WILL.
TELL ME HOW TO FREE HIM FROM YOUR CONTROL.
KILL ME.

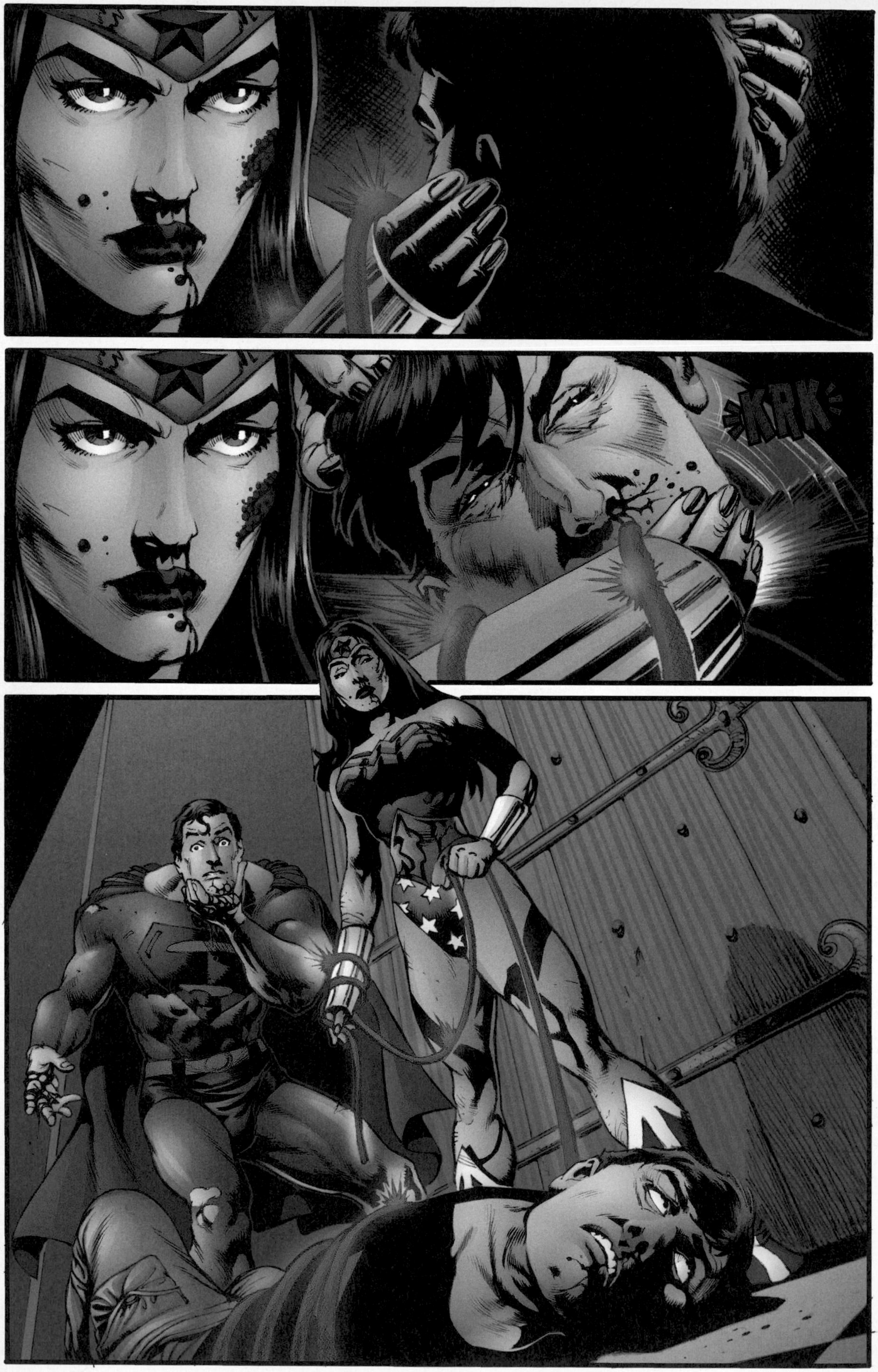
KRK

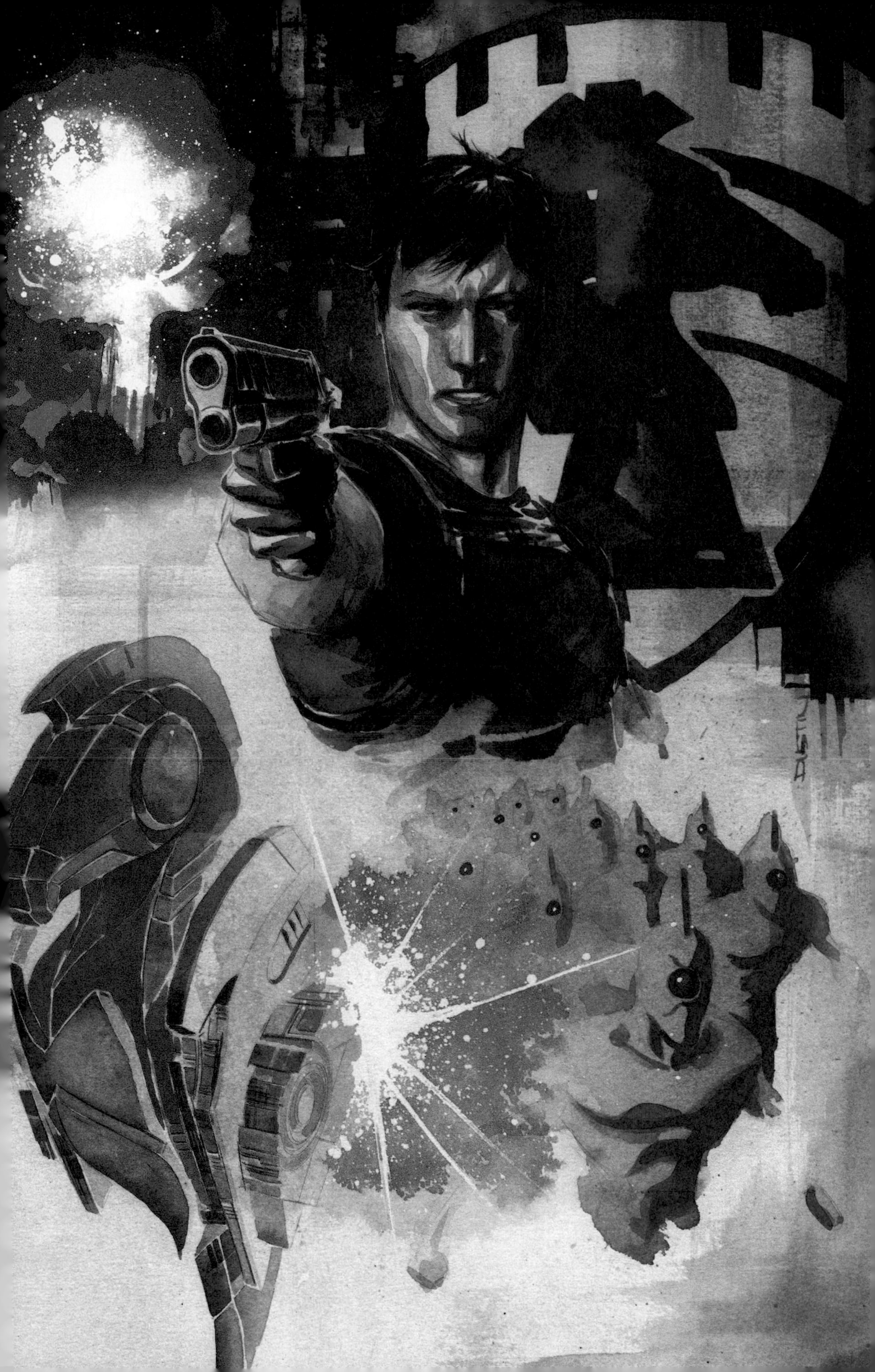

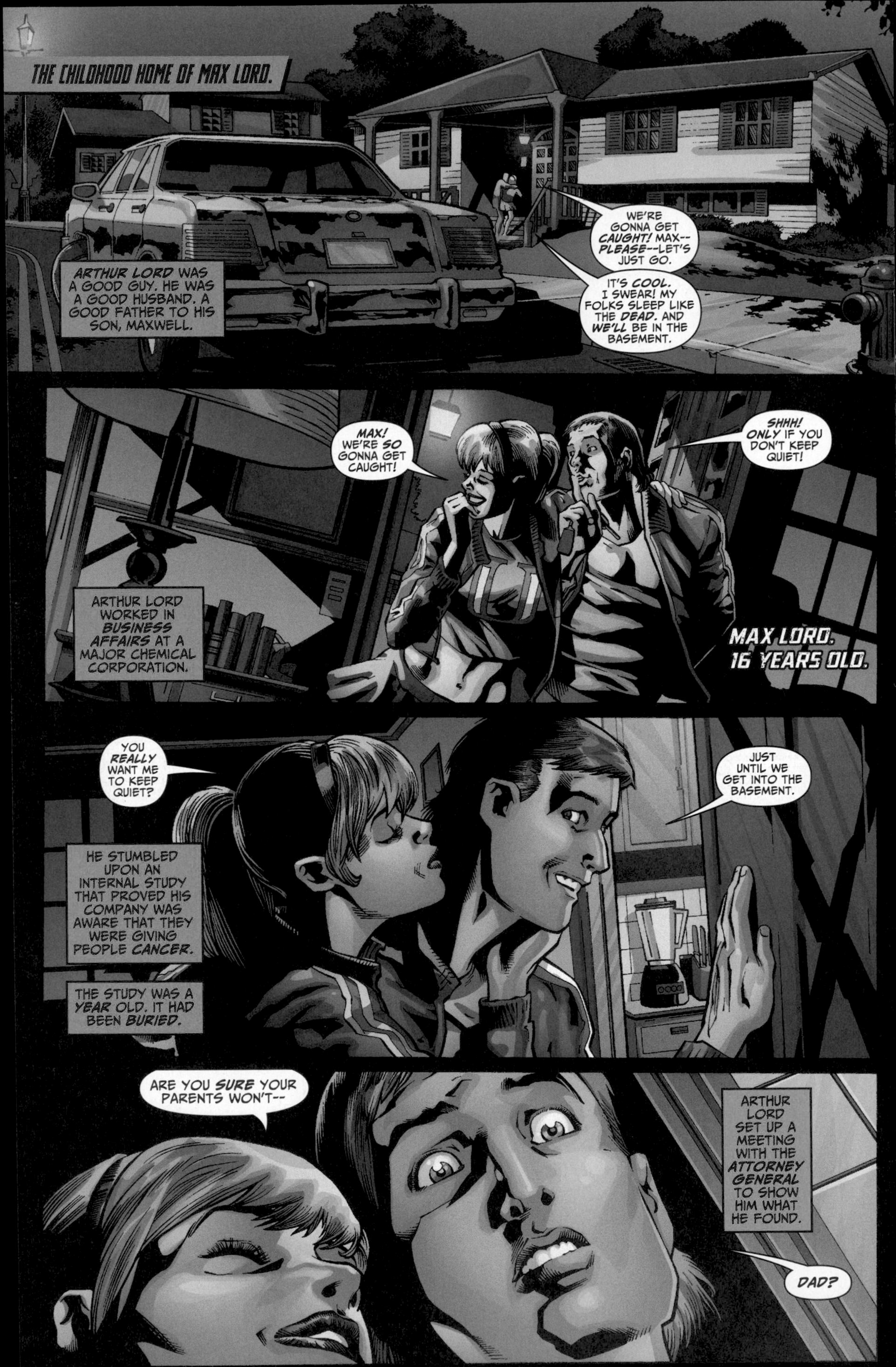

THE CHILDHOOD HOME OF MAX LORD.
ARTHUR LORD WAS A GOOD GUY. HE WAS A GOOD HUSBAND. A GOOD FATHER TO HIS SON, MAXWELL.
WE'RE GONNA GET CAUGHT! MAX-- PLEASE--LET'S JUST GO.
IT'S COOL. I SWEAR! MY FOLKS SLEEP LIKE THE DEAD. AND WE'LL BE IN THE BASEMENT.
MAX! WE'RE SO GONNA GET CAUGHT!
SHHH! ONLY IF YOU DON'T KEEP QUIET!
ARTHUR LORD WORKED IN BUSINESS AFFAIRS AT A MAJOR CHEMICAL CORPORATION.
MAX LORD. 16 YEARS OLD.
YOU REALLY WANT ME TO KEEP QUIET?
JUST UNTIL WE GET INTO THE BASEMENT.
HE STUMBLED UPON AN INTERNAL STUDY THAT PROVED HIS COMPANY WAS AWARE THAT THEY WERE GIVING PEOPLE CANCER.
THE STUDY WAS A YEAR OLD. IT HAD BEEN BURIED.
ARE YOU SURE YOUR PARENTS WON'T--
ARTHUR LORD SET UP A MEETING WITH THE ATTORNEY GENERAL TO SHOW HIM WHAT HE FOUND.
DAD?

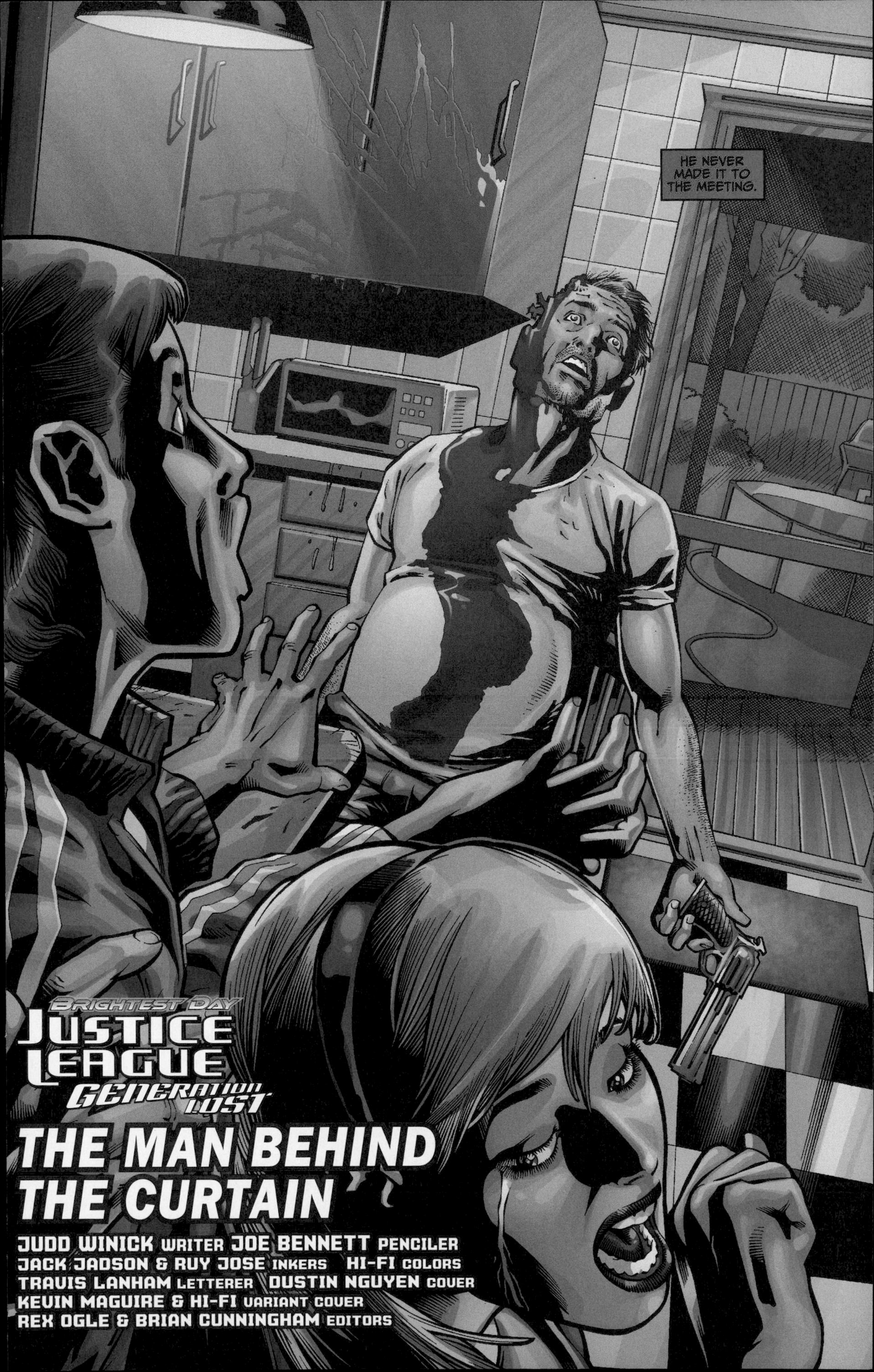

HE NEVER MADE IT TO THE MEETING.
BRIGHTEST DAY
JUSTICE LEAGUE
GENERATION LOST
THE MAN BEHIND THE CURTAIN
JUDD WINICK WRITER JOE BENNETT PENCILER
JACK JADSON & RUY JOSE INKERS HI-FI COLORS
TRAVIS LANHAM LETTERER DUSTIN NGUYEN COVER
KEVIN MAGUIRE & HI-FI VARIANT COVER
REX OGLE & BRIAN CUNNINGHAM EDITORS

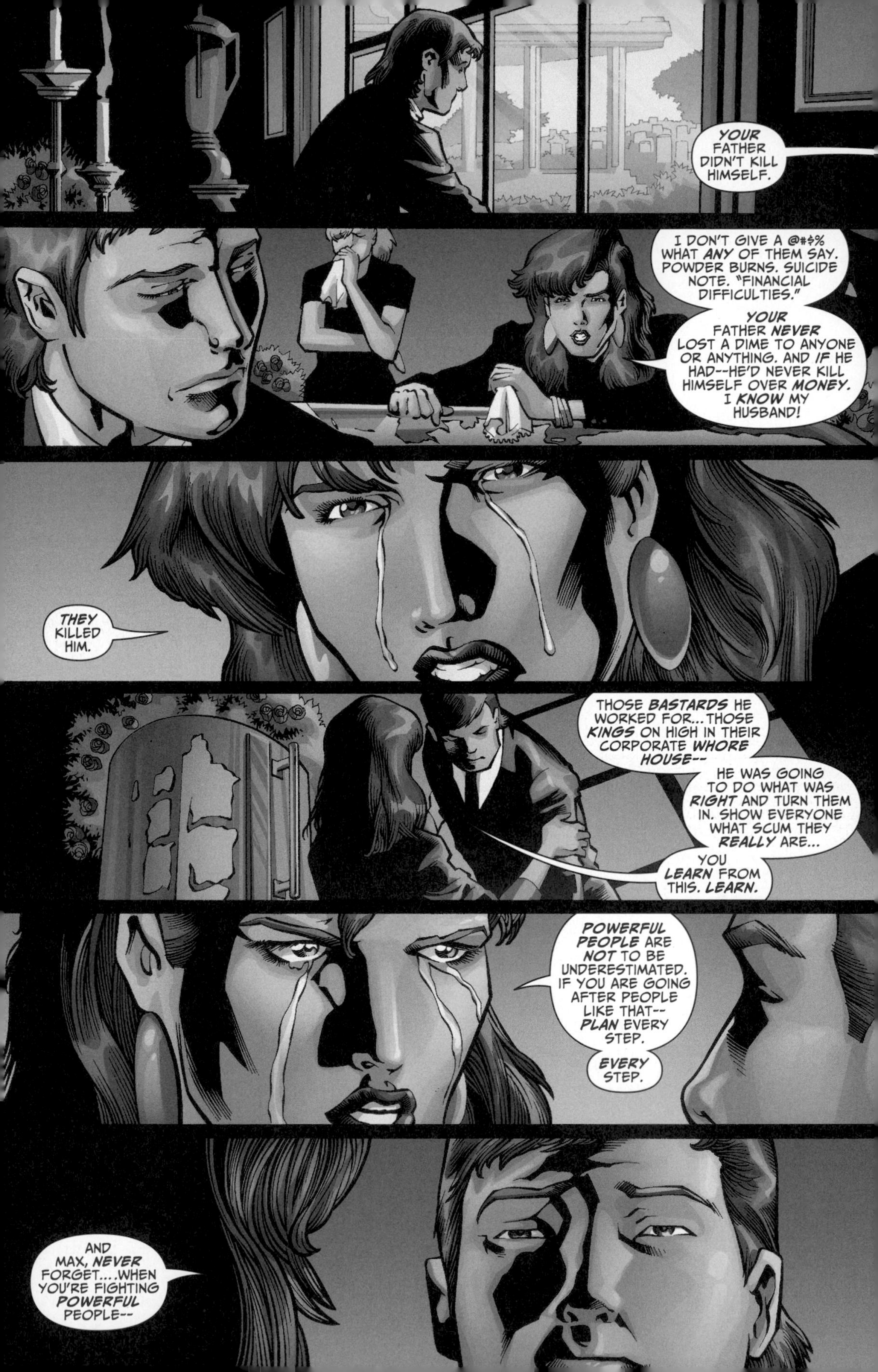
YOUR FATHER DIDN'T KILL HIMSELF.
I DON'T GIVE A @#$% WHAT ANY OF THEM SAY. POWDER BURNS. SUICIDE NOTE. "FINANCIAL DIFFICULTIES."
YOUR FATHER NEVER LOST A DIME TO ANYONE OR ANYTHING. AND IF HE HAD--HE'D NEVER KILL HIMSELF OVER MONEY. I KNOW MY HUSBAND!
THEY KILLED HIM.
THOSE BASTARDS HE WORKED FOR... THOSE KINGS ON HIGH IN THEIR CORPORATE WHORE HOUSE--
HE WAS GOING TO DO WHAT WAS RIGHT AND TURN THEM IN. SHOW EVERYONE WHAT SCUM THEY REALLY ARE...
YOU LEARN FROM THIS. LEARN.
POWERFUL PEOPLE ARE NOT TO BE UNDERESTIMATED. IF YOU ARE GOING AFTER PEOPLE LIKE THAT-- PLAN EVERY STEP.
EVERY STEP.
AND MAX, NEVER FORGET....WHEN YOU'RE FIGHTING POWERFUL PEOPLE--

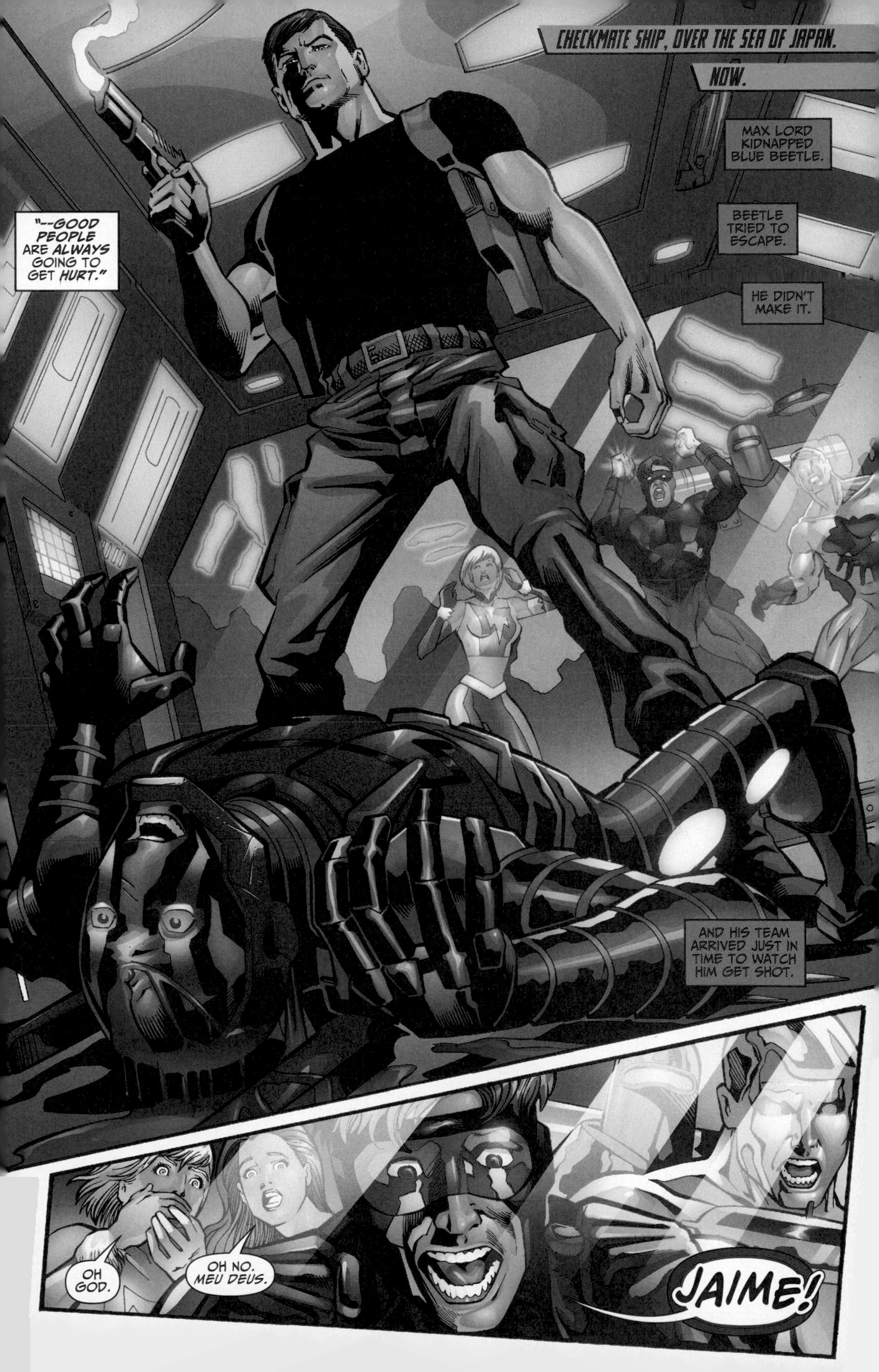
CHECKMATE SHIP, OVER THE SEA OF JAPAN.
NOW.
"--GOOD PEOPLE ARE ALWAYS GOING TO GET HURT."
MAX LORD KIDNAPPED BLUE BEETLE.
BEETLE TRIED TO ESCAPE.
HE DIDN'T MAKE IT.
AND HIS TEAM ARRIVED JUST IN TIME TO WATCH HIM GET SHOT.
OH GOD.
OH NO. MEU DEUS.
JAIME!

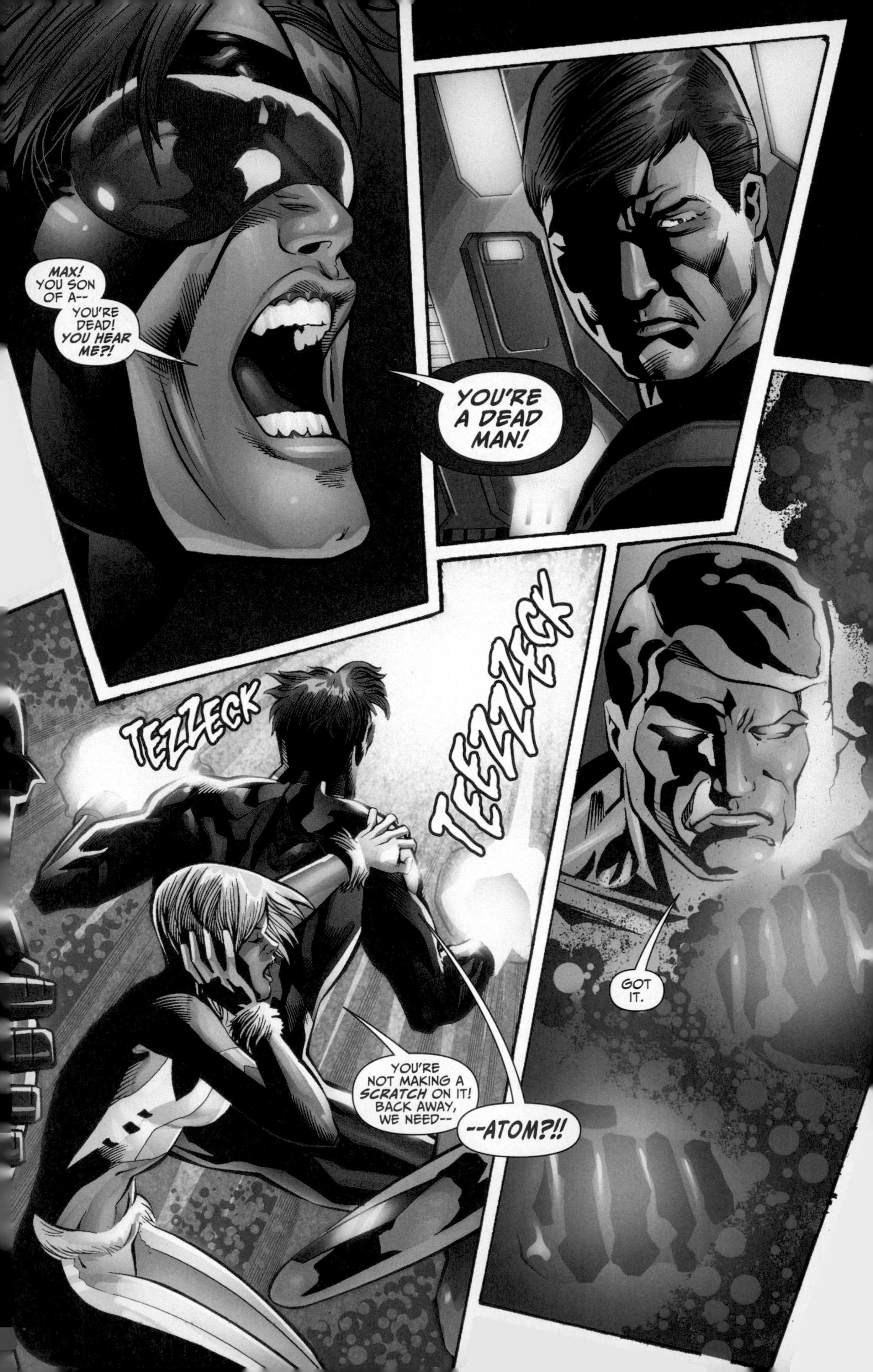
MAX! YOU SON OF A--
YOU'RE DEAD! YOU HEAR ME?!
YOU'RE A DEAD MAN!
TEZZZECK
TEZZZZECK
YOU'RE NOT MAKING A SCRATCH ON IT! BACK AWAY, WE NEED--
--ATOM?!!
GOT IT.

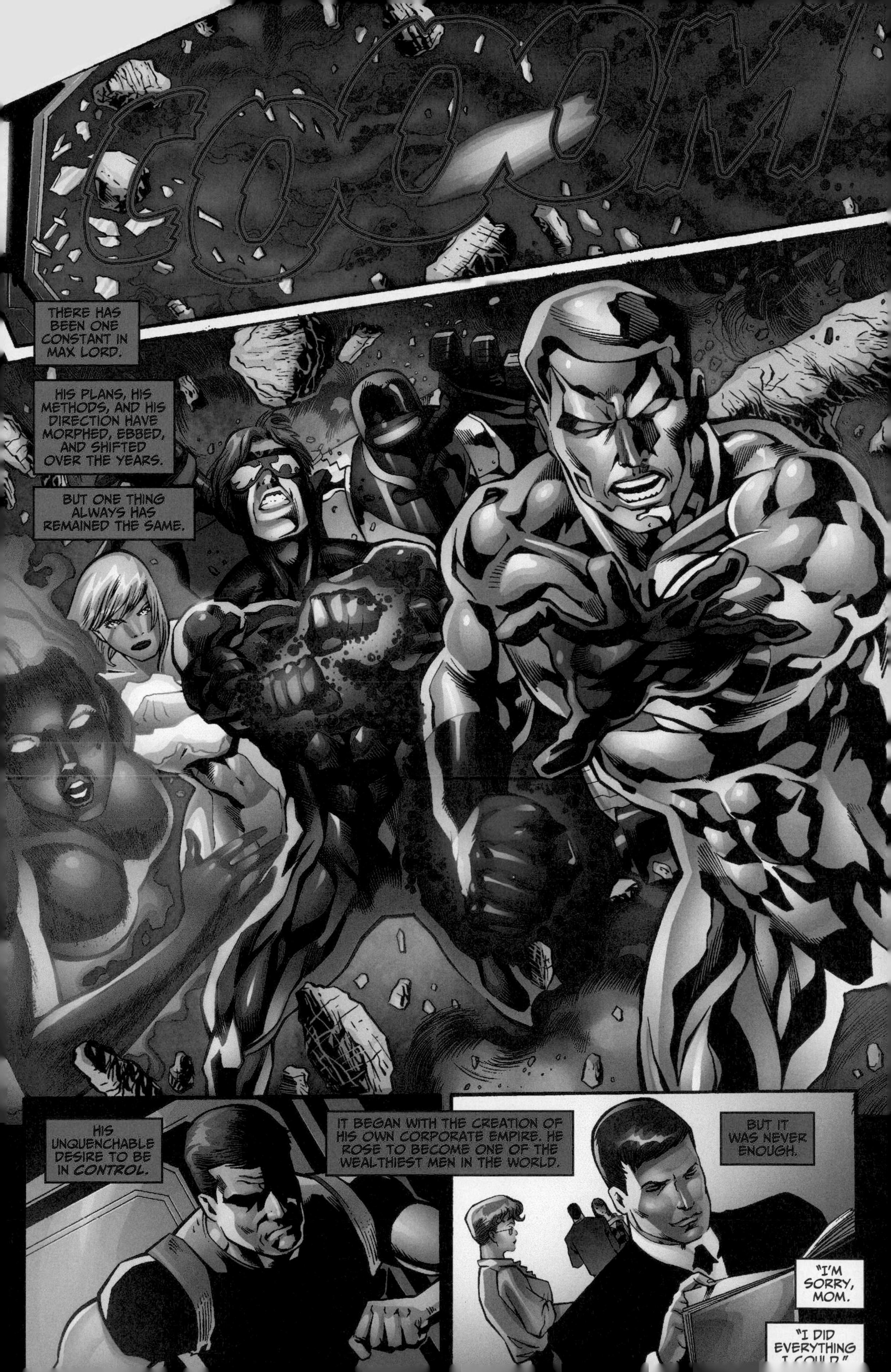
GOOOM
THERE HAS BEEN ONE CONSTANT IN MAX LORD.
HIS PLANS, HIS METHODS, AND HIS DIRECTION HAVE MORPHED, EBBED, AND SHIFTED OVER THE YEARS.
BUT ONE THING ALWAYS HAS REMAINED THE SAME.
HIS UNQUENCHABLE DESIRE TO BE IN *CONTROL*.
IT BEGAN WITH THE CREATION OF HIS OWN CORPORATE EMPIRE. HE ROSE TO BECOME ONE OF THE WEALTHIEST MEN IN THE WORLD.
BUT IT WAS NEVER ENOUGH.
"I'M SORRY, MOM.
"I DID EVERYTHING

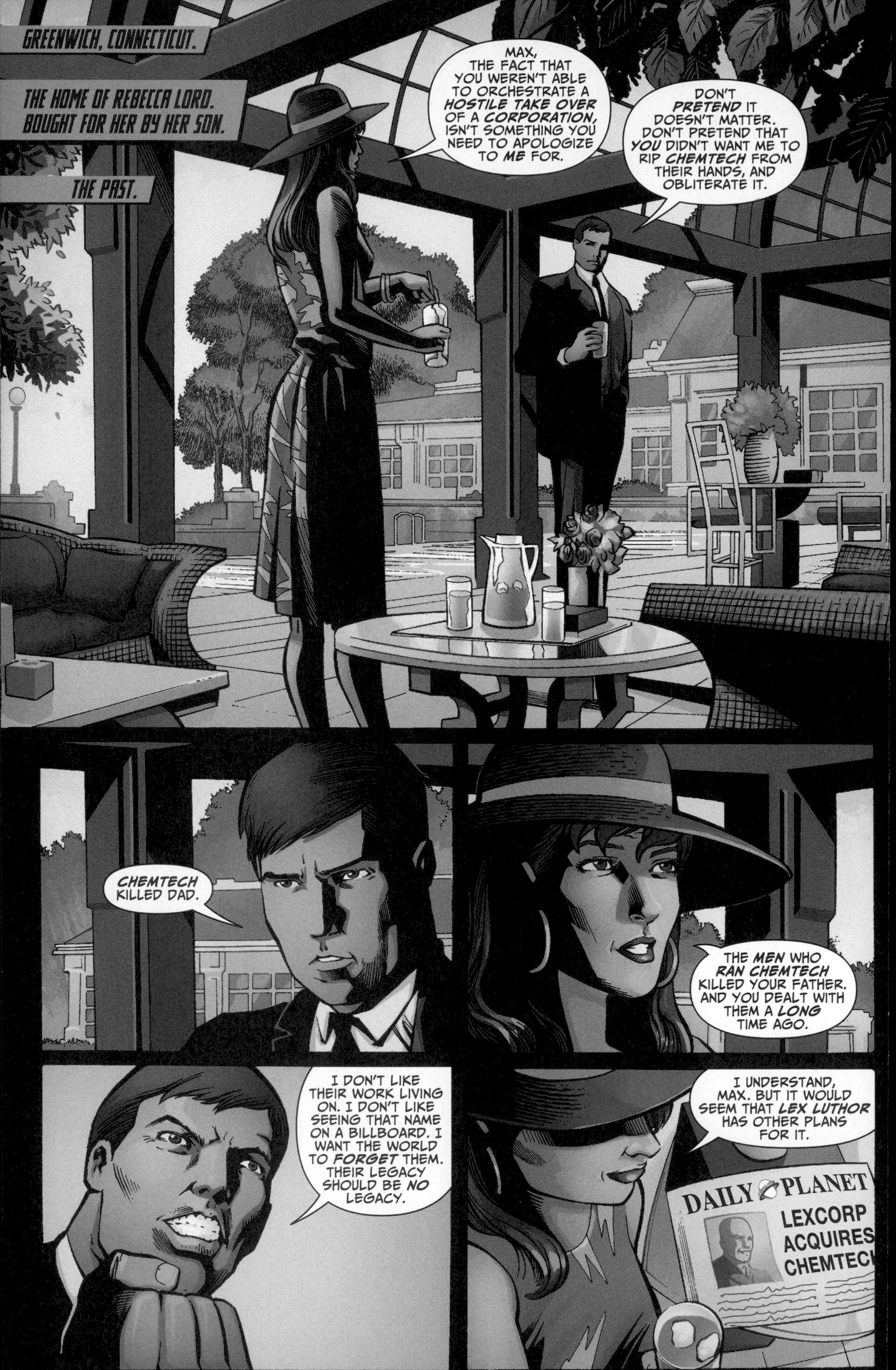
GREENWICH, CONNECTICUT.
THE HOME OF REBECCA LORD. BOUGHT FOR HER BY HER SON.
THE PAST.
MAX, THE FACT THAT YOU WEREN'T ABLE TO ORCHESTRATE A HOSTILE TAKE OVER OF A CORPORATION, ISN'T SOMETHING YOU NEED TO APOLOGIZE TO ME FOR.
DON'T PRETEND IT DOESN'T MATTER. DON'T PRETEND THAT YOU DIDN'T WANT ME TO RIP CHEMTECH FROM THEIR HANDS, AND OBLITERATE IT.
CHEMTECH KILLED DAD.
THE MEN WHO RAN CHEMTECH KILLED YOUR FATHER. AND YOU DEALT WITH THEM A LONG TIME AGO.
I DON'T LIKE THEIR WORK LIVING ON. I DON'T LIKE SEEING THAT NAME ON A BILLBOARD. I WANT THE WORLD TO FORGET THEM. THEIR LEGACY SHOULD BE NO LEGACY.
I UNDERSTAND, MAX. BUT IT WOULD SEEM THAT LEX LUTHOR HAS OTHER PLANS FOR IT.
DAILY PLANET
LEXCORP ACQUIRES CHEMTECH

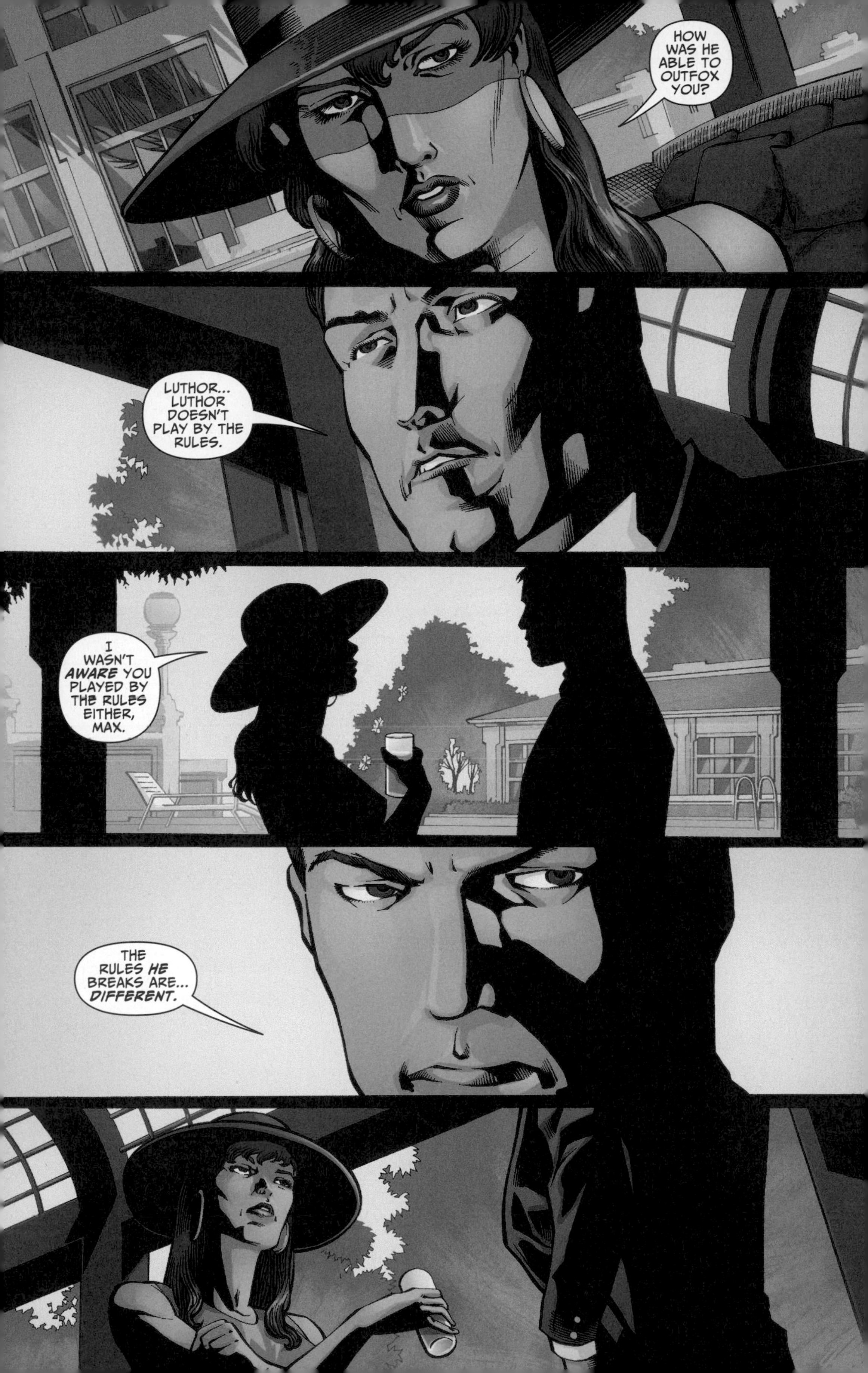
HOW WAS HE ABLE TO OUTFOX YOU?
LUTHOR... LUTHOR DOESN'T PLAY BY THE RULES.
I WASN'T AWARE YOU PLAYED BY THE RULES EITHER, MAX.
THE RULES HE BREAKS ARE... DIFFERENT.

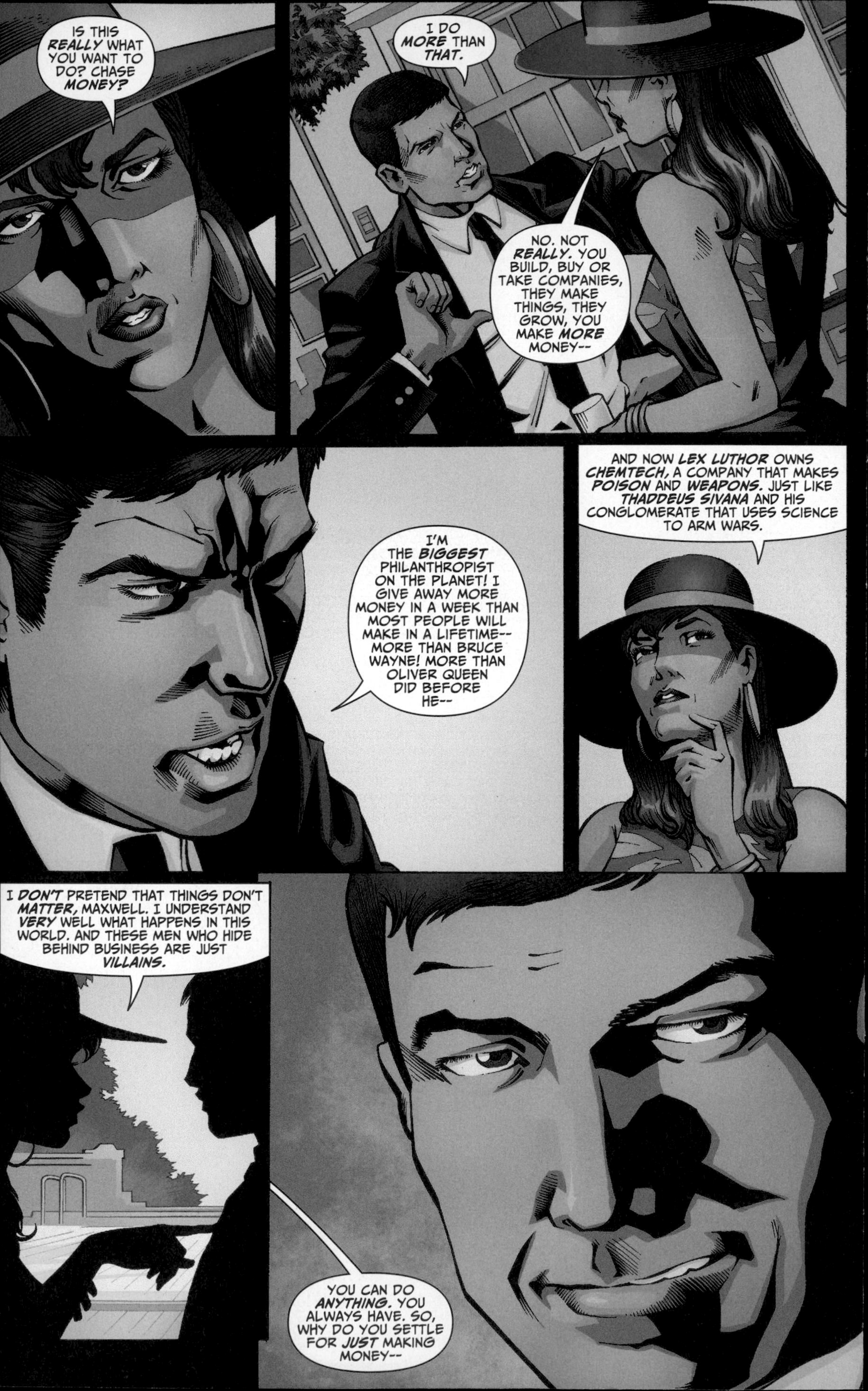

IS THIS REALLY WHAT YOU WANT TO DO? CHASE MONEY?
I DO MORE THAN THAT.
NO. NOT REALLY. YOU BUILD, BUY OR TAKE COMPANIES, THEY MAKE THINGS, THEY GROW, YOU MAKE MORE MONEY--
I'M THE BIGGEST PHILANTHROPIST ON THE PLANET! I GIVE AWAY MORE MONEY IN A WEEK THAN MOST PEOPLE WILL MAKE IN A LIFETIME-- MORE THAN BRUCE WAYNE! MORE THAN OLIVER QUEEN DID BEFORE HE--
AND NOW LEX LUTHOR OWNS CHEMTECH, A COMPANY THAT MAKES POISON AND WEAPONS. JUST LIKE THADDEUS SIVANA AND HIS CONGLOMERATE THAT USES SCIENCE TO ARM WARS.
I DON'T PRETEND THAT THINGS DON'T MATTER, MAXWELL. I UNDERSTAND VERY WELL WHAT HAPPENS IN THIS WORLD. AND THESE MEN WHO HIDE BEHIND BUSINESS ARE JUST VILLAINS.
YOU CAN DO ANYTHING. YOU ALWAYS HAVE. SO, WHY DO YOU SETTLE FOR JUST MAKING MONEY--

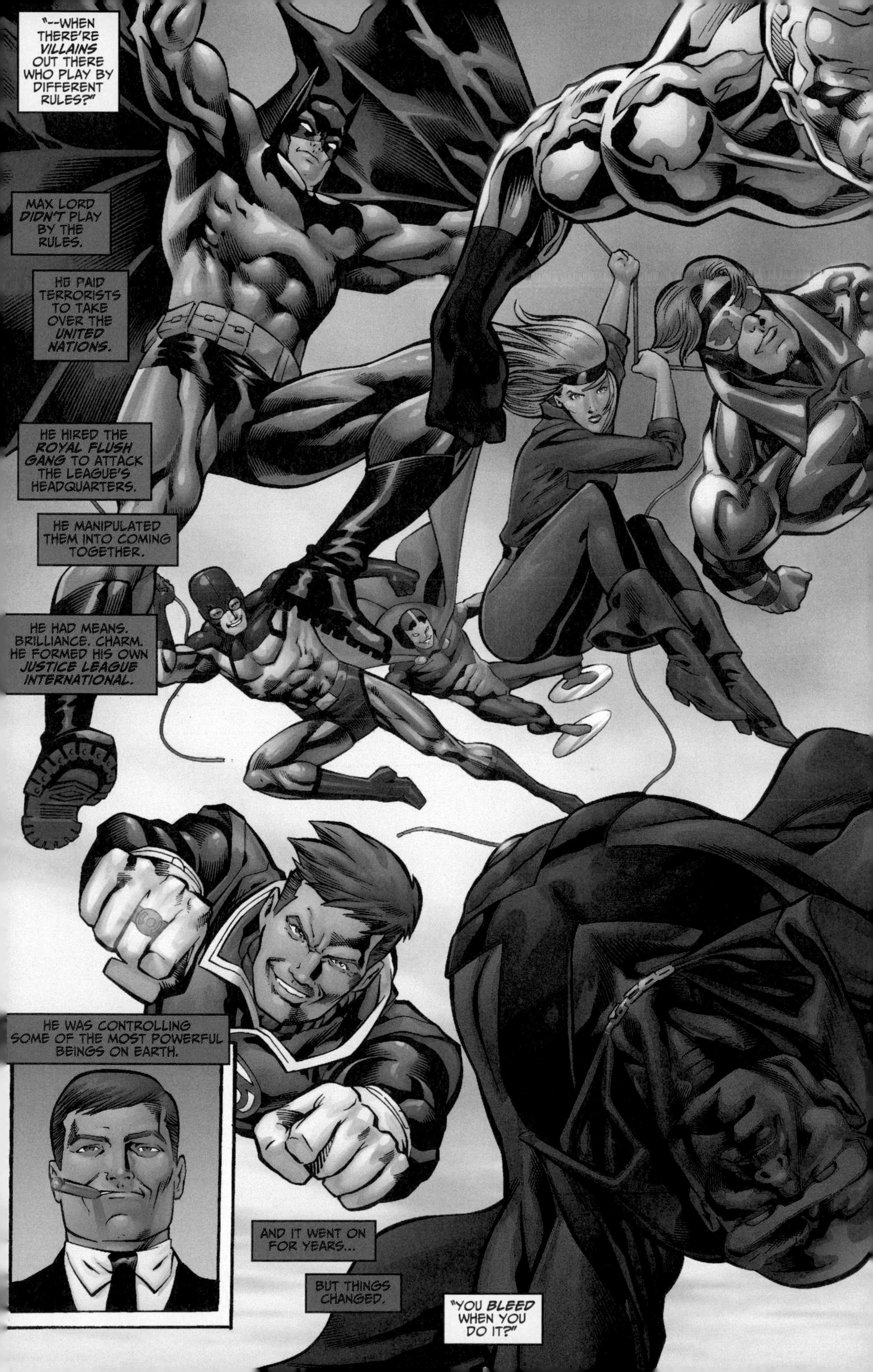
"--WHEN THERE'RE *VILLAINS* OUT THERE WHO PLAY BY DIFFERENT RULES?"
MAX LORD *DIDN'T* PLAY BY THE RULES.
HE PAID TERRORISTS TO TAKE OVER THE *UNITED NATIONS*.
HE HIRED THE *ROYAL FLUSH GANG* TO ATTACK THE LEAGUE'S HEADQUARTERS.
HE MANIPULATED THEM INTO COMING TOGETHER.
HE HAD MEANS. BRILLIANCE. CHARM. HE FORMED HIS OWN *JUSTICE LEAGUE INTERNATIONAL*.
HE WAS CONTROLLING SOME OF THE MOST POWERFUL BEINGS ON EARTH.
AND IT WENT ON FOR YEARS...
BUT THINGS CHANGED.
"YOU *BLEED* WHEN YOU DO IT?"

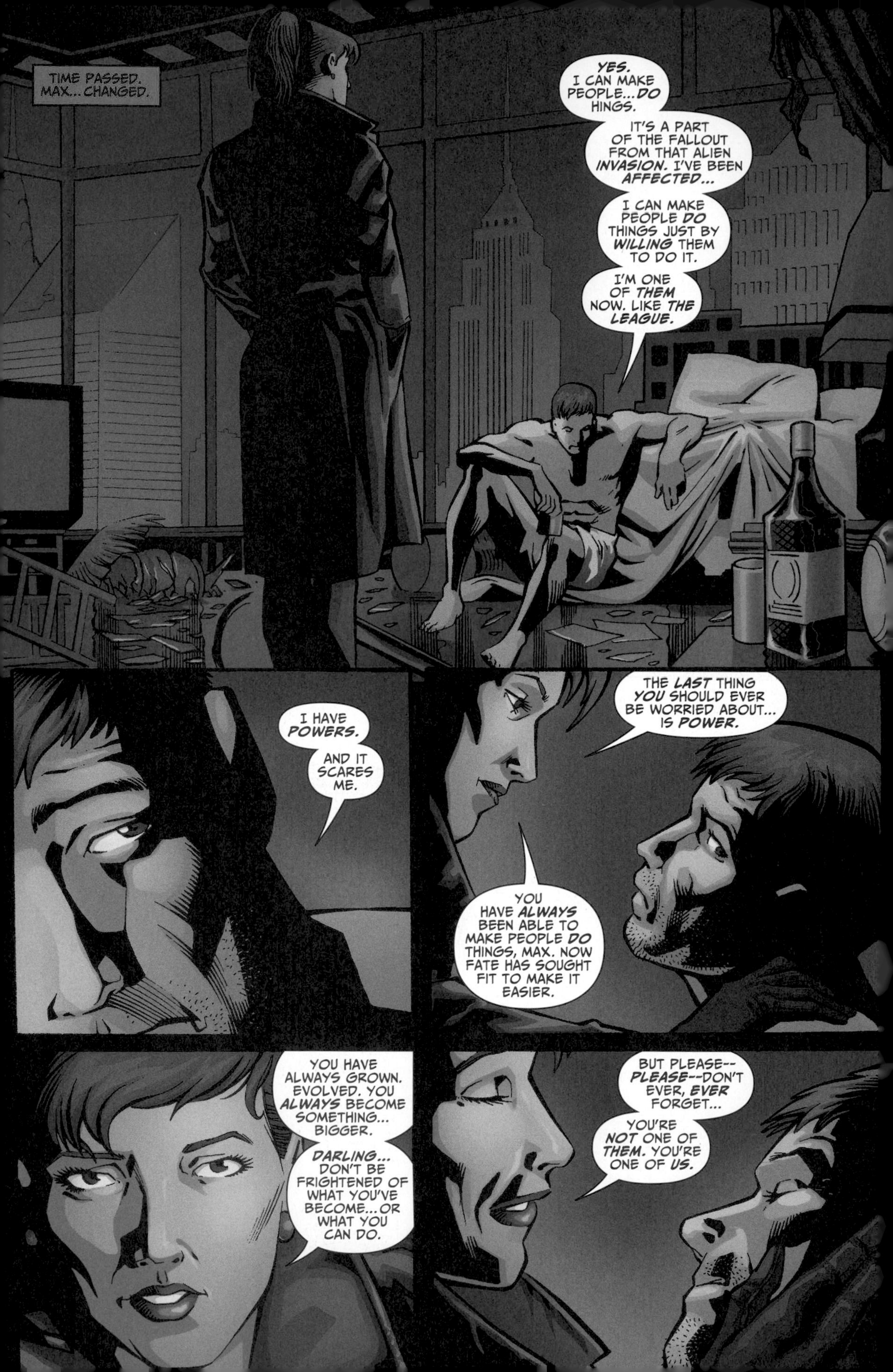
TIME PASSED. MAX...CHANGED.
YES. I CAN MAKE PEOPLE...DO HINGS.
IT'S A PART OF THE FALLOUT FROM THAT ALIEN INVASION. I'VE BEEN AFFECTED...
I CAN MAKE PEOPLE DO THINGS JUST BY WILLING THEM TO DO IT.
I'M ONE OF THEM NOW. LIKE THE LEAGUE.
I HAVE POWERS.
AND IT SCARES ME.
THE LAST THING YOU SHOULD EVER BE WORRIED ABOUT... IS POWER.
YOU HAVE ALWAYS BEEN ABLE TO MAKE PEOPLE DO THINGS, MAX. NOW FATE HAS SOUGHT FIT TO MAKE IT EASIER.
YOU HAVE ALWAYS GROWN. EVOLVED. YOU ALWAYS BECOME SOMETHING... BIGGER.
DARLING... DON'T BE FRIGHTENED OF WHAT YOU'VE BECOME...OR WHAT YOU CAN DO.
BUT PLEASE--PLEASE--DON'T EVER, EVER FORGET...
YOU'RE NOT ONE OF THEM. YOU'RE ONE OF US.

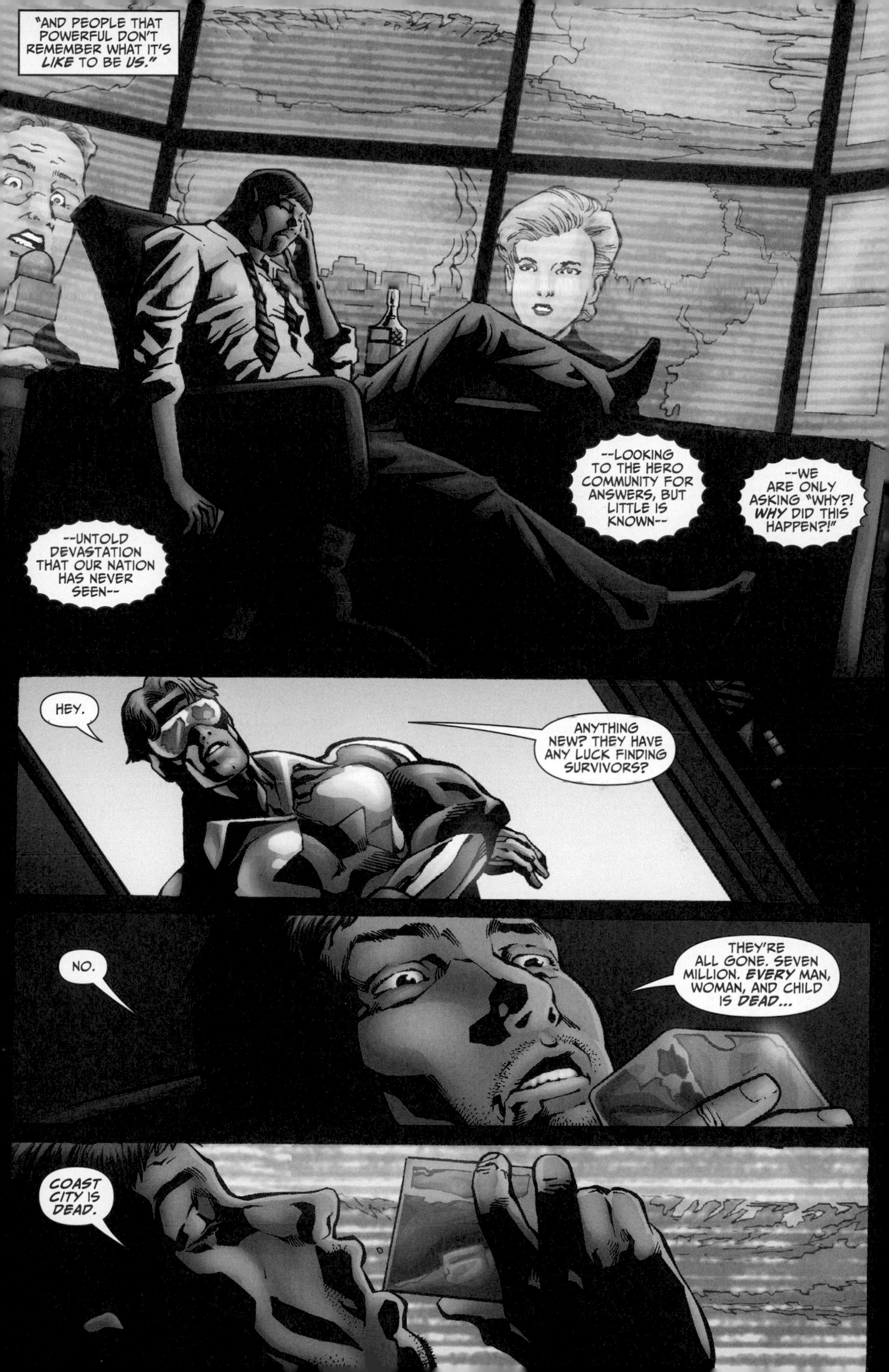
"AND PEOPLE THAT POWERFUL DON'T REMEMBER WHAT IT'S *LIKE* TO BE *US*."
--UNTOLD DEVASTATION THAT OUR NATION HAS NEVER SEEN--
--LOOKING TO THE HERO COMMUNITY FOR ANSWERS, BUT LITTLE IS KNOWN--
--WE ARE ONLY ASKING "WHY?! *WHY* DID THIS HAPPEN?!"
HEY.
ANYTHING NEW? THEY HAVE ANY LUCK FINDING SURVIVORS?
NO.
THEY'RE ALL GONE. SEVEN MILLION. *EVERY* MAN, WOMAN, AND CHILD IS *DEAD*...
COAST CITY IS *DEAD*.

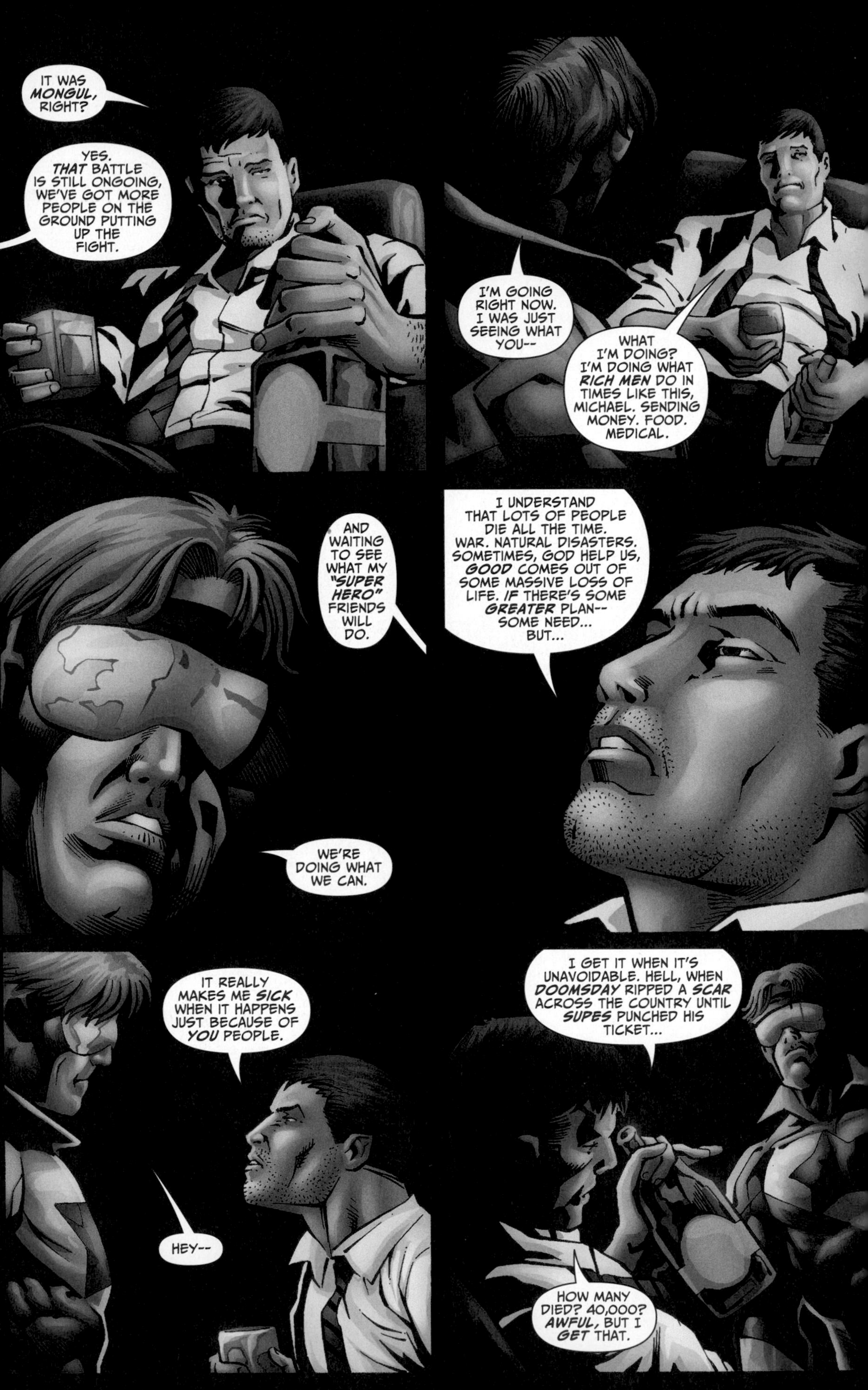
IT WAS MONGUL, RIGHT?
YES. THAT BATTLE IS STILL ONGOING, WE'VE GOT MORE PEOPLE ON THE GROUND PUTTING UP THE FIGHT.
I'M GOING RIGHT NOW. I WAS JUST SEEING WHAT YOU--
WHAT I'M DOING? I'M DOING WHAT RICH MEN DO IN TIMES LIKE THIS, MICHAEL. SENDING MONEY. FOOD. MEDICAL.
AND WAITING TO SEE WHAT MY "SUPER HERO" FRIENDS WILL DO.
WE'RE DOING WHAT WE CAN.
I UNDERSTAND THAT LOTS OF PEOPLE DIE ALL THE TIME. WAR. NATURAL DISASTERS. SOMETIMES, GOD HELP US, GOOD COMES OUT OF SOME MASSIVE LOSS OF LIFE. IF THERE'S SOME GREATER PLAN-- SOME NEED... BUT...
IT REALLY MAKES ME SICK WHEN IT HAPPENS JUST BECAUSE OF YOU PEOPLE.
HEY--
I GET IT WHEN IT'S UNAVOIDABLE. HELL, WHEN DOOMSDAY RIPPED A SCAR ACROSS THE COUNTRY UNTIL SUPES PUNCHED HIS TICKET...
HOW MANY DIED? 40,000? AWFUL, BUT I GET THAT.

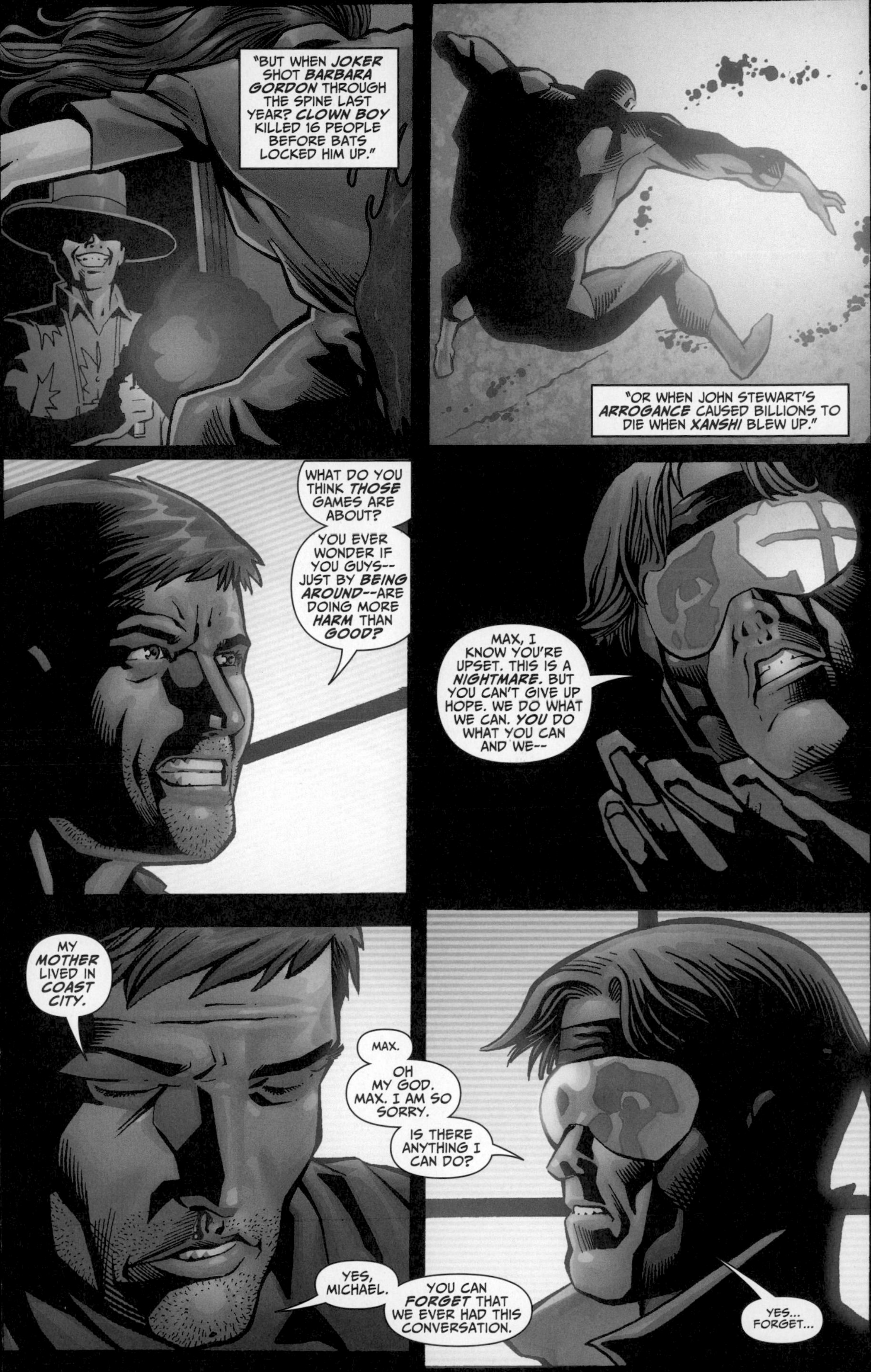
"BUT WHEN JOKER SHOT BARBARA GORDON THROUGH THE SPINE LAST YEAR? CLOWN BOY KILLED 16 PEOPLE BEFORE BATS LOCKED HIM UP."
"OR WHEN JOHN STEWART'S ARROGANCE CAUSED BILLIONS TO DIE WHEN XANSHI BLEW UP."
WHAT DO YOU THINK THOSE GAMES ARE ABOUT?
YOU EVER WONDER IF YOU GUYS-- JUST BY BEING AROUND--ARE DOING MORE HARM THAN GOOD?
MAX, I KNOW YOU'RE UPSET. THIS IS A NIGHTMARE. BUT YOU CAN'T GIVE UP HOPE. WE DO WHAT WE CAN. YOU DO WHAT YOU CAN AND WE--
MY MOTHER LIVED IN COAST CITY.
MAX.
OH MY GOD. MAX. I AM SO SORRY.
IS THERE ANYTHING I CAN DO?
YES, MICHAEL.
YOU CAN FORGET THAT WE EVER HAD THIS CONVERSATION.
YES... FORGET...

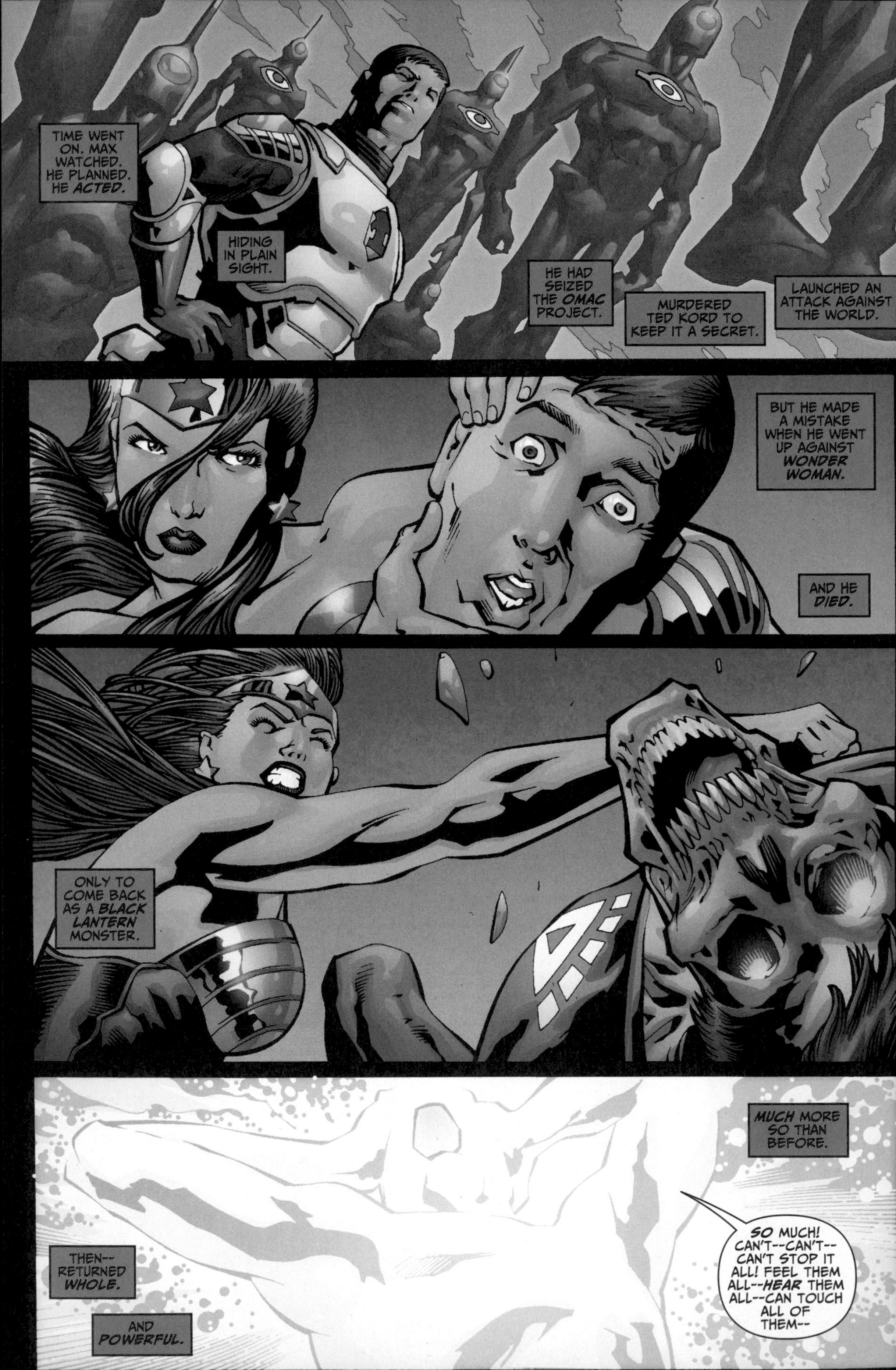
TIME WENT ON. MAX WATCHED. HE PLANNED. HE ACTED.
HIDING IN PLAIN SIGHT.
HE HAD SEIZED THE OMAC PROJECT.
MURDERED TED KORD TO KEEP IT A SECRET.
LAUNCHED AN ATTACK AGAINST THE WORLD.
BUT HE MADE A MISTAKE WHEN HE WENT UP AGAINST WONDER WOMAN.
AND HE DIED.
ONLY TO COME BACK AS A BLACK LANTERN MONSTER.
MUCH MORE SO THAN BEFORE.
THEN--RETURNED WHOLE.
AND POWERFUL.
SO MUCH! CAN'T--CAN'T--CAN'T STOP IT ALL! FEEL THEM ALL--HEAR THEM ALL--CAN TOUCH ALL OF THEM--

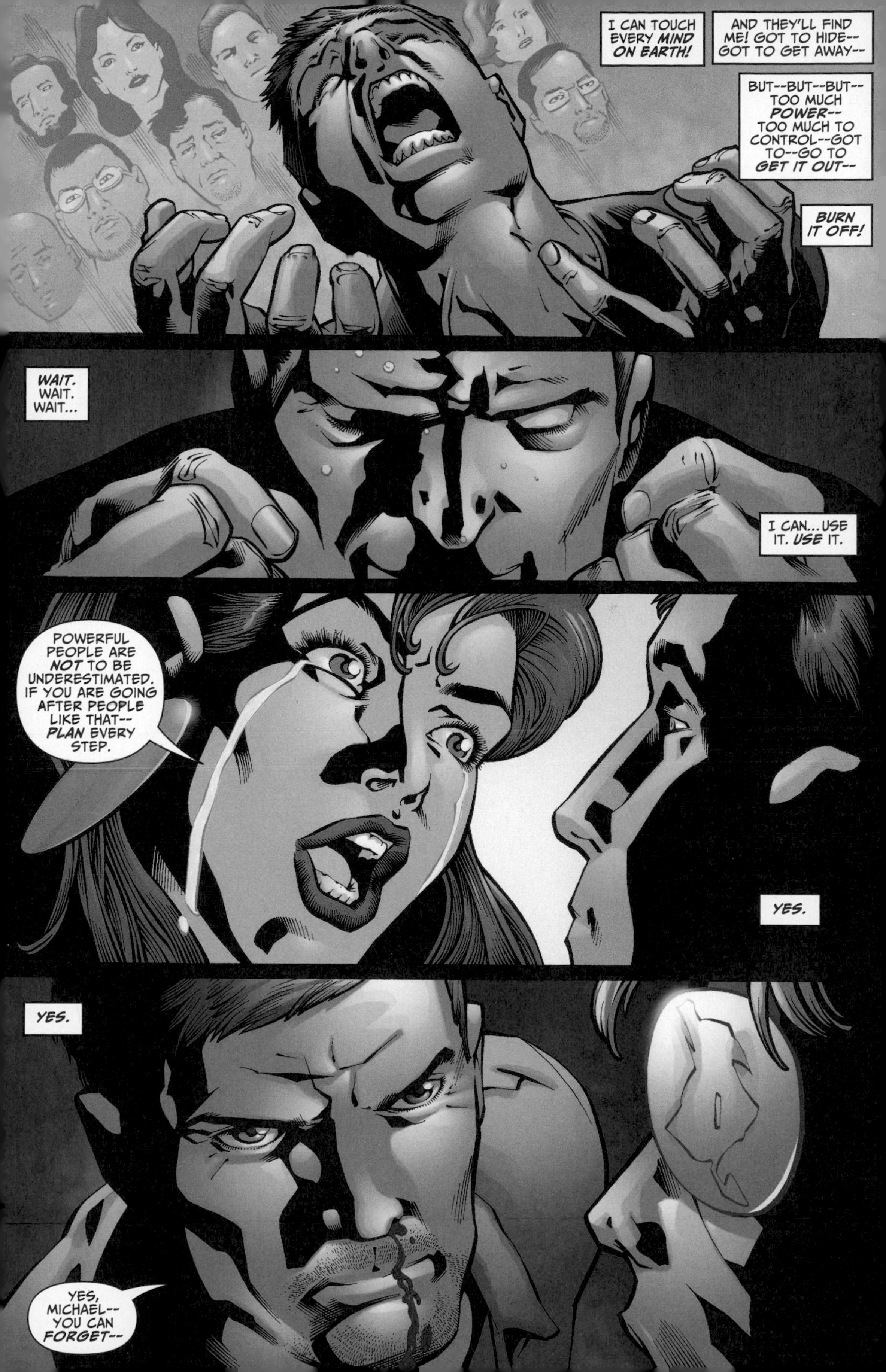
I CAN TOUCH EVERY MIND ON EARTH!
AND THEY'LL FIND ME! GOT TO HIDE--GOT TO GET AWAY--
BUT--BUT--BUT--TOO MUCH POWER--TOO MUCH TO CONTROL--GOT TO--GO TO GET IT OUT--
BURN IT OFF!
WAIT. WAIT. WAIT...
I CAN...USE IT. USE IT.
POWERFUL PEOPLE ARE NOT TO BE UNDERESTIMATED. IF YOU ARE GOING AFTER PEOPLE LIKE THAT--PLAN EVERY STEP.
YES.
YES.
YES, MICHAEL--YOU CAN FORGET--

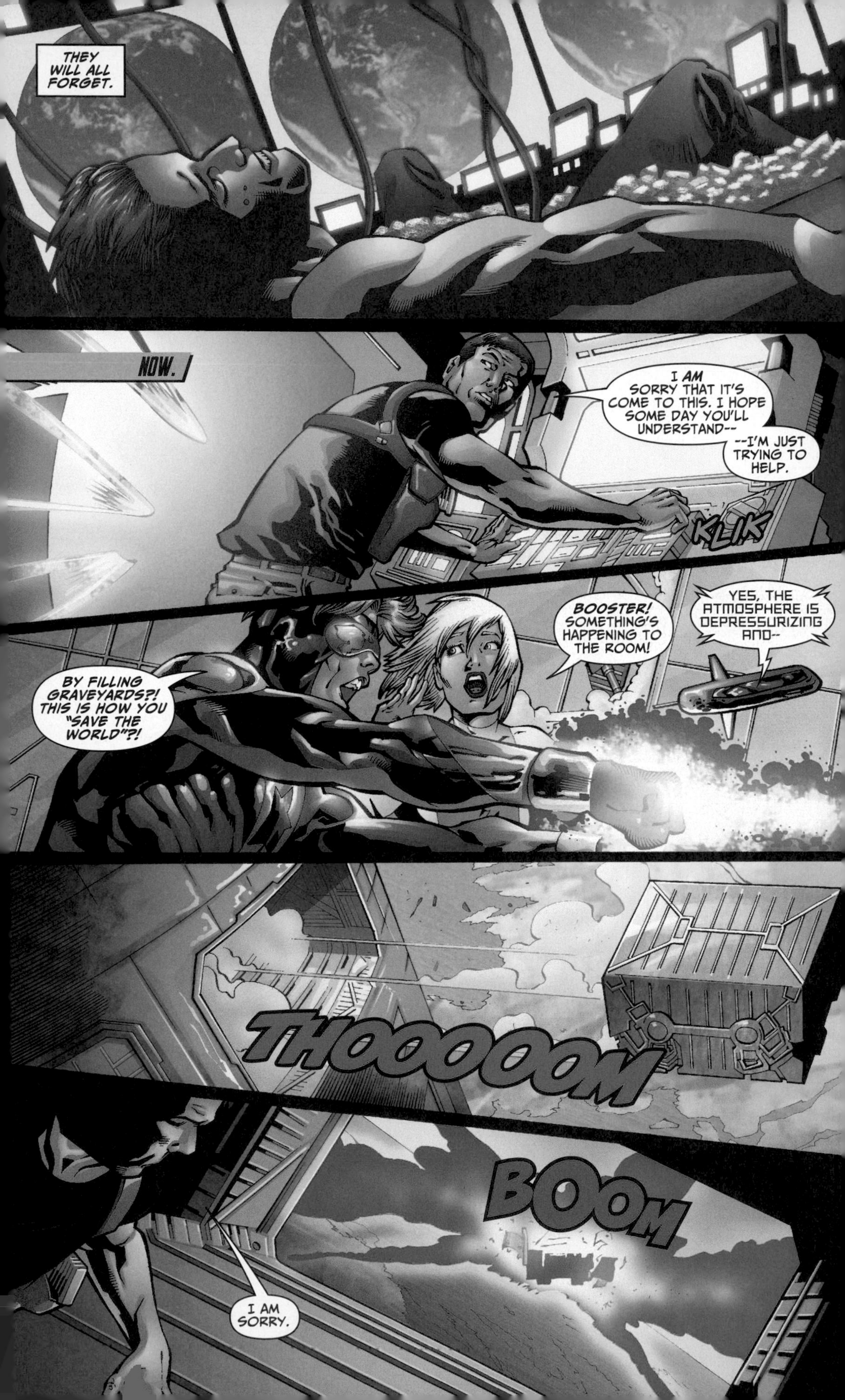
THEY WILL ALL FORGET.
NOW.
I AM SORRY THAT IT'S COME TO THIS. I HOPE SOME DAY YOU'LL UNDERSTAND--
--I'M JUST TRYING TO HELP.
KLIK
BY FILLING GRAVEYARDS?! THIS IS HOW YOU "SAVE THE WORLD"?!
BOOSTER! SOMETHING'S HAPPENING TO THE ROOM!
YES, THE ATMOSPHERE IS DEPRESSURIZING AND--
THOOOOOM
BOOOM
I AM SORRY.

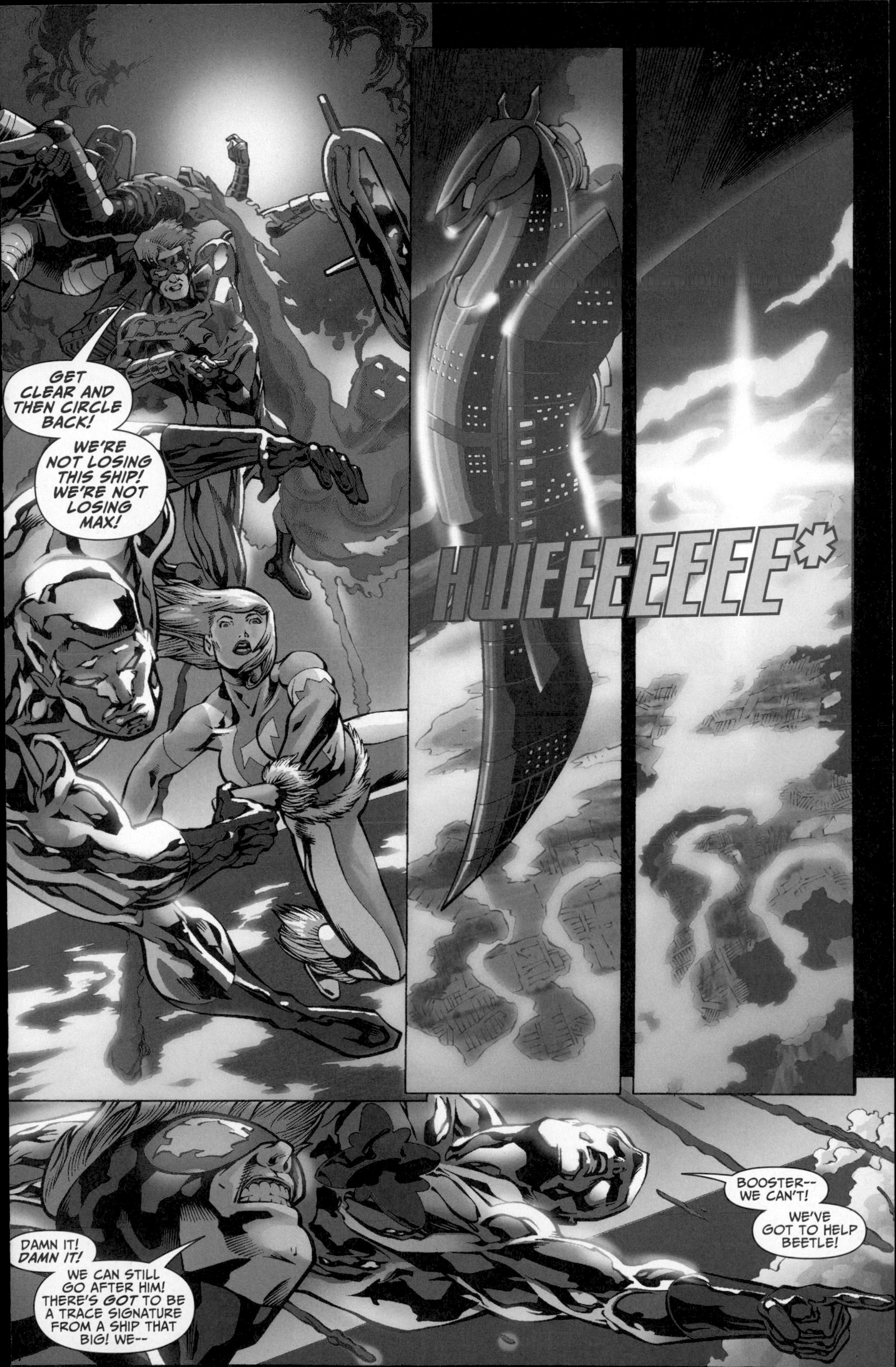
GET CLEAR AND THEN CIRCLE BACK!
WE'RE NOT LOSING THIS SHIP! WE'RE NOT LOSING MAX!
HWEEEEEEE*
DAMN IT! DAMN IT!
WE CAN STILL GO AFTER HIM! THERE'S GOT TO BE A TRACE SIGNATURE FROM A SHIP THAT BIG! WE--
BOOSTER-- WE CAN'T!
WE'VE GOT TO HELP BEETLE!

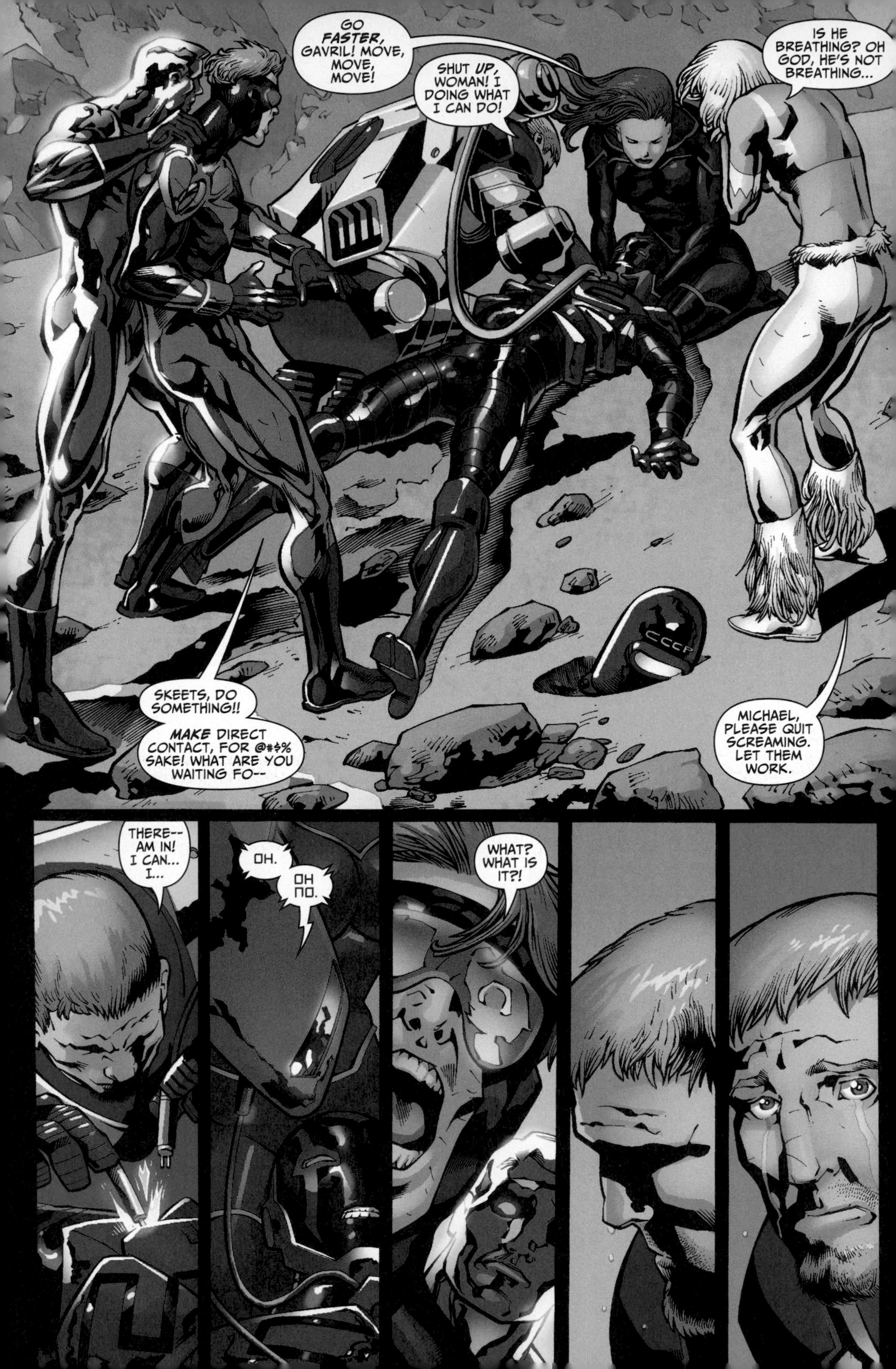
GO FASTER, GAVRIL! MOVE, MOVE, MOVE!
SHUT UP, WOMAN! I DOING WHAT I CAN DO!
IS HE BREATHING? OH GOD, HE'S NOT BREATHING...
CCCP
SKEETS, DO SOMETHING!!
MAKE DIRECT CONTACT, FOR @#$% SAKE! WHAT ARE YOU WAITING FO--
MICHAEL, PLEASE QUIT SCREAMING. LET THEM WORK.
THERE-- AM IN! I CAN... I...
OH.
OH NO.
WHAT? WHAT IS IT?!

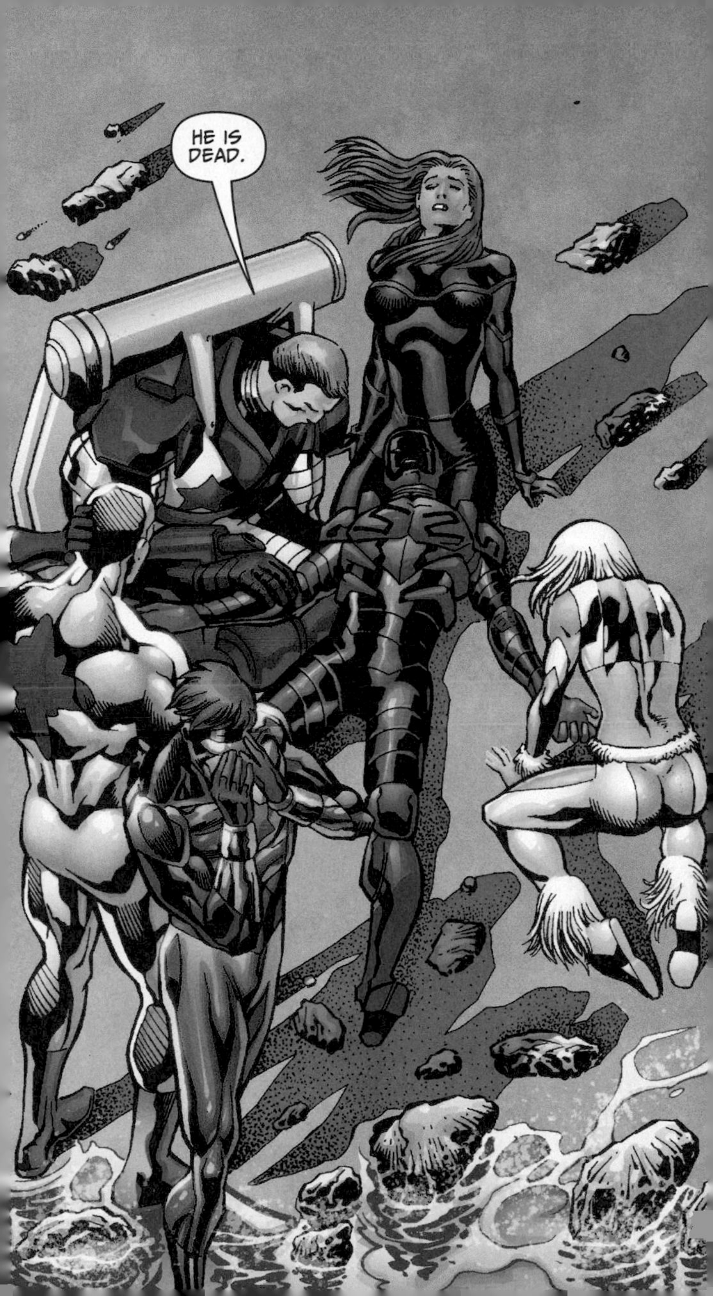
HE IS DEAD.

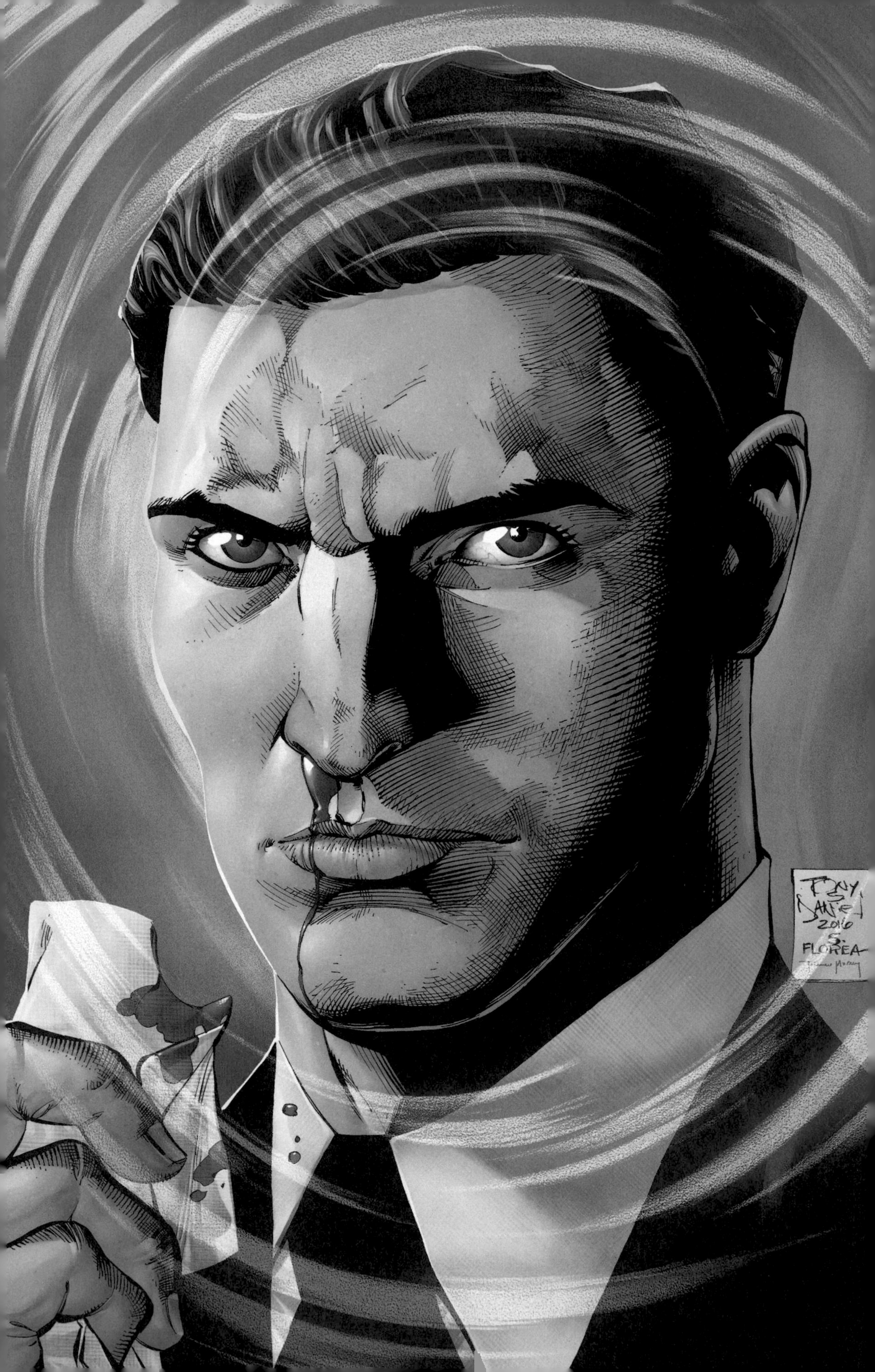
TONY S. DANIEL 2016
S. FLOREA

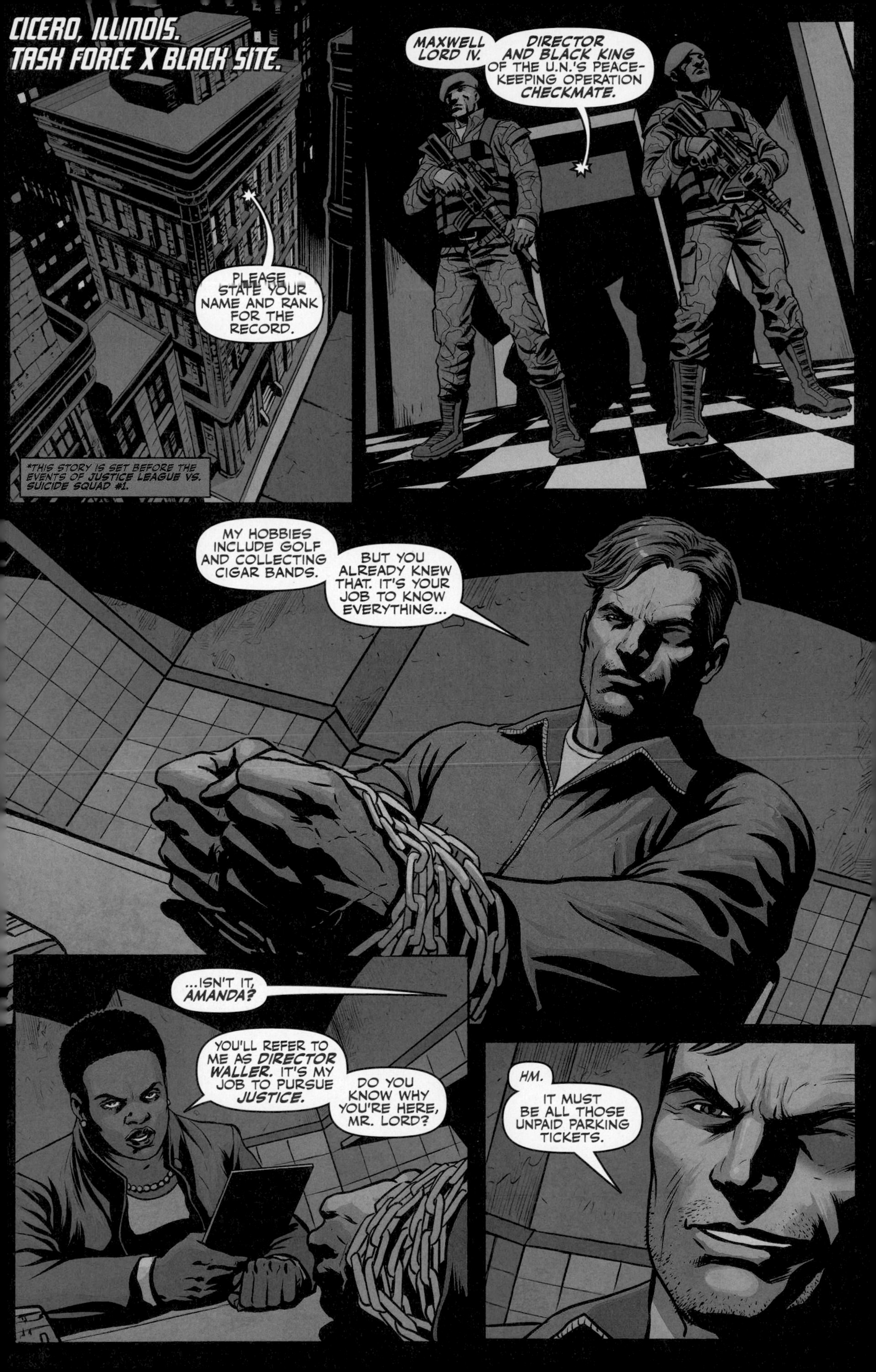
CICERO, ILLINOIS.
TASK FORCE X BLACK SITE.
PLEASE STATE YOUR NAME AND RANK FOR THE RECORD.
*THIS STORY IS SET BEFORE THE EVENTS OF JUSTICE LEAGUE VS. SUICIDE SQUAD #1.
MAXWELL LORD IV.
DIRECTOR AND BLACK KING OF THE U.N.'S PEACE-KEEPING OPERATION CHECKMATE.
MY HOBBIES INCLUDE GOLF AND COLLECTING CIGAR BANDS.
BUT YOU ALREADY KNEW THAT. IT'S YOUR JOB TO KNOW EVERYTHING...
...ISN'T IT, AMANDA?
YOU'LL REFER TO ME AS DIRECTOR WALLER. IT'S MY JOB TO PURSUE JUSTICE.
DO YOU KNOW WHY YOU'RE HERE, MR. LORD?
HM.
IT MUST BE ALL THOSE UNPAID PARKING TICKETS.

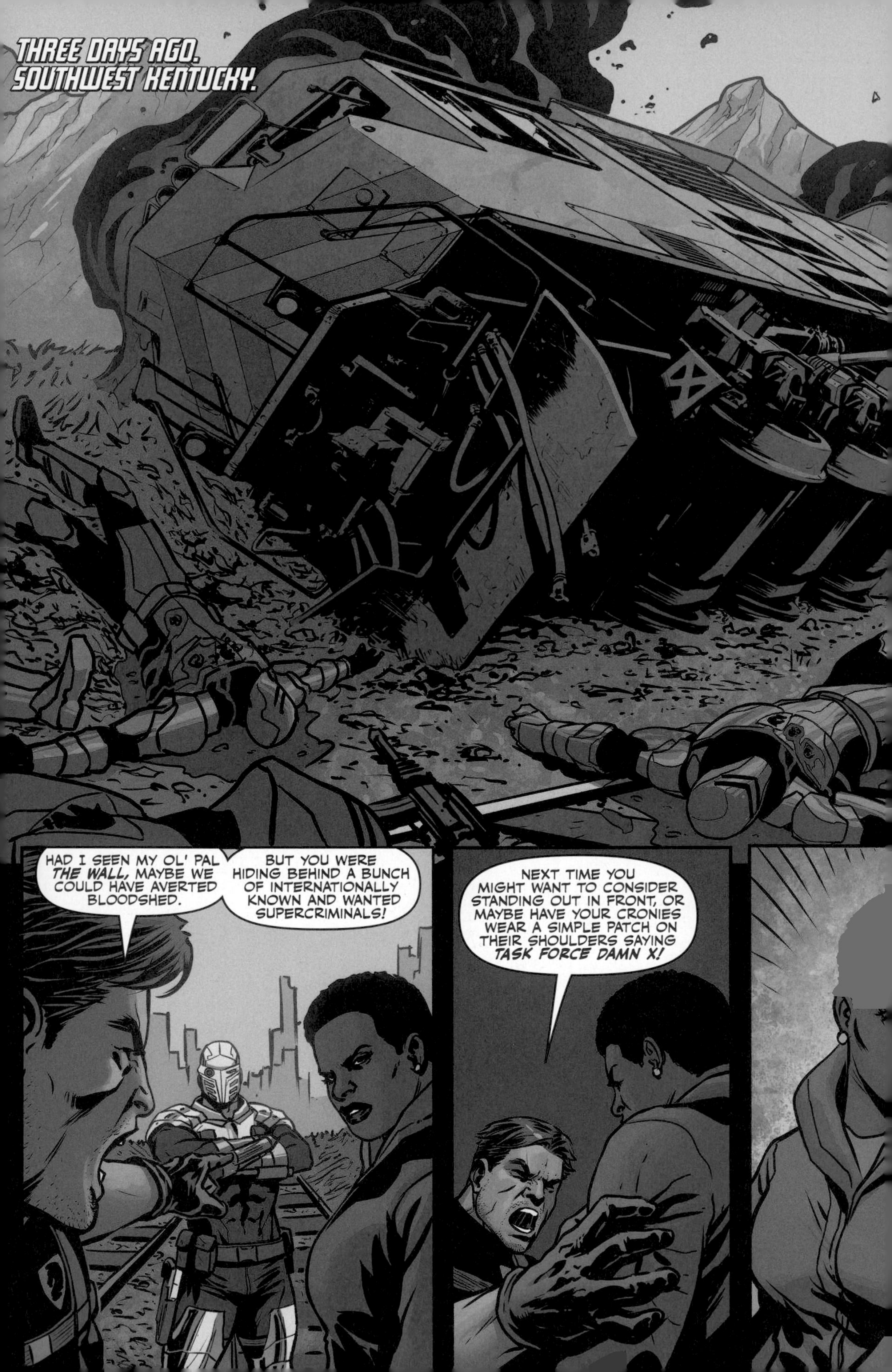
THREE DAYS AGO. SOUTHWEST KENTUCKY.
HAD I SEEN MY OL' PAL THE WALL, MAYBE WE COULD HAVE AVERTED BLOODSHED.
BUT YOU WERE HIDING BEHIND A BUNCH OF INTERNATIONALLY KNOWN AND WANTED SUPERCRIMINALS!
NEXT TIME YOU MIGHT WANT TO CONSIDER STANDING OUT IN FRONT, OR MAYBE HAVE YOUR CRONIES WEAR A SIMPLE PATCH ON THEIR SHOULDERS SAYING TASK FORCE DAMN X!

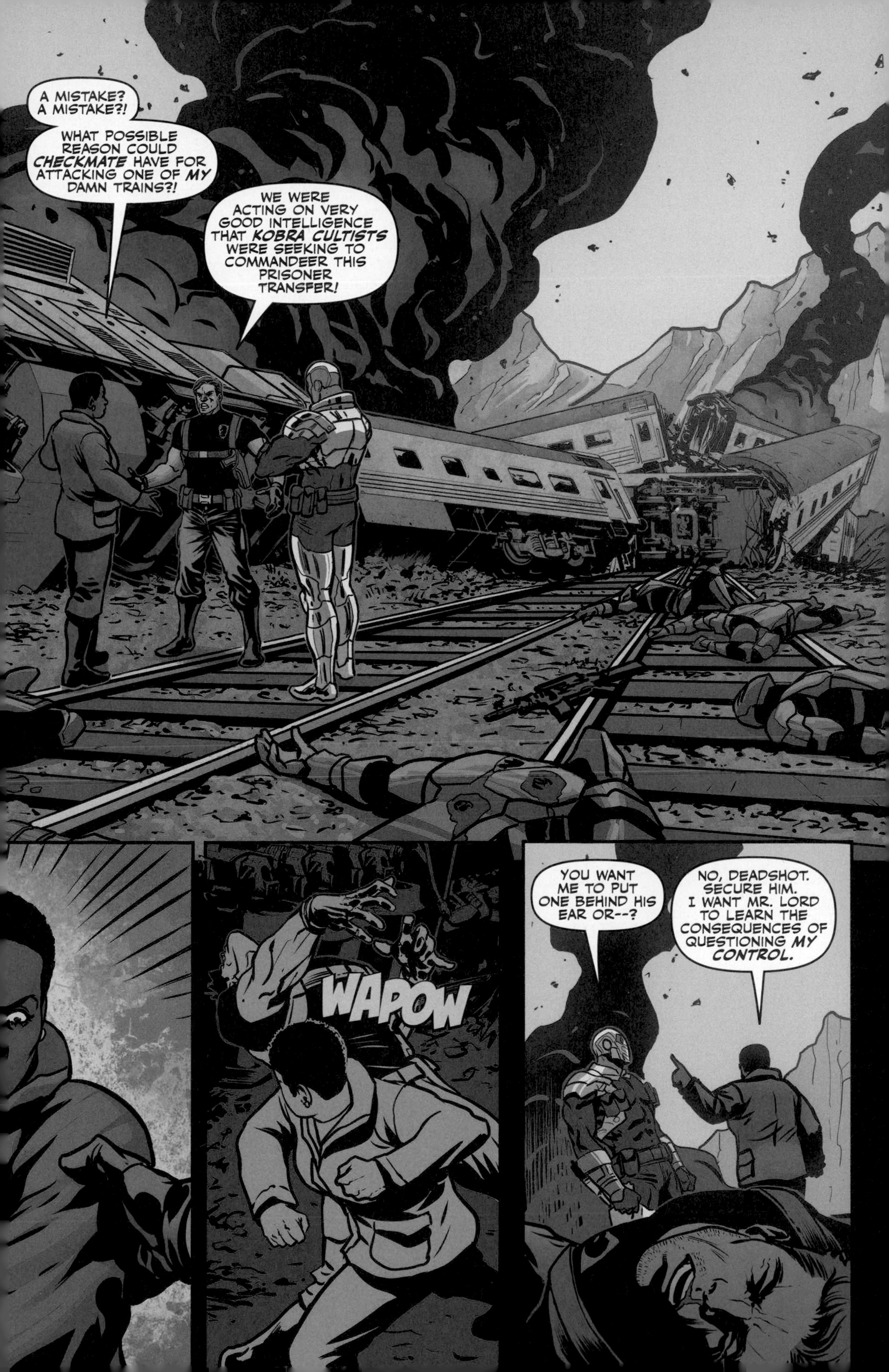
A MISTAKE? A MISTAKE?!
WHAT POSSIBLE REASON COULD CHECKMATE HAVE FOR ATTACKING ONE OF MY DAMN TRAINS?!
WE WERE ACTING ON VERY GOOD INTELLIGENCE THAT KOBRA CULTISTS WERE SEEKING TO COMMANDEER THIS PRISONER TRANSFER!
WAPOW
YOU WANT ME TO PUT ONE BEHIND HIS EAR OR--?
NO, DEADSHOT. SECURE HIM. I WANT MR. LORD TO LEARN THE CONSEQUENCES OF QUESTIONING MY CONTROL.

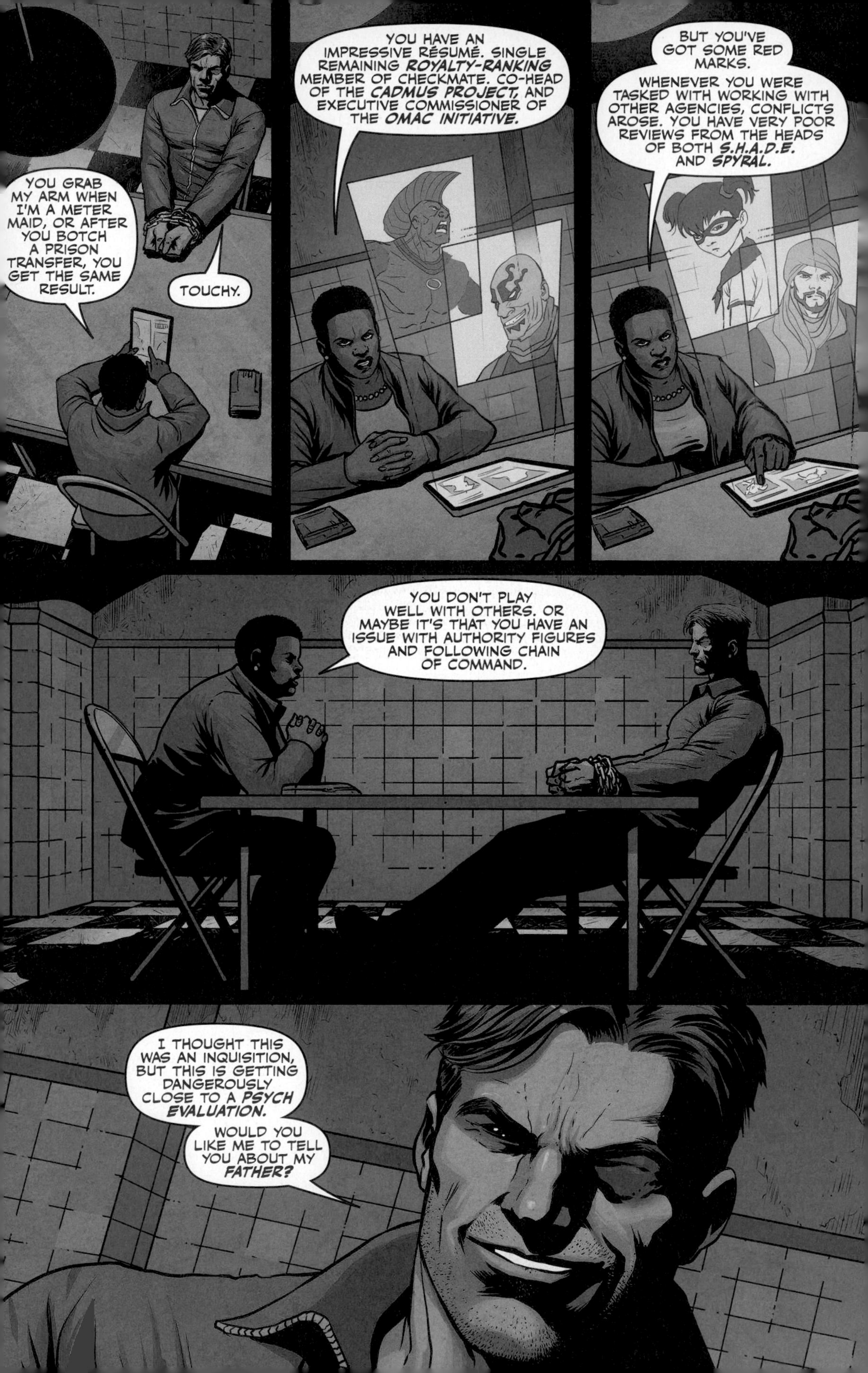
YOU GRAB MY ARM WHEN I'M A METER MAID, OR AFTER YOU BOTCH A PRISON TRANSFER, YOU GET THE SAME RESULT.
TOUCHY.
YOU HAVE AN IMPRESSIVE RÉSUMÉ. SINGLE REMAINING ROYALTY-RANKING MEMBER OF CHECKMATE. CO-HEAD OF THE CADMUS PROJECT, AND EXECUTIVE COMMISSIONER OF THE OMAC INITIATIVE.
BUT YOU'VE GOT SOME RED MARKS.
WHENEVER YOU WERE TASKED WITH WORKING WITH OTHER AGENCIES, CONFLICTS AROSE. YOU HAVE VERY POOR REVIEWS FROM THE HEADS OF BOTH S.H.A.D.E. AND SPYRAL.
YOU DON'T PLAY WELL WITH OTHERS. OR MAYBE IT'S THAT YOU HAVE AN ISSUE WITH AUTHORITY FIGURES AND FOLLOWING CHAIN OF COMMAND.
I THOUGHT THIS WAS AN INQUISITION, BUT THIS IS GETTING DANGEROUSLY CLOSE TO A PSYCH EVALUATION.
WOULD YOU LIKE ME TO TELL YOU ABOUT MY FATHER?

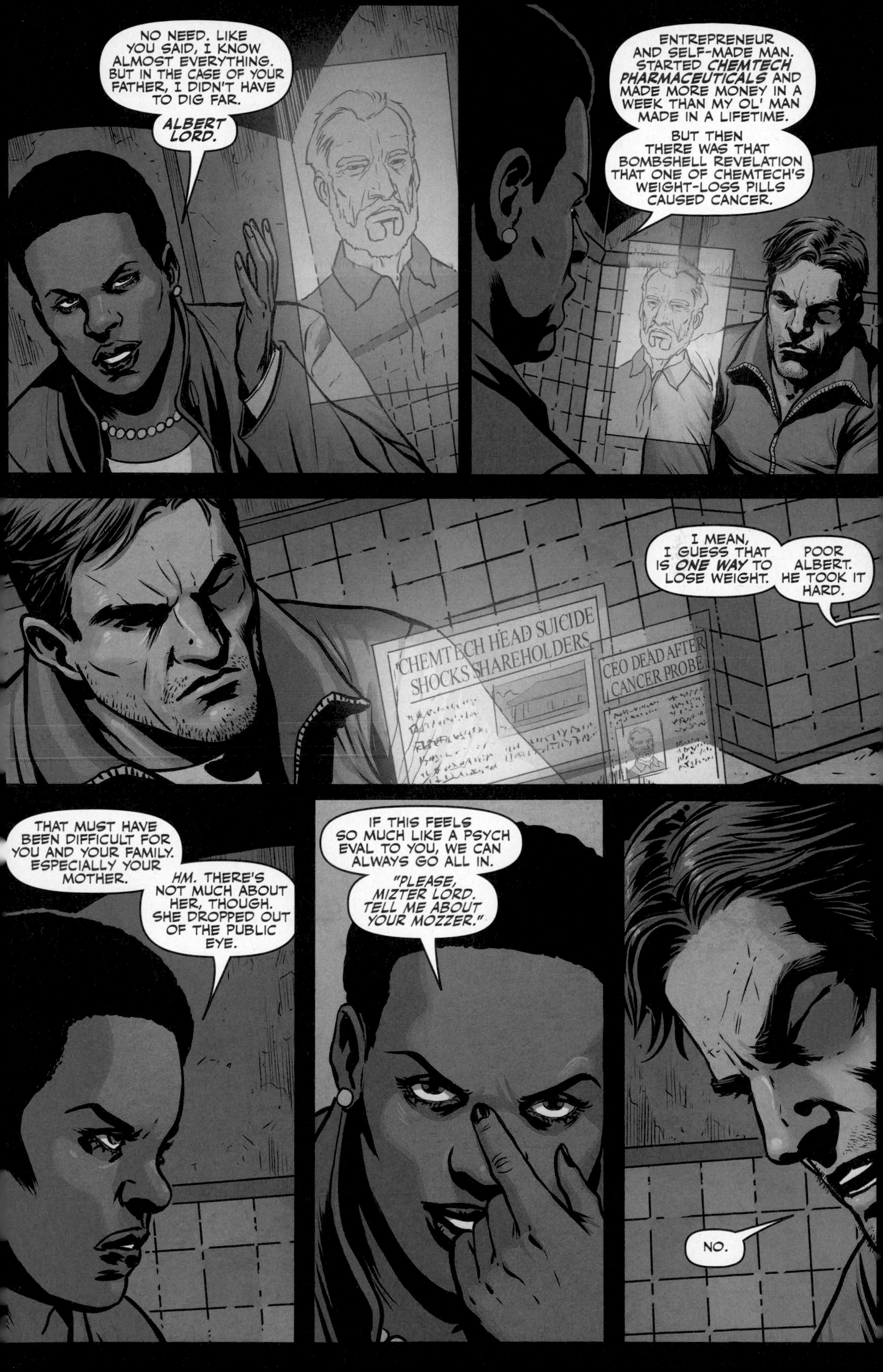
NO NEED. LIKE YOU SAID, I KNOW ALMOST EVERYTHING. BUT IN THE CASE OF YOUR FATHER, I DIDN'T HAVE TO DIG FAR.
ALBERT LORD.
ENTREPRENEUR AND SELF-MADE MAN. STARTED CHEMTECH PHARMACEUTICALS AND MADE MORE MONEY IN A WEEK THAN MY OL' MAN MADE IN A LIFETIME.
BUT THEN THERE WAS THAT BOMBSHELL REVELATION THAT ONE OF CHEMTECH'S WEIGHT-LOSS PILLS CAUSED CANCER.
CHEMTECH HEAD SUICIDE SHOCKS SHAREHOLDERS
CEO DEAD AFTER CANCER PROBE
I MEAN, I GUESS THAT IS ONE WAY TO LOSE WEIGHT.
POOR ALBERT. HE TOOK IT HARD.
THAT MUST HAVE BEEN DIFFICULT FOR YOU AND YOUR FAMILY. ESPECIALLY YOUR MOTHER.
HM. THERE'S NOT MUCH ABOUT HER, THOUGH. SHE DROPPED OUT OF THE PUBLIC EYE.
IF THIS FEELS SO MUCH LIKE A PSYCH EVAL TO YOU, WE CAN ALWAYS GO ALL IN.
"PLEASE, MIZTER LORD. TELL ME ABOUT YOUR MOZZER."
NO.

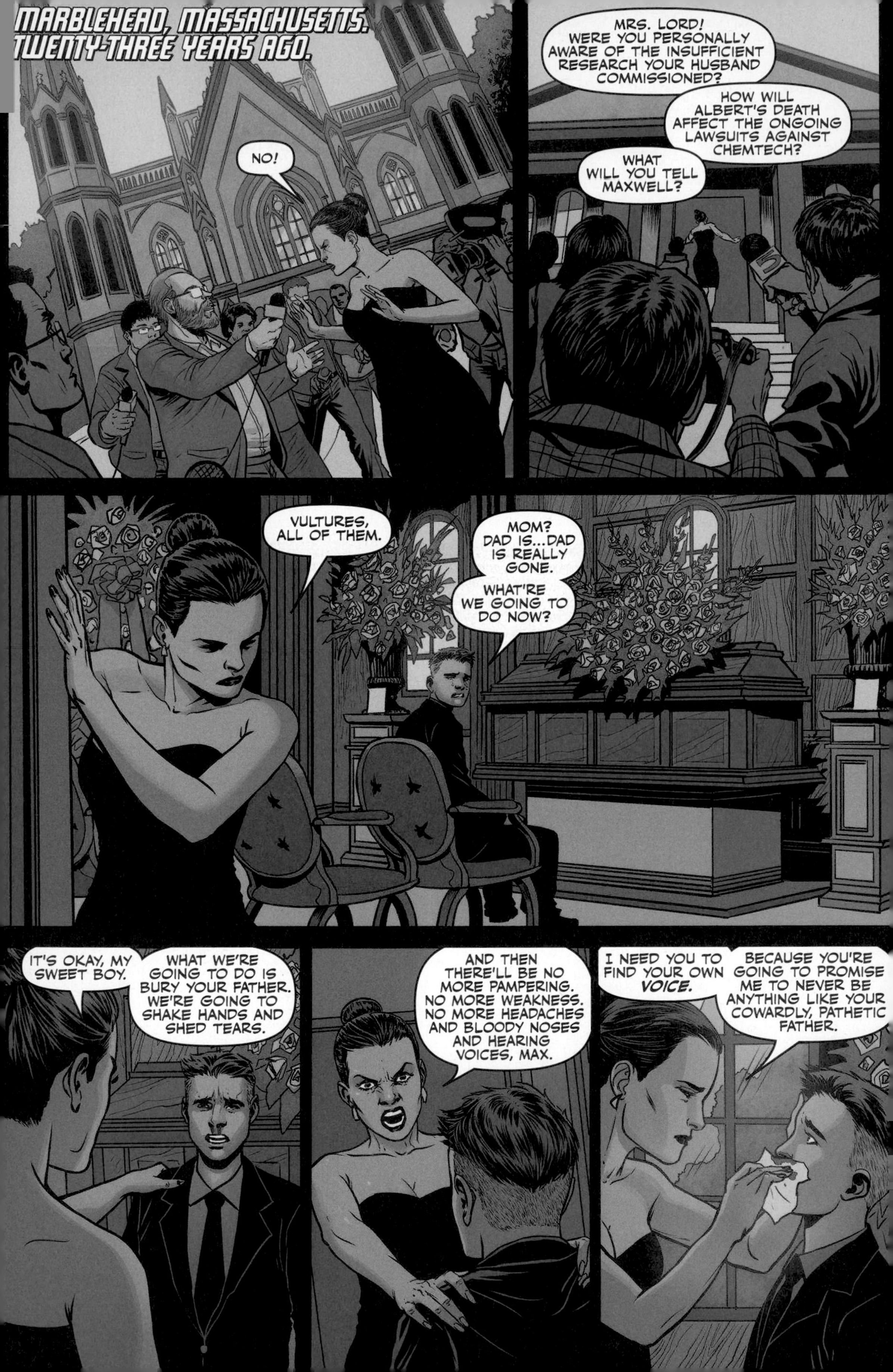

MARBLEHEAD, MASSACHUSETTS. TWENTY-THREE YEARS AGO.
NO!
MRS. LORD! WERE YOU PERSONALLY AWARE OF THE INSUFFICIENT RESEARCH YOUR HUSBAND COMMISSIONED?
HOW WILL ALBERT'S DEATH AFFECT THE ONGOING LAWSUITS AGAINST CHEMTECH?
WHAT WILL YOU TELL MAXWELL?
VULTURES, ALL OF THEM.
MOM? DAD IS...DAD IS REALLY GONE.
WHAT'RE WE GOING TO DO NOW?
IT'S OKAY, MY SWEET BOY.
WHAT WE'RE GOING TO DO IS BURY YOUR FATHER. WE'RE GOING TO SHAKE HANDS AND SHED TEARS.
AND THEN THERE'LL BE NO MORE PAMPERING. NO MORE WEAKNESS. NO MORE HEADACHES AND BLOODY NOSES AND HEARING VOICES, MAX.
I NEED YOU TO FIND YOUR OWN VOICE.
BECAUSE YOU'RE GOING TO PROMISE ME TO NEVER BE ANYTHING LIKE YOUR COWARDLY, PATHETIC FATHER.

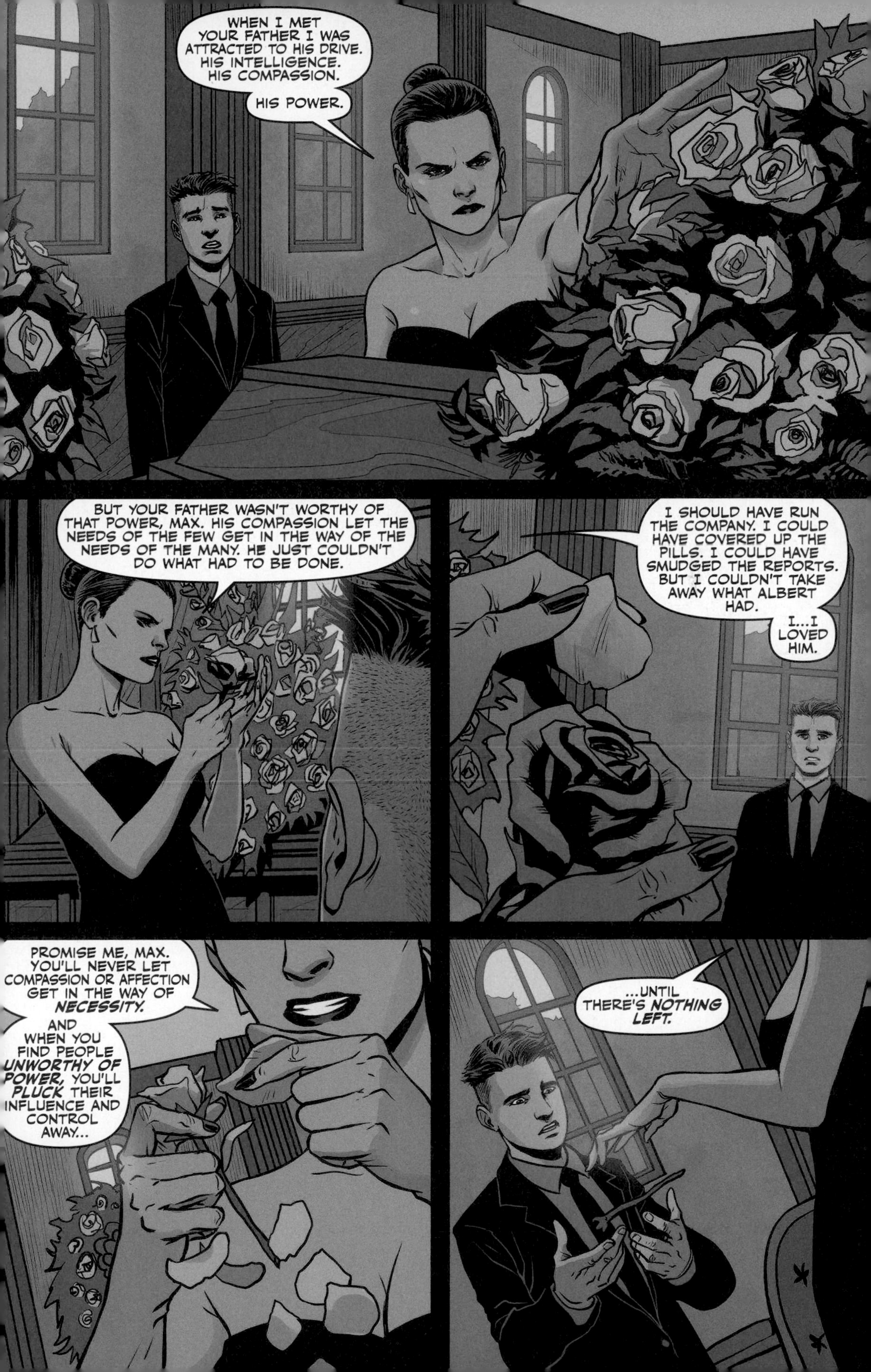
WHEN I MET YOUR FATHER I WAS ATTRACTED TO HIS DRIVE. HIS INTELLIGENCE. HIS COMPASSION.
HIS POWER.
BUT YOUR FATHER WASN'T WORTHY OF THAT POWER, MAX. HIS COMPASSION LET THE NEEDS OF THE FEW GET IN THE WAY OF THE NEEDS OF THE MANY. HE JUST COULDN'T DO WHAT HAD TO BE DONE.
I SHOULD HAVE RUN THE COMPANY. I COULD HAVE COVERED UP THE PILLS. I COULD HAVE SMUDGED THE REPORTS. BUT I COULDN'T TAKE AWAY WHAT ALBERT HAD.
I...I LOVED HIM.
PROMISE ME, MAX. YOU'LL NEVER LET COMPASSION OR AFFECTION GET IN THE WAY OF *NECESSITY.*
AND WHEN YOU FIND PEOPLE *UNWORTHY OF POWER,* YOU'LL *PLUCK* THEIR INFLUENCE AND CONTROL AWAY...
...UNTIL THERE'S *NOTHING LEFT.*

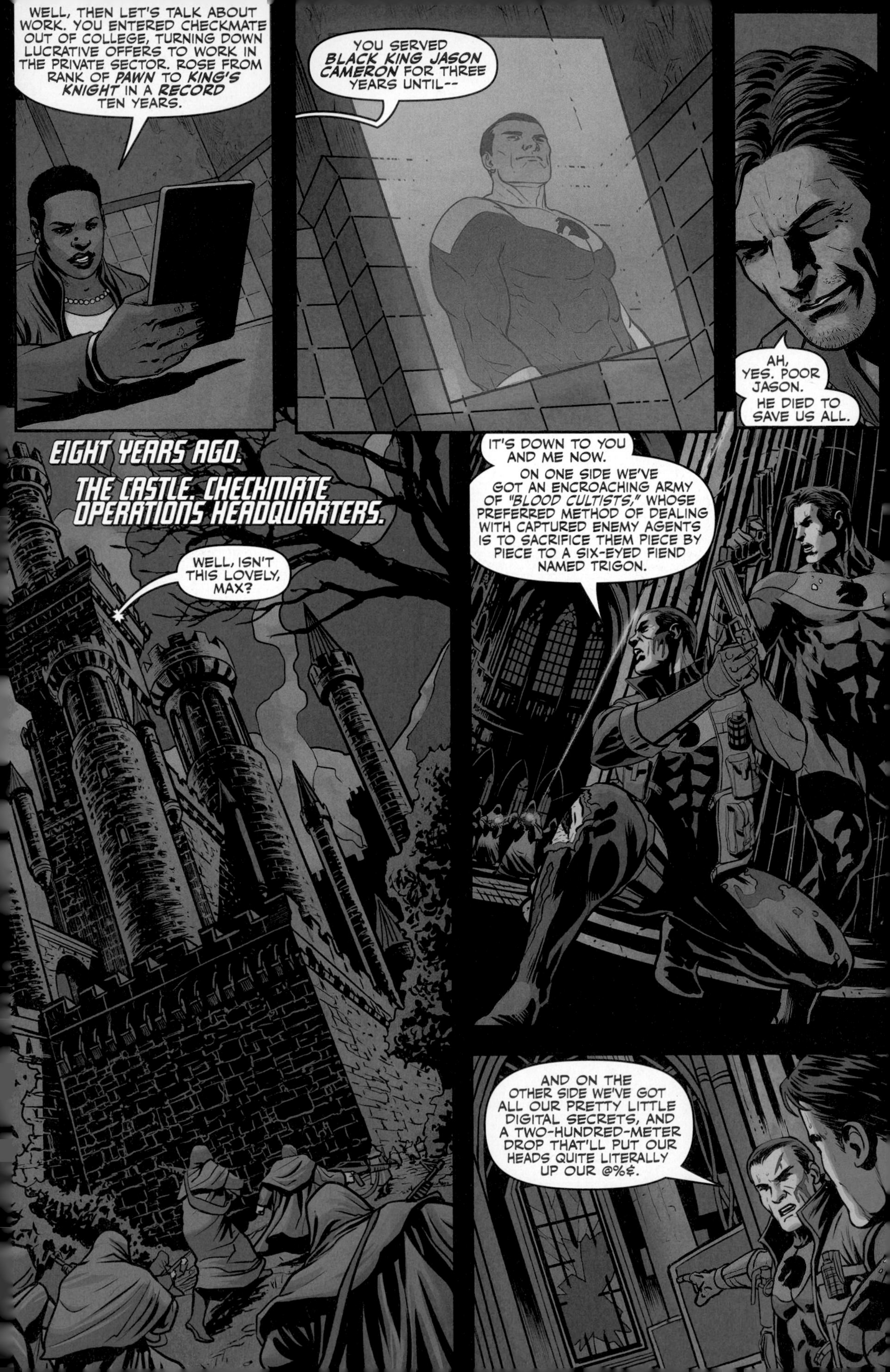

WELL, THEN LET'S TALK ABOUT WORK. YOU ENTERED CHECKMATE OUT OF COLLEGE, TURNING DOWN LUCRATIVE OFFERS TO WORK IN THE PRIVATE SECTOR. ROSE FROM RANK OF *PAWN* TO *KING'S KNIGHT* IN A *RECORD* TEN YEARS.
YOU SERVED *BLACK KING JASON CAMERON* FOR THREE YEARS UNTIL--
AH, YES. POOR JASON.
HE DIED TO SAVE US ALL.
EIGHT YEARS AGO.
THE CASTLE. CHECKMATE OPERATIONS HEADQUARTERS.
WELL, ISN'T THIS LOVELY, MAX?
IT'S DOWN TO YOU AND ME NOW.
ON ONE SIDE WE'VE GOT AN ENCROACHING ARMY OF *"BLOOD CULTISTS,"* WHOSE PREFERRED METHOD OF DEALING WITH CAPTURED ENEMY AGENTS IS TO SACRIFICE THEM PIECE BY PIECE TO A SIX-EYED FIEND NAMED TRIGON.
AND ON THE OTHER SIDE WE'VE GOT ALL OUR PRETTY LITTLE DIGITAL SECRETS, AND A TWO-HUNDRED-METER DROP THAT'LL PUT OUR HEADS QUITE LITERALLY UP OUR @%¢.

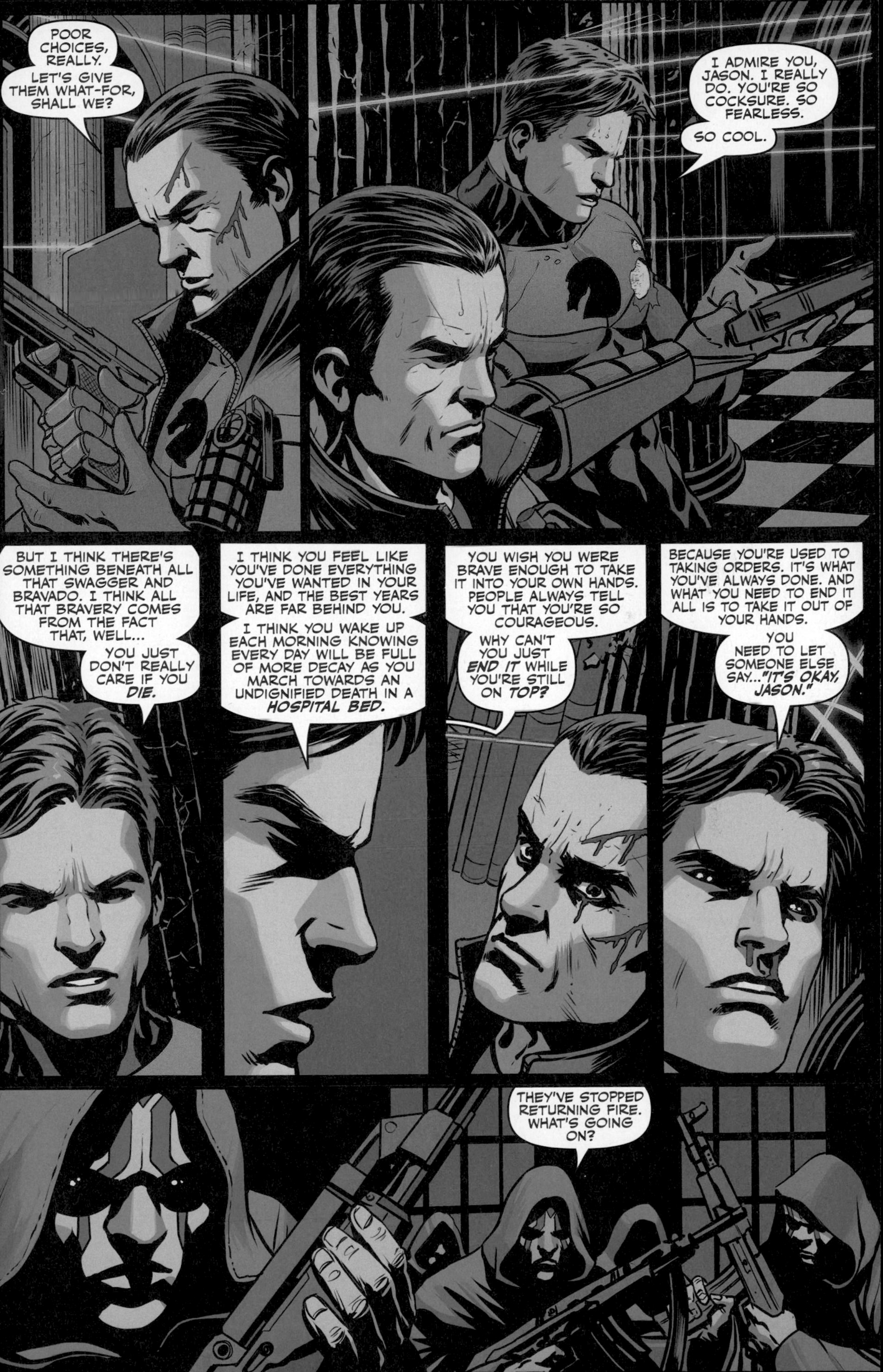
POOR CHOICES, REALLY.
LET'S GIVE THEM WHAT-FOR, SHALL WE?
I ADMIRE YOU, JASON. I REALLY DO. YOU'RE SO COCKSURE. SO FEARLESS.
SO COOL.
BUT I THINK THERE'S SOMETHING BENEATH ALL THAT SWAGGER AND BRAVADO. I THINK ALL THAT BRAVERY COMES FROM THE FACT THAT, WELL...
YOU JUST DON'T REALLY CARE IF YOU DIE.
I THINK YOU FEEL LIKE YOU'VE DONE EVERYTHING YOU'VE WANTED IN YOUR LIFE, AND THE BEST YEARS ARE FAR BEHIND YOU.
I THINK YOU WAKE UP EACH MORNING KNOWING EVERY DAY WILL BE FULL OF MORE DECAY AS YOU MARCH TOWARDS AN UNDIGNIFIED DEATH IN A HOSPITAL BED.
YOU WISH YOU WERE BRAVE ENOUGH TO TAKE IT INTO YOUR OWN HANDS. PEOPLE ALWAYS TELL YOU THAT YOU'RE SO COURAGEOUS.
WHY CAN'T YOU JUST END IT WHILE YOU'RE STILL ON TOP?
BECAUSE YOU'RE USED TO TAKING ORDERS. IT'S WHAT YOU'VE ALWAYS DONE. AND WHAT YOU NEED TO END IT ALL IS TO TAKE IT OUT OF YOUR HANDS.
YOU NEED TO LET SOMEONE ELSE SAY..."IT'S OKAY, JASON."
THEY'VE STOPPED RETURNING FIRE. WHAT'S GOING ON?

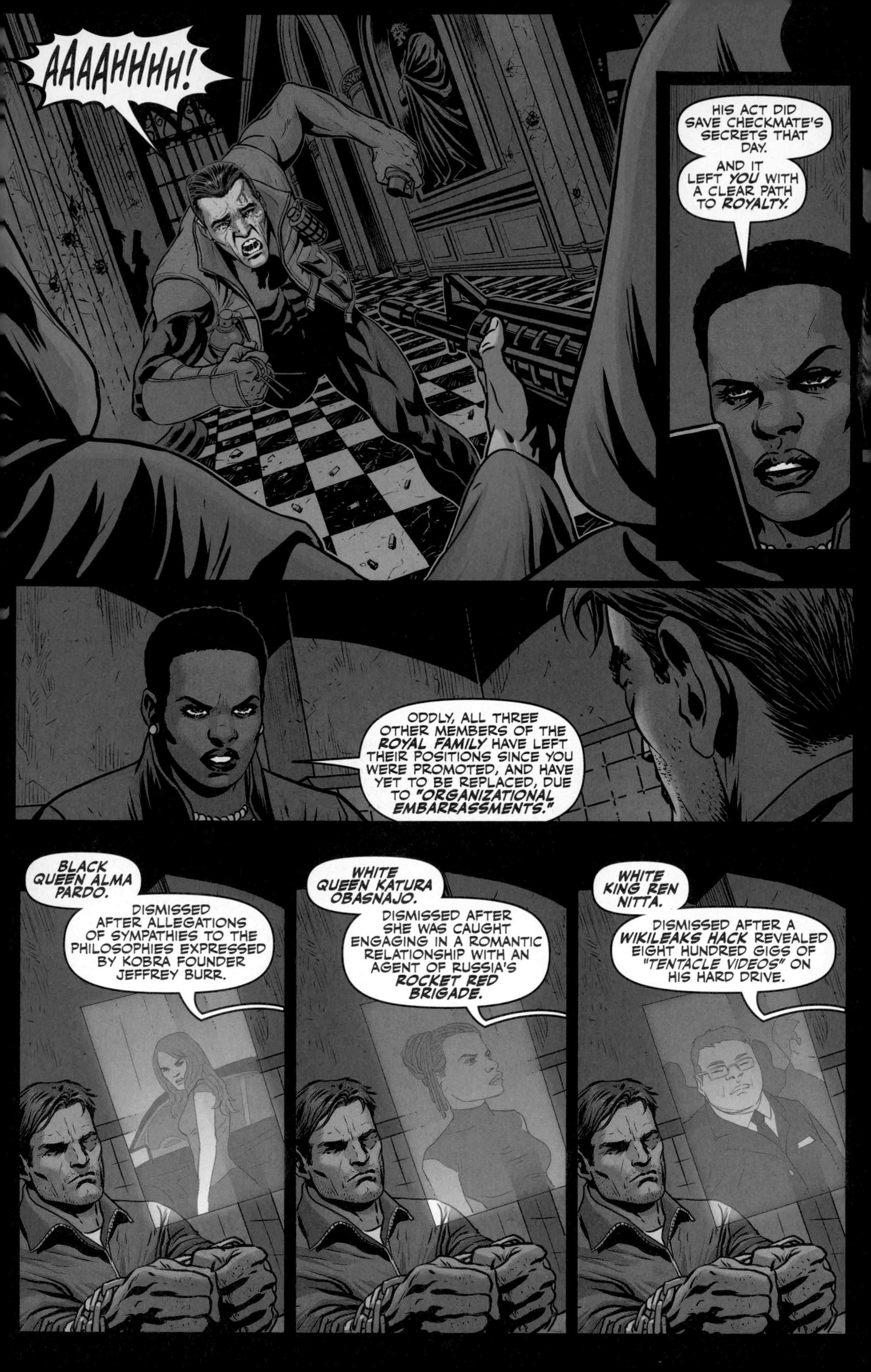
AAAAHHHH!
HIS ACT DID SAVE CHECKMATE'S SECRETS THAT DAY.
AND IT LEFT YOU WITH A CLEAR PATH TO ROYALTY.
ODDLY, ALL THREE OTHER MEMBERS OF THE ROYAL FAMILY HAVE LEFT THEIR POSITIONS SINCE YOU WERE PROMOTED, AND HAVE YET TO BE REPLACED, DUE TO "ORGANIZATIONAL EMBARRASSMENTS."
BLACK QUEEN ALMA PARDO.
DISMISSED AFTER ALLEGATIONS OF SYMPATHIES TO THE PHILOSOPHIES EXPRESSED BY KOBRA FOUNDER JEFFREY BURR.
WHITE QUEEN KATURA OBASNAJO.
DISMISSED AFTER SHE WAS CAUGHT ENGAGING IN A ROMANTIC RELATIONSHIP WITH AN AGENT OF RUSSIA'S ROCKET RED BRIGADE.
WHITE KING REN NITTA.
DISMISSED AFTER A WIKILEAKS HACK REVEALED EIGHT HUNDRED GIGS OF "TENTACLE VIDEOS" ON HIS HARD DRIVE.

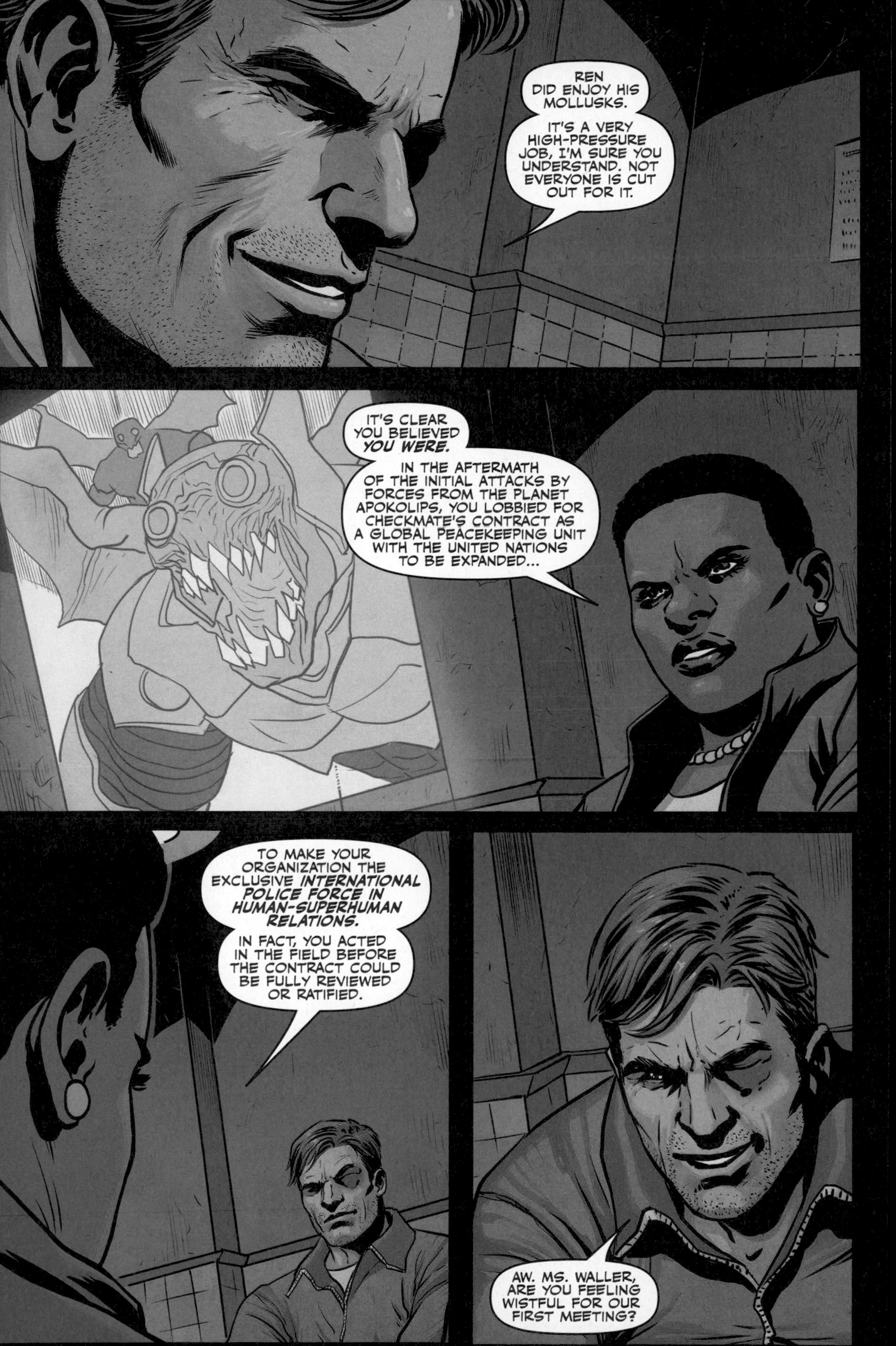
REN DID ENJOY HIS MOLLUSKS.
IT'S A VERY HIGH-PRESSURE JOB, I'M SURE YOU UNDERSTAND. NOT EVERYONE IS CUT OUT FOR IT.
IT'S CLEAR YOU BELIEVED *YOU WERE.*
IN THE AFTERMATH OF THE INITIAL ATTACKS BY FORCES FROM THE PLANET APOKOLIPS, YOU LOBBIED FOR CHECKMATE'S CONTRACT AS A GLOBAL PEACEKEEPING UNIT WITH THE UNITED NATIONS TO BE EXPANDED...
TO MAKE YOUR ORGANIZATION THE EXCLUSIVE *INTERNATIONAL POLICE FORCE IN HUMAN-SUPERHUMAN RELATIONS.*
IN FACT, YOU ACTED IN THE FIELD BEFORE THE CONTRACT COULD BE FULLY REVIEWED OR RATIFIED.
AW. MS. WALLER, ARE YOU FEELING WISTFUL FOR OUR FIRST MEETING?

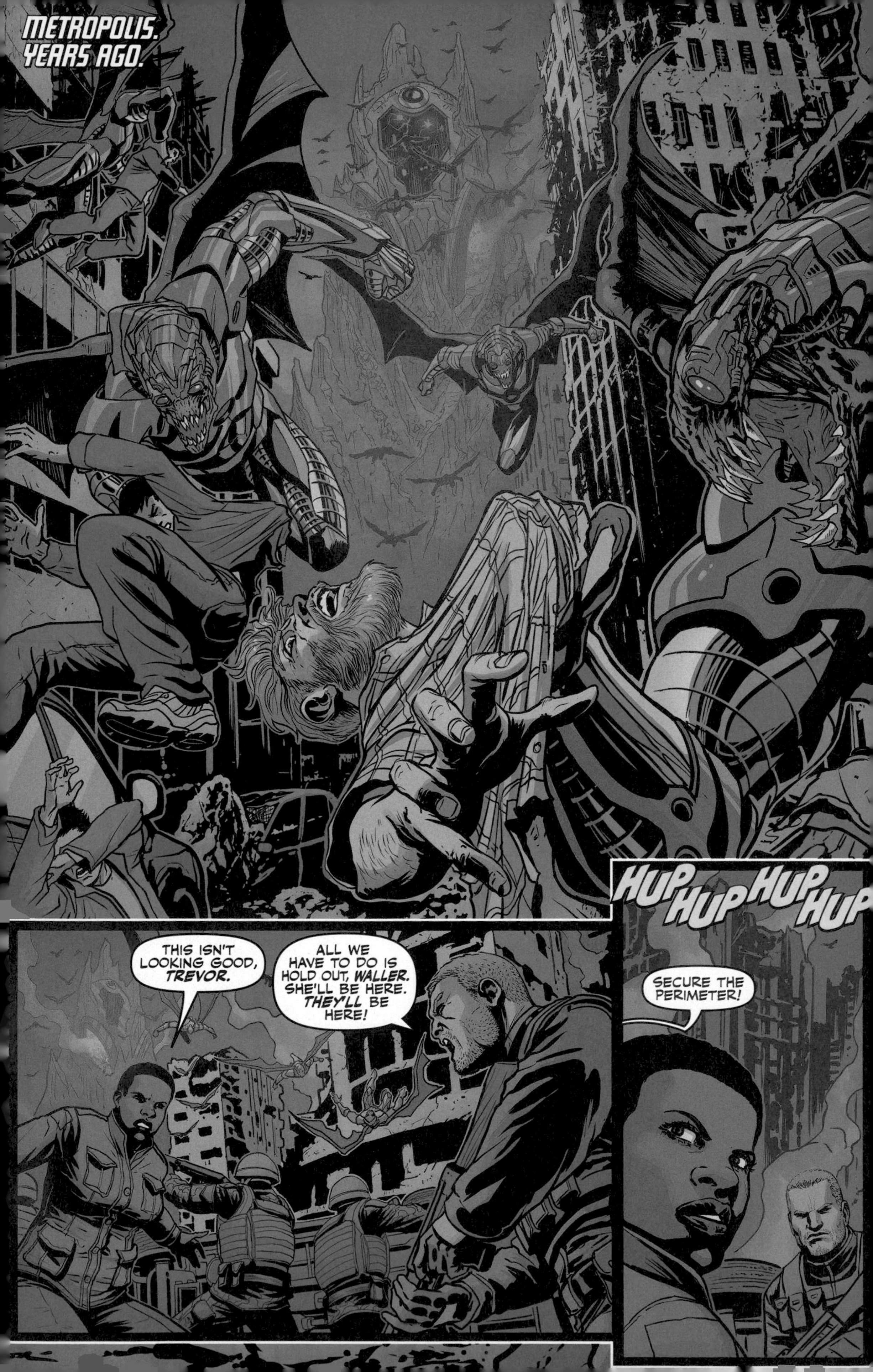
METROPOLIS. YEARS AGO.
HUP HUP HUP HUP
THIS ISN'T LOOKING GOOD, TREVOR.
ALL WE HAVE TO DO IS HOLD OUT, WALLER. SHE'LL BE HERE. THEY'LL BE HERE!
SECURE THE PERIMETER!

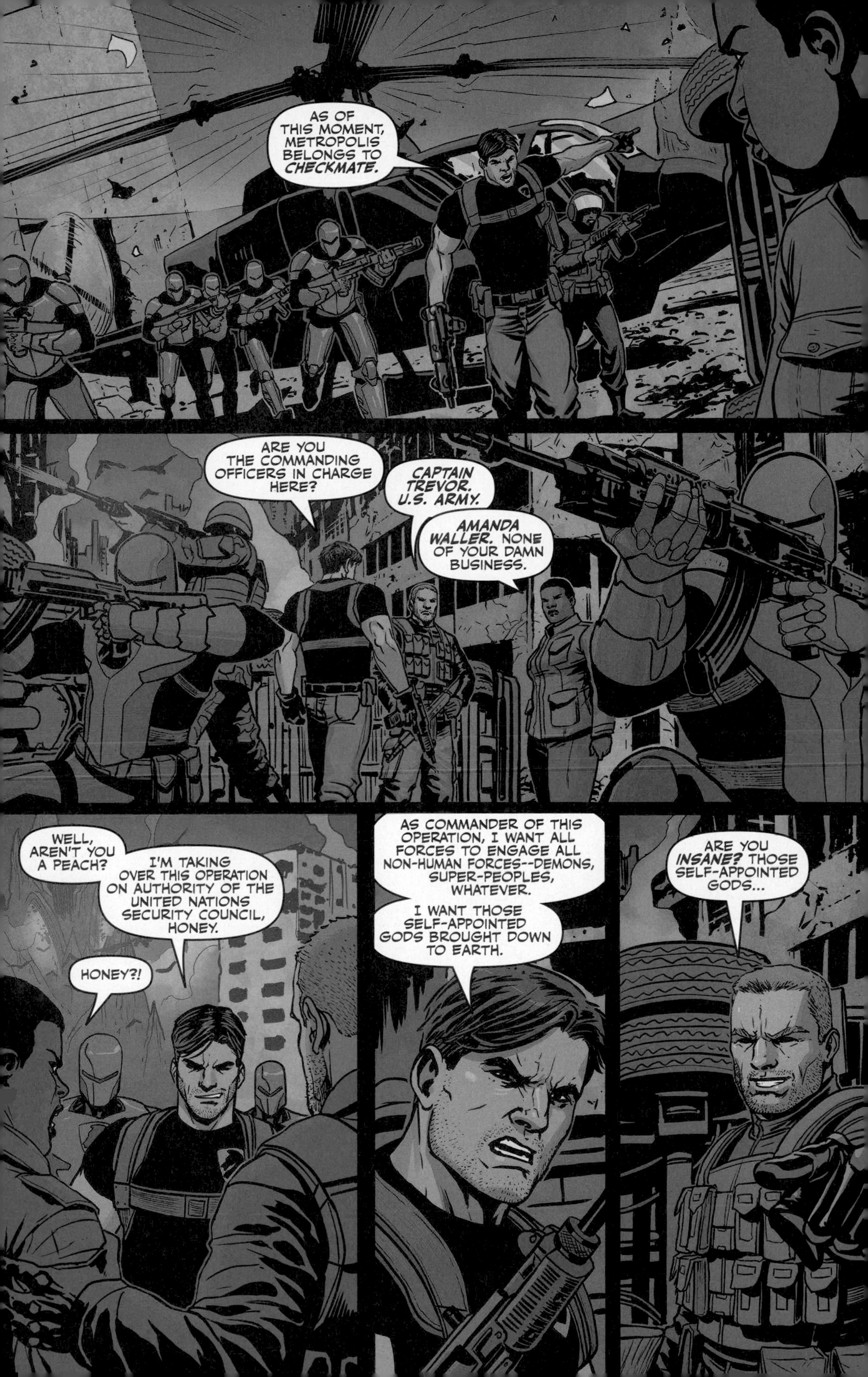
AS OF THIS MOMENT, METROPOLIS BELONGS TO CHECKMATE.
ARE YOU THE COMMANDING OFFICERS IN CHARGE HERE?
CAPTAIN TREVOR. U.S. ARMY.
AMANDA WALLER. NONE OF YOUR DAMN BUSINESS.
WELL, AREN'T YOU A PEACH?
I'M TAKING OVER THIS OPERATION ON AUTHORITY OF THE UNITED NATIONS SECURITY COUNCIL, HONEY.
HONEY?!
AS COMMANDER OF THIS OPERATION, I WANT ALL FORCES TO ENGAGE ALL NON-HUMAN FORCES--DEMONS, SUPER-PEOPLES, WHATEVER.
I WANT THOSE SELF-APPOINTED GODS BROUGHT DOWN TO EARTH.
ARE YOU INSANE? THOSE SELF-APPOINTED GODS...

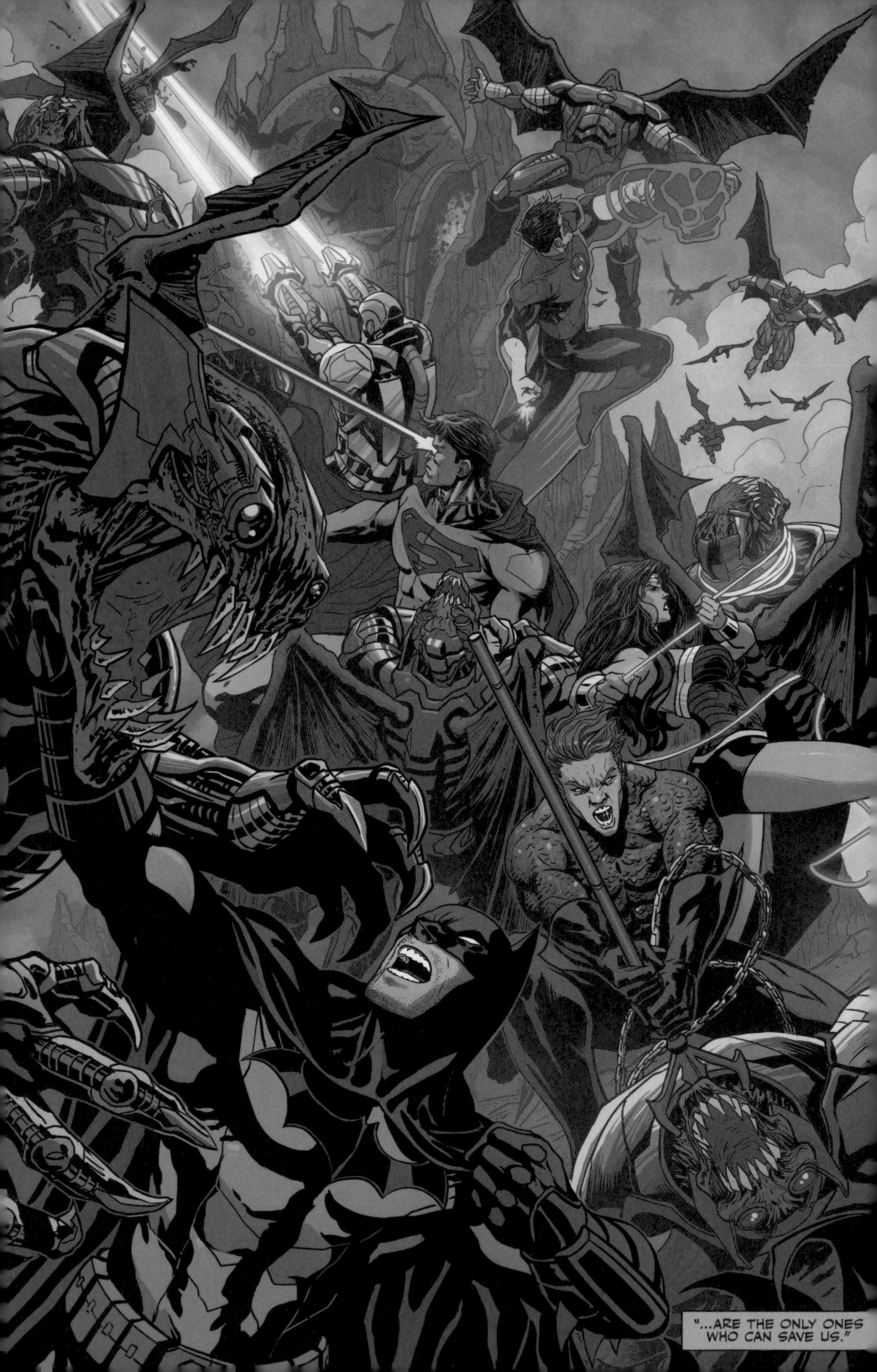
"...ARE THE ONLY ONES WHO CAN SAVE US."

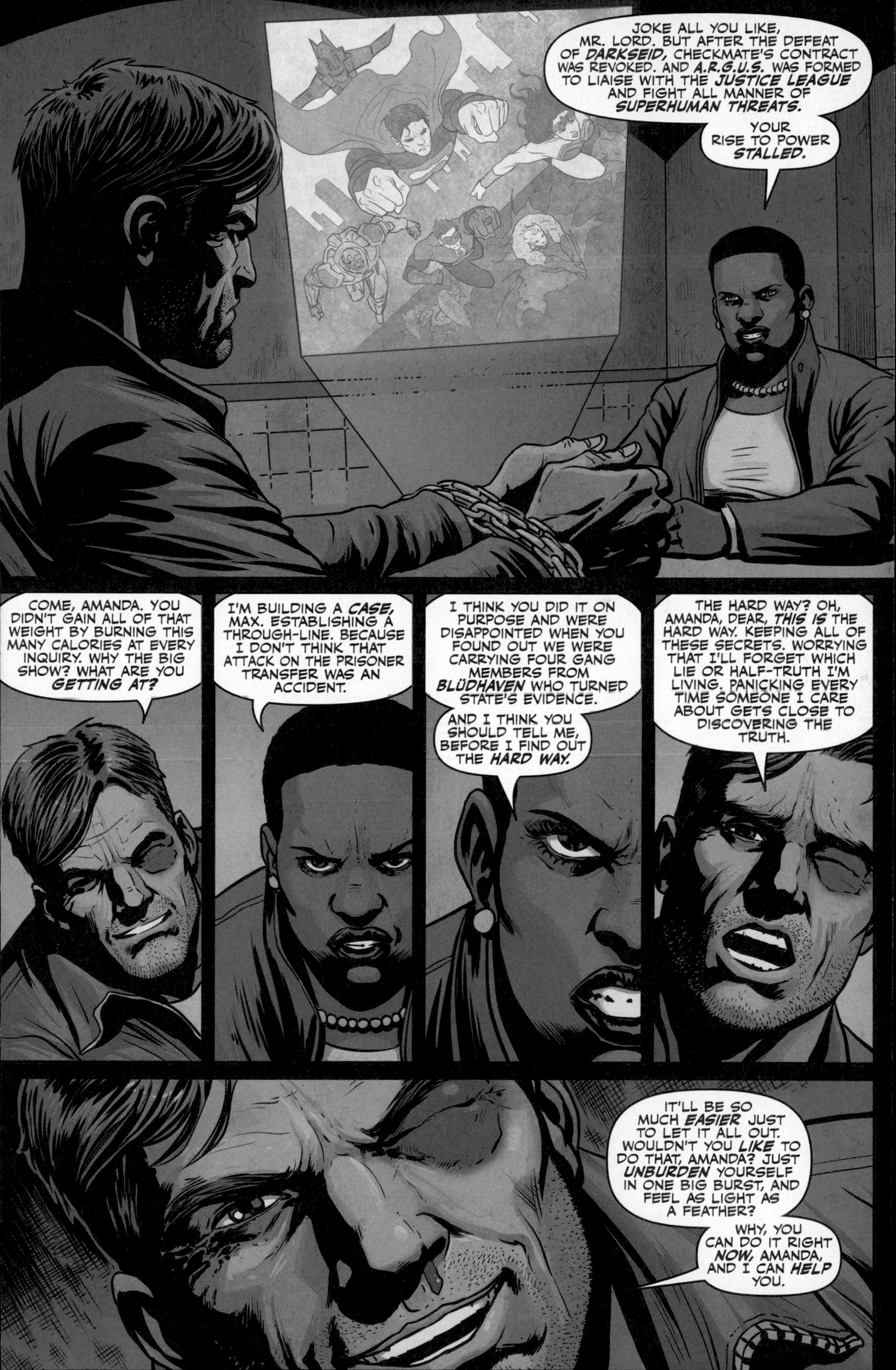

JOKE ALL YOU LIKE, MR. LORD. BUT AFTER THE DEFEAT OF DARKSEID, CHECKMATE'S CONTRACT WAS REVOKED. AND A.R.G.U.S. WAS FORMED TO LIAISE WITH THE JUSTICE LEAGUE AND FIGHT ALL MANNER OF SUPERHUMAN THREATS.
YOUR RISE TO POWER STALLED.
COME, AMANDA. YOU DIDN'T GAIN ALL OF THAT WEIGHT BY BURNING THIS MANY CALORIES AT EVERY INQUIRY. WHY THE BIG SHOW? WHAT ARE YOU GETTING AT?
I'M BUILDING A CASE, MAX. ESTABLISHING A THROUGH-LINE. BECAUSE I DON'T THINK THAT ATTACK ON THE PRISONER TRANSFER WAS AN ACCIDENT.
I THINK YOU DID IT ON PURPOSE AND WERE DISAPPOINTED WHEN YOU FOUND OUT WE WERE CARRYING FOUR GANG MEMBERS FROM BLÜDHAVEN WHO TURNED STATE'S EVIDENCE.
AND I THINK YOU SHOULD TELL ME, BEFORE I FIND OUT THE HARD WAY.
THE HARD WAY? OH, AMANDA, DEAR, THIS IS THE HARD WAY. KEEPING ALL OF THESE SECRETS. WORRYING THAT I'LL FORGET WHICH LIE OR HALF-TRUTH I'M LIVING. PANICKING EVERY TIME SOMEONE I CARE ABOUT GETS CLOSE TO DISCOVERING THE TRUTH.
IT'LL BE SO MUCH EASIER JUST TO LET IT ALL OUT. WOULDN'T YOU LIKE TO DO THAT, AMANDA? JUST UNBURDEN YOURSELF IN ONE BIG BURST, AND FEEL AS LIGHT AS A FEATHER?
WHY, YOU CAN DO IT RIGHT NOW, AMANDA, AND I CAN HELP YOU.

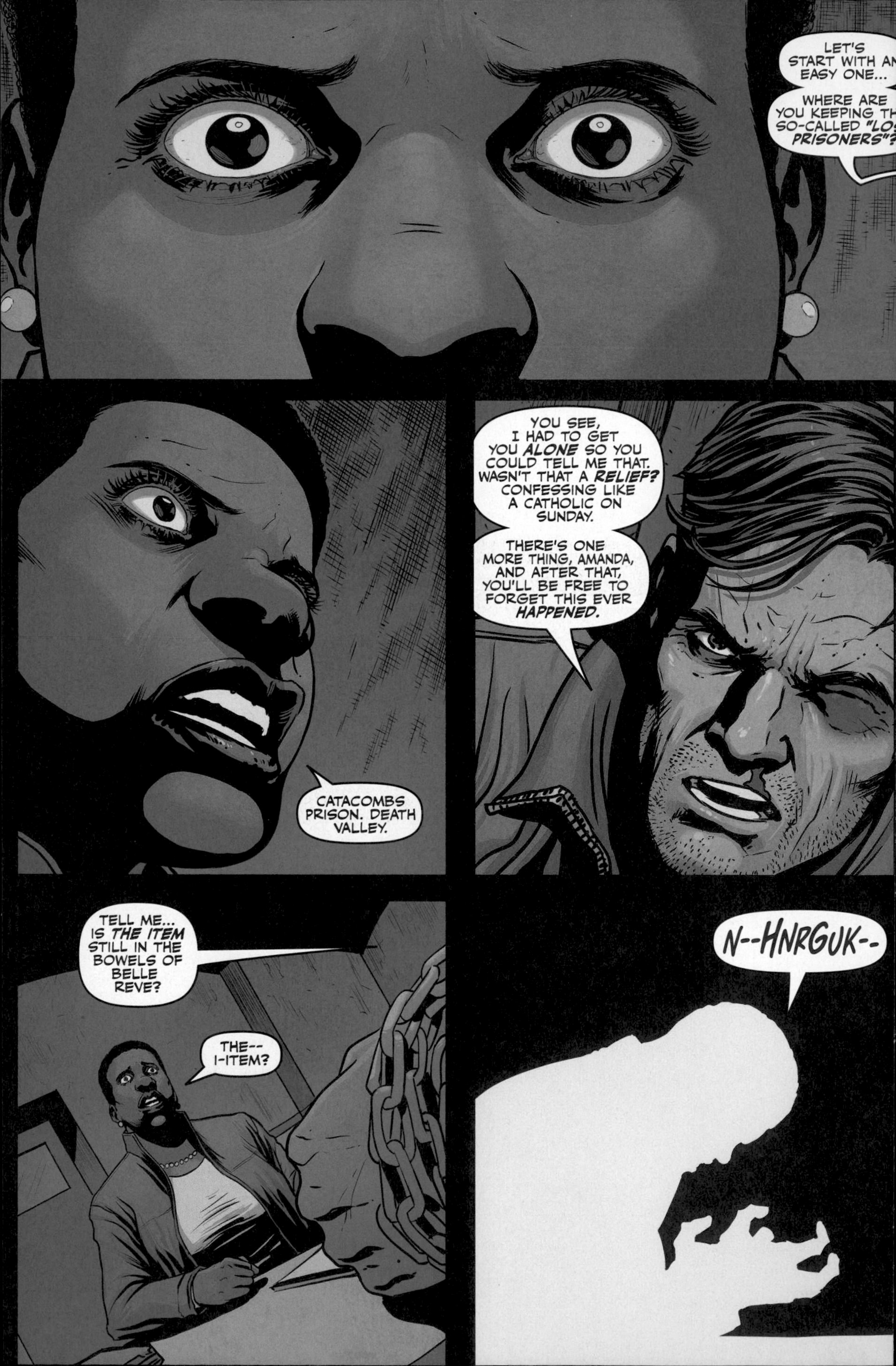
LET'S START WITH AN EASY ONE...
WHERE ARE YOU KEEPING TH SO-CALLED "LOS PRISONERS"?
CATACOMBS PRISON. DEATH VALLEY.
YOU SEE, I HAD TO GET YOU ALONE SO YOU COULD TELL ME THAT. WASN'T THAT A RELIEF? CONFESSING LIKE A CATHOLIC ON SUNDAY.
THERE'S ONE MORE THING, AMANDA, AND AFTER THAT, YOU'LL BE FREE TO FORGET THIS EVER HAPPENED.
TELL ME... IS THE ITEM STILL IN THE BOWELS OF BELLE REVE?
THE-- I-ITEM?
N--HNRGUK--

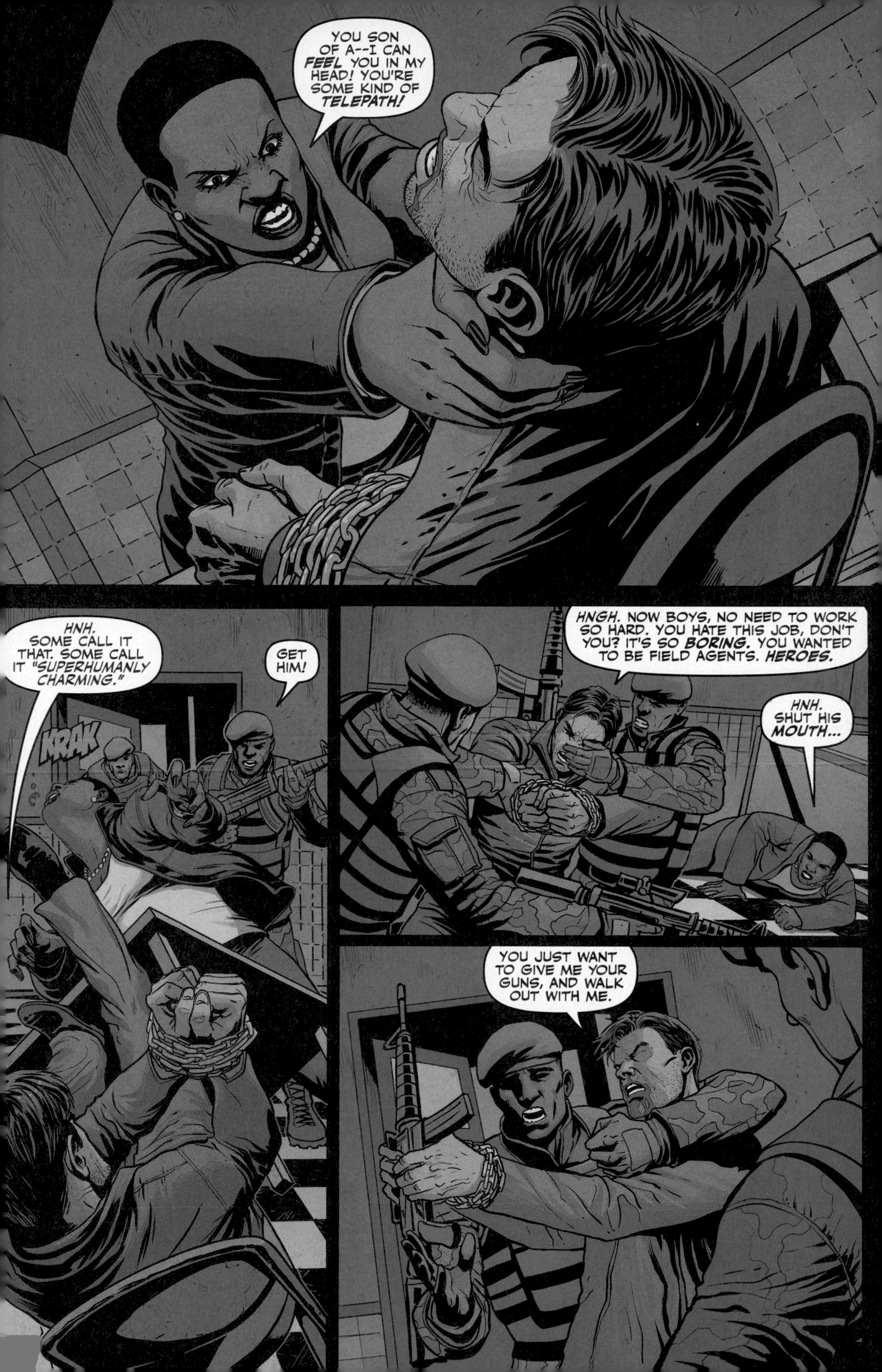
YOU SON OF A--I CAN FEEL YOU IN MY HEAD! YOU'RE SOME KIND OF TELEPATH!
HNH. SOME CALL IT THAT. SOME CALL IT "SUPERHUMANLY CHARMING."
KRAK
GET HIM!
HNGH. NOW BOYS, NO NEED TO WORK SO HARD. YOU HATE THIS JOB, DON'T YOU? IT'S SO BORING. YOU WANTED TO BE FIELD AGENTS. HEROES.
HNH. SHUT HIS MOUTH...
YOU JUST WANT TO GIVE ME YOUR GUNS, AND WALK OUT WITH ME.

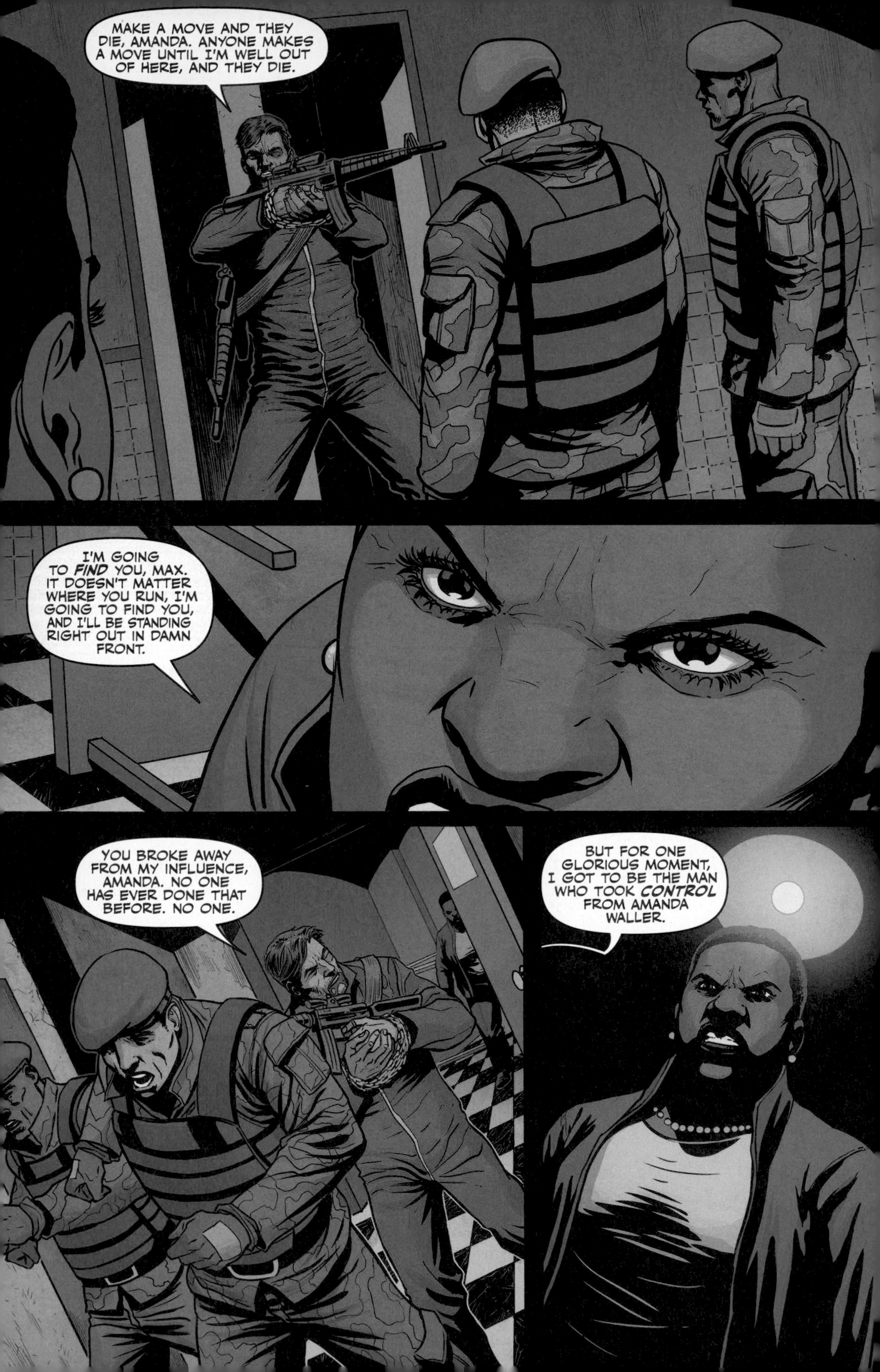
MAKE A MOVE AND THEY DIE, AMANDA. ANYONE MAKES A MOVE UNTIL I'M WELL OUT OF HERE, AND THEY DIE.
I'M GOING TO FIND YOU, MAX. IT DOESN'T MATTER WHERE YOU RUN, I'M GOING TO FIND YOU, AND I'LL BE STANDING RIGHT OUT IN DAMN FRONT.
YOU BROKE AWAY FROM MY INFLUENCE, AMANDA. NO ONE HAS EVER DONE THAT BEFORE. NO ONE.
BUT FOR ONE GLORIOUS MOMENT, I GOT TO BE THE MAN WHO TOOK CONTROL FROM AMANDA WALLER.

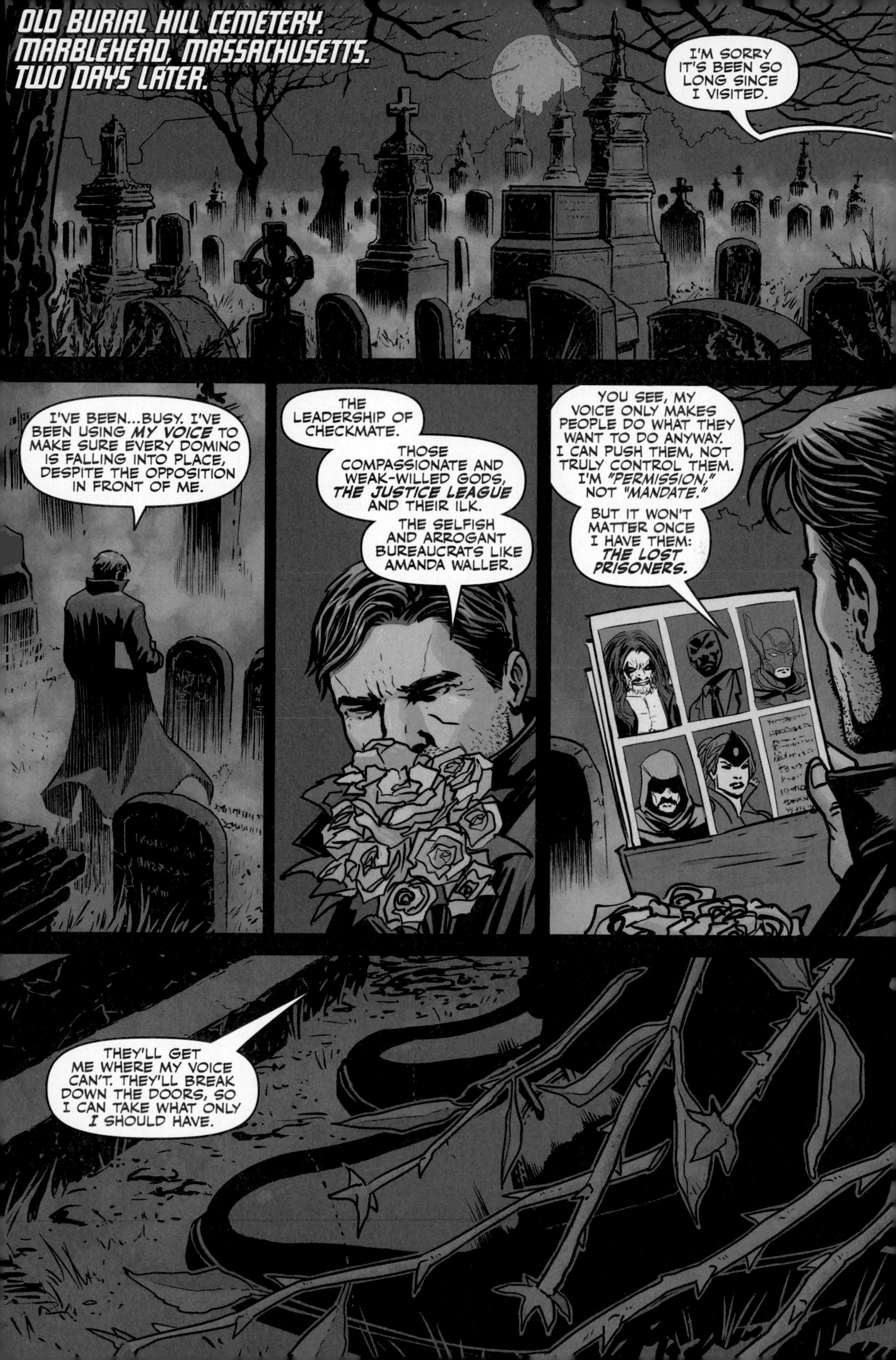
OLD BURIAL HILL CEMETERY. MARBLEHEAD, MASSACHUSETTS. TWO DAYS LATER.
I'M SORRY IT'S BEEN SO LONG SINCE I VISITED.
I'VE BEEN...BUSY. I'VE BEEN USING MY VOICE TO MAKE SURE EVERY DOMINO IS FALLING INTO PLACE, DESPITE THE OPPOSITION IN FRONT OF ME.
THE LEADERSHIP OF CHECKMATE.
THOSE COMPASSIONATE AND WEAK-WILLED GODS, THE JUSTICE LEAGUE AND THEIR ILK.
THE SELFISH AND ARROGANT BUREAUCRATS LIKE AMANDA WALLER.
YOU SEE, MY VOICE ONLY MAKES PEOPLE DO WHAT THEY WANT TO DO ANYWAY. I CAN PUSH THEM, NOT TRULY CONTROL THEM. I'M "PERMISSION," NOT "MANDATE."
BUT IT WON'T MATTER ONCE I HAVE THEM: THE LOST PRISONERS.
THEY'LL GET ME WHERE MY VOICE CAN'T. THEY'LL BREAK DOWN THE DOORS, SO I CAN TAKE WHAT ONLY I SHOULD HAVE.

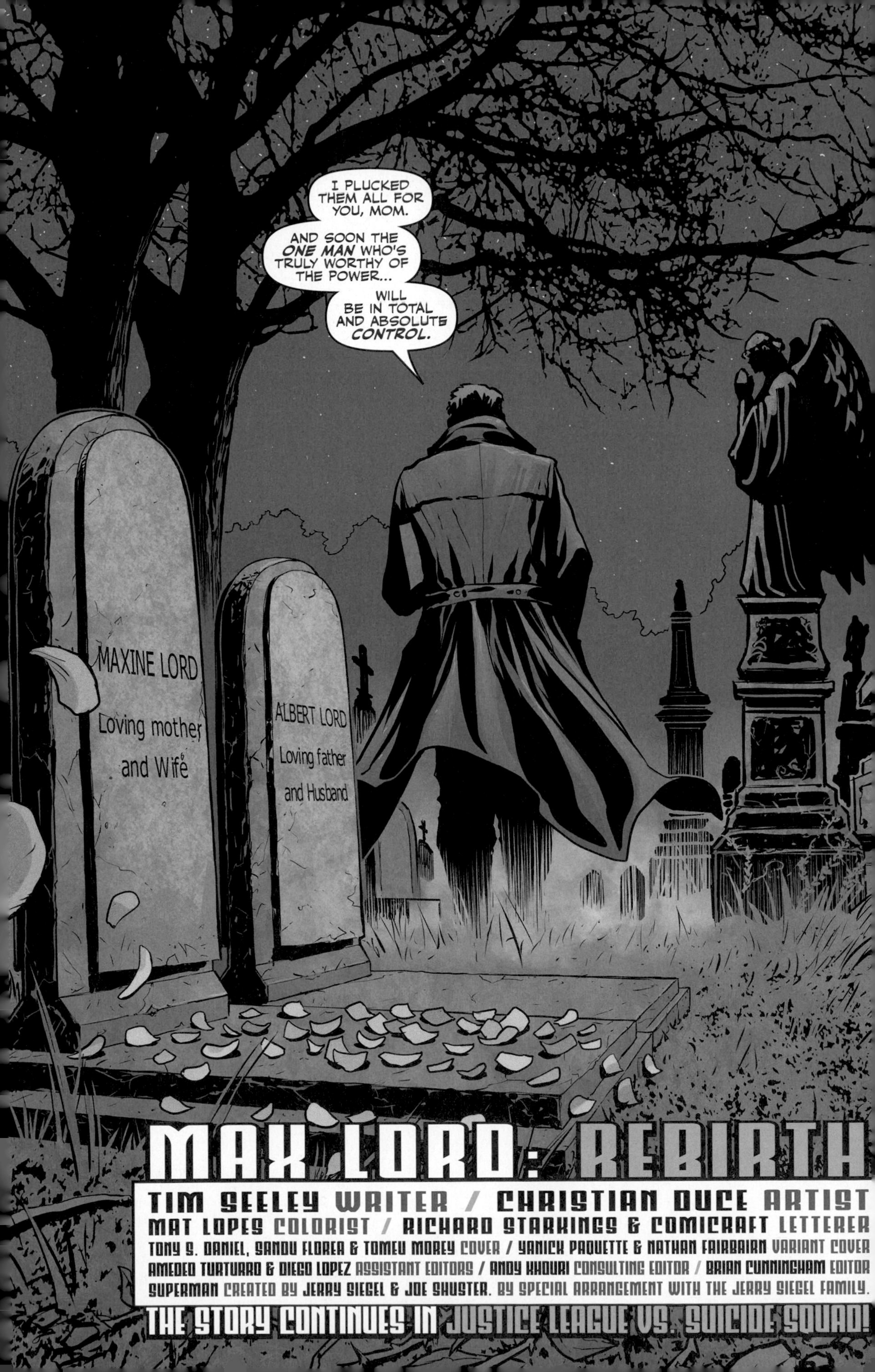
I PLUCKED THEM ALL FOR YOU, MOM.
AND SOON THE *ONE MAN* WHO'S TRULY WORTHY OF THE POWER...
WILL BE IN TOTAL AND ABSOLUTE *CONTROL*.
MAXINE LORD Loving mother and Wife
ALBERT LORD Loving father and Husband
MAX LORD: REBIRTH
TIM SEELEY WRITER / CHRISTIAN DUCE ARTIST
MAT LOPES COLORIST / RICHARD STARKINGS & COMICRAFT LETTERER
TONY S. DANIEL, SANDU FLOREA & TOMEU MOREY COVER / YANICK PAQUETTE & NATHAN FAIRBAIRN VARIANT COVER
AMEDEO TURTURRO & DIEGO LOPEZ ASSISTANT EDITORS / ANDY KHOURI CONSULTING EDITOR / BRIAN CUNNINGHAM EDITOR
SUPERMAN CREATED BY JERRY SIEGEL & JOE SHUSTER. BY SPECIAL ARRANGEMENT WITH THE JERRY SIEGEL FAMILY.
THE STORY CONTINUES IN JUSTICE LEAGUE VS. SUICIDE SQUAD!

Maxwell Lord

GARY MORROW

PERSONAL DATA

Full Name: Maxwell Lord
Occupation: Millionaire Businessman
Marital Status: Single
Known Relatives: None
Base of Operations: New York City
First Appearance: JUSTICE LEAGUE INTERNATIONAL #1
Height: 6′ 2″   *Weight:* 185 lbs.
Eyes: Brown   *Hair:* Brown

HISTORY

Maxwell Lord was an up-and-coming young executive at a major corporation who believed in looking out for number one—himself. No scheme, trick, or amount of office politicking was beyond Lord, who wanted to reach the top quickly and let nothing stand in his way.

The first step in Lord's plan was to get friendly with the chief executive officer of the corporation and become his protege. Eventually, Lord rose in the corporation to the point of being that executive's natural successor, and Lord was willing to do anything to get *his* job . . . even commit murder.

Having learned every facet of background detail about his mentor, Lord knew that he was an amateur cave explorer, a spelunker. Lord took a crash-course in spelunking and then invited his boss on an expedition—just the two of them. However, the executive accidentally plummeted to his near-death even before Lord could do him in. And when Lord had a momentary change of heart and went after the man, he was abducted by an alien computer headquartered inside the mountain, a computer owned by Metron (see *Metron*). The computer, Lord later learned, had gone renegade and intended to have Lord form an international peace group with which it could control Earth. To that end, the computer's programming and knowledge helped Lord become one of the world's richest men and create the multinational Maxwell Lord Enterprises.

When the new Justice League (see *JLI*) was formed, it played into the computer's scheme. Lord became the League's benefactor, infiltrating it from within. But when the computer's owner came to Earth to reclaim it, it would have manipulated Metron and the JLI into destroying one another had not Lord, in a fit of conscience, destroyed it.

Lord continues to be the JLI's benefactor. While he has been forgiven his past transgressions by the League, he is still a manipulator, and the JLI members know better than to trust him implicitly.

Art by Gary Morrow

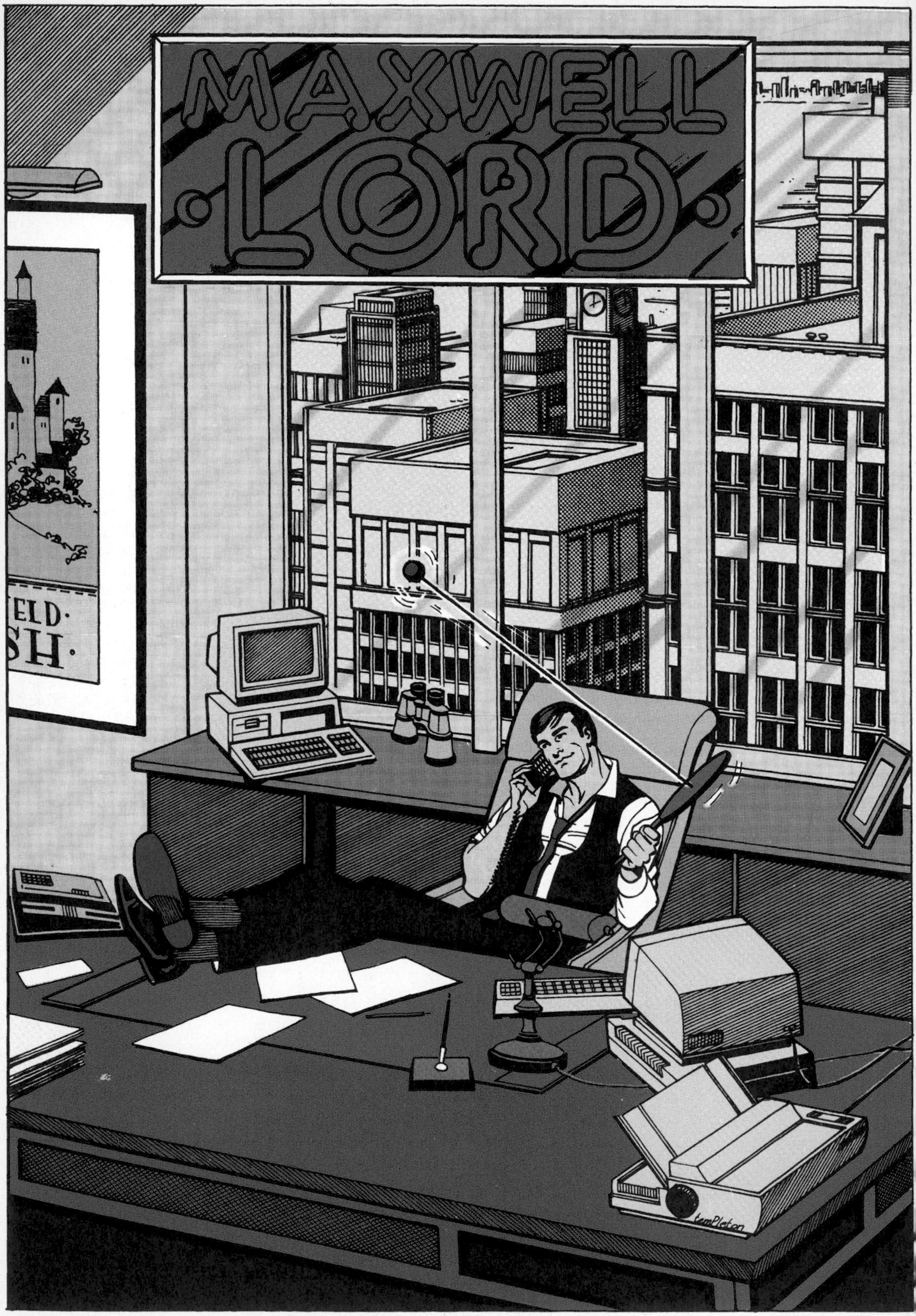
MAXWELL
LORD
templeton